W9-CPE-696

A History of Religions in Korea

Duk-Whang Kim Ph.D.

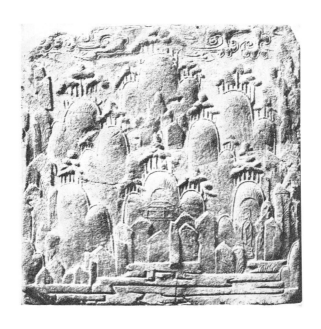

Daeji Moonhwa-sa

The board of Bible translation commitee 1904

The first Korean Catholic father,
Kim, Dae Gun (Andrew)

The first seven Presbyterian ministers 1907

The great Buddhist preist, Seosan Hyujeon

The Dankun Deity

The founder of Chonto-kyo, Choi, Je Woo

The statue of Buddha (Sokgulam, Kyongju)

FOREWORD

Primarily, this book deals with the history and development of religious belief in Korea. The author had been engaged in the research of the spiritual civilizatin in Korea even before the country was freed from Japanese rule, and has produced several pieces of works concerning that particular field of research in the past. However, to this author's findings at the time of writing this research, there were few books available, with the exception of some partial research material dealing with the history of korean religions which gave a complete synthesis of the features and the rise an fall of various local religions. No such books seemed likely to come out in the near future. This was in fact the main reason why the author set his hands to writing this book since the religious development had a vital connection with the author's work.

Also, at this time, entirely no cooperation could be obtained from the religious authorities for the collection of the necessary material for this book, and most of the valuable ones were scattered and lost because of the authorities' factional strife and carelessness. This work, therefore, progressed at a snail's pace. By the time that this work was completed under such unfavorable circumstances, the author felt that half of his hair turned gray, but he could not venture to produce the book because of his lack of credibility in the contents of composition owing to the insufficient references items. The author decided not to publish this work but instead he kept the manuscripts, prepared with such painstaking efforts, in the bottom of his book-file for a long time. But after some years elapsed, there appeared several books in connection with Korean religious history. Encouraged, but having no more resources to add to the old manuscripts, the author decided to publish this book with a sincere hope that it would be a help to the interested readers until such a time as more complete ones reach their hands. It is also hoped that this book in some way, could provide an opportunity for the production of a much better work which would contribute to the academic field.

Errors might have been committed, or there might be some ill-phrases regarding certain religious sects treated in this book. In any case, it is my desire that the readers understand that these errors were not wilfully intended.

Lastly, the author would like to note that the correction of the original manuscript of this has been fulfilled by Do Eung, a son of the author.

August, 1963 Author
at the foot of Chungpa-dong, Seoul

Table of Contents

Part Ⅲ Buddhism(1)

Part Ⅳ Buddhism (2)

Part Ⅵ Christianity(2)

Part Ⅶ Other Religions

Part I

Summary

Chapter 1

The Ancient Period

Mankind is said to be a creature with religious belief, and the Han race (Korean) can be no exception. The belief of the koreans, however, originated from the worship of nature. In the primitive age, the people were so struck with wonders at the mysterious and marvellous formation of nature that they believed that the spirit existed in such universal as well as natural objects as the sun, moon, stars, mountains and rivers, and even in strange animals, rocks and trees. Aside from worshipping the mysterious forces of these creations, they perceived that the spirit also possessed the potential to direct the vicissitudes of human life. Thus, theyoffered tributes and sacrifices in order to avoid the disastrous harms imposed by the spirits, and performed various forms of services to sustain the life of comfort and delight. Generally, this is the form of belief which we call animism today, and this was the prime source of religious life for the Han race.

With some improvements made on such as animistic form of religion, the new Shinkyo belief subsequently emerged in the primeval society. The natural creation was not the only object of worship in this newly developed religion, but the existence of gods managing certain particular fields of work and, at the same time, the existence of the human soul were also believed. Besides this, they believed in the immortality of the soul which would be transformed either as a good or evil spirit according to what one did during his lifetime. Particularly, the soul of one's ancestor was thought to be well in repose and, therefore, possible calamities were avoided when the posterity faithfully attended it. Thus, they began to worship and to give rituals in honour of their forefathers.

Among many natural creations, the worship of the sun had been most particular. As the classic records often quote, 'Where there is darkness there is ghost, and brightness, order and harmony'. It was then believed that the departed spirit was unable to venture any where but become latent in a lighted place. The Han race(Korean) revered the sun, the source of the light as Great Master who generates and nurtures every living thing in the universe and, at the same time, brings delight, order and harmony to mankind by subjugating all the harmful spirits. As such, the sun was regarded as a concrete being in the heaven with many references such as Hanannim(Mighty God in Heaven), Han Earl(Heavenly Soul), or Heavenly God, etc.. In the ancient period, a variety of services was performed to pray for the bliss of the Great Master so as to secure peace of mind and to subdue all the woes of the evil spirits.

The services then were conducted mainly for two purposes. One was to give prayers and wishes to the Master, and the other to suppress, condemn and expel the vicious influences of the evil. And they were executed only by a sorcerer, who was believed to be a unique mediator between man and god. 'The major task of a country consists of military affairs and sacrificial services,' was noted in a Chinese classic Tsochuan. Similarly, the religious functions took over a greater part of the feudalistic social engagements in the primitive age when the governing affairs were so simple, and, thus, the sorcery official even assumed the rule of the state. But, as the ruling system changed later to hamlet and then to tribal units, the reign was turned over to the king, and the mediator of man and god remained only as an official responsible for the religious ceremonies.

Such a form of religion, in which the exorcist executes various rituals for the Heavenly God and conducts magic to conjure the evil spirits, is generally recognized as Shinkyo in korea, although many scholars termed it as shamanism. This was one of the primitive religions that was widely prevalent in Siberia, Japan and among the Ural-Altaics living in the

Manchuria, Mongol territories. On the other hand, some scholars claim it as Sunkyo, Mundankyo or Barkshindo, while still others attempt to put it within the category of Taoism of China because of their similarities in the religious contents. However, it would be proper to call it Shinkyo even if there might be some close affinities between shinkyo and Sunkyo, taking into account the facts that the spirit was worshipped by the ancient belief, and the sorcery official, practicing asceticism in the mountains, preached the revelations of god to the people or performed magic and prepared medicines to eliminate sufferings and anxieties for the preservation of a long life.

The exorcist official was highly looked upon as a man who was a deity or a fairy. A man of deity connotes a man who associate himself with the Heavenly God to officiate at the religious services, and a fairy, a man who practices in order to become a heavenly being.

The first one who came into being as a man of deity or a fairy in the history of korea was Dankun, sometimes referred as Dankun Deity or Dankun Fairy. His forefathers, Hwan Woong and Hwan In, were also the beings of this deified lineage. So were his posterities, who held the reigns over both the religion and state for generations. But they transferred the powers to the descendants who moved into the mountains to perform only religious or divine works.

As the reign of the king expanded from the time when the country was divided by the Three Kingdoms of Kokuryo, Baekje and Silla, the group of the sorcery officials was relegated to street diviners, witches or wizards.Eventually, the followers of the shinkyo religion, that is, the worshippers of the man of deity, turned into special groups mastering the arts of military and the secrets of longevity centering round their idols. The representative examples of this group was the Hwarang Group of Silla and the White-Clothes Hermits(Joui Sonin) of Kokuryo. This is also comparable with the hermit group in China that exuviated from the divine genealogy to found the Odumi religion, which preached the laws of the alchemy and guidance during the periods of the Latter Han Dynasty.

Even after the sorcery officials had been deprived of their influences in the reign, the Shinkyo(korean Shintoism 神教) belief in worshipping the departed spirits still continued to exist among the people. The Shinkyo priests, therefore, came out from their mountain seclusions to resume command of the religious works not only for the people but also for the royal families. The popularity of the belief soon pervaded through the upper and lower classes of the Three Kingdoms. The imperial courts hosted great sacrificial rituals during each season, and the people called upon the sorcerers for the performance of their services in order to invite blessings and to eliminate the misfortunes.

Around this time, the Buddhist monk by the name of Soondo delivered Buddhism to Kokuryo from the Chin Dynasty in China in 325. This was in the second year rule of King Sosoorim, the 17th king of the state. The new foreign religion, well received even by the court, penetrated deeply into the then popular Shinkyo belief and prospered gradually. By the years of King Kwangkaeto, the 19th ruler of kokuryo, the development of Buddhism was so encouraged by the king himself that a total of nine magnificent temples were established in the capital, which is now pyong-yang.

Buddhism reached the Baekje Kingdom about forty years later. Perhaps because it was originally the court religion of India and was the favorite of aristocrats in China, the Buddhism in Baekje won much attraction and curiosity from the royal families and the noble classes. Thus, the religious influences expanded rapidly as the number of converts increased by day and by month. The Buddhist religion was introduced into these states by two different toutes. That of Kokuryo was imported from its adjoining China in the north, while Baekje brought it across the southern sea from the mainland.

On the contrary, Buddshism, which made entrance into Silla about 50 years later than Kokuryo, met exclusion from the courtiers and the people, and its permeation seemed unlikely in the beginning. But in the 15th years of King Bupheung in 528, it found its way to prosperity with the martyrdom of a royalty Yi, Cha Don.

Buddhism, introduced into the Three kingdoms likewise, not only received the royal protection but, since its teachings and preceptions were not entirely inconsistent with those of the native Shinkyo, made a remarkable progress in conciliation with the home religion. As a result, the Three Kingdoms became a great Buddhist kingdom in less than a century with a number of the monuments and temples set up in various places. The Buddhist development also accelerated the artistic and cultural upsurge in construction, sculpture, music and paintings.

From the outset, the Buddhist religion was introduced to the Three Kingdoms with some contradictions to its original nature, for it was rather embraced by the recipient states as a means of national protection and utilitarian purposes without regard to its essential views of selflessness and ultra-nationalism. But the transient view about the human life and the belief in an inevitable retribution, which were the important part of the Buddhist concepts, influenced the people to a conspicuous degree so that many followers of the religion began to feel their lives fleeting. Moreover, in the states of Baekje and Silla, the royal decree was issued to prohibit killing, fishing and hunting, while good was encouraged and vice punished. Under the patronage of each state, Buddhism, the religion of mercy and forebearance, made the most extensive prosperity during these periods of the Three Kingdoms which had the ideal of building their land into the Buddhist Elysium in the East.

While Buddhism was still flourishing, Taoism from the Tang Dynasty also made entrance to Kokuryo at the end of the state and earned an increasing number of adherents both from the imperial court and the people. This was made possible by the deliberations of Yongaesomoon, a powerful subject of the court. Claiming that Confucianism, Buddhism and Taoism were like the legs of a tripod, the subject advised King Bojang to invite the Taoist preachers from Tang. Since Kokuryo was basically a country of strong Shinkyo belief, in which various natural objects were mystified and the sorcerers were believed to be associating with gods of heaven and earth and the departed human spirits, the Taoism of similar essences became well integrated into the religious life of the masses.

When the Silla Kingdom, with the help provided from the Chinese Tang Dynasty, destroyed Baekje and, later, conquered Kokuryo to achieve the unification of the Three Kingdoms, the victorious feats were attributed to the Buddhist doctrines by the unified Silla. Thus, the religion was so stimulated that the Silla state soon became a great Buddhist empire with the establishment of a number of temples, pagodas and statues, and the Buddhist arts and culture developed to the point of extreme elegance. The Silla monks, who went to the Tang Dynasty for study, also contributed greatly in importing Chinese civilizations. Should the periods preceding the Silla's unification be considered as the stages of research and explication of the Buddhist doctrines, the post-unification era was certainly the time of their completion. As the result of the successive return of the monks from the Chinese Dynasty, the Buddhism in Silla began to split into various sects that could be represented by Samron-jong, Chontae-jong, Hwaom-jong, Bupsang-jong, Mil-jong and Yul-jong. During this time, many distinguished priests such as Wonhyo, Uisang, Jajang, Haetong, Myung-rang, Kyungheung, Haecheol, Moohyum, Chaejeung, Jisun, Kukyang, Jinchul, Haengjuk appeared. For about two centuries after the unification, the Silla state enjoyed abundant achievements in Buddshism, and the religious artistic prosperity was unprecedented. The various sectarian religions prestigious of their doctrines and founders, and a number of highly scholastic and virtuous priests came out in succession.

During the years of the 33rd Queen Sungduk of Silla(702-736), Confucianism was introduced from the Tang Dynasty. This, however, does not seem to be the initial inflow. Considering the facts that there were the Confucian learning institutions with the scholars positions of Kukja-paksa and Daehak-paksa already in 372, the 2nd year of King Sosoorim of Kokuryo, and that a Baekje scholar named Wang In(Wani in Japanese) had gone to Japan with the Analects of Confucius and the Chinese letters during the years of the 8th King Koi of Baekje, it was believed to have prevailed sometime in the past. This might be better regarded as the Chinese learning which could not have been anything more than analytic literature or rhythmic prose. But, in the years of Queen Sungduk, Prince Kim, Soo Choong went to the Tang Dynasty and returned with the portraits of Confucius including those of his ten philosophers and 72 disciples. The Queen showed her courtesy in respect of Confucious by having these portraits enshrined in the national learning institutions, and this was the beginning of Confucianism in Silla as a religion. Afterwards, the succeeding kings themselves attended the Confucian shrines to pay homage to the religious founder and to hear the lectures. In the reign of King Wonsung (785-798), the Five Classics of the Confucian Teachings and Three Histories of China were included among the subjects given for the public service examinations. Further, in the periods of King Honkang, attempts were made to develop the religion by sending Prince Kim, Heun and 12 other students, i.e., Kim, Yoon Boo, Kim, Ip Ji, Choi, E Jung, Kim, Sook Koo, Park, Kye Up, etc., to the Tang Dynasty to make exclusive research of the Confucian learning, but these did not achieve much success because of the then powerful Buddhist influences.

In fact, it was not only the Confucianism but also the Taoism that made unsuccssful penetration in Silla, although a man named Kim, In Moon and some others of the upper class society, did extensive readings of the theories of Laotzu, Chuangtzu and Sakya, and Emperior Hyunjong of the Tang Dynasty. They even sent to the Silla Dynasty the Confucians ethical scriptures concerning filial piety during the ages of King Hyosung, according to historical records. The Confucian religion, therefore, could not maintain its treasured values through the establishment of a school anywhere, and some of the Taoist views became intermingled with the Shinkyo belief.

Once the development of Buddhism reached its peak in Silla, the religion began to lose its animation for sometime at the closure of the Dynasty. Then, the Seon-jong(Zen Sect 禪宗), the revolutionary sectarian Buddhism was founded by Great Priest Dharma of China in the 7th centry under the name of Ch'an(Ch'an means meditation on paradoxes and is used to awaken intuitive insight into what transcends logical distinction). The practice, a silent sitting and meditating on whatever illumination arises, flowed in and stimulated a great turning point in the Buddhist sphere of Silla, overwhelming the theoretical Buddhist sect called Kyo-jong(Logic Sect 教宗) that had thus far been prevalent. Simultaneously, most of the Buddhist scholars belonging to the previous sect became underprivileged like the famous Chinese Buddhist named Changui of the Chin Dynasty periods, and their works, giving wide-ranging, discussion and argument about the religion turned out entirely useless. Compared to the theoretically hard Kyo-jong, the Seon-jong taught an easier way to enlightenment and then to Buddhahood and there was an increasing number of followers and monks for this sectarian religion.

Chapter 2
The Koryo Periods(918-1391)

King Taejo, the founder of the Koryo Dynasty, adopted Buddhism as a national religion and enabled it to further develop under the aegis of the imperial households.

Although a man of great capacity who and achieved the unification with an ambition of saving the world, the king was of the belief that the foundation of the Dynasty had been successful only with the graces of Buddha. Thus, Taejo ordered the construction of a total of 3,500 supplemental temples and towers throughout the counties an prefectures of the country in addition to many that were already existing, and sent his fifth son into the priesthood in the latter part of his rule. By virture of Taejo's devotion to the religion, various Buddhist denominations including Kyo-jong and Seon-jong that were on the decline at the end of the Silla Dynasty began to revive with a renewed vigor. The founder of Koryo not only contributed to the revival of Buddhism, but, as he was such a devout Shinkyo believer at the same time, many of the old rituals consecrating the God of Heaven, the Five High or Famous Mountains and the Great River were reinstated along with the Palkwan Festival of Silla, which continued existence even through the golden ages of Buddhism.

The third King Joongjong donated 70,000 suks(10,000 tons) of grain to the great Buddhist temples for the purpose of preparing many learned monks. During the reign of the fourth King Kwangjong(950-975), the priesthood was added in the public official examinations, and the seven higher ranks were given to the Buddhist monks. The first two highest ones among the seven, called Kooksa(the state priest) and Wangsa(the royal priest), were vested on those selected to serve as advisers for the king. Under this system, the Buddhist monks Haego and Danmoon were appointed as the first Kooksa and Wangsa respectively. On account of such protective policies for Buddhism and such superior treatment for the monks, there were many, especially the princes and the sons of the rich and influential noble families, who went into the priesthood. Accordingly, the social standing of the monks was greatly enhanced. Taking advantage of the royal protection, the Buddhist monks were engrossed more in coveting higher ranks, properties and profits than strictly adhering to the sacred religious doctrines. Even worse, they indulged themselves in such disorderly lives of dissipation and debauchery.

While the Buddhists evil practices and degradation ensued, the monks of each different sectarian branch, the so-called preachers of mercy and harmony, had serious discord among themselves, each accusing the other of unorthodox infidelity. At this juncture, the spiritually-awakened Buddhist saint named Uichon, the son of the 11th King Moonjong of Koryo, emerged to infuse a new vitality to the corrupted religion. A beloved prince of the king, Uichon went into the Sung Dynasty in China, where he, touring many famous Buddhist sanctums there, learned the essential doctrines of the five sectarian religions, especially those of the Hwaom-jong and Chontae-jong, from the celebrated Chinese priests. After his return from China, Uichon helped to bring conciliation between the two rivaling sects of Kyo and Seon by advocating the termination of the religious disputes, initiated the Chontae-jong branch that later prospered extensively, and added new life in the religious sphere in general.

Against the Chontae-jong first advanced by Uichon, the Most Reverend Priest Hakil and other priests Danyeon, Jiin and Dukso later made attempts to revive the Seon-jong, but the religion did not improve from its past corruptions despite some of the monks, successful preaching. However, during the years of King Shinjong and King Hijong, Priest Jinul, the state priest, contributed greatly to the restoration of the religion by leading an independent Seon-jong that developed to the Chokye-jong(曹溪宗), the first consolidated Buddhist denomination in Korea, in combination with the Kyo-jong sectarian religion.

True, both Uichon and Jinul can be counted as the most outstanding contributors for the development of Buddhism during the ages of the Koryo Dynasty. But the great achievements the Buddhist religion had rendered for the cultural history of Korea in these periods were the reprints of the complete engravings of the Buddhist canons that took almost 69 years, from the periods of the 8th King Hyonjong to the 11th King Moonjong, to the final completion with all the available national resources. The completed Buddhist letter-blocks were, then, preserved at the Booin temple in the outskirts of Taegu, Kyongsangbuk province, until the years of King Kojong, when they were burnt down by the Mongol invasion. In place of these, Kojong, then taking refuge in Kanghwa Island off In-chon, produced another set of the 84,000 engraved-block letters which took almost 16 years of work.

Although Uichon's restoration of the religious sects and Jinul's esta blishment of more adaptable Seon-jong were greatly favored by the people, there was an increasing amount of waste in both national and private fi-nance, time and endeavor, as a result of the volumnious religious events conducted by the imperial courts and the people. Moreover, the Buddhist monks abused their privileges not only in interfering in politics but also in participating in the power struggles. In private, the monks consumated their lives in satiation and idleness, and some of them were even addicted to the woman and whims in the frivolous community. The Buddhist tem-ples and monasteries, on the other hand, became the source of profiteering as they mobilized their authority in taking the land and servants of the people and engaging in various business activities.

In addition to the thriving Buddhism in the Koryo Dynasty, there were miscellaneous superstitions, for instance, the verification of a prophecy, geomancy and the dual principle or the five primary elements of Chinese philosophy, that were prevalent among the people. Under the influences of the Tang Dynasty, those superstitious belief became popular before the Silla's unification of the Three States. During the periods of Koryo they were so widely professed that even the successive kings and most of the noble classes became the blind followers of the belief along with Buddhism. Various official functions including visitations, religious rites, site selection, palace renovation, etc., were often decided by the forecasts of many fortunetellers or augurers crowded at the imperial palaces. The founder of the Dynasty, King Taejo also believed in the superstitions, but not to the extent of neglecting his royal obligations as did many of the average monarchs from the middle of the Dynasty who were completely swayed by the popular belief.

As the superstitious belief continued its popularity among the royal families and the people, even the public official examination added a subject relating to the art of divination. From the middle of the Koryo Dynasty, numerous superstitious works such as 'Dosunsiki', 'Dosundap-sanka', 'Samkaksan Myungdangki', etc., witten by anonymous writers were widely circulated. The geograpic location of the capital or the individual houses became the common topic of discussion, and the people became entirely dependent on the fortunes told by the geomantic magician for the performance of every little affair of their private life. Being so thoroughly captivated by and unable to do away with the Buddhist ideas and such miscellaneous beliefs, the people gradually lost their self-sustaining or self-esteemed temperaments.

Meanwhile, the local religion of Shinkyo also survived through the shadows of the powerful Buddhism with a great potentiality. As has been previously mentioned, the Palkwan and the Lantern Festivals of the religion with offerings to the gods of heaven, great mountains, rivers, and dragons were consecutively observed by the succeeding rulers of the Koryo Dynasty ever since they were revived by the founder of the Dynasty. The Festivals, originating from the periods of King Jinheung of Silla at the request of the escaped monk named Heyong from the Kokuryo Dynasty, were held at the imperial palaces every winter, and more faithfully and pompously when there were special occasions for the state or the imperial households. From the middle of the Dynasty, however, the formalities of the Shinkyo festivals were seasoned with much of the Buddhist flavours, where by the monks were invited to participat in the feast and a number of the lighted lanterns, the Buddhist symbol of inviting blessings, were used. The Shinkyo belief became so deeply rooted among the masses that the people of Koryo, according to the historical records, took the witches and wizards' conjurations as the sole means of staying free from disease and mishap.

The Taoist conceptions of China were no less influential during these- periods. In 1102, the 7th year of the 15th King Sookjong of Koryo, the Supreme Deity of Taoism was worshipped at the imperial palace under the influences of the Chinese Sung Dynasty. During the reign of the 16th King Yejong, a man named Lee Joong Yak went to China and studied religious principles under Priest Hwang Da Chung, and, in the same period, the devout-Taoist Emperor Huijong of the Sung Dynasty sent two priests to Koryo and helped to establish a Taoist shrine called 'Bokwonkwan' in the Koryo's capital of Kaekyoung, where more than 10 of the religious followers were admitted. Since then, the religion prospered gradually. By the end of the Koryo Dynasty, the number of the Taoist shrines increased to five in the capital and four in the local provinces. But, as they were monopolized mostly by the royal families, the religion itself was not very popular among the people.

Under the pressures of the Buddhist influences, Confucianism did not develop much in Koryo until the middle of the Dynasty. The Confucian school called Kookjakam was established, then the private Confucian schools were started. The Confucian temple to worship the religious founder was setup during the ages of the 6th King Sungjong. Then, as the royal subject Choi, Choong taught the Confucious philosophies during the years of the 11th King Moonjong and eleven other Confucian instructors came out later to promote Confucianism, Confucian learning rose up suddenly,

but it was no more than the learning of the Chinese classics. It also flourished to some extent during the years of the 16th King Yejong as a result
of the king's personal enthusiasm and encouragement for Confucianism
as a religion. He attended the Confucian temple to offer sacrifices and
established the seven religious institutions for fostering Confucianists. Even
so, Confucianism soon became stagnant again.

When the Buddhist sphere was plunged into chaos with various corruptions of the monks at the end of the Koryo Dynasty, the usually
Confucian-minded An, Yoo imported the Sung Dynasty exposition of
the classics from China and mastered the learning together with Kwon,
Boo ; Woo, Tak ; Baek, I Jung. Soon afterwards, the Confucian religion
blossomed to prosperity.

Against the rising influence of Confucianism, some of the famous Buddhist priests such as Ilyeon, Bohur and Haekeun attempted to resuscitate
their declining religion, but were not very helpful in dispersing or eradicating the dake clouds of corruption that had accumulated within the
religion itself. Beside, various invisible feuds between the two different
religious groups continued. Finally, all sorts of misdemeanors committed
by the vicious monk named Shindon during the years of King Kongmin
provided an impetus for the Confucians to begin their open explulsion
movement against Buddhism. Such famous Confucian scholars as Lee,
Saek, Jung, Mong Joo, Jung, Do Jeon and Kwon, Keun were the leading
figures of the Buddhist-opposition. The religious disputes ended with
a revolution launched by the first King of the Lee Dynasty in complete
success for the Confucianists, and, therefore, the Buddhist were expelled
from the imperial courts.

Chapter 3
The Chosun Periods(1392-1886)

Generally, the anti-Buddhist policy was consistently adopted by the Lee Dynasty throughout its five hundred years of history, although the religion flickered with temporary rise and fall in the rules of King Sejo, King Kwanghae and King Jungjo.

Founder of the Chosun Dynasty, Lee Taejo was originally a Buddhist-convert like his ancestors. But it was the only alternative left for Taejo to choose Confucianism, for the internally-decayed Buddhism was not much of an assistance to his founding of the state, and, besides, the rising Confucian power was used as a stepping-stone for the foundation of his Dynasty. Taejo, thus, aroused the Confucian learning by both setting up the great Sungkyunkwan temple, enshrining the famous disciples of Confucius there and by widely appointing Confucian students to government positions. During the years of King Jungjo, another Confucian institution called Obuhakdang was established in the five capital districts. By the time of the next King Taejong, the pro-Confucian as well as anti-Buddhist policies were strictly enforced, where by the number of the Buddhist temples was extremely restricted, the land and the serfs belonging to the temples were confiscated, and the monks were so comtemptuously treated that their existence was totally abandoned by the world.

Lee Tajo's massacre of six faithful subjects including Jung, Mong Joo, charging them as traitors in order to usurp the throne, his further slaughter of the royal descendants in order to prolong the power once it had been seized, and, afterwards, Taejong's atrocious Buddhist suppression brought great commotion to public feeling. But, when the ingenious King Sejong succeeded the reign after Taejong and carried his office well expanding the territories and stimulating learning, there came about unprecedented cultural progress with the appearance of many Confucian talents, and the confused public sentiment was brought to stability.

Inwardly not against Buddhism, Sejong not only often hosted a great Buddhist service to pray for the bliss of his deceased mother and restored the Heungchon temple, but he also built up a magnificent Buddhist shrine called Naebuldang in the palace in the latter part of his rule. In the end, however, the king also endeavored to curtail Buddhist influence by ab-rogating the annual religious event called Yonjon Hwanwon, and the monks' street-roving prayer-procession called Kyunghaeng, and by redu-cing the number of the religious sects to only two of Seon and Kyo from a total of seven permitted by his predecessor, King Taejong. Then, the powerful Confucians rose up with hatred against Buddhism, and there were those who insisted on killing the famous priest Haengho. Even under such severe persecutions, a monk named Kihwa attempted to promote the Seon religion and to bring conciliations between Confucianism and Buddhism.

During the period of King Sejo, Buddhism flourished for sometime. This was made possible by the king's personal intention to seek exoneration from the religion for he was constantly uneasy about the crime he com-mitted in murdering a number of royal subjects including King Danjong soon afte r he became king. The sudden death of the prince, in addition, provided a certain impact for the king. Thus, in order to expiate his guilty-conscience and to pray for his son, Sejo initiated the Buddhist services, widely spread the religious scriptures, established the great Wonkak temple, and respected Priests Shinmi and Soomi.

In the age of King Sungjong, the Confucian philosophy was adopted as the backbone of the state, and Buddhism was again severely persecuted. Even the Confucian subject who had the slightest tint of the opposition religion was not only expelled from the imperial court as an enemy of Confucius, but various Buddhist temples were also destroyed. More of the religious shrines and statues were broken down, and the great Wonkak temple was used as a house for the woman entertainers during the atrocious rules of Yonsankun. The oppressive Buddhist measures were continued by the next King Joongjong, who abolished the subject relating to the monk from the public official examinations, demolished the religious temples, and used the bronze statutes of Buddha for the production of armories. Thoroughly oppressed by the three succeeding kings as such, Buddhism was completely abandoned by the society and was no longer an active religion among the people.

After such a severe Buddhist persecution, those who made up the Buddhist sphere were the groups of various social outcasts, i.e., criminals, idlers, evaders of public obligations or the runaways from the official extortions. They turned out as the vagrants indulged in all sorts of misdeeds and plunderings that caused quite an ill-effects on the general public. Aside from such groups, there were the sincere Buddhists who devoted themselves in pursuits of the religious doctrines and practices, and such famous priest as Seosan, Songwoon, Songwol, Byukan, Pyunyang, Soyo and Hwanjeok emerged during this period.

The Confucian influence of the Lee Dynasty was extended mainly through the three different local institutions called Sungkyunkwan, Hyangkyo(Confucian shrine with school) and Seowon(Confucian school). King Sejong crowned his prince in the first Confucian ceremony ever held by having the prince dressed in religious robes and worshiped at the Sungkyunkwan temple. King Moonjong allocated more male and female servants for the Sungkyunkwan as well as for the four other regional temples. King Sejo, at the request of Lee, Keuk Jeung and Han, Myung Hoi, ordered the construction of more temples such as Jonkyungkak, Jonryechung and Hyungkwanchung. Later, he provided the Sungkyunkwan with material aids ranging from silk-cloth and farm-land. In the end, the Sungkyunkwan temple became a center of religion and politics and, at the same time, a headquarters of the Confucianists. There the succeeding kings conducted a wide range of religious rites including the annual Sukjon and twice-monthly Sakmang Festivals consecrated to Confucius, and offered wine and other tributes at other occassional services. Also, a higher learning institution was set up within the temple to educate many Confucian scholars.

The regional school of Hyangkyo, existed from the years of King Injong of Koryo, was expanded through the local units of the prefectures during the age of King Lee Taejo of the Lee Dynasty, and was restored to normal operation during the rule of King Taejong. The religious ceremonies and the educational system managed by this local temple were the same as those of the Sungkyunkwan. However, from the middle of the Lee Dynasty, some of these Hyangkyo began to deteriorate without government efforts to recover them. In their place, a large number of private schools called Seowon, where Confucian literature and rituals for the famous Confucian philosophers took place, came out in the local provinces. The number of the schools increased to several in one city and about 80 or 90 in total in a province by the year of King Sookjong, and some 650 throughout the country during the reign of King Jungjo(1777-1800). The local Confucian school occupied a large area of farm-land free from taxes and other public duties, and, in the end, became the source of various social activities with all its grandiosity and idleness. The Confucianists of the school, though they preached all the good manners of filial piety, humanity and justice whenever the chances were given collaborated with the factional cliques of the central government and were intent on trapping and crushing the opposing faction.

The social manners regarding the birth, marriage, funeral and ancestral services were naturally Confucianized as the religion was adopted as the guiding principle of the state. In Chosun, the Five Manners and Ceremonies, which were rather the consolidation of the Book of Rites and the Book of Rituals, were generally recognized. Through the years of King Sejo and King Sungjong, they were revised a few times with further rethat was originally prohibited to them, and there were many law cases and were used as the standard for various social events. Thus, the religious altar enshrining the ancestors of a family was set up by the individual house, and the death anniversary services and other Confucian rituals were conducted according to the standard.

At a glimpse, Confucianism seemed to have been predominant over the political religious life of the people through the ages of the Lee Dynasty. But the superstitious belief in the Dual Principles, Geomantic system was just as powerful among the masses, binding the life of the people to a great extent in a popular religion. The office of meteorlogical observation was established within the imperial palace to assume the works relating not only to astronomy but also fortune-telling, and the entire engagements of the royal families such as date, location and direction were decided and executed by the geomancer. The people also followed the advice of the fortunate-teller for the date, location and direction in conducting almost everything that was related to their daily life, i.e., residence, birth, marriage and ancestral services. They also had to perform exorcism, offer tribute or consult the fortune-tellers almost every day in order to be exempt from possible misfortunes. Taking advantage of such human defects, a number of astrologers swarmed up in towns and villages in the rural areas.

The geomantic belief, an exclusive favorite of the royal households and the noble class, was previously taken with an emphasis in selecting a good sunny place, but, in the Lee Dynasty, it was changed to the selection of a good burial-griond, for this was then believed as having a vital relation with the existence of a family and with the viscitutudes of one's posterity for generations to come. Thus, the matter of selecting a good place for burial was rather an important affair of a family, for which everyone exerted all their powers. In some cases, the people squandered all their assets solely for the purpose and in others various disputes over the preservation of one certain site occurred between the different family groups. In addition, there were those making secret burials to a place of so-called good omen

ferences from the Chinese ceremonial records and from the local traditions, involving illegal occupation of the grave-yard.

Taoism was not vigorous even in the periods of the Lee Dynasty. However, the religious temple of Sokyukchon that was built up during the reign of Lee Taejo was promoted to Sokyuk-so in the years of Sejo, and various Taoist gods such as the Trinity, the Supreme Deity, the Most Reverend Laotzu, the Great Gok, the God of rain and water were worshipped and served with rituals at the temple. During the years of King Jeungjong this was closed down by a consistent demand from the Confucian group led by Cho, Kwang Jo. Later, it was restored, but was burnt down again during the Doyotomi invasion from Japan, and, hence, the Chinese Taoism made a complete disappearance from the Korean religious circle.

On the other hand, Shamanism, the ancient Shinkyo belief with the witches and wizards conducting the conjurations, flourished extensively among the people in the first part of the Lee Dynasty. For it was a period of no outstanding religion for the masses with Buddhism pressed into the background, and the Confucianism of less appealing contents was unacceptable to the people. Thus, the ancient belief bulged to the foreground, not only dominating the religious sphere of the people, but also of the imperial courts. The sorcerer's services conjuring various evil spirits were carried out with more enthusiasm from the queens and the royal concubines in the courts, and, eventually, the Shinkyo mediators even took part in most of the official religious rites conducted by the state.

The ancient religion, Shamanism, became wide-spread through the local villages, where a variety of festivals in honor of the tutelary gods were jointly conducted by the residents sharing the same geographical conditions. The village festivals, which were called Dongjae, Dongsinjae, Dangsanjae or Sunghwangjae, were the direct descendants of the Yongko festival, Moochon Festival, Dongmaeng, etc., the state festivals of the Old Chosun.

When Christianity was imported from China during the age of King Injo of the Lee Dynasty, it was no more than a subject of research by the Confucian scholars. But, later, when the movement to practice the faith began, the Christian influence expanded somewhat in the years of King Sookjong and spreaded through the Kyonggi, Hwanghae and Kangwon Provinces during the period of King Youngjo, and reached most of the southern regions during the reign of King Jungjo. Primarily because both the manners and thoughts of Christianity ran counter to those of Confucianism, the imperial court tabooed the new religion as being an unjust science. In the 15th year of King Jungjo, the first big christian persecution took place and another one occurred in 1801, the first year of King Soonjo, there were three excessive oppressions which caused great suffering for the Christian followers. The religious which caused a great suffering for the Christian followers. The religious suppression continued again in 1839, the 5th year of King Hunjong, at which time three French missionaries who had smuggled themselves into the country were captured and killed along with 30 other believers. Then, the imperial court proclaimed an Imperial Edict to eradicate the western religion, and the law governing the administrative unit of five local houses was strictly enforced to ferret out the Christian believers. The secret mission continued despite such hard-pressed persecutions, and, by the years of King Chuljong when the oppressive measures were somewhat softened, the number of the Christian followers increased radically with free missionary activities. In 1859, the 10th year of King Chuljong, they numbered more than 160,000, and western clergymen kept coming into the country.

A Regent Daewonkun, succeeded to the throne following the death of Chuljong, carried out many daring reforms. Not only did he eliminate hundreds of the corrupt Confucian private schools, but also astounded the world by ordering massacres of the Catholics merely out of his political considerations. The Christian foundation that had been secured with the decades of trials by French missionaries and others was also shattered, and the Catholics could not make an outright appearance in public for the ten years rule of the king. But, following the king's retirement, they made every effort to promote the religion under the government's tacit permission. By this time, however, the international situation changed so that the national policy of isolation or repression of the religion was no longer practicable. In March of the 19 th year of King Kojong, the Dynasty of Chosun concluded the treaty of amity and trade with the United States, England and Germany. This gave complete freedom for the foreign missionaries in Korea, and the Catholic gradually recovered from their past injuries.

At the end of the Lee Dynasty, both Confucianism and Buddhism were nothing more than burnt-down ashes, and the western thoughts were misrepresented as having treacherous causes for the country. At this time, a prophetic book called Jungkamrok came into wide circulation from an unknown source, causing speculations that Chosun of the Lee Dynasty would soon perish and, in its place, the Jung Dynasty would be established in the Mt. Kyeryong. It also forecasted where a good refuge would be for the imminent calamities. The people, exhausted by the Suppression and extortion of the upper-class Yangbans and the powers, began to long for the new ideal world. Such a social phenomena at the closure of the Dynasty invited gregarious growth of many forms of guasi-religion. The first such a religious group came about was the Donghak founded by Choi, Je Woo with a proper mixture of the Buddhist, Confucian and Taoist Doctrines. It preached the salvation of mankind, world-wide evangelism, and the preservation of national security and peace to the people. As the religious influence iresistably prospered with an increasing number of converts, the authorities began to doubt that the Donghak resembled the Western religion and believed that it was seducing the public. After four years of mission, Choe, Je Woo was, therefore, captured and put into prison in Taegu, where he later passed away. The legitimacy of the religion, in the meantime, was handed down to Choi's second generation, Choi, Shi Hyung, who systematized the religious tenets as those of a formal religion and worked to implant it firmly into the society. The Donghak was redesignated as Chondokyo by the third founder, Sohn, Byung Hee, which once was the largest religious group in the country with a million followers. Afterwards the Chondokyo was divided by the Sichonkyo, from which yet another branch called Sangjaekyo seceded, while the orthodox group of the Donghak sect initiated the Soowoonkyo. With these secessions, the Chondokyo was greatly weakened.

In the early periods of King Kojong, the Hoomchikyo religion of the old Shinkyo nature, founded by Kang, Il Soon, made an extensive penetration into the masses along with the other branches of the Donghak. But following the death of Kang, Il Soon, many other branches, i,e., the Sundokyo(that later became Bochonkyo), Mookukdaedokyo, Jeungsankyo, Taeeulkyo and countless others also split from the Hoomchikyo. The other religious groups of the old Shinkyo lineage that emerged at the end of the Lee Dynasty were Daejongkyo, Dankunkyo, Samsungkyo, Kijakyo, Sinrijongkyo, Sunghwakyo, etc,. However, all these were not very successful except, perhaps, the Daejongkyo, which made remarkable expansion in Eastern Manchuria with a total of some 30 to 40 thousand followers at its four parishes divided by east, west, north and south.

Chapter 4
The Recent Periods

The recent periods could be marked with the variety of activities of the Protestant Churches and the religious persecution by the Japanese authorities. The Conclusion of the amnity trade treaty with the United States provided an impetus for the influx of many protestant missionaries including Horace G. Underwood and Henry D. Appenzellar of America, who brought forth an immeasurable renovation in the local religious sphere with their outstanding works.

Working from within the different denominations, the foreign missionaries held a united congregation in Wonsan, Hamkyung Province, in 1906 A.D., where they experienced the Graces of Pentecost. In the following year, another congregation of the Korean Christians in Pyongyang struck a spark for the religion, giving a great stimulation movement for the sake of one million souls was initiated. The foreign missionaries not only conducted evangelical works but also rendered their extraordinary services in the fields of medicine, social welfare and education, saving many lives of the Koreans and, at the same time, contributing immensely to the overall development of the native culture. Particularly notable was their service in education. Before the March 1, 1919 Independence Movement, there were no public colleges in Korea as those established in Japan. But the four professional colleges of Soongsil, Yonhee, Ewha and Severance set up by the foreigners were already in existance and producing many patriotic leaders for the national independence. In addition, the establishment of more than 40 senior and junior high schools and 600 primary schools in the local districts, they also made a great contribution in enhancing liberal democratic thought by enlightening the masses with the initiation of various youth movements for women, young men, and boys.

Afterward, the Oriental Orthodoxy Church moved in from Russia and, for some time it seemed it would become prosperous under the auspieces of the imperial court of the Lee Dynasty. But the Collapse of the Dynasty as aresult of the Japanese annexation and, later, the blockade of the supplying sources for its missionary fund as a result of the Socialists Revolution in Russia, offered the church little chance for progress.

Following the First World War, President Woodrow Wilson of the United States proclaimed the 14-article Declaration of Peace and provided the principles for self-determination by a country. Eventually, this also provided a vital stimulation for the local religious groups of Chontokyo, Christians and Buddhists in planning a nation-wide consolidated independence movement on March 1, 1919. The leading members of the movement consisted of 47 persons, among whom 16 were chondokyo, 19, Christians, 2 Buddhists, and 18 from non-religious groups. Although it was initiated mainly by the religious leaders, the entire people of the country took part in the movement that, in the end, brought the tolls 7,509 dead, 15,961 wounded and 47 churches burnt down.

Subsequently, a number of religious leaders were imprisoned, and the authorities repression of all religions was even more intensified. The religious activities decreased for sometime, but soon regained briskness as the people, despondent over the loss of their country, gradually relied on the eternal world as the only means of relief and hope.

The capitalistic exploitation policy of the Japanese government was so severely executed after the Independence Movement that the majority of the local people were reduced to extreme poverty, and thus tended to pursue whatever was good for their immediate survival. Taking advantage of such social trends, some 70 to 80 different kinds of quasi-religions prevailed in the society. Some of them, making false promises of an immortal life, elimination of illness and grudges, or supremacy for the religious founder, swindled money and articles out of the followers, committed lecherous deeds and even carried out murderous acts. The Baekbaekkyo religion, for instance, had the commandments against non-adultery and non-homicide, not only defrauded the individuals' assets or indulged in debauchery, but also some of its leading members acted as a murder group and under the guise of religion took more than 150 of the followers' lives.

With the conclusion of the amicable treaty with Japan in 1876 the 13th year of King Kojong of the Lee Dynasty, various Buddhist sects from Japan launched their propagation in Korea. By the time of the Independence Movement, the total number of the Japanese Buddhist missions reached more than 200 with 130,000 believers, but the majority of them were Japanese residents. The contributions the Japanese Buddhists made to benefit the local Buddhists were very few but they enabled the free passage of the native monks into the capital castle that was banned for more than three centuries by petitioning the imperial government in 1895, the 32nd year of King Kojong, and they introduced the new practice of allowing a monk to lead a family life or to take meat. Since then, the local monks made free entrance to the capital and promptly absorbed the new philosophies of life. Such developments finally led to the promulgation of an imperial decree on religion in 1902.

The Christian religion of Japan was already in Korea before the Japanese annexed the country in 1910. But, since the missionary works were limited exclusively for the Japanese residents, it made very little progress. The Tenrikyo religion, one of the Japanese Shintoism sects, on the other hand, attempted to win the Korean believers, but without much success. However, the establishment of the Shintoist shrines increased in the country ever since the Japanese occupation, and there were more than 900 shrines across the state by the end of World War II. The Japanese authorities forced the Koreans to worship at the temple in order to deprive them of their national spirit.

Since the outbreak of the Pacific War, the Japanese authorities came out with such repressive measures on all the local religions that their religious activities came to a stop. On account of their non-attendance at the Shinto shrines, many Catholic priests were put into prison cells, their churches in Taejon, Yonan, Sinkye and even the one in Pyongyang where bishops lived, were requisitioned by the Japanese army, and evey European minister was either banished or imprisoned. At this time the Protestant Church suffered the severest persecutions. All the foreign missionaries of the Church were forcibly expelled from the country, more than 200 of the church-goers were pressed into confinement en masse where more than so of its churches closed down, and some 2,000 of the church-goers were pressed into confinement en masse where more than 50 of them died. Moreover, the Japanese language was forced to be spoken in the church, the church bells were taken to be used for the production of arms, and the schools operated by the church could no longer exist. In 1942, the Presbyterian Church was consolidated by its Japanese denomination, and the Methodist Church was labelled as a reformed group. Again in 1943, the Holiness church, the Seventh-Day Adventist Church and the Baptist Church were dissolved. At the expense of such unceasing repressions, the number of Protestants that once reached more than 700,000 was decreased to half by the time Korea was liberated in 1945.

The Japanese, however, did not inflict any of its coercive measures on the local Buddhists, for they were quite adaptable to the former's religious policies. But the native Chondokyo religion also underwent the bitterness of losing its central cathedral which was used as a military supply factory and of colsing down some 20 of its provincial churches.

When, at last, the American atomic bomb brought an unconditional surrender from the Japanese government of August 15, 1945, the brothers of faith were released from confinement, and the Koreans regained their freedom of religion.

Part II

Shinkyo

Chapter 1
The Genesis of Shinkyo

The Origin

The Shinkyo(神教) religion, sometimes called Sunkyo(仙教, comparable to Taoism), was an ancient form of religion, in which the Korean people had a faith. While the former was generally regarded as having been originated from the worship of god, the latter was from the god-worshipping man who practiced the spirit ways in the mountains.

In the beginning, however, the Shinkyo developed from the worship of nature. Sometimes, the scholars maintained that the primitive religion grew out of animism that advocates life and spirit for every object ranging from man to such universal and earthly substances as the sun, moon and stars, and the mountains, rivers, trees and rocks. A clear discrimination can easily be made today between animate and inanimate objects and between the organic an non-organic matters. But, since such a judgement was not possible in the primitive age, every strange object was viewed with some sort of delusion.

The Sunkyo, one of the ancient Korean religions, also grew out of the animistic nature. In the earliest time, the people were so struck with horror and wonderment at the mysterious nature that they believed there was spirit and life in almost every strange thing. Seeing the bright sparkling sun, stars, moon, or high mountains that stretch out toward heaven, or a steadily flowing river, or a torrential rain pouring at one time, they thought there unmistakably was a certain vitality or spirit in all these things. Such ideas were later changed and names were assigned to certain particular objects. For example, the sun and the dipper among many other constellations, and the exclusively highest mountain of all mountains. Also, spirits with an invisible existence such as the god of disease was believed to control the good and bad fortunes of a humans life.

Thus, the people thought they could secure the life of comfort and delight and the life of sound longevity only by offering sacrifices through the means of sorcery and worship to the spirits. Man was basically weak and was afraid of the mortality, and it was the ultimate ideal of a man to sustain a long life by ridding himself of all kinds of anxieties, diseases, and horrors. Then, the religious life of revering the spirits began, and this was the foundation of the Shinkyo religion. The other ancient religions which believed in the spirits were mostly derived from a similar back-ground. The religious effects were expected from a certain method of sorcery or excorcism : the mediator was highly regarded as a deity, fairy, sorcerer, witch doctor, or shaman, etc..

The Hannanim and Excorcism

The spirits worshipped in the primitive age were countless, but they could be mainly classified as heavenly god, earthly god, departed human spirit, and other miscellaneous ogres.

The gods of the sun, moon, stars, storm, heat and cold were included within the category of the heavenly god. Among them, the god of the sun was most highly revered, for it was regarded as a concrete being in heaven, a superindentent of the great nature and a source of the light that nurtures every natural creation. Personified with the highest divinity of all gods in heaven, the sun was called with various reverent titles such as Hannanim, Hanwoolnim, Chosin or Chonje(all meaning God or Em-peror of Heaven). It was, therefore, customary for most of the countries in the Orient to make entreaties to Hannanim for blessings at every national occasion or festival. Sometimes, it was part of a state affair to plan a regular festival for the specific purpose of offering prayers and tributes to the god of the sun. The Yongko festival of the Booyeo State, the Moochon festival of the Ye State, the Dongmaeng of the Kokuryo and the Palkwan festival of the Silla Dynasty are good examples of this practice.

Among the earthly gods, the most popular one was the god of the mountain.   According to the Samkuk Saki, the chronicle of the Three States, the three different categories of rituals for the mountains —— the major one called Daesa (grand fete) for the three mountains of Naryerk, Kolhwa, Hyollye : the medium one called Joongsa (middle fete) for the five others including Mt. Dongtoham : and the minor one called Sosa (small fete) for still 24 others including Mt. Buaak —— were conducted in the Silla Dynasty during autumn. Also, in Kokuryo, similar mountain festivals were held along with the rites for heaven on the March 3 Hunting Day every year.

The god of Mt. Bark or called Barksan among many others was worshipped with a special emphasis. The word 'Bark' signified light or god. In the ancient periods, the people, seeing that the sun rises over the top of a high and rugged mountain, felt a great inspiration, and thought that the summit provided a junction between heaven and earth. Thus, the name of Mt. Bark or the lighted mountain was normally given after every high mountain, where the earthly god was believed to exist and the site of offering rituals for the heavenly god was selected. Such high mountains in the country as Mts. Baekdoo, Taebaek, Sobaek, Baekwol, Baekwoon, Bulham, Bulyu, etc. were those regarded as Mt. Bark. Among these, Mt. Baekdoo with its mysterious features and steepness was considered the source of all mountains in the Orient. The ancient people had a belief of worship and respect toward the mountains. Hence the theory that Hwanwoong Deity descended Mt. Baekdoo and initiated the foundation of the first ancient kingdom of Korea.

It was another belief of the ancient people that man was composed the dual elements of flesh and soul or spirit, and, after death, the former would deteriorate while the latter would still exist either by ascending to heaven or descending to the under world as an evil causing various misfortunates for mankind. In order to cope with the possible mischief from the evil spirit, the people conducted Shamanistic practices and offered sacrifices.

The souls of one's ancestor were given more faithful devotion and sincere care than any of the obscure ones, for they were believed to give more blessings to their posterities if they were served well.

Other sundry spirits, to which the people became adherent, were innumerable. They include such things as ghosts, demons, ogres, etc., and even the birds, beasts, trees and rocks were believed to possess a soul. Among them, a village tutelar god called Sonang was most popular.

In addition, the heavenly god, the earthly god, the human soul, and the other miscellaneous gods and ghosts were also believed to possess certain mysterious powers, and it was not certain as to when and in what manner they would bring harm to humans. As a result, it was inevitable for man to consecrate various rites in order to pacify them in advance. The annals of the Three States compiled by Jinsoo of the Chin Dynasty of China gives the following quotations about the rituals :

'In May of every year, the ghosts are served with sacrificial rites in the Tri-Han Dynasties, whereupon the people spend days and nights singing, dancing and drinking.'

The Book of the Latter Han Dynasty, a history written by Bumyup of the Sung Dynasty, of this quotes :

'In Ma-Han Dynasty, they serve the ghosts with sacrifices, dancing and singing every day, after the people complete ploughing in May.'

The Book of the Chin Dynasty, another history compiled by Bang, Hyung Ryung and Lee, Yeon Soo during the period of the Tang Dynasty, says :

'It was a custom of the Tri-Han Dynasties to have a high regard for the ghosts, for which the people provided festivals with singing and dancing in May every year after the planting was over.'

The Excorcist
In the ancient era, the religious influence was so powerful that almost

everything from politics to the daily life of the people was imbued with religious tints. Therefore, the religious service for the sake of the heavenly god was an integral part of the rule by the state or the mode of living along with military affair. The Tso Chuan, a Chinese Commentary on Spring and Autumn Annals, explains that the two affairs relating to religion and military constituted the major task of a country. Thus, the head of a tribe or the king of a state was not only endowed with the power to rule over the national affairs but also over the religious ones at the same time. During the theocratical periods, the governor of a state had heavier roles as an administrator of the religious rites or as an excorcist.

By being in the middle of god and man, the excorcist revealed the divine will to man, and communicate the human wishes to god. Moreover he assumed the works of furnishing the blessings from various spirits and, at the same time, forestalling the comings of misfortunes. When a man encountered a certain difficulty that was humanly impossible to be solved, or contract a disease or bad luck, he consulted the divine will or called upon various forms of conjurations and oracles. Even in the trial society, the excorcist had to be the one exceptionally well versed in astronomy, geography and medicine with an uncommon wisdom and virtue. The magic performer dwelt in a shrine built under the spiritual mountain with a hedge around it. This place was considered a divine area, so completely out of the territorial jurisdiction from the state that even if a criminal took a refuge in it, the authorities had no right to seize him. Also a magician, doctor and prophet, the excorcist or the sorcerer was the highest ideal of man, revered as Shinin(Deity) or Sunin(Fairy), since he was engaged in the divine works of inviting blessings, chasing away the calamities or practicing the spiritual ways of longevity in the mountain.

In the old theocratical age, the head of a clan group controlled the state and religion either as a king or an excorcist. But, as the ruling style of the state became complicated later with cultured progress and with the outcome of a strong tribal society, the political power spontaneously overcame the religious one, and the king held only the reign over the state, leaving the religious matters in the hands of the sorcerers. Even after religion and state were completely separated following the formation of a centralized government during the Tri-Han Dynasty periods, the social status of the witches and wizards was nevertheless reduced. But the kings and the people still depended on them for divine blessings as well as the elimination of disease and bad fortunes from the vicious spirits.

The Worship of Ancestors

One peculiar feature of the ancient Shinkyo was the admiration of ancestors, motivated mainly from a conception that the soul is immortal. Believing that man was composed of flesh and soul, the ancient people thought that if should a man die, the flesh would corrode away but the soul would remain unperished. That is, if the soul stays within the body the man is alive, but if it leaves the man is dead. The soul that left the body was believed to be continuing its existence either in heaven or in the lower world according to the good and bad that it had done in its previous life. Furthermore, the happiness of the descendants was also thought to be attainable only by offering good services to the souls of the ancestors. This conception fostered an ancestral worship among the off-spring, who provided troublesome sacrifices for their forefathers, set up shrines or even employed grave-keepers for the ancestral tombs.

Filial peity, one of the old ethical practices, was another motive for ancestral worship. Under the old family system, this was a natural outcome for the large group of a family which lived together, worked together, respected their one common head together and became attached to the communal life. The love and grace received from the head of a family were gratefully remembered by his posterity, and his works were inherited.

Along the Daedong River and around Mt. Koowol in Hwanghae province and in other areas of Manchuria, there were the scatterings of the grave stones called Koindol, a great flat stone put up on the burial ground like a table that was used for offering sacrifices. These were constructed by the descendants in order to give ancestral services.

The Dankun Deity

The founder of the ancient Chosun, Dankun, generally referred as a man of deity or a fairy, was the first one to appear as a saint of the Shinkyo religion in the history of Korea as in the case of the deified saint Yellow Emperor or Huangti, the founder of China. The word Dankun implies Dankul meaning the sorcerer, who healed the sick, the distressed, and governed the people with the will of God. Dankun had the greatest power within his empire and, therefore, was most respected. His forefathers, Hwanwoong and Hwanin, lived under the god-descended tree in Mt. Taebaek and unified several other clans living there to form the first tribal state that later developed into Ancient Chosun.

Following the will of his forefathers, Dankun ruled well over the people with a broad concern for the welfare of mankind and was himself so highly virtuous that various tribes of the neighborhood gradually submitted to his dominion. According to the memoirs of historical books, the Dankun descendants reigned over Chosun for 2,000 years until Wiman established the new empire. They then retreated to the divine village of Assita, where they ended their successive rule of Old Chosun. Up to the present, there have been many contending arguments about the history of Dankun. But the fact that his dominion had lasted for about 20 centuries means that his divine position as Dankul or the sorcerer had been successful for that length of time. Soon after the ruin of Ancient Chosun, Dankun and his descendants retreated into the mountain and became the witches and wizards assuming only spiritual divine works.

The lineage of Dankun was followed by Hwangum at Mt. Baekdooak, one of the eight hermit shrines in Seokyung(now Pyongyang). Cho, Yeo Juk, one of the group practicing fairy witchcraft at the time of King Sunjo of the Lee Dynasty, wrote in his Chung Hak literary collections that the heavenly God Hwanin was the very founder of the fairy belief in Chosun. His son, Hwanwoong succeeded him in governing both religion and state, and that Dankun, after a thousand years of preaching magic, went into the mountain to become a fairy being. In view of this, the Dankun generations of Hwanin, Hwanwoong, Hwangum, and their succeeding ones thereafter were presumed to have been sorcerers and fairies.

The place where Hwanwoong first made his descension in Mt. Baekdoo was called the city of god. But the opinions vary whether this took place in Mt. Baekdoo, Mt. Myohyang, Mt. Mani, Mt. Koowol, etc,. However, the divine tree, through which he was said to have come down, could be compared with the god-tree that is worshipped as a tutelar in a village today. As for the city of god, it must have been so named because many people of the deity converged at the area when Hwanwoong and Hwangum carried out witchcraft.

The Samshin-san (meaning the three-god mountain)

Instead of meaning the three mountain gods, this represents Mt. Baekdoo, where three gods or three fairies of Hwanin, Hwanwoong and Hwangum dwelt. Mt. Baekdoo was originally called Barkan, the first syllable of which meant the light or the divine light. Thus, it was the mountain of light or of divinity. The mountain had the highest peak in the Orient over which the sun rose and was the juncture of heaven and earth, was a place to give sacrifices to god, and was itself the god for regional sacrifices.

Hwanwoong, the son of Hwanin, established the first city of god under the god-tree in Mt. Taebaek, bringing all the tribes around the mountain under his domination. After marrying with another divine family, he gave birth to the Dankun deity, who then founded the kingdom of Ancient Chosun. Ever since, Mt. Baekdoo was called the Samshin-san after the three divine figures.

Not only had Hwanin been an exceptionally virtuous deity, but his son Hwanwoong also provided many graces for the people with his ideal rule to make man magnanimous. In establishing Ancient Chosun, Hwangum also adopted the same line of rule with such a benevolence that popular feeling was greatly converted. The prestige and the spiritual teachings of these three divine characters were greatly covered by ensuing generations, who believed that the personal fatality, safety, and the soul after death were supervised by the three gods. An article in the Memoire of the Three States said to the effect that Hwanwoong descended the City of God to supervise some 360 sorts of affairs for mankind. Considering the three gods inhabited in such high mountains as Mt. Koowol, Mt. Mani and Mt. Myohyang, the people later called those high mountains Mt. Taebaek. They set up the Samsung Shrine in Mt. Koowol to offer sacrifices for the three gods, the religious altar in Mt. Mani for the three fairies, and many people began to think that Dankun Wanggum had lived in Mt. Myohyang. One of the old practices to give sacrificial rites on National Foundation or the Day of Dankun's Accession on October 3 are still observed today.

It was also called the Day of Taebaek or the Day of Hyangsan because of an optical illusion that the 'lighted(or Bark) mountain', where the three gods dwelt, was any highest mountain. However, the Travelogue of the Western Region written by Cha, Surl Rak proved that Mt. Myohyang was neither Mt. Taebaek nor Mt. Koowol the three-god mountain. With regard to this, it said, "Although the Dankuns were said to have descended of the fairies borne in Mt. Myohyang because of the many old remains there of heavenly makings, Taebaek stands for the Mt. Baekdoo, but not the Mt. Myohyang. But the name of Taebaek was given to it ever since someone practiced the immortal ways in the mountain during the age of Dankun."

By all indications, however, the three deities seemed to have had lived in Mt. Baekdoo. The report that they were perpetuating their lives on such a fairy elixir as ginseng spread throughout the country and across the neighboring Chiness states of Yen and Ch'i Dynasties. Emperors Wei and Suan of the Ch'i and Emperor Chao of the Yen, the believers of the deity and fairy, then were convinced about the legends of this three-god Mt. Baekdoo in the Orient.

Then, there was various supposition about the geographical location of this Samshin-san. For instance, the Annals of the Sacrifice and Worship in the historical records of the Han and Chou Dynasties of China inferred that it was only a mirage appearing in the Gulf of Bohai. In the History of Chou Dynasty, it is quoted : "The mirage of appearing at the sea-side gives the form of a lofty tower, while the other one appearing at the prairie gives the shape of an imperial palace···" Tungfang Shuo, an adroit and eloquent humorist during the Former Han Dynasty, wrote in his Travelogue about the Ten Fairy Islands, the Book of Marvels and in other works as if the three-god mountain was Mts. Kunlun in Chosun, home of the gods and fairies, and explained, "Mt. Hsienpu of the Kunlun had a nine-fold castle built around it that reached some miles in height." In addition, many necromancers then asserted that the three mountains of P'englai, Fangchang and Yingchu in the Gulf of Bohai were the very mountains of the three gods. At any rate, it was known to the Chinese people that the gods and fairies had been living in these mountains where there was a medicinal herb that enabled man to live a perpetual life. Many Chinese people including the emperors were fascinated to hunt for the medicinal herb in the mountains. Some of them even became insane after taking the wrong herbs.

When the Chinese necromancer named Sufu of the Ch'in Dynasty attempted to get the elixir for the Dynasty's Founding Emperor, he must have been sure of getting them. The Emperor also had his faith in the medicine. So, as soon as Sufu wrote to the ruler explaining about the three-god mountain in the Gulf of Bohai and about the fairies living there and producing the medicines he was permitted to look for the divine being with the help of thousands of young men and women. But, once he had gone, he never returned nor did he find the mountain. One story relates that Sufu arrived at Cheju Island off the southwestern coast of Korea. However, Sufu's theory about the mountain seems to have been based on an illusion of a high mountain in Korea that was reflected over the sky of Bohai. Affected by the popular imagination of the Chinese necromancers, the Confucians of Chosun also thought that Mt. Kumkang, Mt. Chiri and Mt. Halla were the fairy mountains.

In actuality, neither the Chinese nor the people of Chosun knew about the real location of the so-called Samshin-san. Where, then, mountain is no other than Mt. Taebaek. The other records related that it was situated somewhere in the sea of Bohai, and there the fairies existed and the immortal herbs grew, the white birds and animals lived and the palace with gold and silver was built. The General Topography of the Tang Dynasty of China said in part : "To the south, there is a white mountain. All the birds and animals living in it, and all the trees and grasses growing in it are white···" The Songmak Kimun said : "Mt. Jangback(Long White Mountain) that stretched over a thousand miles across the East from its iced peak is where the white-robbed merciful goddess inhabited. Even the birds and animals living in the mountain are all white, and man can not dare put a foot into it···" In view of the fact that there are still a number of the white birch-trees, white deers, white hogs and white eagles living in Mt. Baekdoo and quantities of the sandalwood are produced in this mountain area, it seems that this is where the so-called Samshin-san or the three-god mountain is located.

The Dogmatic Contents

In a way, the Shinkyo religion with its worship for the various souls and spirits belong to polytheism, but it later developed through and was inherited by the three major tendencies such as the excorcism, denominational Shinkyo and folklore Shinkyo.

As has been previously mentioned, the old religion embraced a wide-range of contents, but there were no definite doctrines based on the philosophical and theoretical backgrounds as could be found in Buddhism or Christianity. Perhaps, they might not have been necessary with this particular form of religion, because it could survive through the people for generations from the ancient times. The strong influences of Buddhism and Confucianism during the Koryo and Lee Dynasties deprived the religion of its chances for formation of its doctrines. But at the closure of the Lee Dynasty, the work barely possible with the emergence of a sectarian

Shinkyo called Daejong-kyo.

The unconditional worshiping for Hannanim(mighty God), nature, ancestor, and the admiration for purity were the main creeds of the Shinkyo religion.

The Hannanim or Heavenly God was the supreme and eternal god of all, reigning over life and death, fortune and misfortune of all mankind, and nurturing every living thing in the universe. He was absolutely believed to save mankind with his spiritual power, when man offered whole-hearted prayers and sacrifices. Depending on the degree of one's sincerity, therefore, the man would either receive his Graces or Damnation. Whereas the God abhored the vice and impurity, the man always endeavoured to do good and behave decently.

Beside, the other gods including ghosts, human souls, natural gods and miscellaneous ogres were also believed to possess spiritual power, with which they would impose various harm on man unless man engages in sincere devotions. If any harm was done, the man used the conducts of sorceries, incantations, conjurations or prayers to ask blessings from the Absolute Power of Heaven.

Thus, the worship for the Power and elimination of the devil were regarded indispensable in inviting the happiness and welfare of the world. The soul of a man was believed to be immortal by ascending to heaven as a good spirit if one had conducted virtuous deeds during his lifetime, and this stimulated the people to do only good. Hwanwoong's ideal and philosophy of ruling were derived from this Shinkyo religous belief.

Another characteristic of the Shinkyo was the reverence toward light and purity. Therefore, spiritually sinister thoughts or physical pollution were all considered a crime. The practices of the people looking up on the east, where the sun rises, and of the people enjoying the wearing of white clothes also originated from this Shinkyo concept.

The religious formalities of Shinkyo varied in many ways, but they were mainly executed by the sorcerers who were regarded as the sole arbitrators of man with the divine spirits, although this attitude was changed to a great extent in later periods.

Chapter 2
Shinkyo of the Three Kingdoms

The Hwa Rang

This was a particular religious group practicing the method and technique of longevity during the periods of the Three Kingdoms when the state and religion were no longer an integral part of the rule so that the sorcerers were only engaged in the sacrificial works of the country or village. The Shini kyung, or the Book of Marvels, quotes : In the Orient, there lived the men wearing the plain white belt, and the women the colored clothes. They always face each other politely but do not violate, do respect each other but not disparage, venturing their lives for the sake of the others in calamities or perils. They are the people called men of virtue.' In fact, they were the group of men regarded as the fairy class in the first part of the unification of the Three Kingdoms. The men of the fairy class, in turn, represented the Hwa Rang group of the Silla Dynasty who cultivated the ways of god and the fairy, acquired the arts of military and disciplined their spirits. There was a similar group called Jooi(or Black-robed Hermits) in the Kokuryo Dynasty.

The Hwa Rang group was also referred to as Poongryu, Sungrang, Wonhwa, Kookson, etc,. In a preface to the Ranrang Monument, Choi, Chi Won wrote : 'In this country, there is an occult religion called Poongryu. As described in the History of the Fairy(Sunsa) the origins of the religion, the Poongryu is, in fact, a compound of the three religions.' A positive study cannot be made on this fact as the historical record is no

longer available. Choi, however, further wrote : 'Engaging exclusively
in the works of non-interference and in the performances of the doctrines
of silence, it assimilated a sect of the Laotzu philosophy of the Chou
Dynasty.' This proves that the Hwa Rang group was a sect in pursuit
of the ways of gods and fairies. H eretofore, many had a view that the
Hwa Rang was merely a group of warriors or ascetics, neglecting the fact
that it was, instead, the highest national religious sect of the Sunkyo creed.
The three religion combination, for the system it may be true, the Hwa
Rang was already nationally established by the 37th year of King Jinheung
of the Silla Dynasty(576) when the Buddhist influence had been in full
bloom and the Confucian morals deeply penetrated in the higher class
aristocrats. Over a length of time, the Shinkyo religion could well have
intermingled with the two other foreign religions to some extent. True,
Hwa Rang was the group of young warriors with asceticism as its object,
but its central concept was based on the Shinkyo of spiritual worship and
Taoism of non-interference with nature, flavored with some Confucian
doctrines. In the beginning, it was a band of the followers of the Shinkyo
religion, learning the divine principles and manners from the sorcerers.
After the religion made a complete secession from the state the sectarian
Shinkyo was formed, and this was the very Hwa Rang Group. There was
another Shinkyo sect called Soongchon-kyo in Silla. With the development
of these sects, various canons of Shinkyo were written called Sunsa(the
History of the Fairy), Shinji Bisa(the Annals of God and the Phrases of
Secrets) that described the religious doctrines, the fairy ballads and dances
necessary in performing the di vine works composed and designed, and
the pilgrimages to the spiritual mountains conducted together with the
practices of writing, archery, horse-riding and mathematics.

Although such a Shinkyo sect as Hwa Rang was basically founded as
a religious tenet, it also took a greater role for a group of young warriors
because of the national need. Some examples were the Army of Hangma
(Defeating Devils) established by the Buddhist monks during the periods
of King Hyeonjong of Koryo Dynasty for the purpose of national defense,

and the Army of Volunteer Monks organized the periods of the Lee Dynasty's King Sunjo to resist the Japanese invading troops.

The Joui Sunin(or the Black-robed Fairy Group)

Like the Hwa Rang group of Silla, this was an organization of young warriors of the Kokuryo periods, practicing both the disciplines and doctrines of the military and Shinkyo religion. The origin of this group could also be traced back to the sorcerers of the theocratical age. About the second century, Chang Do Ryung of the Han Dynasty found the Odumikyo religion in China based on the sutras of Laotzu, which taught the military arts and the Taoist practices concerning room manners. The immortal group of Kokuryo assimilated the Chinese patterns, as it is described in the History of New Tang Dynasty : 'In Kokuryo, there is a grand house called Kyungdang built by the road-side, where young men and women recited sutras and practiced archery in groups.'

There are few records available that could lead us to a clear understanding of the Kokuryo fairy group with the exception of what Kim, Boo Shik, a distinguished scholar of Koryo Dynasty, related in the History of the Three Kingdoms with some excerpts cited from the Book of the Sui Dynasty of China. All the historical evidences in relation to the Hwa Rang or the Joui groups have long disappeared. Kim, however, only mentioned that there was 'the Joui group in Kokuryo'. But the Koryo Dokyung, a sketch book of Koryo written by Su Ko of the Sung Dynasty, said : 'The married monks, in their fine white linen dresses with the black belt around their waist, lived in the country with their families, but without carrying the Buddhist commandments or wearing surplice. They always endeavoured in public works as cleaning the road, clearing out the ditch or repairing the castle. When the war broke out, they would volunter themselves together with their colleagues with provisions for the battle and be courageously willing to go forward to the battlefront. Altouth they were, in fact, the underlings of castration, they were called monks simply because their appearance with the head and beard shaven gave the

impression of a Buddhist priest.' All those explanations correspond with
the inherited traditions of the Kokuryo's fairy group. It was perhaps because of the height of the Buddhist prosperity in the earlier part of the
Koryo Dynasty, when the cropped haircut or shaving were the prevailing
mores of life, that the group was compared with the married monks. The
Joui fairies were also regarded as eunuchs after Kokuryo perished by Silla
because they were castrated to one of the low classes and were treated as
such. Such a social attitude and treatment toward the Kokuryo warrior
group has undoubtedly been continued for sometime even after the foundation of the Koryo Dynasty. This is similar to the Buddhist monks who
in the higher position during the age of Koryo but were degraded to one
of the eight low social classes including butcher, bier bearer, etc——after
various Buddhist persecutions during the periods of the Lee Dynasty.

The Introduction of the Odumi Religion

The famous scholars of the Lee Dynasty often tended to accept the
Sunkyo religion of Ancient Chosun as a lower branch of Taoism of China.
But, in fact, the Chinese religion was first introduced in Korea during
the years of King Youngryu in the later part of Kokuryo Dynasty.
According to the History of the Three Kingdoms and the History of the
New and Old Tang Dynasty, Li, Yuan, that is, the Founding Emperor
Kao Ts'ou of Tang dispatched the Taoist priests with the images of their
god to Kokuryo in the 7th year of King Youngryu as a means to improve
goodwill relations. In so far as the historical records are concerned, this
was the beginning of Chinese Taoism in Korea, and it was then called
Odumi-kyo(or religion).

At the time, the popular Shinkyo belief began to harmonize with the
new foreign religion, for the two had many things in common, such as,
offering sacrifices to constellations, mountains and rivers, or performing
sorceries through the medium. Therefore, when the Taoist preachers began
the lectures on the Laotzu scriptures in Kokuryo, thousands of interested
persons including the followers of Shinkyo and even King Youngryu

himself attended, according to the History of the Three Kingdoms. The number of the converts to the Odumi religion seemed to have increased radically within a short period of time. The king later sent another envoy to learn the religious doctrines and formalities in Tang Dynasty.

'The three religions of Buddhism, Confucianism and Taoism are like the legs of a tripod. Although the prosperity of Buddhism and Confucianism is remarkable in our country, the Taoist improvement is lagging behind because its magic practices are not well projected.' counseled a dexterous minister named Yonkaesomoon to the king in the 2nd year of King Bojang of Kokuryo. In view of this remark, it seems that there was not as many Taoist followers as the others even though it was 30 years since Taoism was first introduced. Taking the minister's advice, King Bojang sought out the Taoist propagation from T'ai Tsung of the Tang Dynasty by sending his envoy in March of the 2nd year of his rule. T'ai Tsung, in turn, dispatched 8 Taoist priests including Shu Ta to Kokuryo. The Taoism brought in during the two different philosophies of Laotzu and Fairy, the religious sect of which was organized by Chang Taoling in the years of Emperor Shunti of the Post Han Dynasty. After practicing the ways of immortal longevity in Mt.Ku Ming, Chang came to propagate the religion, healing the sick with his three-sense technique, prohibiting drinking and killing, and carrying out the aid projects for the travellers. He also had the believers of his religion pay a tribute consisting of five bushles(Odu) of rice(mi) by every individual house, from which the name of the religion originated. Using the teachings of Laotzu as its scriptures, Chang's Taoist sect had three separate religious classes for the followers such as Kuijol for new comers Kanryung or Jaeju, and Ridu, these gradually expanded. Through Chang's 2nd and 3rd generations, the religious influence predominated the entire territories of the Han Dynasty, and these landlords or viceroys. Before he was subjugated by Ts'ao of the Wei Dynasty, Chang Sung, the fourth successor of the religion, removed the religious headquaters to Mt. Lunghu in Kiangsi, where it also flourished.

Though it might have been the precedent of Taoism in Kokuryo, Chang

Taoling's Odumi religion lacked the theoretical systems of other religions. It had an ambiguous attitude on whether the heavenly being really existed, or, assuming they do, if an ordinary person could become one of them. Afterwards, the theoretical foundation of the religion was systematically laid out by the two famous Chinese Taoists, Wei Peyang of the Post Han and Ko Hung of the Chin Dynasty. During the age of the Tang Dynasty, the Taoist priests decided to place Laotzu as the founder of the Chinese state on the sophisticated grounds that the surname of Laotzu matched with that of the country. In approval of the sophistication, Emperor Kao Ts'ou established the Temple of Laotsu, and Emperor Tai Tsung worshipped the Taoist founder more than Buddha. Emperor Kao Tsung bestowed the highest title of respect on the Laotzu Temple and ordered everyone under the rank of marquis to learn the Taoist scriptures, and provided the public servant examinations with religious literature. Such developments resulted in a great thriving of the Taoist religion in Tang Dynasty of China along with the Buddhism and Confucianism.

The Shinkyo Religion of Baekje

When the state of Baekje was established in the territories belonging to the Jin-han and Ma-han Dynasties, there were more than 50 tribal states already in existence. The Annals of the Wei Dynasty in China gave a following description on the Three Han Dynasties of Korea : 'One man from each tribal state was selected the master of sacrifices offered to God in Heaven, and he was called the son of Heaven.' Likewise, the religion and state were already divided in these periods, the sorcerers executing the sacrificial rites regarded the son of heaven, and their dwelling place regarded as the divine area. The sorcerers lived in a spiritual mountainwith the hedge built around their places, and assumed the roles of mediators between man and god.

Such Shinkyo beliefs of the Three Han Dynasties directly descended to the Kingdom of Baekje and gained a great momentum as a popular religion until Buddhism was introduced. With regard to the Shinkyo deity and fairy of Baekje, the Samkuk Yoosa(the historical memories of the Three Kingdoms) relates the following in its Volume Ⅱ :' In a provincial district of kun, there are the three mountains called Ilsan, Osan and Boosan. During the golden prosperity of the kingdom, the deities(or the fairies) lived on each of the three mountain tops, flying uneasily from one summit to another in the mornings evenings.' The mountain quoted here seemed to have some connection with that of the Samshin-san, or the three-god mountain, and the one who became a deity then must have been believed to be able to fly. Not long age, an old square tile that had the sketches of the three forested mountain tops and the picture resembling a Taoist temple and prist, was discovered. Along with the other historical records, this illustrates that the deified figures had been living in the mountain even during the age of Baekje. Especially after the Buddhist religion was introduced with many converts from the royal families, the Shinkyo sorcerers who officiated at the religious affairs of the state were driven out.

The Chinese Taoism, on the other hand, apparently did not flow into the Baekje Dynasty, but the ideas of Laotzu-Chuangtzu were no less influential because of the number of books relating to Buddhism, Confucianism and Taoism which were brought in from China as a result of the state's frequent surface communication with the mainland. According to the Samkook Saki(the History of the Three Kingdoms), the Kokuryo army invaded Baekje during the years of the latters' King Keunchoko. Crushing the invading troops at the place called Bankurlyang, the prince of Baekje(who later became King Keunkoos) pursued the invaders to the area northwest of Sookok Castle. At this time, General Mak Ko Hae pleaded to the prince in command : 'I have been aware of the Taoist maxim that said one must learn how to be satisfied so as not to be in disgrace, and when to halt to save himself from danger. Since we have made many gains already, do we still have to continue our pursuit?' It was said the prince then stopped his advance to overcome the Kokuryo army. In view of this, there seemed to have been many generals who believed in the Taoist conception in Baekje. A pundit like Dr. Wang In(Wani in Japanese) who migrated to Japan from Baekje, was also said to have been a Taoist-mined scholar. As such, the doctrines of Laotzu-Chuangtzu, even if not a religious form, permeated throughout the country along with the Confucianism.

The Taoism and the Downfall of Kokuryo

Following the arrival of the eight Chinese Taoist priests including Shuta from the Tang Dynasty, King Bojang of Kokuryo not only abolished the Buddhist temple to replace it with the Taoist one but he placed the Taoist priests in higher positions than others in religious ceremonies. He also ordered the Chinese priests to assume the roles of appeasing the nature or giving invocations to the Dragon God. Thus, the Taoist influence grew up in the royal palace of Kokuryo with an increasing animosity from both the Buddhists and Confucians.

Bodok, a famous Buddhist priest at the close of the Kokuryo Dynasty who established eight temples with his followers and headed the Yonbok temple in Mt. Banyong, beseeched the Taoist-minded king many times that the destiny of the state was in danger because of the radical tendencies of the imperial court. But King Bojang, did not listen. Dissatisfied over the imperial government, Bodok took a secret leave from Mt. Banyong toward south in the 9th year of the king, and reestablished his sanctuary in Mt. Kodae located in Wansan prefecture of the Baekje Dynasty. After Priest Bodok had left, Kokuryo seemed to have continued for some time. But the disunity within the political powers, and the strife among the flesh and blood of the powerful retainer named Yonkaesomoon soon erupted. At this time, that is, in the 27th year of King Bojang, the united forces of the Silla and Tang Dynasties launched attacks, and the 700-year-old Kokuryo Dynasty finally collapsed.

Although Kokuryo that worshipped Taoism crumbled, the Silla Dynasty with her devotion to Buddhism achieved the unification of the Three Kingdoms, and, Silla believed that her religion had overpowered Taoism. Therefore, there was not a trace of Taoism in Silla, for it was constantly ignored while Buddhism was extensively encouraged.

The Palkwan Festival

This was one of the Shinkyo ceremonies of the Kokuryo Dynasty relayed to Silla by the Buddhist Priest Heiryang. The priest was the one who looked after the safety of Keojubu, an agent sent from Silla to Kokuryo. Later, when Kochibu launched an invasion against Kokuryo after he was promoted to a higher government position in the 32nd year of King Jin-heung, Priest Heiryang accompanied his former protege into Silla, where he was given the religious title of Seungtong, and advised the king to observe the festival. The Palkwan feast was initiated and conducted in an amphitheatre in early winter with many people including the sovereigns and servants participating in dedicating sacrifices to gods and nature, and to enjoy drinks, refreshments, songs and dances together. Palkwan came after Tongmaeng festival of Kokuryo and similar events conducted by other states were the Yongko festival of Booyeo, The Moochon festival of Ye and the Jaechon festival of Ma-han Dynasty. According to the Koryo-sa(the History of Koryo), one hundred activities including songs and dances were performed after the festival was over. These were inherited from Silla. Shin, Chae Ho gave the following explanation about 'the hundred activities' in the chosun Sangko Moonhwa-sa(the History of Ancient Culture in Chosun): 'The first performance is called Hanmaeng(meaning Fighting in the Water), in which two contestants stand face to face in the water, and fight with splashes and stones to decide the victor. The second one is called Soobak(meaning Striking with Hands), whereby the two fighters strike one another with their bare fists to win the contest, and this latter developed into judo in Japan and Chuanfa in China. The third game is the art of fencing, which was most emphasized by the warriors of Booyeo, the fairy group of Kokuryo and the Hwa Rang group of Silla. The fourth is archery, for which the Chinese people regarded the Koreans in the ancient period as most skillful and talented. The fifth is the game of ball-striking, or called Kyugku, in a specially-provided ball-ground. The sixth is the game of hitting a man with a bullet. The seventh is horse-riding, and the eight is the game of hunting. There should be more games of different varities. As it was said of hundred abilities, but the before-mentioned games of eight kinds were the main events of the festival as the name Palkwan(eight parts) implied.' The formalities and the games of this Shinkyo festival, which dated back to the ancient Dankun era when they were no more than a primitive religious ceremony, might have gone through many changes with the elapse of time. They were finally inherited by the Koryo Dynasty.

Similar religious events of the Palkwan were also observed in the Chinese dynasties as Chin and Liao, and in Japan, where they shared religious and racial heritages similar to those of Koreans.

Chapter 3
The Conciliation of Shinkyo and Taoism

Shinkyo and the Founder of Koryo

Though he was a faithful Buddhist, King Taejo, the founder of the Koryo Dynasty, was so devout that he did not neglect to offer sacrifices for various Shinkyo gods such as the sun, five mountains, great rivers, etc.. Even in December of the first year of Taejo, the period of King Kyungmyung of Silla, the post Baekje Dynasty was indespicably powerful. But, wishing to fulfill the great achievement of unifying the three kingdoms, Taejo revived the Palkwan festival in the ball-ground with lighted laterns shining in the area all through the night, and, at the same time, performances of the hundred sports, songs and dance, together with the masquerade show of parading the dragon and phoenix-shaped horse-wagons took place. As was the case in silla the festival in Koryo was opened with a libation for the local gods and was followed by various entertainment ranging from offering liquor, cakes, music, and dancing to sports. As it is explained in the Koryo Dokyung(the Illustration Book of the Koryo Dynasty), such festive events were handed down from Silla and Kokuryo.

King Taejo, in his later years, even attempted to preserve the Palkwan festival as a national event throughout the succeeding reigns of Koryo by leaving a ten-article injunction to his successor. "My wishes are with the lighted lantern festival and the Palkwan······ which is to serve the Heavenly God, the five mountains, the famous mountains, the great river and the dragon god. Let no villainous subject in the later years propose any amendments to the formalities of this festival for god," said the King in one of the articles. "From the beginning, it is my heart-felt wish that sovereigns and subjects should be pious on this occasion and should enjoy the even together," the King continued.

Ever since, the Palkwan festival was conducted prosperously for some time through the ensuing years, even though some of its formalities were seasoned with Buddhist flavors to some extent. But, during the years of the sixth King Sungjong, the sovereigns and subjects adhered only to Confucianism and Buddhism, and the observat ion of the festival became stagnate on the grounds that it had incurred extreme burdens with all its miscellaneous events. Hence, the festival was not observed for about thirty years. At the request of a man named Choi, Hang during the eighth King Hyeonjong, however, it again came to life and continued through the successive reigns of the Koryo Dynasty as an important national event. The event then was held for two days, during which time the local ma-gistrates presented to the king their congratulations, and literatures. Many foreign envoys or merchants paid tributes to the king or executed their business transactions with commodities.

The Admiration for Shinkyo

As the prosperity of Buddhism reached its height in Koryo, the Buddhist temples and statutes were erected in the spiritual mountains or places, where the Shinkyo gods were worshipped. But the History of Koryo related that the Shinkyo belief was equally pervasive among the local populaces addicted in serving various ghosts or spirits. On the other hand, the royal households were so susceptible to the Taoist influence prevailing in the Sung Dynasty of China that numerous Taoist gods including the Five Sovereigns High in Heaven, the Polar Star, Mars, Venus, etc., were worshipped with sacrifices during the periods of King Moonjong. The Supreme Deity of Taoism was enshrined in the royal place by King Sook-jong ; and the image of his Primal Celestial Excellency, the highest god of Taoism, was enshrined in the Occhok Pavillion in the 2nd year of King Yejong and sacrifices were offered.

During the years of King Injong in the middle of Koryo, the Palsung-dang(meaning a shrine for eight saints) with the description inside of the images of the eight Taoist deities was constructed within the imperial palace at the request of Jung, Ji Sang, a royal subject, and a separate religious palace in honor of the deities was built in Mt. Songak, where the divine beings were reported to be living. According to the collection of the Jung, Ji Sang's writings, the eight saints or deities signified, first of all, the Mt. Taebaek Fairies of Mt. Baekdoo : second, the Transcendentals of Mt. Yongwui : third, the Angels of Wolsung : fourth, the Pyongyang Fairies of early Kokuryo : fifth, the Mt. Mokmyok Fairies of early Koryo ; sixth, the Hermits of Mt. Songak : seventh, the Deity of Mt. Jeungsongak : and, lastly, the Goddess of Mt. Duak. The origins of these eight deified characters can not be traced. But, considering the names of the high mountains, the eight deities tried to attain immortality by pursuing asceticism in the spiritual mountain.

By the middle of Koryo, the Sunkyo religion became so amalgamated with Buddhism that its pure tenets were barely visible. Instead, the two religion were mixed and the Hyangdo group appeared, and the eight deified characters were inferred as half-deity and half-Buddha or Boddhisattva.

The 18th King Uijong of Koryo not only admired the Sunkyo religion himself within the imperial court, but also encouraged the belief in Buddhism and Sunkyo by issuing a four-point message to the people in the 22nd year of his rule in Sokyung(now Pyongyang). The message read :

First, the Buddhist services shall be respected with a great-value.
Second, the Buddhist monks shall be treated with reverence.
Third, the Buddhist Trinity shall be protected.
Fourth, the customs of Sunkyo shall be observed continuously.

The Establishment of the Taoist Temples

Under the influence of the sung Dynasty in China, the imperial courts of Koryo were already serving many celestial gods including Supreme Deity of Taoism at the time of the 15th King Sookjong. But the first Taoist temple was not built until the next ruler King Yejong, sent a man named Lee, Joong Yak to China to specialize in the principle doctrines of Taoism. At this time, Emperor Hui Tsung of the Sung Dynasty was very fascinated by and so absorbed in the religion of Taoism which was in its golden age in China. Learning the religious minute and formalities from the Chinese priest named Huang Dachung, and observing the Taoist prosperity in Sung, Lee, Joong Yak returned and transplanted the religion in Koryo. Later, in the 5th year of King Yejong, two Chinese Taoïst priests were sent to Koryo from the Sung Dynasty in china. Then, the first Chinese- styled Taoist temple, called Bokwon-koong or Bokwon-kwan, was established with the cooperation of the two foreign priests, and the religion was taught to the interested people. In Volume III, the Annals of Joongkyung(the capital of Koryo, which is now Kaesung), there is the following quotation about the Taoist temple. "It is located in the north of the Imperial Household by the Taehwa Gate. The images of the Taoist Trinity are depicted within the temple, and Kings Yejong and Uijong made personal visits to offer sacrifices in it." The Taoist Trinity signified the primordial powers of heaven, earth and water.

According to the works written about the temples by Kim, Dam, an official of Koryo during the 4th year of King Taejong, there were more Taoist temples such as Sokyuk-jon, Jungsa-eup, Daechung-jon, Kooyo-dang, etc. set up in Kaesung after the Bokwon-kwan, and another temple called Taeil-jon was presumed to have been established in such local towns as Hwanyung, Chongju, Boopyung and Kusung.

The temple Kooyo-dang, among others, was the one originally set up in Kanghwa by King Kojong when the king took refuge there from the invading Mongol troops, but reestablished in the capital castle of Kaekyung after it was retaken. The name Taeil, also called Taeul, of the local temple meant the God of Heaven, to which the consecutive emperors of China from the Han Dynasty served with sacrifices.

The Frequent Taoist Services

After Taoism was introduced in Koryo, the frequencies of offering sacrifices in honor of the Taoist gods as well as the local gods increased in volume.

For instance, in his 2nd, 10th, 18th, 19th and 27th years, King Moonjong hosted the services himself respectively for the Taoist idols of Polar Star, Taeil(or Sun) Constellation, Mars-Jupiter and the hundred gods located at the temple, the ball-ground and the imperial palace. He also served-sacrificial rituals personally for the local gods of heaven, earth, mountain and river in his 5th, 14th, 20th and 25th years at the amphitheatre.

The next king, King Soonjong died after he was enthroned only three months, and the succeeding one, King Sunjong, was no less devoted to the services than his predecessor. Thereafter, there were few royal successors who followed the Taoist religious services.

The Mixture of Taoism and Buddhism

The Taoist religion introduced into the Koryo Dynasty at the time of King Yejong from the Sung Dynasty made a good impact into the imperial courts and the people, in combination with the local Shinkyo devotion admired heaven, earth, mountain and river which was inherited from Ancient Chosun. As the royal household favoured both Buddhism and Taoism as the court religion, the two not only existed compatibly and in harmony, but gradually also became intermixed. The people followed the royal tendeney to believe Buddhism along with their local gods. Thus, in the religious ceremonies and manners, there were many combined elements from the two religions.

The Palkwan Festival was, for instance, itself a Shinkyo ritual handed down from the age of the Three Kingdoms with the mixture of Taoist flavours. But by having the lighted lanterns hung and by allowing the

Buddhist monks to attend the festival, it turned out to be a melange of all religious formalities. When the Palsung-dang shrine was built in the Rimwon Imperial Palace in Pyongyang to enshrine the eight Taoist fairies in the 8th year of King Injong, there were quibbles that Taoist fairies were the real Buddha or Boddhisattva from India. After the middle of Koryo, on the other hand, there were many instances, whereby the Supreme Deity of Taoism was worshipped at the Buddhist temple as if it were the Sakra Devanam Indra, the celestial emperor of Buddhism. The Great Bear, another Taoist god in heaven, was also served in the Buddhist shrines with prayers for seeking blessings and eliminating misfortunes. Even in a Chinese transliteration of the Saddharma Pundarika, one of the Buddhist sutras, there was a line explaining··· the Supreme Deity of Taoism can also be represented by the Sakra Devanam Indra···, Many Chilsung(seven stars) Pavillions dedicating to the Great Bear were built in the Buddhist shrines after the middle of Koryo, mainly because of the worship of the constellation by the Esoteric Buddhists and especially because of the Chilsung festival which King Moonjong initiated in the court.

The Arrival of Suh, Sa Hao in Koryo

In the 19th year of King Kongmin at the end of Koryo, a Taoist priest by name of Suh, Sa Hao was dispatched from the Ming Dynasty in China to assist in giving the sacrificial services for the major mountains and rivers in Koryo.

When the eight Chinese Taoists arrived in Kokuryo at the period of King Bojang from the Tang Dynasty, and, later, the two in Koryo during the years of King Yejong from the Sung Dynasty, they had played the roles only of religious missionaries. But Suh Sa Hao's visit was made with the more political objectives to enhance the prestige of his country. The Hankook Dokyosa(the History of Taoism in Korea) written by Lee, Neung Hwa gives the following excerpts of the Suh's writings on his services in Koryo. 'The reason Ming's court sent imperial priest Suh, Sa

Hao to consecrate sacrifices for the gods of Prominent Mountains and Rivers in Koryo is··· because the Koryo Dynasty honors with respect Ming's court's achievement of world unification, and expresses an allegiance to the Ming's government···' Although the priest from the Ming Dynasty was purely on a political mission, his visit, needless to say, accelerated the development of Taoism in Koryo.

Chapter 4
Shinkyo of Lee Dynasty

The Sokyuk-su Pavillion

King Lee Taejo, the founder of the Lee Dynasty, abolished all the
existing Taoist temples and established the Sokyuk-su pavillion in place
of them. This was done in November of the first year of the king at the
written advice from the Board of Rites, which said to the effect that the
services should be simple and solemn rather than intricate in the number
of the temples. As a consolidated Taoist shrine, the Sokyuk-su pavillion
was first built in Songdo in August of the third year of Taejo, but was
destroyed later to be reestablished at Seoul.

Lee Taejo had his devotion not only in Confucianism, but also inwardly
in Buddhism and Taoism. Even before he was enthroned, Taejo built a
religious altar called Jesung-dan in Doronpo, a village about 8 miles south
of Hamheung Prefecture, and send a eunuch to consecrate the sacrificial
services to the Evening Star on the annual Dano festival day, which falls
on the fifth of May according to the lunar calendar. Assuming the reign
after Koryo was overthrown, the king immediately launched the project
of establishing the Taoist pavillion and shrines in order to pray for the
fortunes.

The Sokyuk-su pavillion set up by King Taejo was so completely rebuilt
again by King Taejong later that its original features underwent great
changes. During the years of King Sejo, the Taoist temple was promoted
to Sokyuk-su from its previous Sokyuk-jon, and a ranking government

official along with four other lower grad official were appinted to be responsible for its management. This makes us presume that the Taoist services that time had been valued with great importance.

Generally, the Sokyuk-jons in the earlier part of the Lee Dynasty seemed to have been patterned after the Taoists shrines in China. The principle gods that were enshrined and served in the temple, according to the Yijo Shilrok(the Authentic Historical Records of the Lee Dynasty), had been the Supreme Deity, Laotzu and the Dipper among many others. Where as the first two gods, placed on the highest two altars of the temple, had the image of a man-god, the last one, the Dipper, was on one of the lower altars with an image of a goddess.

The Taoist managing staff of the Sokyuk-su pavillion were nutured and selected on the basis of their talents through and elimination test given in the scripture books of Taoism such as Kumdan, Youngbokyong, Yon-saengkyong, Taeilkyong, Okckookyong, Chinmookyong, Yongwangk-yong.

The Removal of the Sokyuk-su(pavillion)

When King Joongjong acceded to the throne after the atrocious ruler Yonsan-kun, many including the scholar Lee, Bong made an entreaty to remove the Taoist temple. It was difficult for the pious-minded king to abolish the traditions inherited from his ancesters all at once so he showed a negative response to the request, and the matter was left pending for the next ten years of his rule. Finally, however, at the persistent demand of the group of Confucians headed by Jo, Kwang Jo, the temple was closed, and its building was used as a public office in the 13th year of the king. In one story, the Confucians were said to have badgered the king with their importunities one night until it was so late that all the royal servants were either out side or in bed, and the king was simply forced to give in to their demands. As a result, Jo, Kwang Jo and his Confucian group were abhored by the king, and when the Confucian leader was falsely accused and condemned to death in the following year by the opposition faction led by Hong, Kyung Joo and Shim, Jung, he did not receive sympathy from the royalty. Since the Sokyuk-su was abolished against his will, King Joongjong attempted continuously to reinstate it, but could not realize it in the light of solid opposition from the Confucians. But in his 17th year in power, the king decreed the rivival of the temple and other Taoist services of the previous years on the pretext that it was the last will of his dying mother. Oppositions stormed in from many corners of the Confucian schools such as Sungkyun-kwan, Hongmoon-kwan, etc. but did not succeed in rescinding the royal ratification.

The revived Sokyuk-su continued its existence with its previous Taoist services until the years of King Sunjo. In the consequence of the 7 years Toyotomi War that began in the 18th year of Sunjo, that is, 1585 A.D., the Taoist temples had been burnt down along with the other public offices, and were never recovered thereafter.

The Jechon(sacrificial rite for Heaven) at Mt. Mani

According to the History of Koryo, the peak of Mt. Mani in Kanghwa Island was designated as a place where the Dankun deities had conducted the sacrificial rite for heaven, and the Samrang castle at the mountain was known to have been built by Dankun's three sons. The Dankuns quoted here seemed to indicate the existence of the deified personages, who ruled both the religion and state in the primordial age, and the castle as dwelling place for the three fairies as its name Samrang signified.

During the Lee Dynasty periods, the libations were held there in spring and autumn. In the 6th year of King Yeonsan-kun, a regular palace was built by an imperial order, despite the opposition from the government council body called Uijongboo and from the Confucians. The opposition was rejected on the ground that the palace was needed in order to provide a place for the festivals for the constellation of gods. In the years of King Injo, the governor of the Kanghwa Prefecture, was instructed to build up a religious altar and a shrine in the mid-slope of the mountain to carry out the religious services.

The Worship for Kuan Yu

This was introduced into the local belief after the arrival of the rein-forcements from the Ming Dynasty in China during the Toyotomi War. Kuan Yu, originally a seller of beancurd, was a famous general of the Shu, one of the Three Dynasties in China. Joining Liu Pei in 184 A.D. together with Chang Fei, he strived for the foundation of the Minor Han Dynasty, and became a famous hero for his deep fidelity and excellent bravery. In China, the god of bravery was highly revered in Taoism from the age of the Sung Dynasty, and, therefore, the Shrine of Kuan Yu temples were set up in the 31st year of King Sunjo by the commanders of the Ming troops, one by Mao Kuo Ch'i in Songju in Kyongsang province, another by Ch'en Lin in Kangjin, still another by Lang Fang wei in Namwon, and the last one by Hsieh Hoo Chen in Andong respectively.

In Seoul, the temple was built by the Ming General Ch'en Yin, who had been recuperating from an illness outside the present South Gate, at the foot of Mt. Mokmyeok(which is now Mt. Nam) in the 32nd year of King Sunjo. The royal household donated some of the expenses for its construction, and, when it was completed, the king himself attended the shrine to extend the courtesy of bowing twice before the divine portrait of Kuan Yu. In the following year, four thousand pieces of gold were sent from the imperial court of the Ming Dynasty through Wan Shin Te for the construction of another temple. King Sunjo, accordingly, ordered the Board of Rites to build a giant temple outside the Gate Heungin fol-lowing the Chinese patterns. Thus, there was a total of two Kuan Yu temples in Seoul and four in the provinces.

Kuan Yu was widely trusted in particularly by the Ming Dynasty war-lords, for there was a supersitition that, if one had good faith in Him, His spirit would appear in the battlefield and would destroy the enemy. The Ming generals, therefore, believed that the Japanese defeat from the Toyotomi War was solely on account of the spiritual help of their idol.

Hence, the generals of the Lee Dynasty in their armored suits and head-pieces worshipped at the Kuan Yu temples twice every year.

The Belief in the Witches and Wizards

Coming into the period of the Lee Dynasty, the Buddhist religion which had deeply penetrated into the population became a target of suppression and of gradual liquidation. In place of it, Confucianism was adopted as a state religion, but only to be embraced by the few aristocrats. Separated from the masses and deficient of real religious substances, the newly-adopted state religion was unable to satisfy the spiritual vacuum or uneasiness of the people, attributed to poverty and disease. At this moment of religious panic, the hidden desire of the people was to find some satisfaction from the Shinkyo belief that had been the underlying basis of the local faith from the ancient periods. Thus, the activities of the witches and wizards became ever more conspicuous, as the people tended to cling to them because the social unstability, caused by the factionalism and disunity of the ruling class and the uneasiness of the farming class, increased. By the time of King Youngjo, the total number of the sorcerers reached no less than 4 to 5 thousand, and could have well exceeded the figure during the reign of King Soonjo, taking into account of the fact that over two thousand of them were only recorded in the Financial Department of the Survey of Important Political Affairs of the Lee Dynasty(called Manki Yoram) as having paid their income taxes. Although they were treated as outcasts by the state, they were so firmly bound up with the people that there were few people who did not subscribe for their assistances in relation to the worldly affairs, fortunes and misfortunes, or few houses that did not have the sorcerer's written amulets pasted on them. Such devotion to the witches and wizards was especially popular and influenced among house wives, as well as court-ladies and royal concubines.

Should a royal prince or concubine be caught with an illness, then the medium would be called up to the court temple Injung-jun to recite incantation or to give prayers. While the state medium was appointed for the Sungsook-chung(the hall for the Constellations), the witches were summoned to petition the gods at the national festivals for rain or for the tutelar god. In the end, the witches and wizards entered the royal palace so frequently causing such a disturbance that they had once been expelled from the palace during the years of King Sungjong for the disturbances they created in collusion with the court-ladies or the ladies-in-waiting. But, afterwards, they were summoned again to do only their recitations of incantation day and night, although this was again prohibited later by King Joongjong. Still later, the superstitious belief to ward the medium had been rectified to some extent in the face of the strong oppositions from the Confucian group of Jo, Kwang Jo, but its popularity among the people remained unchanged.

The witches and wizards, as have been described previously, belonged to a school of the ancient Shinkyo religion. Standing in the middle of god and man, they assumed the works of executing religious ceremonies of conjuring the evil spirits by means of incantations, prayers and fortune-tellings, or wishing the blessings from God. They conducted these services not only for a certain individual, but also for the villages and towns with various festivals. The method of their services was colored by the Buddhist or Confucian influence. The gods they worshipped were mostly the celestial and natural ones inherited from the past including the three gods called Samshin or Sansung Jaesuk. The witches and wizards called a number of their gods with three reverences such Daekam(great supervisor), Daewang(great king) or Shin(god). Other examples were Junnae Daekam (god of chamber), Tojoo Daekam(god of land), Soomoon Daekam(god of gate-keeping), Wangrae Daekam(god of comings-and-goings), Bookoon Daekam(god of prefecture), Koonwang Daekam(god of king), Kunjoo Daekam(god of building), Upwang Daekam(god of bussiness or assets), Yongkoong Daekam(sea god), Hokoo Daekam(god of plague), etc.. Also revered as Daewang and shin were Jookwang Daewang (god of extensive memorialization), Chokwang Daewang(god of first space), Okwan Daewang(god of five senses), etc., and Baekdoo-san Shin (god of Mt. Baekdoo), Mokmyeok-san Shin(god of Mt. Mokmyeok), Halla-san Shin(god of Mt. Halla) to name only a few.

The Sunghwangje Festival

This was one of the popular ceremonies of god conducted by the witches and wizards most widelly during the ages of the Lee Dynasty. In Seoul, the festival was held twice a year in spring and autumn, and in local villages, two to four times a year under the auspieces of the state or local government.

Initiated at the time of King Moonjong of Koryo to repress disorders in the castle, the Sunghwang-je festival devoted to the tutelar god of a village seemed to have been cast out from the San-je(mountain festival) and Sunang-je(village festival) of the Ancient Chosun period or the compound of the two, for the god of the Sunang-je later became the principal of the Sunghwang-je festival. The Sunang-je festival also seemed to have been derived from the Palkwan-je of Kokuryo and Silla, for there were many similarities both in gods and religious formalities of the two festivals. The three gods called Sanshin(of mountain), Doshin(of town) and Byulshin(separate god) were sometimes served as the principal at the Sunghwang-je, for which the local governor was responsible to offer the cows or hogs as tributes. After the formal festival proceedings, the witches played the music to console the gods and to pray for the welfare of the villagers. And all the attendants, both the official and people, the rich and poor, dined together in front of the shrine, and enjoyed the wrestlings, swings, dances, andother entertainments.

The Popularity of Sacrificial rite for Village, Dong-je

If the Sunghwang-je, prevalent in most of the towns, were to be the official rites them Dong-je was purely the people's, held in cooperation with all the residents of a village to serve the god of their area. In otherwords, this was another village feast sponsored solely by the people who shared the common geographic living condition to pray together for happiness and for elimination of misfortunes. Depending on the village, it had different designations like Dong-je, Dongshin-je(village god), Sanshin- je(mountain god), or Dangsan-je. The master of ceremony of the festive event had to be the most spirited, virtuous and blessed man elected by the village people, and, after the election, he must alienate him-self from women, drinking and smoking in order to keep his body clean for the festival.

The festivals were usually observed at the shrine, under the deified tree, or at the altar set up in the village. The gods of the festivals varied in each village, but generally they had one common relation with the village tutelar god. In some places, however, the Gods of Plague or human spirits were worshipped at the festival. At the Dong-je, all the attendants made bows and prayers before the shrine for the welfare of their village, and they shared the blessed drinks and the consecrated meats together after the festival.

Chapter 5
The Daejong-kyo Religion

The Origin

The Daejong-kyo was the revival of ancient Shinkyo which was transmitted from the Old Chosun periods with various changes in its form
of belief. Through the later generations, the ancient Shinkyo religion
survived as the excorcist for example, in such a local festival as the Palkwan
and Dong-je, and by such a sectarian religious order as the Hwarang or
Jinjong-kyo. It was from the last example, that is, the sectarian Shinkyo,
that the Daejong-kyo originated.

Thus, the founder of the Daejong-kyo corresponds with that of the
ancient Shinkyo, that is, the Dankun Deity who, after his descent in Mt.
Taebaek with his vassals with devotion to welfare of mankind established
the first kingdom of Chosun.

The sectarian Shinkyo continued its existence through many succeeding
dynasties under the diversified names such as Daechon-kyo of the Booyeo
State, Chonshin-kyo of Tri-Han, Soongchon-kyo or Hwarang Group
of Silla, Jinjong-kyo of Balhae, and Baechon-kyo of Liao or Kim Dynasty.
During the periods of Koryo, it was referred as Wangkum-kyo or Jae-
kaseung, although it prospered little by virtue of Buddhism. During the
Lee Dynasty, it was almos t completely subdued by the Confucian influence
except what remained of the witches and wizards and some of the local
festivals. However, at the clos ure of the last dynasty, the Shinkyo religion
was restored with the upsurge of a national spirits.

The immediate history of the Daejong-kyo could be traced back to October of 1904 A.D., when a man called Baekbong went over to north of Mt. Baekdoo, claiming that he had been endowed with the revelations of the Dankun Deity, and discovered the old scriptures in one of the stone-boxes at the Daesoong-jon, the Dankun sanctums. The scriptures were handed down to Doo, Il Baek, who in turn, transmitted them to La, Chol in December of 1908. Inaugurated as the first bishop of the religion, then called Dankun kyo, La, Chol initiated the evangelistic mission at the Chuiwoon-jung pavillion in Je-dong, Seoul, on the 15th Full-Moon Day of January(lunar month), 1909 A.D.. At this time, there was a great consciousness rose high in the wake of the Japanese annexation in the following year. Uneasy about its further mission following the annexation in 1910, the Dankun-kyo was renamed Daejong-kyo in September of the same year and moved its headquarters to Eastern Manchuria.

La Chol, the initiator of the Daejong-kyo whose original name had been in Young, was the man who passed the higher public service examinations at the age of 29. On charges of attempted murder of the traitorous official who signed the Protectorate Treaty with Japan in 1905, he was sent on a ten-year exile in Ji Island off the south-west coast of the peninsular at the age of 45, but was exonerated a few years later. Then, in December, 1908, with the spiritual enlightenment he attained from Priest Baek Bong, La, Chol worked on the systematization of the Dankun-kyo doctrines, and preached extensively even after the religion was redesignated Daejong-kyo. In the year when he should have been 54, he climbed up Mt. Koowol and immolated himself, leaving the self-reproachful passages to the effect that he had failed in his undertaking to save the people from the national dishonour, that nothing had been accomplished from his eight-year missionary works, and that all the brethren should repent and lead a good life. He also left a will that Kim, Kyo Hoon should succeed him as the second bishop of the Daejong-kyo.

After the removal to Manchuria, the religion expanded its power by dividing into four parishes at the east, west, north and south. Finally, the

number of the followers reached more than 20,000. But, in 1942, the
Japanese authorities' suppression of the religion resulted in the imprisonment of the 22 executive members of the parishes including the then Bishop
Yoon, Se Bok. Among the members, ten died in jail. Some of the religious
leaders, meanwhile, hid from the Japanese officials and endeavoured their
efforts in secret mission. After the liberation, the headquarters of the religion again moved back to Seoul in January of 1946, and, then, the platform was entirely revamped with the selection of Kim, Joon, Lee, Hyon
Ik, Lee, Keuk No and Lee, Shi Young to the many executive positions
of the religious body. Such persons as Jo, Wan Koo, Jung, Yeol Mo,
Jung, In Bo, Kim, Seung Hak, Sung, Ha Shik, Myung, Je Se, Jung,
Kwang, Yoon, Bok Young and Uhm, Joo Chon were also those who
helped in the reconstruction of the religion.

The Doctrines

On the basis of the scriptures founded by Baek, Bong, the doctrines
of the Daejong-kyo were composed in combination with Buddhism,
Confucianism and Taoism elements.

The Doctrines, first of all, say that man will be blessed by being respectable and obedient toward God, the Lord of all creatures ; the second,
to cultivate true-heartedly the spiritual nature endowed by God ; the third,
to unite the race with love ; the fourth, to pursue happiness by means
of tranquility ; and the fifth to make man deligent and laborious in all
his pursuits.

These were the five essential points of the Daejong-kyo, needed to be
integrated in order to fulfill the three essences of nature, life and spirit.
In creation of all living beings, the mightiest, the most intelligent and
the most virtuous God bestowed on them those three elements, which
should be mind, body and temperment in case of a man. When the mind
that could be compared with the nature is virtuous, it shall be blessed,
but, on the contrary an unvirtuous mind will be cursed with a disaster.
Should the temperment, that is the life, be pure, one will enjoy a long

life, or else, meet with premature death. Should the body, or the spirit, be rich, one will be noble, or otherwise, be lowly. Only by cultivation of these essences through adjustment, retraint and prohibition, man can be in a position to be called by God.

Also, there were the following rules in the Daejong-kyo, similar to the Five Commandments of the Hwarang-do group of the Silla Dynasty:

1. Be loyal to the state.
2. Be dutiful to parents.
3. Be faithful to friends.
4. Be valorous at war.
5. Be fair and just when taking one's life.

The following eight additional rules of the religion were supposed to have been the pledge-words used at the Palkwan festival of the Koryo Dynasty :

1. Do not kill.
2. Do not steal.
3. Not be obscene.
4. Do not make improper remarks.
5. Do not drink liquor.
6. Not be seated in a high seat.
7. Not be luxurious.
8. Do not observe nor listen to the things that are not righteous.

The System

At the headquarters of the religion, there was the Chief Bishop who held the power over all the religious functions. The three offices called Chonbum, Chonri and Chongkang, and the other activities such as the Biblical Assembly, Research Room and Mission came under the Chief Bishop. The provincial headquarters and the religious assembly were organized in each province.

The service of worshipping animals was performed regularly on Sun days. The four great anniversaries, i.e., the Kaechon-jol(the National

Foundation Day) on October 3rd, the Uhchon-jol(the Ascension Day) on March 15, the Joongkwang-jol(the Double-lighted Day) on January 15, and the Kakyung-jol(the Auspicious Day) on August 15th were respectively observed by the religion.

There were the five different ranks of Sakyo, Jungkyo, Sangkyo, Jikyo and Chamkyo vested on the religion followers, and the holders of the top two ranks of Sakyo and Jungkyo were called 'Big Brother'.

The Dankun-kyo

When the Dankun-kyo was redesignated Daejong-kyo following the Japanese annexation, some leaders of the religion like Jung, Hoon Mo opposed the change and separated from the Daejong faction with its independent church in Shiheung, Kyonggi province, and attempted to expand the religious in fluence throughout the country by having set up their branch church in Kyongsang and Cholla provinces. As a result, the number of the believers exceeded 10,000 by the year 1938 A.D.. However, with the outbreak of World War II, the religion made a complete disappearence from the domestic scene.

The doctrines of the Dankun-kyo were generally similar to those of the Daejong-kyo.

Part Ⅲ

Buddhism(1)

Chapter 1
The Foundation of Buddhism

Sakya

Buddhism is one of the oldest religions in the world founded by the self-awakening of Sakya moni, who was born in India in April, the year 565 B.C. Sakya, originally named Sitarta, was born as the only son of King Chingfan of the state of Kapilavasta, after the king was well over 50 years of age. The king was maried to Princess Maja of King Anusyaka of the Chulivasta, another ancient state of India.

The prince Sitarta was raised by his aunt, Madame Kyodonmi, in his childhood, for his mother passed away seven days after his birth. He was so gifted with sagacious talents from his childhood that at the age of 7 he was already thoroughly conversant in grammar, arts, logic, theology, medicine, etc. taught by a Brahminic scholar named Bhadra and in Brahminic sutras taught by Pisamitra. He also had such a devotion to the military arts that he won fame for bravery in winning fights with the warriors.

King Chingfan's expectation for the future of his son was undoubtedly great. However, the prince, though he was talented with intelligence and bravery, was also endowed with a contemplative and philosophical nature that he was often immeersed in deep meditations. Lest he should be seized with taedium vitae by his gloomy character, the king, as a means to alleviate his agony, crowned him prince at the age of 15 and built three diffecent delux palaces suitable for the hot, rainy and cold seasons with the decorations made of gold, silver and other valuable treasures for his own use. A number of women entertainers were called into the palaces to console the prince with their expert singing and dancing. At the age of 16, the prince was espoused with the then paragon of beauty, the daughter of King Shanchio of the Chulivasta. Despite such extreme material and physical pleasures provided by his father, the crowned prince always hoped to leave the palace in order to satisfy his curiosity about life.

In the year in which the prince became 29 years old, a son was borne to the royal couple. Thinking that his son could succeed to the throne in place of him, the prince was delighted and attempted to carry out the long-cherished dream of leaving when the opportunity came. Then, one day on a stroll around the castle, he saw an old man at the east gate, a sick person at the south gate, and a funeral procession at the west gate. This experience, which was later conveyed in a legend as the Experiences at the Four Gates, gave the prince an enlightenment that man could not escape from the four trials of birth, age, sickness and death. The prince, then, severely felt the transiency of life and was ever more determined to take leave of the palace.

At last on the 8th of December the same year, Sakya secretly left the Kapila Castle to become a bonze, and headed for the state of Magadha, where there were many learned scholars and priests. There, he met a learned ascetic by the name of Bhagapi, from whom he received the teachings but this did not dispell the doubts he had in mind. Then, he left for the capital of the state, the Wangshe Castle, where he inquired from two ascetics about the principle ways of the priesthood, but again, was not satisfied. In the end, feeling that spiritual awakening comes only from self-devotion, he crossed the spiritual river of Nilien to enter into the Woods of Penance in the Village of Yurupinla, for many of the Indian ascetics who were pursuing purlification of their souls went into the mountains for mortification. After 6years of sufferings in the Woods, that is, the dawn of the 8th of February the year when he was 34, Sakya suddenly attained spiritual awakening and reached the stage of Nirvana.

The former prince of the Kapilavasta felt that the ecstasy he was experiencing after the achievement of the highest degree of enlightenment was too precious to be enjoyed by himself alone. Thus, he resolved to save the mankind by embarking on the work of enlightening the others, which he began by giving his first sermon of Four Truths to five of his previous followers in Luyehyuan. He extended this through the states of Petsari, Magadha, Kapila, Shewei, Wangshe, etc. for 45 years. Finally, his disciples swelled to thousands and his position as a great saint of India became firmly founded. With his last preaching of the Four Truths for Deliverance that helped Subhadra, a sage of the Kusinagra Castle, to achieve the spiritual enlightenment, Sakya passed into Nirvana in February when he was 80 years of age. His body was cremated and his remains, divided in eight parts, were given to kings of the eight states, who had a close connection with Sakya. Among many of Sakya's followers, there were ten great disciples including Suribu and Moginlin.

The Formation of Buddhism

The founder of Buddhism, Sakya originally had no intention to creat a religion, but, rather, aspired to save himself from the actual world full of agonies, and to awake the people spiritually. Also, he did not insist on the worship of the personified gods, as the Brahmas worshipped a unique god of the universe in Brahminism, nor did he mention such religious formalities as divine services or prayers, but only gave sermons about the laws that control human life and the universe of the material world, and about the final objectives of self-cultivation in one's life. In this sense, there was no religious elements in the original nature of Buddhism.

However, Sakya's atheistic, non-prayer and pessimistic philosophies were gradually modified along with the formation of the religious bodies by his disciples, who worshipped their master as Buddha, a divine being. Late r, such a thing às the religious ceremony, precept and prayers were also systematized by the disciples to give form to a religion in Buddhism. The first ones to complete the foundation of the Buddhist platform were the five disciples including Chiao Chinju, who was the messanger the king sent after the prince when he was practicing ascetism in the state of Magadha, and remained his servants ever since. But, beside them, Yehsu, the son of a rich man from the state of Baranas, was the first disciple converted from Sakya's sermon in Luyehyuan, from which 56 other prominent disciples emerged including Fuluna. Then, a series of conversions to Sakya was followed by a number of leading philosophers and gifted people such as Yurupinlakayeh, a famous priest of the Magadha, with his 500 followers ; Gayakayeh, Yurupinlakayeh's brother, with his 300 followers ; Natikayeh with his 200 ; Suribu, the most renowed sage the, with his 250 ; Moginlin, later known as one of the two great saints of Buddhism along with Suribu ; and Chuhsila. In the third year after his awakening, Sakya was requested by his father to preach in the Kapila, where he also earned more than 50 converts at one time including Ahnandha, Ahnuludha and Kapina, who later became famous disciples of Sakya. In the fifth year, 500 women of the Sakya lineage also entered Buddhism, which made such a remarkable expansion until the death of its founder.

The Doctrines of Buddhism

Sakya's doctrines, in summary, were to help the people attain spiritual enlightenment and, thereby, reach Nirvana, the eternal comfort. The contents of almost every Buddhist scripture amount entirely to this. At any rate, the doctrines of the old Buddhism were expounded with the Four Noble Truths and Eight Paths of Canonization(or Righteousness).

The Four Noble Truths signify 1. The truths of pain, accumulation, riddance, and deliverance. The truth of pain is a pessimistic view that reality is all suffering and this, in turn, is based on a transient conception that the life of love and hatred, birth and age, and ailment and death is in constant mutation. 2. The Noble Truth of the Cause of Pain explains the reason for all the pains and sufferings of the reality which Sakya himself realized came from ignorance and passion. 3. The Nobel Truth of the Cessation of Pain is arrived at from the above two processess, once the worldly pains and their causes are acquired. And 4. the last truth of deliverance is the stage of reaching Nirvana. According to Sakya, the method of the Buddhist salvation is neither in pursuit of pleasures nor of mere asceticism, but in the moderation of the two ; The Eight Paths of Righteousness are enumerated below :

1. Right View	Having a right intelligence about the Four Truths, that is, not to possess a heretical view.
2. Right Thought	To speculate rightly about the principles of the Four Truths, that is, not with wickedness.
3. Right Speech	Avoiding wicked remarks.
4. Right Behavour	Avoiding such improper practices of killing and stealing by observing the commandments.
5. Right Livelihood	Keeping away from the five ways of viciousness by leading a just life.
6. Right Effort	Devoting oneself for deliverance.
7. Right Mindfulness	Striving for the right views and thoughts at all times.
8. Right Concentration	To regard Nirvana more than a fixed contemplation.

The above 8 paths as the commandments of daily life were referred to as 37 guiding articles at the time of Sakya's death. They were also called Three Learnings, which meant commandment, comtemplation and Intelligence.

Sakya, in a sense, stressed the law of equality, in contradition to the then prevailing system of four social classes of Brahminism, by preaching that whoever believes in the Truth and carries out the Paths would be delivered into Nirvana.

Although these doctrines are the fundamental laws of Buddhism, there is another underlying principle that constituted the basic philosophy and that is the law of cause and effect. According to this law, the generation of every thing in the universe, physical, spiritual or phenomenal, is only possible by cause and effect, but not without one or the other. For example, the grain can not ripen with only with the seed, but also with the effects of the land, water, sun and labour. Likewise, all the deeds of the human beings, controlled by karma, the law of the cause and effect, would bear their respective results through the three stages of existences. There w ere 12 typical causes and effects, on with which Sakya comtemplated while he was meditating on himself and his life under Boddhendrum.

They are :

1. Darkness of the Mind   Bewilderment(Ignorance of the truths)

2. Deed   Karma(The Fundamental of the physical Deed)

       These are the causes of the past or the Truth of Accumulation.

3. Discernment(the Action of the Mental world)
4. Namarupa(the. Tangible world)
5. Six Places(the Objective World of Consciousness)
6. Stimulation(the World of Sensation)
7. Suffering(the Interrelationships with the Objective World)

       These are the effects of the present, or the Truth of Pain.

8. Affection(the Attachment to the Objective World)
9. The Takings(the Attachment to the Objective World)
10. Existence(the Material and Immaterial Beings)
11. Life(the Concrete Human Life)
12. The Death of Old Age(the Mutation of Birth, Age and Death)

       The effects of the future, or the Truth of Pain.

Sakya saw that, with the cause and effect of Darkness, Death results and so with those of Deed, Discernment, and, so on down through the 12 causes and effects, where man will receive the painful effects of agony, sadness and the death at an old age.

In connection with the law of cause and effect, there are the Three Standard Imprints of Buddhism, a formula that is necessary in order to understand the religion. The standards explain first of all, the attitudes that all deeds are mutable ; secondly, that all laws are of selflessness, that is, the denial of ego, self-perception and self-attachment ; and lastly, that Nirvana is the world of tranquility, into which one, who attains the selfless vision enabling a true observation of the transient world could enter.

Chapter 2
Buddhism of Kokuryo

The Introduction of Buddhism

It is reported that Buddhism, which dominated the spiritual arena of the Korean people for about ten centries from the middle of the era of Three Kingdoms, was first introduced from the Former Ch'in Dynasty of China in June of the 2nd year of King Sosoorim of the Kokuryo Kingdom. According to the History of the Three States(Vol. 18), the Ch'in's Emperor Fuchien then dispatched to Kokuryo a monk named Shuntao with an image of Buddha and the Buddhist sutras, and the Kokuryo's king and his servants went so far as to meet him at the gate and to pave the way for his missions.

The Former Ch'in was a state established(B.C. 897-221) on the northern territory of China by an ancient tribe called Ti(氏). It was one of the five Tartar and Turkish tribes of Hsiungnu, Chieh, Hsienpi and Chiang occupying the border regions of the state of Chin, that was set up after the downfall of the Three States of China. The Ch'in state, though she enjoyed territorial unification for sometime, plunged into a state of anarchy with an increase of famine. The five tribes rose up and rivalled for power for more than a century. But with the exception of Ti that formed the Former Ch'in, other tribes failed and disappeared. At the time of Emperor Fuchien, almost all the territories of northern China was brought under control by the powerful state of the Former Ch'in, which also achieved a remarkable cultural civilization by encouraging Buddhism and Confucianism.

Kokuryo always maintained amicable relations with the state of Ch'in as a diplomatic strategy because of the hostilities from her adjacent country of Former Yen that was established by the Hsienpi tribe in western Manchuria. Finally, when the state of Former Yen was destroyed the Ch'in's emperor Fuchien, a high official of the Yen, Mu Yung P'ing sought political asylum in Kokuryo. Instead of providing a refuge, Kokuryo then deported the hostile Yen's official to Emperor Fuchien, and because of this the relations of the two countries became closer. It was at this time that the Buddhist monk, Shuntao, was sent from China.

The Arrival of Three Buddhist Monks

Beside Shuntao, the first Buddhist monk to arrive in Kokuryo from the Former Ch'in, there were two others, Atao from the Latter Wei Dynasty 2 years after Shuntao, and T'anshin from the East Chin 25 years later.

However, there is no authentic record available to give a clear identity about the monk Shuntao. The Biography of Buddhist Priests in Korea only relates, 'It is not known what sort of man Shuntao was. He was a man of great virtue, high ideal and deep benevolence because he saved mankind, and he was so devoted in the Buddhist mission that he travelled extensively across the country.' Some have a vague opinion about the country Shuntao came from. But in this writer's opinion, he was a monk of high virtue from the state of Former Ch'in that was set up by the ancient tribe of Ti, who earned many followers with his enthusiastic efforts in Kokuryo.

Concerning Atao, also call Atao Wotou, who came into Kokuryo in the 4th year of King Sosoorim from the Wei, the records contain contradicting stories. The Biography said to the effect that it is not certain whether he was originally from West India, or from the Wu Dynasty in China or was the man who went over to the Wei from Kokuryo and came back to Silla again later. But according to the Commentary of the Three

Kingdoms of Korea(Vol. 3), he was born to Kokuryo's mother, Ko, Do Nyoung, and the Wei's envoy named Wochumo. At the age of 5, Atao was allowed by his mother to enter into Buddhism and went into the Wei to meet his father when he was 16. In Wei, he studied Buddhism for 3 years under the Priest Hsuanchang and returned to Kokuryo to devote himself to the development of the religion. Afterwards, he went over to Silla for the Buddhist missions and completed his life there.

The Buddhist monk, T'anshih of the East Ch'in, who came into Kokuryo with volumes of Buddhist sutras in the 5th year of King Kwangkaeto, that is, 25 years after Shuntao, was a man originally from the Shansei region of China. He was reported to have conducted many miracles after his achievement of Buddhist doctrines. It was also said that the monk had white legs, for which he was called White-legged Priest, because his legs did not get satined or soiled when he crossed a dirty stream.

Although the aforementioned three monks are recorded as the first missionaries of Buddihism in Kokuryo, the Liang Dynasty's Biography relates that Priest Chin Tun from the Tsin Dynasty exchanged messages with a Kokuryo monk before their arrival. In view of this, we can assume that there were Buddhist-converts already in Kokuryo before the three monks began their mission.

The Establishment of the Buddhist Temples

King Sosoorim of the Kokuryo set up two Buddhist temples for the two foreign missionaries, Shuntao and Atao, around the Royal Palace, and had all the royal families and subjects profess this religion at the temples. The first temple built for Shuntao was named Sungmoon temple, to commemorate the name of the gate, Sungmoon, to which the king personally went out to welcome the foreign priest on his arrival, and the other one was designated Ibulan temple, the reason for which is not very clear.

King Kokookyang, the successor of King Sosoorim, who was also converted to Buddhism, supported the religious development in Kokuryo by issuing a royal message to the people to believe in the religion. King Kwangkaeto, the 19th king in the reign of Kokuryo, not only left his distinguished services both in the political and military fields, but also was so devoted to Buddhism that he established nine gigantic temples in the then southern capital, Pyongyang, one year after he was enthroned. Few records say anything about further institution of the Buddhist temples, although there seem to have been many, following King Kwangkaeto, with the exception of the Kumkang temple that was sent up in July of the 7th year of King Moonja according to the History of the Three Kingdoms (Vol. 19.)

The Development of Buddhism

With the encouragement shown by King Kokookyang and King Kwangkaeto, Buddhism was transmitted throughout the country, gradually emasculating the heretofore popular local religion of Shinkyo. As a result, many local people crowded to the temples to become Buddhist-converts and many went across to the Chinese Dynasties of Former Ch'i, Ch'en, Liang, Sui and Tang to learn the doctrines first-hand, and many went over to the Baekje and Silla Kingdoms and even to Japan to convey the religion.

Among the Kokuryo's Buddhist students who went to China and became famous were the three saints, Lang, Sil and In, of the Samron sect(三論宗, Tri-theory) Buddhist Sect began by an Indian saint, or Boddhisattva, named Nagarijuna and his disciple, Aryadeva. According to the History of Buddhism in China, Saint Lang went into the provinces of Kiangsu and Anhwei and learned the doctrine from an Indian saint named Kumarajiva, who was then in the Liang Dynasty, at the Chungsan Temple. A disciple of Saint Sil, Saint In went into Ch'en, but after its downfall, moved into Szechwan, where he had done extensive research of the doctrines and preaching at the same time. The other famous bonzes, among many, were Payak of the Chontae-jong sect, who learned the doctrines in the Ch'en and Jihwang of the Exoteric Sect, who studied in the Sui.

Chapter 3
Buddhism of Baekje

Maranandha

The first man to introduce Buddhism in Baekje, one of the three Korean kingdoms, was an Indian monk by the name of Maranandha. This occurred 14 years later then Kokuryo. The Indian Buddhist, then preaching across China, was accompanied into Baekje by one of her envoys to the Eastern Chin Dynasty in September of the first year of the kingdom's 15th King Chimryu.

At this time in China, there were many famous monks from India and from the countries bordering Western Chin, who engaged in preaching and intranslation of the Buddhist scriptures. For example, Dharmaraksa, an Indian Buddhist saint often regarded as Burning Boddhisattva, came into the Western Chin and completed more than 300 volumes of the translations. Afterwards, Kumarajiva came into the Latter Ch'in from a country in Western Chin, and, with the help of the other monks, translated 100 volumes of the Mahayana sutras. At the southern state of Eastern Chin, the religion also prospered greatly under the imperial protection of the succeeding emperors. And the Buddhist followers increased to a great number, partly because of the extensive influences of the many Indian Buddhist preachers but also because of the constant wars between the states of China.

It was at this time that the Indian monk, Narandha, met the Baekje official in Eastern Chin, and he did not object to his mission in Baekje.

Upon his arrival at the Baekje's capital of Hansan(new Yangjoo-kun, Kyonggi province), the foreign Buddhist was welcomed into the Royal Palace personally by King Chimryu himself, and was courteously treated. With the conversion of the king and his royal subjects to the religion, Buddhism again began to spread among the people.

According to the History of the Three states(Vol. 24), the Hansan temple comparable to those of the Kokuryo, was built in the Baekje capital in February of the year after the arrival of Maranandha, and the temple was put under the management of the foreign Buddhist and ten other local bonzes. Although King Chimryu died a few months after the temple was constructed, the religion continued to be prosperous.

Monk Kyumik and His Learning

No historical records are available to give an authentic picture of the ups and downs of Buddhism in Baekje for the 142 years after King Chim-ryu. But during the years of the 25th King Sung it was adopted as a state religion and it developed steadily with a number of converts from the people, the nobles and commoners alike, and with the establishment of Buddhist monasteries and towers in many places.

Such a thriving of the religion is, of course, attributed to the encoura-gement of the Royal court. On the other hand, the efforts which a high priest named Kyumik made toward the prosperity of the religion were no less great. He was the man who went into China to research the works of the Buddhist doctrine in the 4th year of King Sung, and theninto India, where he studied the Buddhist literature for more than five years and learned the Buddhist precepts from an Indian priest named Pedaldha. On his return to his home country with the original texts of the Abiwun's Collections of the Five Buddhist Precepts, Kyumik was received by King Sung, and, later, was allowed to complete 72 volumes of the statutory translations along with 28 famous local bonzes at the Heungyoon temple. Hence, the Baekje's Buddhism developed with a special emphasis on its precepts and formalities. Later, 36 volumes of the Buddhist rules were written by two local priests, Wunook and Haein. King Sung, in his 29th year, sent his envoy to an erudite, Maosi, in the Liang Dynasty in China for the doctrines of Nirvana, and the envoy returned also with one of the Liang's Buddhist handicraft artists and a painter.

The Export of Buddhism to Japan

The Royal Court of the Baekje Kingdom did not only enable the prosperity of the religion in her country, but also extended it to her neighboring country of Japan. King Sung, sent a six-foot tall Buddhist statue in his 23rd year to the Imperial Court of Japan and, again in October of the 30th year, another bronze statue and the Buddhist doctrines with a letter of solicitation containing the following effects:

'This precept is the best of all the statutes which Confucius of the Chou Dynasty could not attain. Sould you have faith in it, you will receive an endless blessing by achieving the highest awakening, the Buddha. This precept is now widely professed by the countries of India, China and even ourselves. It is, therefore, advised that you esteem it highly in your country.' At first, the sovereigns and subjects of the Japanese Imperial Court hesitated to believe. But a few converts began to appear, and later they increased gradually. In his 32nd year, King Sung again dispatched 16 Buddhist priests including Wunhae and Dosim to help develop the religion in Japan.

Thus, the Buddhist was introduced to Japan was by King Sung. But the one who really raised the Buddhist culture in Japan was the 27th King Uiduk, who ruled for 44 years. The year he was enthroned, King Uiduk sent 9 priests to replace the 7 previously sent to Japan including Dosim, and, later in his 24th year, dispatched much Buddhist literature along with, scholars and monks. Many more Buddhist architects, stone-masons, potters and the like, were sent to build up monasteries, temples and towers in the neighboring state.

At the request of Emperor Bintats of Japan, more Buddhist monks such as Illa, Eunsol, Yeono, etc. went over to the island country in the

31st year of King Uiduk, and, in the following years, additional Buddhist scholars and lawyers including Ryongjo, Ryongui, Hejoong, Haesook, Doum, etc., were sent to Japan with various Buddhist relics. The Japanese envoys and bonzes also travelled to Baekje to learn the religious doctrines. As a result of such frequent exchanges between the two countries, the Buddhist civilization of Japan reached its peak during the age of Emperor Shogo. Furthermore, the Japanese attitude toward the Baekje monks was so friendly that many monks claimed allegiance to Japan. Among them, Kwon Reuk's allegiance to that country with all his works in Buddhism, astrology, topography, etc. in the 3rd year of King Moo was considered a great loss for the Baekje state, for he was a famous scholar-priest with profound knowledge in many foreign writings.

The Prohibition of Killings

Following the death of the devout Buddhist Kings Uiduk and Hye, King Bup, no less ardent in the religion than his predecessors, asceded the throne. Upon assuming the reign, the king issued a decree to forbid killings and to release all the captive animals such as birds, hogs and fishes. This action was taken to carry out mercy, one of the Buddha's basic philosophies. Following the royal orders, the ceremonies to release the live animals were held in various parts of the country.

King Moo's Establishment of the Grand Monastery

The merciful King Bup then launched the construction of the greatest Buddhist monastery called Wangheung temple, but died in the following year without seeing its completion.

However, the project was completed in 35 years by the following 30th ruler King Moo. After the completion, the King often went to the temple together with his Empress, the former Princess Sunhwa of King Jinpyung of the Silla Dynasty. The present location of the Wangheung temple is presumed to have been located by the Baekma river in Booyeo, Chollabuk province, the capital of the Baekje Dynasty.

Chapter 4
Buddhism of Silla

The Beginning

Buddhism was introduced into the Silla Dynasty about 50 years after Kokuryo. But, unlike Kokuryo and Baekje, where the religion was received with royal favours, it went through many thorny paths, sometimes costing the lives of a few martyrs, before it was firmly founded in Silla.

The first pioneer of the Buddhist mission in this last of the Three Kingdoms was believed to have been a man called Jungbang from the Kokuryo, who was seized and put to death by the Silla authorities. The next missionary, Myulhubi, also from Kokuryo, with his strange appearance of cropped head and clothes, was again taken by the Silla people as a sigh of a bad omen, and was, therefore, executed.

However, in the years of King Nulji, a Kokuryo monk named Mookhoja filtered in and was secretly engaged in the Buddhist mission at the house of a man known as More. At this time, an envoy from the Liang Dynasty in China brought incense hitherto unknown as to its name and use as a gift to the Silla Dynasty. This provided an opportunity for the Kokuryo monk to come from his hideout with an explanation for the Kokuryo monk to come from his hideout with an explanation for the foreigner's present. He told the imperial court that the incense was used for burning while serving the Buddhist Trinity of Buddha, Dharma and Samgha, and that the spiritual responses were certain to come should one pray through this means. Coincidentally, just at this time, the princess was ailing. At the request of the King, Mookhoja performed the Buddhist services for her recovery, and the princess soon regained her health. As a result of this, the king and the royal families began to embrace the religion, but its penetration to the people was blocked by a strong opposition from the subjects surrounding the king.

The Death of Yi, Cha Don

During the age of the 21st King Bicheo of the Silla Dynasty, another monk named Ado came in from Kokuryo with his three followers, and conducted the evangelical mission, staying at the More's house(Ado and Mookhoja may be the same person, according to the Historical Memoirs of the Three Kingdoms, the Samkook Yoosa).

The 23rd ruler, King Bupheung, a Buddhist-convert, upon coming into power, attempted to raise the religion by consulting the opinions of his subjects. All except one, Yi, Cha Don, who entreated the king to carry out the attempts even at the expense of his own life, opposed. The king at first rejected the appeal of the only devout Buddhist subject, but Yi, Cha Don was so determined to sacrifice his life for the sake of the religion that he was later turned over to the hands of the executioner on charges of opposing the public opinion. At the moment of execution, he was said to have left the following remarks.

"I am being put to death for the cause of the sacred law of Buddha. With the Almighty Spirit of Buddha, some mysteries shall happen following my death."

Strange enough, as soon as the was beheaded, his parted head was said to have flown across the sky and landed on a ridge of Mt. Kumkang in Kyungju, and gallons of milk-white blood poured out of his neck, and a great earthquake occurred. After this marvellous happening, many anti-Buddhist subjects and soverigns pledged their allegiance to the religion. This was in the 15th year of King Bupheung. Yi, Cha Don, at the age of 26(according to the Samkook Yoosa, he was 22), was therefore long remembered by the Silla Buddhists as a great martyr. A tower commemorating his martyrdom was built by his followers 306 years later, in September of the 9th year of King Hunduk, atthe Baekyul temple.

King Bupheung

The name of King Bupheung, the first son of King Jijeung, was one given posthumously for what he had done to raise Buddhism. Following Yi, Cha Don's martyrdom, the king, originally a devout Buddhist, gained control over all the opposition forces of the religion to proclaim a royal decree to prohibit the killings and huntings.

In his 21st year, the 23rd King Bupheung of the Silla Dynasty established a great Buddhist monastery, the Heungryun themple, the construction of which took him only six years to complete despite the frequent wars with the states of Kokuryo and Baekje. The King, naming himself with a Buddhist title of Kongbup, used to recite sutras using the beads in his hands at the Heungryun temple, where he also held great memorial services in honor of Yi, Cha Don every year. His Empress was also a devout Buddhist, who later became a priestess at the Youngheung temple.

The Development of Buddhism

During the 36 years of King Jinheung, the successor of King Bupheung, the development of Buddhism reached its height with the establishment of a number of temples and statues, i.e., Hwangryong temple, Bunhwang temple, Damsok temple, Bupju temple, Jiwon temple, and some six-feet tall bronze statue at the Hwangryong temple, and other sculptural works. The religion, then, madea complete entry into the lacal belief.

In the 10th year of the same King, the Buddhist relics were conveyed to the country for the first time in Korean history from the Liang Dynasty in China by the Buddhist scholars who went there to study. With the consequent return of other students, namely, Usin from India in the 14 year, and Myungkwan from the Ch'en Dynasty in the 26th year respectively, an abundance of Buddhist scriptural literature flowed in to make Silla's Buddhism lustrous.

The religion, was fostered and continued its prosperity through the succeeding reigns of Kings Jinji, Jin pyung, Sunduk, Jinduk, etc., during which time many students went to China for their research in Buddhism, and made a remarkable contribution in importing the Chinese culture. And through these periods, the Silla's artistic technology improved to the point of rare elegance and elaboration with the creation of a great number of Buddhist works in art, not to mention the temples.

Priest Wonkwang

Among the many high priests who emerged in the years of the 26th ruler King Jinpyung, Priest Wonkwang, who attained the Nirvana of Spiritual Perfection in China and later became a great moral leader in Silla, was the most outstanding. According to the Haedong Koseungjun(the Biography of the Monks in Korea), the Priest, whose original surname was Park who came from a town called okkyung, left for the Ch'en Dynasty in China at the age of 25, and achieved the Buddhist enlightenment after years of learning from the many famous priests there. Then, he went into the state of Wu, where he taught his learnings to the Chinese aspirants so well that his name was instantly known through the country, and his followers quickly increased. In the capital of the Sui Dynasty, he also became famous for his teachings.

At the news of Wonkwang's rising fame in the mainland, King Jin-pyung, in his 22nd year, recalled the Silla Priest from China to become a spiritual leader in his home country which was frequently involved in warring with the neighboring states of Kokuryo and Baekje. In Silla, the Priest, despite his old age, wrote a letter asking for reinforcements from the Sui Dynasty at the request of the king, and initiated the Five Commandments for the Hwarang Group that played a great role for the state. Priest Wonkwang died at the age of 99 in the 52nd year of King Jinpyung at the Hwangryong temple. The Five Commandmentsthe aged priest drafted for the Hwarang-do were :

1. Be loyal to the state.

2. Be dutiful to parents.

3. Be faithful to friends.

4. Be valorous at war.

5. Be fair and just when taking one's life.

The Most Reverend Priest Wonhyo(or popularly called Wonhyo Daesa)

Born in a Buddhist village of the present Yangsan-kun in the 39th year of King Jinpyung form a family named Seol, Priest Wonhyo was the most famous after Priest Wonkwang in Silla. He was called Sudong in his childhood, when he first began to learn the religion. Wonhyo's main schooling in Buddhism came from the Saddharma Pundarika which he had learnt from Priest Rangji of the Bungo temple in his earlier years, and,later, the Sutras of Nirvana from a Kokuryo monk named Boduk.

When he was 31 years old, the priest achieved a self-awakening while he was on his way to the Tang Dynasty to study Buddhism with his colleague priest Uisang. Enroute, a storm arose at night and they were forced to spend the night in a cave. Wonhyo became so thirsty in the middle of the night when it was dark he drank something which felt like water. When he awoke the next morning, it was rainy and gloomy, and to his surprise, Wonhyo discovered that the place they slept on was a grave, and the water he gulped the previous night was the stagnant water of the skull. Giving up everything, he came to sudden self-realization ; If your spirit is alive, all the laws exist, but if it is dead, all the laws are non-existent. The whole world and the very laws therein are the work of the spirit, without which noting exists. Hence, what is the use of going to Tang ? I shall not continue this trip.' Thus, the self-awakened saint separated from his company and returned to Silla with the belief that self-realization comes from one's own belief in one's own mind and not from the schooling of others.

Priest Wonhyo, who gained a reputation for his extensive knowledge in all the scriptural theories of various Buddhist sects, felt that the doctrines of the religion should not be the monopoly of the monks at the temples, only but, instead, should be breathed into the life of the people. Therefore, he set out on the bohemian life of a commoner, sometimes playing the Kumoonko(a stringed instrument) at a shrine or at an inn, or sometimes sitting in comtemplation at the mountain, or sometimes singing and dancing through the villages. One of the songs he composed said to the effect that the one who was capable of everything could only rise above the life and death was very popular among the people. Wonhyo, by having illicit intercourse with the princess at the Yosuk Palace, which was a total transgression, had begotten a son, Sul Chong, who also was so intelligent that from his childhood he was already well-versed in the Buddhist literatures in his early ages ; later, he became one of the ten highest sages in Silla.

Wonhyo died at the age of 70 at the Hyol temple in the 6th year of King Shinmoon, leaving a total of 81 volumes of writings, many of which became popular even among the Buddhist scholars in china and Japan.

The teachings of the Buddhist Ascetic Jajang

The one who made a distinguished service in the broad propagation of Buddhism in the Silla Dynasty and, at the same time, became a great favorite of the imperial court, was Jajang Yoolsa(or Ascetic Priest Jajang) during the period of Queen Sunduk. According to the Memoirs and History of the Three Kingdoms and The Biography of the Monks, Jajang was a son of Kim, Moo Rim, a Buddhist of converted royal stock, who decided to devote his son to the study of the works of Buddha even before he was born. Although his parents died before he was really devoted to Buddha, Jajang, growing up, entered the priesthood himself and practiced asceticism, abandoning allhis assets. His devotion to the religion was so determined that when he was persuaded and even threatened by the then King Jinpyung to accept a government position, he responded that he would rather live a day for the sake of religious precepts than live a hundred years in transgression.

In the 5th year of Queen sunduk, Jajang went to Tang Dynasty and, after receiving a spiritual inspiration from Great Saint Wenshu at Mt. Chingliang, spent three years there cultivating and teaching the Buddhist doctrines. At the request of the Queen, he returned home with more than 400 boxes of the Buddhist sutras and other religious material. Appointed by the Queen to the highest priesthood in the country, Jajang promoted the religion by his preachings at the Imperial Palace and Hwangryong temple, from which the number of the converts incerased radically.

With the approval of the Queen, the Buddhist ascetic built a nine-story tower at the Hwangryong temple as a prayer to Buddha for the destruction of the nine enemy states around the Silla Dynasty. Each story of the tower, from the first to the ninth, signified the states of Japan, China, Wu, and other wild tribes in the north of Tolo, Yingyu, Tungus, Tan, Hsiungnu and Yemaek. The tower, completed after three years, was one of the three most valuable treasures of the Silla Dynasty along with the 6- feet-tall Buddha's bronze statue set up at the Hwangryong temple and the pearled belt of King Jinpyung. Incidentally, the two states of Kokuryo and Baekje perished 30 years after the tower was constructed. Afterwards, Jajang established the additional temples of Tongdo temple, Wonyong temple, Sooda temple, and set up towers in ten other palaces. He also left some 15 volumes of literary works about Buddhism.

Chapter 5
The Unification by Silla and the Monks' Advance Abroad

The Unification of the Three Kingdoms

In the 7th year of King Mooyeol of the Silla Dynasty, the state of Baekje was staggering in exhaustion and suffering a slackening of popular spirit because of her courageous but dissipated and luxurious King Uija. Taking advantage of the situation, King Mooyeol attacked and destroyed the Baekje Dynasty with reinforcements from the Tang Dynasty in China.

After the subjugation of Baekje, Silla was eyeing Kokuryo, which had been entangled in the discords of the sons of the then prime minister Yonkaesomoon, resulting in factional strife among the ruling class. At this time, the Tang Dynasty requested Silla for relief and the two united forces again conquered the Kokuryo state. This was in the 8th year of King Moonmoo of the Silla Dynasty.

Although the Silla state thus achieved the unification by conquering her two neighbors that had been enemies for almost 7 centuries, the results were not altogether to her advantages, for she had to encounter new pressures from the powerful Tang in China. The relation of the two previous partner states so deteriorated that Emperor Kaojong of the Tang Dynasty, at last, prepared for an all-out attack on Silla. At this juncture, Priest Uisang of Silla, then studying in the Chinese Dynasty, made a quick return to his home country and reportd the facts to King Moonmoo. Then, the king, by having Priest Pyungrang pray for the settlement of the national crisis and by performing a secret Buddhist rite at the Sachonwang temple,

temple(the Emperors of Four Heavens) specifically built for that purpose, was said to have defeated the invading forces from China at sea and, in the 12th year of the king, driven the Tang's land forces across the northern boundary.

In Silla, it was taken for granted that both the unification and the defeat of the Tang Dynasty invasion were only possible by the graces of Buddha. Thus, the religious services admiring his Graces were ever more preeminent and became so prosperous that, in the end, Buddhism entered its golden age in the country. The political ideals and all the cultural developments were based on the religion, all the intelligentsia of state acknowledged the supremacy of the Buddhist monks. In the capital of Silla, 808 Buddhist temples were ereched ; other works such as stone-statues of Buddha, towers, mushroomed everywhere. From almost every house of the village the sound of the recitation of the sutras reverberated.

Afterwards, the relations between Silla and Tang improved to some extent. Frequent raids on the three coasts of Silla by the Japanese bandits, however, were the matters of great concern for the ailing King Moonmoo. The King left his last injunction to Priest Jiui that he would like to be buried in the East Sea, where he could become a dragon and defeat Japanese assaults. His successor, King Shinmoon, fulfilled his will the first Buddhist funeral service ever held in the Silla Dynasty.

The Increase of the Monks' Travels to Tang

Following the unification and the highest achievement of Buddhist prosperity in the country, a great number of the monks went to the Tang Dynasty to study religion. They made a great contribution not only for the development of Buddhism, but also for an overall improvement of the culture in Silla by both direct and indirect importation of Chinese civilization. The tendency of going to the Tang Dynasty by the local monks was especially prevalent then, for it was generally considered a way to attain the fame and reputation of a high priest in the country.

The first Buddhist who went to China for study from Silla was Priest

Kakduk in the age of King Jinheung. He was the man who brought the Buddha's relics from the Liang Dynasty for the first time in Korean history. The other monks to follow Priest Kakduk before the Silla's unification were Wonkwang and Damyuk, who returned from the Sui Dynasty in the 22nd year of King Jinheung ; Hyeonkwang, Myungkwan and Jimyung, who went to the Ch'en Dynasty; and Anham, Jajang, Wonseung, Hyetong, Woncheuk, Uisang, etc. went to Tang.

The other famous monks, who were many from the various Buddhist sects, of the post-unification era, were reported to have gone to mainland China, where the Tang Dynasty accomplished a great territorial unification after Sui and achieved a brilliant culture. Namely, they were the priests Seungchon, Hyochoong, Sung, Bumsoo, Damjang, Sungrim and Wonpyo from the Hwaom-jong sect ; priest Buprang and 50 others from the Seon-jong sect ; priest Sunkyung and 4 others from the Bupsang-jong ; and priest Myungrang and many others from the Shinin-jong sect.

When they returned from China, they not only endeavoured to promote Buddhism in their home country, but also cultivated such fields as mathematics, history, medicine, law, literature, architecture, arts, etc.. The stone cavern in Mt. Toham, the Dabo and the Sukga Towers at Bulkuk temple, which still exists in Kyungju, Kyongsang province, today, are considered the best of the great artistic products of this period.

Some of the monks did not return to the country after their study in the Tang Dynasty, but, instead, earned their fame there by mastering the sacred principles of Buddhism or by leaving volumes of the distinguished literary works of the original Buddhist scriptures.

As a result of the Sillaians frequent travels to China for the purposes of study or trade, there were many residence areas or temples established for the use of travellers at such Chinese coastal towns as Chingchou, Chuchou, Haichou, Tenchou, etc.. The most famous among them was the temple set up at Mt. Ch'in in Tengchou prefecture by a Sillaian named Chang, Bo Go. The temple's annual earning was said to have reached 500 suks of grain, and it was staffed with more than 30 persons.

The Monks Travel to India

As was the case with the Sillaian monks going to china, it was then popular for the Chinese Buddhists of the Tsin and Tang Dynasties to go on pilgrimage to the Holy Land of India, the mecca of their religion.

Accordingly, many of the Sillaians, then studying in China, followed the fashion to visit the Holy Land, but, with the exception of Priest Kyumik of the Baekje Dynasty, none of them returned to their home-land. Ariabalma, one of the monks from Silla in Tang, was described in the Memoirs of the Three Kingdoms(vol. 4) as having passed away at the Narandha Temple of India when he was over 70 years old, while he was engaged in researching the Buddhist doctrines there. The other Buddhist priests of Silla, recorded either as dead or unknown after their travels to India, were Heup, Hyeontae, Kubon, Hyeonkak, Haeryun and two unknown priests.

However, there were two high priests from Silla, Hecho and Daebum who left distinctive marks on the History of Buddhism in China with their visits to India. Priest Hecho was a man of the King Sungduk era, who went to Tang at an early age. Later, after about ten years of travels through the sacred places of India, Hecho returned to China to engage in the translations of the original sutras. The priest died at the age of 54, leaving a number of works including the five volumes of his Travelogues to India, which remained as highly-placed documents for the Chinese History of Buddhism. Priest Daebum, on the other hand, was a man of the King Mooyeol period, who earned his fame after his research work in India and, later, rendered his services for the development of Buddhism in China by staying in the Tang Dynasty.

Besides, there was another priest by name of Wonpyo, who went to the Tang during the years of King Kyungduk of Silla. He also made a visit to India and brought 80 volumes of the Hwaom Sectarian Surtas to China.

Chapter 6
The Secession of the Kyo Religion

The Kyo Religious Secession

When Buddhism was first conveyed to each of the Three Kingdoms, there was no classification of any religious denominations. Rather it was received unconditionally until the end of the Three Kingdoms, merely on the basis of the sutras and other religious material brought from China. For example, according to the actions of high priests like Wonhyo, Won-kwang, Jajang, etc. of silla at the closure of the tripartite dynasties, there was no sign of any sectarian movement within the religion.

But, following the Silla's unification, various Buddhist sects began to appear under the influences of the Sillaian Buddhists from China, and, for a century, and, for a century thereafter, it was a period of the Kyo religious secession.

The Chontae-jong Sect

The doctrines of this was originally explicated by the Chinese Buddhist Saint Huiszu of the Ch'en Dynasty, and the sect was formally founded later by Saint Chontae at Mt. Chontae in China.

According to the Biography of the Monks of the Sung Dynasty, the Chontae-jong was first imported to Silla by its Priest Hyeonkwang in the age of King Jinheung. Hyeonkwang was a man from Woongju(now Kongju in Choongchongnam province), who went to the Ch'en Dynasty and mastered the religious doctrines from the Chinese Saints Huiszu and

Chihja. After he returned from China, the Sillaian priest built up a temple in Mt. Ong in his hometowm and engaged himself in the propagation of the sect. At one time, there were a number of followers, but the chontae-jong did not prosper as an independent denomination in Silla successfully.

The Hwaom-jong Sect

While the Chontae-jong was founded in southern China, the Hwaom-jong had originated from the north. The doctrines of the sect were first framed by Tushun of the earlier part of the Tang Dynasty, enlarged by Tushun's disciple Chihum, and were later completed and codified by other Chinese Buddhist scholars.

The first one to convey the Hwaom-jong in Silla was the Priest Uisang, who returned in the 11th year of King Moonmoo after learning the basics of the sect from the Chinese Saint Chihum for 11 years in Tang Dynasty. Uisang established ten temples throughout the country including Boosuk temple, in Mt. Bookak, Bumu temple, in Mt. Keum jung, Hwaom temple, in Mt. Chiri, and others. He gained many followers, and, among them, Ojin, Jitong, Pyohun, Jinjung, Jinjang, Doyung, Ryangwon, Sangwon, Neungin and Uisook were his ten notable disciples.

Afterwards, the Buddhist denomination was broadly extended through the country with the return of Priest Seungchon from Tang in the first year of King Hyoso. He brought many religious materials concerning the Hwaom-jong from China and handed them over to Priest Uisang. Priest Bumsoo also returned home following Seungchon to contribute furthering the mission of the sect.

The Bupsang-jong Sect

Also called Yooshik-jong or Jaeun-jong, the principle conception of the Bupsang-jong was that every phenomena of the world, concrete or otherwise, was the product of human consciousness.

This Buddhist denomination was also founded by one of the Chinese monks named Hsienchang of Tang Dynasty, who learned the secret principle from the Marandha Temple in India. His disciple, Jaeun, later accomplished the foundation work of the religion as an independent denomination and his name was often cited to identify the sect.

Priest Woncheuk, of the royal lineage of Silla, who received schooling from Hsienchang in Tang, was the first missionary of the Buddhist sect in his home country. Woncheuk was one of the five highest priests in China with his wide range of knowledge in both the Mahayana and Hinayana sutras and other Buddhist theories. He made a short trip to silla during the years of King Shinmoon, but returned to Tang again and died there. He had two disciples in Tang, both high priests Seungjang and Dojeung from Silla··· the former remained in China but the later returned home in the 6th year of King Hyoso to cultivate the foundation of the Bupsang-jong.

But the one who really made great efforts for the development of the sect in Silla and, therefore, was regarded as its prime initiator, was Priest Kyungheung. After his research into the theories of Consciousness in Tang, Kyungheung did much to propagate the religion in the country by authoring some 250 volumes of the religious books. He was treated as the Most Reverend Priest, or called Kooksa(國師), by King Shinmoon.

The Mil-jong Sect

This consisted of the two other branch denominations ; one, the Shininjong or Moondooroo introduced in China during the epoch of the West Ts'in Dynasty from India, and, the other, Jinun-jong transmitted by the two Chinese Buddhists, Sunmui and Kumkangchih, during the period of the Tang Dynasty.

However, the first person to transmit this sectarian religion in Silla, of the Shin-jong branch, was the Priest Myungrang, who had been in Tang for the four years during the reign of Queen Sunduk. This was presumed to have been some 80 years before the other sect, Jinun-jong, reached Tang. Priest Myungrang earned the reputation, after his performances of the secret petitions to the Moondooroo at the Sachonwang temple of sinking the Tang's invading war-vessels at sea at the time of King Moonmoo.

The Jinun branch of the Mil-jong sect was fostered in Silla by Priest Haetong, who learned the doctrines from the original transmitter, the Chinese Priest Sunmui, in the Tang Dynasty. Haetong, even after 3 years of schooling there, could not attain the final realization. He was said to have put a burning brazier over his head, at last, to make it. After the attainment, he was also said to have healed the ailments of the Tang's princess and of the princess of King Hyoso in Silla.

Belatedly, in the 9th year of King Hyoso, a Buddhist monk named Myonghyo want to China to learn another Jinun branch of the sectarian religion that originated from Kumkangchih in Tang Dynasty. Myonghyo was assumed to have relayed the school in Silla later.

The Yul-jong sect

As the character 'Yul' stands for and generally means the religious commandments of Buddhism, this sect was founded on the basis of a systematized philosophy of the Quartering Commandments that originated from India 100 years after the death of Sakya and, later, was translated and completed in China by the Tang Dynasty's Nansan.

The first one to introduce the religious sect in Silla was Priest Jajang, although the memoirs of the Three Kingdoms record that Priest Jimyung went to the Sui Dynasty in pursuit of the religion earlier than Jajang. Jimyung left for the Sui in the 24th year of King Jinpyung, but there is no authentic record of his missions in Silla afterwards. However, Jajang built up the Tongdo temple in Mt. Youngchui after his return from Tang, and engaged in the extensive propagation of the religion by giving preachings of the commandments twice a month at the temple. Priest Wonseung, Jajang's contemporary, who went to Tang in the 49th year of King Jinpyung and mastered both doctrines of the Kyo(教) and Seon(禪) religions, also helped in raising the Yul-jong sectarian religion in Silla.

In summary, all the denominational schools of the Kyo-jong Buddhist religion that had been founded and developed in Silla are as listed in the following:

Name of the Sect	Founding place	Founding Temple	Founder	Royal Epoch
Chontae-jong	Woongju	Ongsan-temple	Hyeonkwang	King Jinpyung
Hwaom-jong	Youngju	Boosuk-temple	Uisang	King Moonmoo
Bupsang-jong	Kyongju	Samrang-temple	Kyongheung	King Shinmoon
Yul-jong	Yangsan	Tongdo-temple	Jajang	Queen Sunduk
Bupsung-jong	Kyungju	Bunhwang-temple	Wonhyo	King Moonmoo
Yeolban-jong	Chonju	Kyongbok-temple	Boduk	King Mooyeol
Mil-jong	Kyongju	Kumkwang-temple	Myungrang	Queen Sunduk

Chapter 7
The Promotion of the Seon(Zen) Religion

The Introduction of the Seon(Zen) Religion

With the introduction of the Seon religion from China about three hundred years after the first inflow of Buddhism, many changes began to take place in the local Buddhist sphere. That is, all the previous sectarian religions became castrated, and almost all the books thus far written in relation to the difficult Buddhist doctrines were viewed as insignificant.

The Seon(Zen) religion had a comparatively easy dictum in its practical approach to Buddha, while the other sects heretofore had been based only on hard conceptional theories in such written forms as sutras. The principle idea of the Seon, however, was that when a man had a Buddha in his mind, he could become one, without depending on the recorded scriptures. In other words, man originally Buddha-natured but he needed to have his own self-awakening.

It was related that the Seon was first transplanted in China by Boddhi Dharma of India during the epoch of Division between North and South, and the sectarian religion prevailed in the North by one of the two high priests of the time, Hyenung, was called the South Seon, while the other in the South by Shinsu was the North Seon. Because of its simplicity, the sectarian school of the Seon religion was said to have been conveyed extensively when Dharma initiated it in China.

According to the Choi, Chi Won's writings and the other historical records, Priest Buprang, who had been schooled by the Seon's fourth founder Taosin, in the Tang Dynasty during the Queen Sunduk age, was the first relayer of the religion in Silla. His disciple, Shinhaeng, followed suit and conveyed the northern school of the religion after 3 years of learning in Tang during the years of King Haekong.

About 40 years later, the southern school was brought in by Priest Doui. He was said to have spent 36 years in Tang in pursuit of the school from the 5th year of Queen Sunduk to the 13th year of King Hunduk, and more than 40 years in preaching at the Jinjong temple in Mt. Seorak after his return from China. But Doui's years of evangelical mission which were continued by his disciple Priest Kyumik did not produce many effects.

Priest Hongchup and Mt. Silsang

Although both Sinhaeng and Doui were considered a scorn to the in-docile Buddhist world then, they passed away without realizing their dreams of the extensive mission of the Seon religion. The Most Reverend Priest Hongchup, who went to the Tang Dynasty after Doui and received the indoctrination of the sectarian school from the learned Chinese monk named Hsit'ang, initiated the school in Mt. Chiri. By this time, the situation turned favourable toward the religion so that he could easily work in establishing a firm foundation for the Seon.

Priest Hongchup, also nicknamed Founding Priest Namhan, went to China in the years of King Hunduk of Silla and returned in the first part of King Heungduk reign. While he was promoting the religion of Seon at the Silsang temple in Mt. Chiri, he earned many converts including Prince Sunkang of King Heungduk and more than a thousand disciples including Pyungwoon, Suchol, etc.. Even though his learnings in Tang were recorded to have been much later than Doui's, Priest Hongchup and his school in Mt. Silsang, the sectarian name for Mt. Chiri, were marked as the originators of the Seon religion in Korea. His disciple, Priest Suchol, as the next successor of the school, advanced the religion to a great extent, and died in the 7th year of King Jinsun, and Suchol's fol-lowers again continued the religious promotional works through the later generation.

The Nine Mountain Schools of the Seon Religion

Priest Hongchup's School conveyed from Hsit'ang of the Tang Dynasty was one of the nine others founded still later. All these schools, in the end, were consolidated and became the Chokye-jong religion of today. The eight mountain schools were :

The School of Mt. Dongri······This was founded in Mt. Dongri, southeast of Koksung-kun, Mooju(now Kwangju), Chollanam province, by Priest Haechol in the first year of King Munsung about 13 years after the Mt. Silsang School. Haechol, whose surname was Park from Kyungju, went to Tang in the 6th year of King Hunduk, and returned in the first year of King Mungsung after some three years of studying the Seon religion at the Boosa temple in the western province of China. Whilehe was conducting indoctrination in the school after setting up a cloister in the mountain(Dongri), Haechol often received letters of consolation from King Munsung, and raised up such great disciple priests as Dosun and Shisun.

The School of Mt. Kaji······Initiated by Priest Chaedeung about one year after that of Haechol in Kwangju on his return from Tang in the 2nd year of King Munsung. Chaedeung, after being enlightened by Priest Doui's disciple Kyumkeo, went to China in the 2nd year of King Hikang. The school Chaedeung initiated was later moved and formally founded in Mt. Kaji in Yuchi-myon, Jangheung-kun, Chollanam province and became so influential that there were more than 800 followers. Priest Doui was regarded as the principle founder, while his disciples, Kyumkeo and Chaedeung, died at the age of 77, and were given the posthumous title of Bojo by King Hunkang.

The School of Mt. Sungju······This was founded by Priest Muyeom, who returned from Tang in the 7th year of King Munsung, at the Sungju temple in Kongju, Choongchongnam province. Muyeom, originally a priest of the Hwaom-jong of the Kyo Buddhist religion went to China in the 13th year of King Hunduk where he studied for more than 20 years with the Chinese Seon Priest Juman at the Bulkwang temple in Honanfu and with Priest Puch'eh in Mt. Makok of the Puchou region. His learnings was so great that the Chinese people regarded him as the great Boddhisattva in the Orient. Upon return to his home country, Muyeom received special treatment from royal families, while a throng of followers came to listen to his teachings when he initiated the school. For his wide-spread fame, he later earned the Buddhist entitle of Kwangjong from the 49th King Hunkang, at the same time, he taught almost two thousand distinguished disciples. The remains of the school were in Misan-myon, Boryong-kun, Choongchongnam province.

The School of Mt. Dokul······This was founded by Priest Bumil, who learned and practiced under the Chinese Priest Yumkwan, in Tang for six years. He entered Tang at the time of King Heungduk, but returned home in the 9th year of King Munsung because of Tang's Buddhist persecution. Setting up his school at the Kulsan temple, he spent forty years promoting the religion of his learnings and won ten enthusiastic followers, including Rangwon and Rangkong.

The School of Mt. Saja······This was established by Priest Jeolchung on the tenets of the southern school of the Chinese Seon religion that was conveyed by Priest Doyun, who went to Tang in the 17th year of King Hunduk and came back the same year Priest Bumil returned, that is, in the 9th year of King Munsung. As soon as Doyun settled down in Mt. Poongak, a crowd swarmed before his door like a mob. Among them, was Jeongchung, who later moved to Mt. Saja of Wonju-kun, Kangwon province, with his followers where he formed one of the nine Seon religious schools and became Doyun's closeast disciple. Afterwards, the number of the school adherents continued swarming in from all corners of the country ; the 49th King Hunkang, being attached to the religion, constructed the Heungyong Monastery for the school in Mt. Saja that was brought then under the administrative jurisdiction of the central government called Jungsa-sung.

The School of Mt. Huiyang······Priest Jisun founded this school at the Anrak temple in Mt. Hyonke in the 3rd year of King Kyungmun, but later transferred it to Mt. Huiyang in what is now Hunkyung-kun, Kyongsangbuk province ; this was done during the years of King Hun-kang at the request of one of his disciples named Simchoong, Jisun received the schooling mainly from the local Seon Priest Haeun at the Susuk temple. On account of its wide-spread popularity, the temple of the school was designated 'Bongum' temple by royal decrees of King Hunkang. In view of its geneology, which, according to one the Choi, Chi Won's records, was in the order of Ssangbong, Buprang, Sinhaeng, Joungbum, Hyeun, Jisun, etc., this school constituted the revival of the Seon religion that was first introduced in Silla by priests Buprang and Sinhaeng. The founder, Jisun, had many famous disciples like Yangbu, Sungchok, Kehui, etc., by whom the school was greatly promoted.

The School of Mt. Bongrim······This was founded by Priest Shimhi in Jinrye, Changwon-kun, Kyongsangnam province, who learned from the Most Reverend Priest Heyonwook, who was highly revered even by Silla's four kings Minae, Shinmoo, Munsung and Hunan. Entering the priesthood at the age of 19, the founder toured the famous mountains and places in the country, and then practiced the Seon religion for six years in Songkye from the 2nd year of King Jinsung. At this time, he already had many followers, later, he moved into Mt. Seorak ; from here he was summoned by King Jinsung, but did not comply, but preached his Seon religion in Mt. Tak Myungju. In the end, however, Shimhi in-augurated his school in Jinrye by setting up a cloister under the name of Bongrim temple. By this time, he had such a large throng of followers that, when he was recalled by King Kyungmyung to preach at the imperial palace, 80 senior disciples sat on the platform with him.

The School of Mt. Sumi······Among the nine mountain schools of the Seon religion, this was the last one founded by the Most Reverend Priest Ieom with the opening of the Kwangjo temple in Mt. Sumi located northwest of Kaekyung(now Kaesung) held to be the first capital of the Koryo Dynasty. The founding priest of the school in the last stage of the Silla Dynasty had six-years of study under the Chinese priest Taoying

in Tang. Following his return from China in the 15th year of King Hyokong, Ieom won his fame through the missions in Mt. Seungkwang and
Mt. Youngkak ; eventually, he was awarded a special courtesy by the royal
households. When the school was established in Mt. Sumi by an imperial
decree of the Koryo Dynasty, it also had a throng of pursuers, of whom
Cheokwang, Doin and Jungneung were later the notable successors of
school.

THE NINE MOUNTAIN SCHOOLS OF THE SEON-JONG AND THEIR FOUNDERS

Name of Location	Name of School	Founder & Temple	Royal Epoch
Mt. Silsang	Silsang-temple	Hongchup of King Heungduk age	Namwon-kun
Mt. Dongri	Daean-temple	Haechol of King Shinmu age	Koksung-kun
Mt. Kaji	Borim-temple	Chedeung of King Munsung age	Jangheung-kun
Mt. Sungju	Sungju-temple	Muyeom of King Munsung age	Boryong-kun
Mt. Dokul	Kulsan-temple	Bumil of King Munsung age	Kangneung-kun
Mt. Saja	Heungnyong-temple	Doyung of King Munsung age	Nyongwol-kun
Mt. Huiyang	Bongum-temple	Jisun of King Kyungmun age	Munkyung-kun
Mt. Bongrim	Bongrim-temple	Shimhe of King Jinsung age	Changwon-kun
Mt. Sumi	Kwangjo-sa	Ieom of Koryo's Founding Emperor age	Haeju

Chapter 8
Buddhism in the Early Part of Koryo

The Buddhist Devotion by the Founder of Koryo

With the fall of the Silla Dynasty, the country was in a turbulent state; the insurgent groups raved and various forms of superstitions grew so widely prevalent that the most of the famous Buddhist monks disappeared into their mountain sanctuaries. Nevertheless, the people, though confused, did not lose their faith in the Graces of Buddha for the recovery of social orders and national peace.

King Taejo, the founder of the Koryo Dynasty, was born of a faithful Buddhist family, with a legend in connection with Buddhism. Even before he usurped the throne, being in a powerful position, he established ten great Buddhist monasteries in and out of Kaesung such as Bupwang temple, Jawoon temple, Wangryun temple, Sana temple, Naejaesuk-won, Chonsun-won, Shinheung temple, Wontong temple, Munsu temple and Jijang temple, and prayed to Buddha for the achievement of his political ambitions and for the prosperity of the religion as well. His conviction was that one could solve all his problems only if he had an ardent faith in religion.

Once, therefore, he had concluded the foundation of the Koryo Dynasty following the peaceful overthrow of the Silla regime, King Taejo attributed all his accomplishments to the might of Buddha. Accordingly, the King not only to build the Kaetae temple in Yeonsan to glorify the Buddha's Graces, but also to give a new vitality to the declining religion by pro-

viding courteous treatment to the monks ; he encouraged Buddhist services and est ablished many temples and monasteries. He thought this
was the way to win again the hearts of the people towards a love for
Buddhism practiced for the past 400 years.

According to the History of Koryo(Vol. 2, the Koryosa), the founder
of the Dynasty was related to have constructed a total of 3,500 Bibo
(Supplement) towers and temples throughout the country at the suggestion
of a monk named Dosun as a means to save the people from the rebellious
rampages in the country-side. On the completion of this gigantic project,
even though at the expense of the taxpayers, the imperial court gained
the confidence of the people with its "Buddhism-first" policy.

This policy was inherited by the successive kings of the Koryo Dynasty
for 500 years thereafter, mainly because of the last injunctions the founder-
King Taejo made to his assistant, Park,Sul Hee, a year before he died.
The injunctions were made in ten articles, three of which were to the effect
that the Buddhist religion should be the foundation of the state.

The Appearances of the Talented Monks of the Seon-jong

Along with the policy encouraging the Buddhist religion by the Koryo
Dynasty, many talented monks came out of their mountain seclusion and
supported King Taejo in his attempts to win the popular support, extending, at the same time, the religious influences of their own schools.

Among the famous monks who appeared at the time of King Taejo
were Priest Ieom of the Mt. Sumi School, who won the deep respect of
the king himself as a result of his predominant Seon religion, and Priest
Kyungpo, who brought another source of the Seon religion after his 30
year stay in Tang Dynasty and sustained his fame through the three reigns
succeeding King Taejo. The others were Priest Keukyang of the Mt.
Huiyang School, who returned from China after his 20-year study in Seon-
jong in Tang and, for his reputations, received royal treatment through
the four kings succeeding King Taejo ; Priest Hyeonhui, treated with
special consideration by King Taejo as the Most Reverend Priest after

his return from Tang ; Priest Yeom who earned more than 50 disciples after his return from Tang ; and the Most Reverend Priest Chanyu, who enjoyed the special courtesy of the royal households through the four reigns succeeding King Taejo and established a great Seon school in Mt. Haemok before his death at the age of 90. Still others were Priest Yungda of Mt. Dongri and Priest Choongshim of Mt. Youngbong.

The Department of the Monks and the Systems of Wangsa and Kooksa

Taejo's successor, King Hyejong, passed away only one year after he was enthroned while the third King Jungjong remained in office for three years. During that time, Buddhist learning was promoted by distributing 70,000 suks(10,000 tons) of grains to various monasteries.

Following the short-lived Jungjong, King Kwangjong accomplished many things for the development of Buddhism in Koryo. He established a number of temples, sent 36 monks to the Sung Dynasty in China for study, and, in later years, being guilt-stricken by his executing many innocent lives on false advises, issued a decree to prohibit the killings, to release captive lives and to hold Buddhist rites extensively.

The most notable accomplishment by Kwangjong, above all, was the establishment of the systems governing the public service examinations and the ranks of the Buddhist priests. The examination system set up by the monks department was enacted in the 9th year reign of Kwangjong at the suggestion of Ssuangi, a naturalized person from the Posterior Chou Dynasty in China. The ranks awarded to the monks of the Kyo-jong religion(Dogmatic Buddhism) in each promotional step were in order of Daesun, Daeduk, Daesa, Jeungdaesa, Samjeungdaesa, Sujwa and Seung-tong, while those of the Seon-jong(Zen Sect) were Daesun, Daeduk, Daesa, Jeungdaesa, Samjeungdaesa, Seonsa and Daeseonsa. The last ranks of Seungtong and Daeseonsa were the highest positions attainable by the two main sectarian Buddhists. In the 19th year of Kwangjong, the system of the Wangsa(meaning Royal Priest) as an instructor for the king, and the Kooksa(meaning Most Reverend Priest) as a model of the state, was instituted, and those who held the rank above Samjeungdaesa were qualified for the positions. With the enforcement of the systems, it went without saying that many distinguished monks from various walks of life appeared afterwards, but the first ones to obtain the two supreme positions were Priests Danmun and Hyeger respectively.

Consequently, the profession of the monk was then considered a most honorable one in the society of Koryo ; those appointed to the two highest positions of the religion could also participate in discussions of national affairs along with the government ministers.

Danmun and Kyunyeo

In line with the promotional policies of Buddhism in the early part of Koryo, a number of famous monks came out, not only from the Seon-jong Sect as illustrated in the preceding pages, but also from the Kyo-jong, i.e., Priests Hyeger, Danmun, Kyunyeo, etc..

Royal Priest Danmun, first of all, was a monk who belonged to the Hwaom-jong branch ; he was born in the 4th year of King Hyokong of Silla from the family of Ko in Kwangju. Leaving the world at the age of 5, he studied under Priest Shinom at the Jangui templ e in Mt. Bukhan and perceived the Buddhist precepts at the age of 15. The Priest won a personal favour from King Taejo with his effective prayers for an easy birth by the Empress in Taejo's 9th year reign ; he was appointed an instructor of the Hwaom-jong religion at the Chonsung-jon Pavillion by King Hyejong, the Lord Abbot by King Jungjong when he held the religious congregation at the Kuryongsan temple, and the Chief Priest of the Kuibup temple. Finally, he became Royal Priest later honored by the 4th King Kwangjong.

A great erudite of the Hwaom-jong Sect, the famous Priest Danmun was offered the position of Kooksa(the most reverend priesthood) by King Kwangjong when he was 75, but refused to spend the rest of his life in mountain seclusion. Upon his arrival in Mt. Kaya, he was said to have been enthusiastically welcomed by his followers as if he were the real Buddha. Danmun died the following year at the age of 76, leaving a number of famous disciples like Youngchan, Ilkwang, Myunghoe, Yun-kyung, Anhyeon, Hongkyum, etc..

Another famous monk of the Hwaom-jong was Priest Kyunyeo, who earned the respect of religious circle for his outstanding literature and Buddhist virtues. Born in Hwangju in the 7th year of King Kyungmyung at the closure of the Silla Dynasty, Kyunyeo was so ugly that his parents were said to have abandoned him in the street at the time of his birth, but he was raised again by the parents who became repentent after seeing a crow had protected him with its wings when the child was left abandoned on the street. The Priest left the world at the age of 15 and pursued his study with the learned monks at the Buheung temple and Youngtong temples. While he was growing up with his Buddhist learning, the Hwaom-jong religion was divided by the two antagonistic branch schools of Mt. Namak(Mt. Chiri School) and Mt. Bukak(Busuk temple School), the former originated from Priest Kwanhae and the later from Priest Huirang in the last part of the Silla Dynasty. Though he was of the Mt. Bukak School, Priest Kyunyeo brought an end to the school's factional disunity along with Priest Inyu.

In addition, Kyunyeo attempted to popularize the religion by rewriting and readjusting the contents of more than 30 religious books his prede-cessors had written in connection with the Hwaom-jong doctrines. The Priest,who died in the 24th year of King Kwangjong at the age of 57 while he was the Chief Priest of the Kuibup temple, also left a number of Buddhist literary work that became very popular in the local religious sphere.

Chapter 9
The Multiplicity of the Buddhist Services

The Hundred Thousand Monks at the Ritual

The development of Buddhism made in Koryo especially during the reign of King Kwangjong was more than that wrought during the Silla's unification period. But that of Koryo was accompanied by a multiplicity of various religious services.

More common were the Buddhist rites, all sorts of scriptural lectures, the establishment and renovation works of the towers and temples during the age of King Hyeonjong, who also revived during the year he was enthroned both the Lantern and Palkwan Festivals that had been observed from the time of Taejo, but abolished at the time of Sungjong. In the 9th year of Hyeonjong, almost 100,000 monks attended and served food in a ceremony enshrining the Buddhist relic at the Kaekeuk temple.

Hyeonjong's successor, Dukjong, was no less attached to the religious feasts. The year he assumed the throne, Dukjong provided food for 30,000 monks at the festival balling-grounds and toured the Wejasuk-won, Wangryun temple, and Hyeonhwa temples almost ten times. The next King Chung-jong served food for 10,000 monks at the out-door ritual in the 2nd year of his reign, and had almost the same number of Buddhists, conducting seminaries for priesthood at the Hoekyung-chon Pavillion in his 7th and 9th years. On his birthday, Chungjong executed the 7 day prayer-meetings at the various temples with both the officials and monks participating.

Such mutitudinous Buddhist activities were continued by the succeeding King Munjong, perhaps, even more frequently, and these scales and varieties resulted in a great deal of abuse in money and time by the royal households, extortion from the local populace, and finally, the corruption of the government and the Buddhist temples. The expenses for all those religious services were, of course, paid for by taxes collected from the people. In a sense, Buddhism at this time was looked upon by the royal family, the aristocrats and the commoners alike as a religion of prayer with realistic benefits. Thus, the people tended to become solely dependent on Buddha's Graces for their living.

The Kyunghaeng

This is a prayer procession through the streets conducted by the sutra-reciting Buddhist monks. It originated in the 12th year of King Chungjong, when the King sent his royal attendent Choi, Jean to burn incense at a festival ground called Kujong, and sent out a prayer procession after him through the street ; the Kyunghaeng was performed annually through the first part of the Lee Dynasty.

As it paraded through the three streets of Kaekyung, the capital of Koryo, the procession, with the incense fire in the lead, was followed by columns of people carrying the prajna-paramita-sutras hung over their neck with colorful threads, and by thousands of sutra-reciting monks, a formally-dressed directing official in the rear. This was a great attraction for the general public. Originally, Buddhist rite was held indoors, the monks circling around the Buddha, memorizing their sutras. But the imperial court of Koryo extended its scale as a means of exhibiting the power of Buddha protecting the royal family, praying for blessings for the people.

The Kyunghaeng was held whenever there was a special occasion for the royal household, for the state and for the capital. It soon became very popular throughout the country.

The Lantern Festival

One of the oldest local events, along with the Palkwan Festival, this was observed as an important national function through the entire reigns of Koryo, although it was abolished for some 30 years from the period of the 6th King Sungjong on the grounds that it was troublesome ; it was celebrated again from the 8th King Hyeonjong as mentioned previously. Whereas the Lantern feast was held in Silla on February 15th to pray for an abundant harvest and prosperity for the royal family, it was conducted in koryo as a Buddhist rite at the temples at no particular time. The date was once changed to January 15th during the years of King Uijong, when the lighted lanterns were hung for two days, and the offering services in honour of Buddha were performed by the Imperial Palace and every local town.

The festival was usually observed on any particular occasion such as Sakya's birthday, the completion of a temple, etc., for more than two days, with as many lanterns lighted as possible. In the 21st year of Munjong, it was held for five days and nights to celebrate the completion of the Heungwang temple ; a total of 30,000 lanter ns were said to have been put up in the two day ceremony to enshrine the newly-made Buddha's statue in the 27th year of the same King.

During the festival of Koryo, there were prayers for the peace and security for the state and the royal households ; the foods and refreshment provided were shared in merriment by both the government officials and the people.

The Bad Effects of the Services

For the execution of various Buddhist religious services and for the construction of the countless number of temples, the imperial courts of Koryo consumed and expropriated an exhorbitant amount of national treasury and resources, not to speak of the individual consumption of private houses, accrued from their own ways of services. As a result, this caused great damage to the people in general.

The expropriation was to such an extent that even royal courtiers like Lee, Yang opposed the requisition of laborers and engineers for the construction of the Daejeungkwang temple in the 18th year of King Hyeonjong. But to the Buddhist-devoted ruling class, such a thing as damage to the people was a matter of little consequence. At an all-government official counsel of national affairs held by the 6th King Sungjong, according to the History of Koryo(vol. 93), a participant named Choi, Seung No was said to have suggested the abolition of all the religious activities because they were only stimulating pauperism and idle life among the monks and other parasites.

In fact, a great number of offenders, parasites and other idle groups tended to find escape from responsibilities and an easy life in the temples as a result of the government's protective policy for Buddhism.

Chapter 10

The Prosperity of Koryo and The Golden Age of Buddhism

The Prosperity of the Mil-jong

As approved to its decline in the Tang Dynasty of China, where the religion was first introduced into Silla, the Mil-jong Buddhist sectarian religion became quite popular among the literary people and in the imperial palaces of Koryo.

The Most Reverend Priest Jonghyeon, who won the favor of the royal household and much respect from his followers with the performances of many miracles during the years of King Munjong, was representative of this sectarian religion. Jonghyeon studied the sectarian religious philosophy under Priest Yungchol at the Chiljang temple when he was 13,and earned fame with his lectures in the 15th year of King Sungjong. Through the reigns of Hyeonjong and Dukjong, he received courteous treatments from the royal family ; later he was appointed to the religious rank of Seungtong because of his accomplishments. In the years of Chungjong, the Mil jong priest set up his first sectarian temple, Sayeon temple, in Mt. Samkak. It was during the age of Munjong that he was given the titles of Wangsa(royal priest) and then Kooksa(most reverend priest) respectively because of the numerous miracles he had performed ; for instance, he made rain fall with the works of his sutras. The Priest died at the age of 83, and his religion was succeeded by disciples like Youngneom, Insang, Shimchon, Jolwoon, etc,.

The Golden Age of Buddhism

Throughout the entire history of Koryo, the period covering about five hundred years of the reigns of the three rulers of the 11th King Munjong, Sunjong and Sookjong could be marked by an era of extreme prosperity for the Dynasty. During this period, Buddhism also reached its culmination with an unprecedented multiplicity of religious activities, and reverence for Buddha and the monks.

Munjong's devotion for the religion was also record-breaking. The completion of the reprints for the Koryo's famous collections of Buddhist Literature(covering sutras, laws and treaties) that took about 60 years since the work was first begun by King Hyeonjong, was first one of his great achievements. He had such a great regard for the priesthood that he sent his precious sons, the 4th Hoo(Who later became Priest Uichon), the 6th Kyu and the 10th Kyung, to the Buddhist world, and, in order to show his respect for the monks, the King personally invited to his kingdom all the aged bonzes above 80 years of age from across the country in the 5th year of his rule. In addition, he once set up a system enabling one son out of every individual home having, at least, three sons to become a monk.

Aside from the preachings he himself received from the Buddhist saint every June, Munjong annually sponsored the 7-day prayer meetings and seminars at the various temples throughout the country on his birthday in December. They were repeated many times more in a year to pray for the welfare of the royal family and the state.

Among the many Buddhist constructions he had carried out with the forage of the national resources, despite the opposition from his subjects, the gigantic monastery of Heungwang temple, established with the measurement of some 16,800 sq. ft. in the present Kaepoong-kun, Kyonggi province, was the most remarkable. The construction of the temple took 12 years from the 10th year of Munjong.

Although Seonjong, the Munjong's successor, died three months after he was enthroned, the next 13th ruler of Koryo King Sunjong was no less attached to the Buddhist rites. During his 11 years of reign, Sungjong spent almost every day with one kind of devotional service or another. The only big religious assemblies he held were the three seminars given at the Hoekyungjon Pavillion in his 2nd, 4th and 6th year in office respectively with 30,000 monks attending.

Moreover, Sunjong even changed the entire formalities of the royal household to those of Buddhism, and always had the sutra-carrying Buddhist priest lead his way whenever he was taking leave of his palace. The other remarkable accomplishments he had fulfilled were the establishment of the Daekok-chung temple and Daehongho temples and the 13-storied gold tower in the imperial palace. Also the publication of 4,740 volumes of the Buddhist literary collections at the Heungwang temple were noteworthy.

Following Heonjong, the short-lived successor of Sunjong, Sookjong held the reign for 10 years. During this time, he exerted more of his time and efforts for Buddhist works than for state affairs. His entire reign was full of religious undertakings such as conducting seminars and rituals at the Hoekyung-jon pavillion and at the Heugnwang temple, visiting all the famous monasteries in the country, and building a number of the Buddhist shrines, towers and instruments. Sookjong also had his young 5th son, Deungun, enter the priesthood.

The Appearance of the Daekak Kooksa (meaning the Most Reverend Priest of High Enlightnment).

The Daekak Kooksa Uichon gave Buddhism in Koryo gave a new vitality. The 3-century long disharmony between the sectarian religions of Kyo-Jong and Seon-Jong was brought to an end after Uichon founded his Chontae-jong school and emphasized the universality of all religious views.

Priest Uichon, the 4th son of the 11th King Munjong, was a brother of the 13th King Sunjong. Following the will of his father, Uichon learned the Hwaom-jong religion from the Royal Priest Ranwon of King Kyungduk at the Youngton temple when he was 13, and pursued his studies of not only the Hinayana(Exoteric) and Mahayana scriptures but also of Confucianism. In order to continue his researches in China like other famous monks, Uichon besought royal approval for his trip to the Sung Dynasty, but was constantly turned down by his father Munjong, by the next King Soonjong, and even by his brother, King Sunjong. Thus, in April of the 2nd year of Sunjong, he finally stowed away at night on a Chinese commercial liner with his two followers including Sukae. Arriving in the Sung capital in July, Uichon toured around the famous temples for a month at the courtesy of the Sung Dynasty's Emperor Chuljong.

Afterwards, he travelled through Hangchow and Mingchow in China, discussing, consulting and researching the doctrines of various schools of all the sects from such renowned priests as Priest Chingyuan of the Hwaom-jong, Priest Tsongchien of the Chontae-jong, Priest Yuanchan of the Kyo-jong, and from 50 other Chinese Buddhists including Huilin, Pangchi, Huailien. After a 14 month stay in China, Uichon returned home at the call of Sunjong with more than a thousand volumes of comprehensive Buddhist writings and with a pledge to transmit the Chontae-jong in Koryo.

Sunjong appointed Uichon, when he returned, to be the Chief Priest of the Heungwang temple, the head temple of the Hwaom-jong. Setting up an office for the religious literary collections at the Temple, he collected the Buddhist books from Japan, China, and from the local source, and put out a total of 4,740 volumes of sutras. Prior to this undertaking, Uichon compiled all his gathered material 'A New General Catalogue of All Religious Literatures' in a three-volume series, in which the works of the famous local priests such as Wonhyo, Uisang, Daehyeon, Kyungheung and 20 others were included. This was called Koryo Sokjangkyung, or a series of the Buddhist collections of Koryo. Beside this, he also exchanged Buddhist writings with the famous Chinese priests in the Sung Dynasty.

After his further prusuits of self-cultivation at the Sunam temple　in

Mt. Jokye in Sunchon in the 9th year of Sunjong and at the Hongwon temple and the Haein temple in the 11th year of the same king, Uichon was reappointed the Chief Priest of the Heungwang temple by Sookjong. When he was at the Kookchung temple, he began to expound the Chontae-jong religion with a stress in the theory of a universal view of all the different religions. To be a true Buddhist, he claimed, one must not be prejudiced against certain religions or conceptions. With this attitude of mind a gradual reconciliation took place between the Seon-jong and Kyo-jong.

The use of the minting coins as a unit of currency initiated at the time of Sookjong was one of the many contributions Uichon made for the state. He learned the merits of the system while he was in the Sung Dynasty. The use of coins was once enforced during the years of Sunjong and Mokjong, but gradually this use gave way to the old practice of using the grain as the method of transactions.

Uichon died in September of the 6th year of Sookjong at the age of 47, and, in honor of his great achievements both for the state and for the religion, he was given the posthumous title of Daekak(the Greatly Enlightened) and was revered as the Most Reverend Priest by the King.

The Establishment of the chontae-jong

The Chontae-jong established in Koryo by Priest Uichon was the same religious sect first introduced in Silla from the Ch'en Dynasty in China by Priest Hyeonkwang, as has been described previously. It was the one originally founded by the Chinese Priest Chihja on the basis of the teachings of the Saddharma Pundarika, called Buphwakyung, because of its orthodox doctrines. The original scriptures of the Buphwakyung which belonged to the Mahayana Buddhism, were translated into Chinese classics long before the sect was founded by Lachih, a man of the Six Dynastic period of China.

However, the religion was not successfully propagated either in Silla or Kokuryo in spite of the attempts made by Priest Hyeonkwang of Silla,

Priest Pnayak of Kokuryo, and others such as Bupyeung, Rieung, and Soonyoung of the Silla's unification period, because it was not listed as one of the five major sectarian religious or 9 mountain schools of Silla, or the 6 major religions of Koryo.

At any rate, when Priest Uichon gave the lectures on the Chontae-jong doctrines at the Kookchung temple, more than a thousand scholar-monk-swere gathered to listen raising quite a sensation. Afterwards, the 5th son Deungum of King Sookjong, who later became the Most Reverend Priest Wonmyung, became a follower of Uichon. As the popularity of the Chontae-jong was on the rise, many temples of other religions were converted, and Uichon chose the promising monks from various sects and schools, and gave them a position in his religion, thus decreasing the rivalry between all the different denominations including that of the Kyo and Seon.

The Uichon's Chontae-jong, also called Chontae Buphwaom-jong, Wondon- jong, dae-jong or Daekyo, held the view that it was the only pure religionof true Buddhism, while regarding all the others only as methodical ones. In other words, it had its own practical dogmas called Osipalkyo(or Five Times and Eight Teachings) explaning how one should become a Buddha, as compared to other commentary Buddhism explaining the meaning of Buddhism.

The Seventy District of Buddhist Temples

In Koryo, where the successive kings made their conversion to Buddhism, there were countless numbers of sizable temples, towers and monasteries built in the capital of Kaekyung and other local areas. In the capital alone, there was a total of 70 temples, forming a great Buddhist city, according to the History of the Sung Dynasty(on the Koryo Part).

The 70 temples in the capital were :

Bupwang temple, Wangryun temple, Jawoon temple, Ilwol temple, Naejaesuk- Won, Oejaesuk-won, Sakun temple, Chonsun-won, shinjung-won, Shinheung temple, Munsu temple, Wontong temple, Jijang temple,

Daeheung temple, Kuyo-dang were set up before the Taejo's foundation of Koryo ; Anhwa temple, Bojae temple, Kaekook temple, Myeonsung temple, Kwangheung temple, Ihyelk temple, Naechonwang temple were established after the Taejo's foundation of Koryo ; Bongeun temple, Kuibup temple, Honghwa temple, Yuam temple, Samkyu temple were built in the years of Kwang jong ; Heungkook temple, Jinkwan temple, Hongho temple, Chonsu temple, Munchon temple, Myoryoon temple, Hwangmyung temple, Koesan temple, Bokwoon temple, Buleun temple, Yongheung temple, Shipwang temple, Kwonjun temple, Jeungsan temple, Haean temple, Keonsung temple, Seoboong temple, Jawoon temple, Sook-neung temple, Daewoon temple, Daeadn temple, Hongwon temple, Myot-ong temple, Bongoem temple, Bojae temple, Doil temple, Bongsun temple, Inkyung temple, Heungwang temple were established after the time of Kyungjong.

The Heungwang temple, among all the temples, was the one King Munjong constructed which took 12 years of man's labor. Completed in the 21st year of the King, the scale and greatness of this temple was as good as the imperial palace. On the opening of the temple, Munjong held a 5 day lantern festiva l with thousands of lighted lamps hung on both sides of the street connecting the imperial palace and temple and enlisted one thousand famous monks to reside in the temple. Later, a castle was built aroud the temple, and a gold towe r was erected in it.

The Anhwa temple, originally built at the time of Taejo, was renovated in April of the 13th year of Yejong, and the occasion was marked with a three-day celebration. The make-up of this temple, where the scrolls and the statues sent from Emperor Huijong of the Sung Dynasty were preserved, was in comparably luxurious. The Hongho temple established in the 10th year of Sunjong in the Eastern region of Kaesung, and the Kookchung temple completed in the 2nd year of Sookjong at the wishes of Empress Dowager Inye and used as the headquarters of the Chontae-jong by Uichon, all deserve to be commended.

The Royal Priest Sohyeon and the Promotion of the Bupsang- jong

Of the various Buddhist sectarian religions, it was the Kyo-jong religion that developed most extensively in Koryo. If the Chontae-jong were to be placed under the category of the Kyo-jong, all the religious influences of the Kyo-jong denomination derived entirely from the Chontae-jong or the Hwaom-jong schools, especially after Priest Uichon appeared. The other religious schools were all inactive, except, perhaps, the Bupsang-jong, which gained its vitality for sometime during the years of Munjong and sunjong due to the works of Royal Priest Sohyeon.

Sohyeon, whose surname was Park, studied the theory of intellectualism and the religious sutras under Priest Haerin of the Haean temple at the age of 17. Becoming a Daeduk from among the congregation at the Wangryun temple and earning the title of Joongdaesa in the 23rd year of Munjong, Sohyeon was summoned to the imperial palace school the 6th prince Taeng of Munjong, who later became a Seungtong at the Bupju temple. Having been promoted to the rank of Seungtong by the next King Sunjong, the Bupsang-jong priest, well conversant not only in the Buddhist scriptures but also in the Confucian classics and in poetry, corrected and republished 353 volumes of religious books which his predecessor Jaeun had produced. For 22 years, he lectured to his followers about his religious doctrines, and sponsored annual Buddhist rites at the Bupsang-jong temple.

Upon his death in the first year of Sookjong at the age of 59, Sohyeon was conferred with the posthumous court rank of Wangsa(Royal Priest) and the title of Haeduk by the King. He braced up the Bupsang-jong with more than a thousand followers including Prince Taeng, and was, therefore, regarded as one of the two greatest authorities of the Kyo-jong religion along with Uichon.

Chapter 11
The National Faith and Crisis

The National Faith

Although ultra-nationalism, ultra-racialism and the denial of reality were the important parts of the essentials of Buddhism, the religion was received and professed by both the Three Kingdoms and Koryo as a means for the realization of national purposes. This could be supported by many instances, i.e., King Bupheung of Silla embraced the religion on a pragmatic ground that, if he had a faith in it, the state would prosper and the people would live in peace. Priest Wonhyo, a great celebrity in the religious sphere during the middle of Silla, exerted his efforts in enhancing the nationalistic ideology by expounding the doctrines of the national Buddhist Sutras called Kumkwang Myungkyung. So was Priest Wonkwang, who left many achievements in strengthening the power of the state and in arousing the popular spirit that constituted the back-bone for the Silla's unification during the age of King Jinpyung, and Priest Jajang of the period of Queen Sunduk, who established a nine-storied tower in the Kwangyong temple in thehopes of defeating Silla's neighboring enemy states.

Such a tendancy was also inherited in Koryo, where the Founding King Taejo established many Buddhist temple to pray for the accomplishment of his many ambitions, and where the successive kings conducted countless numbers of Buddhist constructions and rituals as a means to enjoy the good welfare and peace of the state. As a result, the imperial household of Koryo only tended to rely on the Graces of Buddha whenever the destiny of the state was in crisis.

The Invasion of the Kitan Tartars and the Collection of Buddhist Literatures

As the Kitan Tartars of the Liao Dynasty in China made an easterward advance destroying the state of Balhae, a country bordering in north of Koryo, the rulers of the uneasy Koryo Dynasty which followed Kwang-jong set up their dilpomatic relations with the Sung Dynasty on the other side of Liao, making Koryo's collision with the Kitans inevitable.

In October of the 6th year of King Sungjong of Koryo, the Kitans built their triple fortress along the Yalu River and blocked the Koryo's passages to the Sung and the Nuchen. In December, two years later, an army of the Kitans intruded the northwestern region of the country, but was turned back at the expense of the strong diplomatic negotiations by Koryo's envoy Suhi. The second invasion with an army of 300,000 Kitans from the north was launched during the political upheaval in Koryo, in which the 7th King Mookjong was slaughtered by the revolutionary leader Kang, Jo, and thus, the capital Kaekyung fell under the hands of the invading forces without much resistance. Hyeonjong succeeded Mook-jong who fled to south in the Cholla province, but soon returned to the capital after the retreat of the foreign troops and concluded the peace treaty with the Liao Dynasty.

The Kitan invasion inflicted great damage on the people of Koryo with their rampant violence and plundering. In order to repel the consequent foreign instrusion by the Graces of Buddha, Hyeonjong initiated the re-printing of the letter-blocks for the great Collections of the Buddhist Li-teratures based on the original texts brought from the Sung Dynasty. This work succeeded through Dukjong, Chungjong and was completed in the age of Munjong, requiring 60 years. The Collection in a total of 5,048 volumes were then preserved at the Buin temple in Taegu, but were des-troyed after the Mongolian invasion in the later period. Incidentally, the Kitans made another attempt to invade Koryo in the 9th year of Hyeonjong while the king was still working on the Collections, but retreated without success.

The Kangma Army

Anxious because of the constant threats from the enemy in the north, the imperial government of the Koryo Dynasty established the Hangma (meaneng Destroying the Devil) Army organized with the Buddhist monks at the 9th year of Sookjong. At the suggestion of Yun, Kwon, the army was later reorganized into the Shinkikun (or the calvary) and the Shinbokun (or the infantry). The monks, when the country was at peace, were given trainnings for both services and were called in for immediate action at the time of a national emergency.

This system of national defense played an important role later during the Mongolian invasion and the Japanese invasion of the Lee Dynasty period.

The Invsion of the Mongols and the 80,000 Letter-Blocks of the Buddhist Collections

For about a century and half after the complete withdrawal of the Kitans in the north, the Koryo Dynasty enjoyed peace without any foreign invasions until the Mongolian attacks during the reign of the 23rd King Kojong.

The Koryo Dynasty eliminated the trouble-making remnants of the Kitans with the help of the Mongols of the Yuan Dynasty in China. Because of this, the Mongols approached Koryos with a highhanded attitude, sometimes compelling the latter to pay burdensome trubutes to their envoy in Koryo even behaving discourteously in the royal palace. But the immediate cause of the Mongols first invasion which took place in the 18th year of Kojong was the death of their envoy named Chukuyeo, who was murdered on the way to his country after his mission in Koryo in January, the 12th year of the King. The two countries then held contradicting views over the death of the envoy···the Mongols accusing Koryo of its responsibility, and the Koryo protesting that the murder took place over the Yalu River where it had no jurisdiction. In any case, the first invasion by the Mongols, who pressed to surround the capital Kaekyung,

was withdrawn peacefully because their commanding general Salita received bribes.

Although a temporary peace was purchased, the Koryo Dynasty, still
uneasy about their further repercussion, removed its capital to Kanghwa
Island in the 19th year of Kojong. The move was taken by the Mongols
as a hostile action, and, thus, the powerful outsiders reinvaded the Koryo
territory in the 22nd year of the King and, this time, through the entire
country.

While in the island capital, the King and his subjects were engrossed
in various Buddhist rites praying for the defeat of the invading enemy.
But no solution appeared. In the 23rd year of King Kojong, the Collections
of the Buddhist Literature that had been the work of the four succeeding
reigns since Hyeonjong were completely burnt down to ashes together
with the Buin temple by the Mongols. Kojong, in his 24th year, undertook
the work of reengraving the Buddhist scriptural characters, devoting a
long letter of earnest prayers to Buddha. The work was completed 16
years later with a total of 81,137 printed blocks, popularly called 80,000
Daejang-kyung. But, considering the fact that there were the two letters
on both sides of a block, the number should be 160,000.

As Wonjong succeeded to the throne following Kojong, the government
of Koryo adopted a conciliatory policy toward the Mongols, who then
held the northern half of the country under their control, and moved its
capital back to Kaekyung again. For about a century after this, Koryo
was under the influence of the Yuan Dynasty.

Chapter 12
The Appearance of Priest Jinul and the Approximation of the Kyo-jong and Seon-jong

The Flourishing Seon-jong

Despite the loss of some of its high priests in consequence of the Chon-tae-jong activities initiated by Priest Uichon, the Seon-jong Buddhist denomination became unflinchingly popular among the people. A man like Lee, Ja Hyeon, for instance, abandoned his official position of Jinsa and promoted the religion during King Yejong and King Injong periods by renovating the Munsu-won temple in Mt. Chungpyung, Kangwon province, setting up more than ten of its temples and hermitages, and by absorbing himself in the Seon-religious contemplation. Many famous Buddhists such as Damyeon, who later became a high priest, flocked to the school.

The Most Reverend Priest Hakil, one of Lee, Ja Hyeon's contempraries, was another promoter of the Seon religion against the Chontae-jong. Accounted as having healed many patients with his attainments of the Seon doctrines and absorption of the Sutra of Great Wisdom, Hakil himself made efforts to propagate the religion, even declining Uichon's invitation to give lectures at the Hongwon temple. He was entitled with the position of Daeseon temple in the 9th year of Yejong and became a Royal Priest in the first year of Injong. He was also asked by Injong to stay at the Kyungam temple, but he fled into Mt. Woonmun in Chungdo-kun, Kyongsangbuk province, where a throng of Buddhist scholars gathered from all directions to hear his teachings.

Another contributor to the Seon-jong's development along with Hakil was the Royal Priest Tanyeon, who had taught Yejong, the prince of Sookjong. Tanyeon received the religious indoctrination from the Priest Jookhyeon and Lee, Ja Hyeon. Later, he was appointed by King Yejong to the rank of Seonsa and by Injong to the post of Royal Priest, and then he gave counsels for the royal families on most of the state affairs. In the later years, he taught the Seon students at the Dansok temple in Jinju.

The other promoters of the Seon religion at a later date were Priest Jiin of the King Uijong period and Priest Hyosun of the Myungjong.

The Appearance of the Most Reverend Priest Jinul

Although the Seon-jong Buddhist denomination of Koryo, as in the case of Silla, had been the mere extension of that transmitted from China, a great reformation was brought up when Priest Jinul originated the Independent Seon school in the years of King Shinjong. Regarded as one of the two greatest authorities along with Uichon in the Buddhist religious field of the Koryo Dynasty, Priest Jinul earned his reputation by his learnings and virtues solely as a private monk, bringing an innovation to this sectarian religion, while Uichon led the whirlwind in the Kyo-jong religion as an official monk being a favourite of the kings and the sovereigns. The rise of the two priests, however, was marked as epoch-making in the history of the two separate Buddhist religions in Koryo.

With a secular name of Jung and a pseudonym Mokwooja, Jinul entered Buddhism at the age of 8, and passed the priest's examination when he was 25. After studying the religious books compiled with the preachings of the Tang Dynasty Priest Hyeneung at the Chungwon temple in Changpyong and the Hwaom-jong theories together with its collected sutras at the Bomun temple in Mt. Haah, Jinul spent a number of years in pursuit of both the Seon and Kyo religions at the Keojo temple in Mt. Kong in Youngchon, and continued his research in Mt. Chiri in the first year of King Shinjong. He was awakened after reading the passage, 'the Seon (meaning the religious meditation) is nowhere, whether there is silence, noisiness, the cause and effect of the sun and moon, distinctions of thought'. He taught thousands of his followers, many of them from the noble and royal class, at the Kilsang temple in Mt. Songkwang, Sunchon-kun, in the 3rd year of Shinjong. Then, the Seon religious learning became unprecedently vigorous, and Jinul built up many temples including Baek-wunchung temple, Jeokchui-am and Zowol-am.

When he died at the Kilsang temple at the age of 53 in the 5th year of Hijong, Jinul was awarded by the King with a posthumous entitle of Bozo Kooksa (the Most Reverend Priest). He also left numberous literary works on Buddhism, and his religious legitimacy was succeeded by many famous monks such Jinkak, Chungjin, Jinmyung, Haedang, Jajung, Wonkam, Jakak, Damdang, Myomyung, Jawon, Hyekak, Kakom, Jung-hye. Hongjin, etc.

The Combination of the Two Religious Theories

Until the appearances of Priest Uichon of the Kyo-jong and Priest Jinul of the Seon-jong, the two Buddhist sectarians rivaled each other, disparaging the other as heretics or challenging the religion with the Truth.

Despondent over such antagonisms, Uichon advocated a theory of combining all the different religious precepts, emphasizing that one must pursue not only the Buddhist doctrines, but also the introspection, that is to say, one must practice both the Seon and Kyo religions. In addition, since the prejudice of the Buddhist monks was taken as a cause of the rival, Uichon picked up many intelligent Seon priests and had them exercise his theory at the Kokchung temple, the head temple of the Chontae-jong. Uichon earned many sympathizers to his theory, not only because he was an authority of royal lineage but also because of his great reputation as a priest, and the religious rivals gradually terminated.

About a hundred years after Uichon, during which time Seon-jong was at a low ebb, Priest Jinul emerged, and restored the nine mountain schools of the Seon religion and upheld another theory of combination for fixed religious beliefs. He realized that there was not much difference between his religion and those of the others as far as the religious meanings were concerned. Therefore, Jinul attempted to win the Kyo-jong over to Seon by ending the biased attitude of the Seon priests, Jinul's view, which he inherited through the Lee Dynasty as a precious religious reference, also won many followers.

Through the works of these two priests, the Seon and Kyo sectarians finally ceased their long squabbles and came to a reconciliation

The Seon-jong and the Family of Choi

Compared to Uichon's Kyo religion that prospered with the conversions of the successive royal households, Jinul's Seon religion extended its influences under the protection of the Choi, Choong Heon's family, the heredical power-holder of the imperial government of the Koryo Dynasty. Jinul, of course, had many disciples such as Priest Haesim, Priest Yose and Priest Seunghyong to carry on his religious power base.

Choi, Choong Heon was the victor of the power struggles among the subjects in the imperial court in the years of the 19th King Myungjong by exterminating the last opponent Lee, Ui Mun and his clans who usurped the powers the previous years by murdering the 18th ruler, King Uijong. By slaughtering the other encumbering subjects, Choi held the entire authority of the court within his hands, and this power was succeeded through to his fourth generation for more than 60 years from the period of King Myungjong, Shinjong, Hijong, Kangjong to that of Kojong. The kings were then the mere figure-heads of the state.

Such an atrociously powerful Choi not only revered the Seon religion himself but encouraged others to profess it by giving rewards to diligent believers and reprimanding the negligent, and by sending his own son into the priesthood. He also held many Buddhist rites inviting the famous Seon priests. Accordingly, many of his flatterers followed suit and sent their sons to enter the religion, and many monks of the Kyo-jong even made conversions to Seon-jong. His son, Choi, Yi, and his grandson, Choi, Hang, though he had been such an immoral person to kill all the families on his mother's side, did much to promote the Seon religion by setting up the temples and by providing excellent treatments for its priests.

Chapter 13
The Degradation of Buddhism

The Corruption of the Monks

Just as every phenomenal event generates growth, maturity and corruption, so Buddhism that grew up through the years of Silla and matured
to its culmination in the years of King Munjong of the Koryo Dynasty,
began to fade and corrupt at the time of its full maturity.

Although the true nature of the religion was in mercy, purity and un-
selfishness, the monks, enjoying all the imperial favors, the freedom from
the economic burdens and the reverence from the general Buddhists believers, were easily exposed to corruption. These corruptions became very
conspicuous following the years of Munjong. They were more than those
of the medieval Christians. The irresolute monks indulged themselves in
eating meat and in marrying, even worse, leading a dissipated life of
worldliness against their beliefs.

Already in the 10th year of Munjong, that is, only about a hundred
years after the foundation of Koryo, some of the monks absorbed themselves profit-making businesses, as well as in the frivolous living, defaming
the pious name of the temple. Such a great Buddhist figure as Priest Uichon
of the Kyo-jong and Preist Jinul of the Seon-jong came out during these
periods to assume the roles of rebuilding the sound pillars of Buddhism
but their efforts were useless in stemming the degeneration of the monk's
worldly ways of living.

From the middle of Koryo, the monks' corruptions were even worse.

It was so had that an increasing number of Buddhists led a matrimonial life after having illegal inter-course with a woman. Moreover, learning the bad practices from the government officials, they obtained their religious ranks with various bribes giving silks and other ornaments. When King Choongyeol visited Kyungju in June of his 7th year, he found out that more than half of the total monks in the area were married and living with their families.

Some of the corrupt monks organized themselves into a group of rascals causing much trouble. The two sons, Manjong and Manjon, of the powerful subject Choi Wu at the time of the 29th ruler, King Kojong led the hooligans, robbing the people of their fortunes, and accumulating a great amount of profit by extorting creditors, and controlling many Buddhist temples. Attired in Tartar fashions and riding horses, they overran various places, drinking, dancing, plundering, and, even worse, raping married women and humiliating government authorities. As a result, the people were frightened and suspicious of the monks.

The Religious Austerities of the Tibetan Monk

It was not only the Koryo monks that were degenerated in their religious austerities, but the Tibetan Buddhists seemed to have been just as corrupted. Once a Tibetan monk arrived in Koryo with all the royal welcome in the 2nd year of King Choongyeol, he claimed that they did not take special food, especially meat and liquor, but they did keep themselves apart from women. But within a few days, he moved in with a prostitute. In addition, he conducted a 4-day Buddhist rite by placing a man 3 feet tall made out of wheat dough on the altar, as well as another 108 pieces of small attendants, lanterns and towers made of the same material. After the ritual, he threw them all out of the west gate of the main castle.

Dumb founded at the sight of such strange conduct, the monks in Koryo criticized that the Tibetan religious ceremonies were all fictitious.

The Heresy of Buddhism

The corruption of Buddhism was not only limited to the religious short-comings of the monks, but the essentials of the religion itself were adulterated with such heretical superstitions as the geomantic system, and the dual principle or the five primary elements of Chinese philosophy.

Such heretical tendancies in Buddhism originated from the Tang Dynasty in China, where Buddhism, Taoism and Confucianism developed in turn, and were popular among some of the noble calss at the end of Silla after the return of the monks from the Chinese Dynasty. Some of the Buddhists then even linked the destiny of Silla with the geomantic system or attributed every human affair to the superstitious dual principle. The Buddhist monk Dosun who appeared during this time and was also famous for his divination.

The founding ruler, King Taejo of Koryo established the supplementary Temples throughout the country according the fortune-telling of Dosun. The succeeding royal households and the aristocrats of the Dynasty followed the heresy so blindly that they carried out every royal function ranging from the removal of the capital, the king's visitation, the prayer-meetings, ground selection for the construction of the palace, in accordance with the Buddhists prophecies.

From the middle of Koryo, the heretical adherence became even more popular among the Buddhists. Various books of divination such as the Records of Dosun, the Records of the Blessed Site in Mt. Samkak, etc. (Dosun-ki, Samkaksan Myungdang-ki, etc.) were in circulation among the monks, dazzling the popular feeling and, in some cases, confusing the political situation. During the years of Injong, a dexterous monk like Myochung came out with the theory of wind and water, and compelled the king to build up the Daehwa-koong palace in the western capital of Seokyung ; the project was met with revolts from some of the opposing Confucian groups. Blindly taking the counsel from his eunuch Youngui that the state would prosper and the lives of the kings be lengthened by the devotional services, King Uijong conducted the rituals at the temples outside the imperial palace for such a long time that a great amount of national treasure was spent. He also believed his Buddhist subject's advice that the Mongolians would surrender if the king would establish religious seminaries in a temporary palace in the Kanghwa Island. King Wonjong executed the meetings for 120 days. There were many other countless examples in which the rulers came to the heels of the heretical views of the Buddhists.

The More Rampant Buddhist Services

In order to pray for the security of the imperial courts and to glorify Buddha, the royal households of Koryo from the middle of the Dynasty conducted a multiplicity of services on every occasion both big and small, at the temples, in the capital. Also, the capital bustled with the prayer-processions called Kyunghaeng and the people of all classes carried out their own Buddhist rites. Men and women monks clamored about their Manbul Festival (an entertainment for the men and women Buddhists. This practice was prohibited at the time of Sookjong). The worldly monks moved about in groups to offer rice.

The following examples are quoted to show how multitudinous the religious events were from the middle of Koryo. These are the only notable ones held during the first year of King Yejong.

January····· Observed a hundred-day festival at the Munduk-jong pavillion.

February···· Observed the Lantern Festival.

March······· Renovated the Hwangyong temple in the eastern capital.

April········ Observed the Lantern Festival.

May········· Conducted the Buddhist services at the Sanho-jung pavillion and the Cultivation Gathering at the Yeonchin-jon.

June········ Received the Precepts of Boddhisattva at the Keonduk-jon; Conducted seminaries on the Kumkwang Sutras at the Keonduk-jon, the Buddhist services at the Sanho-jong, the Kyunghaeng(Prayer Procession) in Kaekyung, and the sutra-recitation services in five districts of Bu.

July·········· Conducted Cultivation seminaries on the Prajna-Paramita-
Sutras at the Hoekyung-jon, the lecture-meetings on
the Hwaom Sutras at the Jangryong-jon, the festivals for
all souls at the Jangryong-jon, the prayer-meeting for rain
by the sutra lectures, and invited the famous priests to
lecture on the Mokryon Sutras.

September·· Conducted the Sutras conjuring misfortunes at the Keonduk-jon, the seminaries on the hundred disciples at the
Hoekyung-jonand served food for 10,000 monks at the
court and 20,000 in the province, and appointed Yun Kwon
to inspect the Chonsu-won of the Bupwang temple.

October····· Conducted the mercy-seminaries at the Munduk-jon and
the Prajna-Paramita-Sutras seminaries at the Keonduk-jon.

November·· Conducted the Palkwan Festival, and travelled to the Shin-
jeung- won of the Bupwang temple.

The other activities carried out by the kings of Koryo were, perhaps,
more numerous and an immeasurable amount of fortune was used.

Just an Cho Ik, a historian of the Ching Dynasty of Ching, pointed
out in one of his books that the corruption of Lamaism, or the Tibetan
Buddhism, had been one of the major causes that led to the downfall of
the Yuan Dynasty, the Buddhist corruptions in Koryo, in fact, were also
the main reason for the collapse of its the Dynasty.

The Profiteering by the Temples

The land granted by the royal households and the land offered by followers was sufficient for the monks to operate a temple. But, despite the
fact, the monks accumulated a lot of assets by exacting fortunes on the
pretexts of religious services or by engaging themselves directly in mer-
cantilism and other profit-making undertakings. With the margin of profits, they invested in the procurement of the greater farm-land, and,
moreover, possessed a great number of men and women servants, who

were considered moveable properties in the society of Koryo. Therefore, the real estate owned by the monks stretched out to tens of miles, in complete disregard to the equal land system of Koryo.

Since the temples were the sources of good profits, the religious sectarian struggled to obtain the good temples, using various means. The sect which had connections with the royal households or the powerful authorities used their influence to possess the temples with an abundant source of fortunes. In consequence, a temple which belonged to the Seon was annexed by the Chontae-jong one morning and one of the Hwaom-jong's was turned over to the Seon by the next morning, and sometimes, without the knowledge of the temples concerned. There was no such practice as an honest exchange between the temples and the religious sects. In addition, the monks of the resourceful sects indulged in obscenity and other corrupt practices without shame just as much as the indiscreet men of nobility in wealth and sex.

Taking advantage of the fact that the temple was the place of abundant resources and the monks were specially priviliged by the state to exemptfrom all national duties, many of those seeking easy living crowded to the temples. Of course, the priesthood was then considered an honorable profession, whereby its highest Wangsa(Royal Priest) and Kooksa(the Most Reverend Priest) advised on state affairs and received the courtesy due to a disciple from the king. Thus, many from the royal family, the nobles and the commoners alike came to the temples with their high ideals and ingenuous motives to learn the teachings of Buddha and to save the people. But many more were idle groups with the intentions of leading sumptuous lives by becoming monks, or of evading various public obligations such as military services and taxes ; still more were social offenders like murders, rapists or burglers trying hide. Therefore, the sanctity of the temples gradually became discolored by such miscellaneous groups of villains.

The Priests Interference in Politics

Another heretical practice in Buddhism was the priests' growing concern in the fields of politics that helped pave the way for national ruin.

After the establishment of the system of Wangsa and Kooksa in the years of King Kwangjong of Koryo, the priests' participation in the state affairs became even more active, for the two highest priests assumed the important role of protecting the national destiny with their religious po-wers. The Kooksas and Wangsas were in a position to advise the kings, and the other high priests in the ranks of Seonsa and Sujwa were often summoned by the royal households for their counsel or to be responsible for some great temples. But most of the virtuous priests declined royal favors and preferred religious pursuits at secluded temples like Seungkyung temple. Priest Uichon was one of this category and so were Tamjin Hakil, Jikyum Kesim, Seunghyung, Jiin, Honwon, Bowoo, etc..

However, the majority of those who participated in politicking were the worldly monks of little religious virtue. During the years of Injong, there was a vicious monk Myochung, who used the personal trust of the royal family and powerful subjects to advance the theories of invading the Kim Dynasty, and to change the dynastic title of Koryo, inciting a rebellion by the opposing Confucians. He was the one who persuaded the King to set up the Daehwa Palace in Seokyung, as has been previously noted. At the time of King Uijong, the monk Hoejung from the Chongji temple earned the royal favor by conducting the arts of divination while also conducting various evil practices.

In the years of the 19th King Myungjong, the monk Suhae from the Bupwun temple, and Hyeonso from the Kaekuk temple were arrested by Lee, Ui Bang on changes of their political conspiracy with one of the meritirious retainers named Lee Ko ; in January of the 4th year of the same king, some two thousand Buddhist monks from the temples of Joongkwang temple, Hongho temple, and Hongwa temple intruded into the imperial castle in protest of the warrior's dictatorship and collided with the army of Lee, Ui Bang. About 100 Buddhists were killed and all of the temples were burnt down after the incident. Later, the dictator Lee, Ui Bang was stabbed to death by one of the monks named Jongam in collaboration with Jung, Kyun, a son of the court official, Jung, Jeung Bu. Afterwards, Jongam and his followers enjoyed their authority in the court for some time, but were expelled later.

The monks were deeply involved in the power struggles during the ensuing reigns of Shinjong and Hijong. In the first year of Shinjong, the monks from the Heungkook temple cooperated when Choi, Choong Hyeon's servant Manjuk attempted to spearhead an uprising to seize power by stimulating public and private servants. In the 5th year of Hijong, nine royal subjects, including Hanki, were killed by Choi, Choong Hyeon because their conspiracy to murder the powerful dictator was betrayed by one of the monks from the Kuibup temple. On the contrary, a number of the worldly monks, on secret orders from the king, unsuccessfully attempted to assassinate Choi at the court. As a result, Choi dethroned King Hijong, expelled him to Kanghwa Island, and gave his support to King Kangjong.

While some of the Buddhist groups cliqued with the powerful Choi during the age of Kojong, the other monks from the Heungwang temple, Kyungbuk temple and Wangryun temple, the veterans of the monk army, battled with Choi's Army in the capital. Then, Hundreds of the monks were slaughtered as the battle ended with their defeat.

The Shindon's Confusion of the State Affairs

The monks interference in politics reached a climax with Shindon in the age of King Kongmin, and was completely terminated thereafter.

Shindon, whose Buddhist name was Pyunjo, became a monk in his early age, for his mother was a maid-servant at the Ockchon temple in the Youngsan prefecture. He was secretly called into the imperial palace by the king because of strange coincidence that his countenance was similar to that of the monk the king had dreamt of as having saved his life. Though he was illiterate and lacked virtue, Pyunjo accentuated this similarity, and monopolized the royal affections with his arts of divination. In the end, many of the noble class sought blessings from this monk and many of the royal subjects attempted to achieve court favors from him. One day, Pyunjo visited the house of one of the officials named Kim, Ran. Knowing his desires, Kim provided two virgins for the visitor. The other official named Choi, Young accused Kim of immoral meddling. Informed of the accusation, Pyunjo set a trap for Choi, causing him to be relegated to one of the accusation, Pyunjo set a trap for Choi, causing him to be relegated to one of the lower official positions.

Without knowing of such misconduct of Pyunjo, King Kongmin appointed him to a marquisate in the hope of coping with various corrupted situations in the government. Accordingly, the monk carried out an all-out and aggressive reforms, dismissing many royal subjects such as Lee, Su San, Kyung, Chon Yeo, Lee, Kong Su ; he employed those officials of poor lineage to abolish aristocratic influences ; he rearranged the land-ownership system ; and gave freedom to the men and women servants. Though his political and social revolutions were supported by the lower class of society, he was severely criticized by the upper class for his radical and clumsy methods of administration. However, he was engrossed in courting royal favor by flattering the king on one hand while indulging in various irregularities such as sensual pleasures and bribes, calumniating many royal subjects in collaboration with the vicious groups.

Beside, he was a man of such despicable dual-personalities as to call out loud acclamations every time the King bowed to the newly-appointed Wangsa Seonhyeon and Kooksa Chonhi in their inauguration ceremony in the 16th year of King Kongmin, but to murmur to one of the subjects, 'There is nothing better to see in the world than the Sangkam(the King) bowing.'

In front of the king, however, he always behaved himself with clean manners, drinking tea, eating vegetables. These hypocrisies of Pyunjo did not last long, for the Confucian subjects as well as the upper classes began to impeach him for his various misdemeanours. Fearful of royal punishment, the monk took the lead and attempted unsuccessfully to murder the king. He was later sent into exile in Suwon, and died there. Pyunjo's misrule did not end up with his death alone, but also provided and impetus for the Confucian subjects to initiate the expulsion movement for the Buddhist religion itself, finally leading to the collapse of the Koryo Dynasty.

Chapter 14
Buddhism at the End of Koryo

The Five Sects and the Two Classes

At the end of Silla and in the first part of Koryo, there were such Buddhist denominations as the five kyos of Keyul, Bupsang, Bupsung, Yeolban and Wonyung-jong that belonged to the Kyo(teaching) sects, or called Kyo-jong, and the nine mountain schools of Kaji, Silsang, Dokul, Dongri, Saja, Sungju, Huiyang, Bongrim and Sumi of the Seon(zen) sects.

But with the ups and downs of the sectarian movements, they were refered to as the five Kyo sects and two classes following the middle of Koryo. There were many contending views but, no conclusive one as to the five Kyo sects and the two classes. Some claimed that the five Kyo (teaching) denominations consisted of Keyul, Bupsang, Bupsung, Won-yeung and Chontae-jong and the two of Seonsook and Chokye. The others maintained that the five were Keyul, Bupsang, Bupsung, Yeolban and Wonyeung-jong, and the two the Seonsook and Chontae ; while other insisted that the Kyos meants Jaun, Hwaom, Siheung, joongdo and Nam-sang- jong, and the Jongs(Classes) the Chokye and Chontae.

In fact, there were more sectarian branches in Koryo Buddhism. With Uichon's initiation of the influential Chontae-jong, they were(the five Kyos and the two jongs) generally reorganized and redesignated as Hwaom (Wonyeung)-jong,   Jaeun(Bupsang)-jong,   Joongdo(Bupsung)-jong, Siheung- jong, and Namsan(Keyul)-jong ; the other two, the Chokye-jong and Chontae-jong were the very compound of Seon(zen) and Kyo (teaching) religions. The origin of the Siheung-jong was supposed to have been a branch of the Chontae-jong.

These religious denominations were recognized by the imperial court; each of them had its own executive office called Jongmuwon, where there was the head priestral director to conduct the selection of the monks: the other miscellaneous sects, were not previliged to conduct the selections. The Chontae-jong was divided into the Chontaeyuja-jong and the Chontaebupsa-jong.

Chonyoung and Choongji

When the twilight loomed large in Buddhism at the end of Koryo, the Most Reverend Preists Chonyoung and Choongji, both the fifth and sixth successor of the Chokye-jong, came out respectively during the periods of King Kojong and King Choongyeol, and elevated the Seon(zen) religion greatly.

Chonyoung, whose secular surname was Yang, became a monk under Priest Haeshim in the 12th year of Kojong and, in the 23rd year of the same King, passed the Seon(zen) priestal selection examinations. After learning the religious disciplines from the Priests Chungjin and Jinmyung, he was appointed to the ranks of Seonsa in the 35th year of Kojong by virtue of Choi, Woo's reverence(a son of Choi, Choong Hyun). In the 37th year of the King, he became a superindentent of the Seonwon temple, a Seon temple previously built by Choi, Woo. Two years later, he was designated head Priest of the temple by then Chief Priest of the Chokye-jong Jinmyung, who later selected Chonyoung as his hierarchic successor because of his growing reputation and matured discernment. When he was appointed Daesun temple by the King, Chonyoung received marked royal courtesy ; the King himself served the food-table and provided official escorts for him when he returned to Mt. Chokye.

By widely promoting Buddhism with his many disciples, Chonyoung played the roles of the Beacon-light for the declining Seon-jong at the time. He died at the age of 73 in the 12th year of King Choongyeol and was given the posthumous title of Kooksa by the King.

Choongji was a man born in the 13th year of Kojong in Jeongan, Choongchong - buk province, with a secular name of Wi. At the age of 19, he passed the public services examination with top honors, later serving as an envoy to Japan. Being disappointed with his public career, he returned to the Seonwon temple and was schooled by Priest Chonyoung to become a monk. Then, touring around various temples in the south, Choongji nourished his knowledge. Although he had wanted to become a priest of high virtue rather than an administrative head priest of a temple, the surrounding priests selected him as the Chief Priest of the Kamro temple in Kumhae Prefecture. Afterwards, with his followers thronging to the temple from all corners of the country, he revitalized the fading Seon religion. Choongji was supported by his disciples as the sixth successor of Seon-jong succeeding Chonyoung ; he was given the posthumous title of Wonkam Kooksa by the king when he died at the age of 67 in the 18th year of King Choongyeol.

The Rising of Ilyeon

Ilyeon, along with Chonyoung and Choongji, was one of the famous priests who swayed the country with his great learning during the periods of Kojong and Wonjong. He was the one who left numerous literary works including the Samkuk Yoosa, or the Memoirs of the Three Kingdoms.

With a secular name of Kim from Jangsan-kun, Kyungju, Ilyeon entered Buddhism at the age of 9 and, learning from the lectures at the Seon temples, passed the priest selection examinations of Seon-jong at the age of 22. After solidifying his religious pursuits through the tours of the Bodong- am, Samun-am and Muju-am shrines, he became a Seonsa in the 33rd year of Kojong when he was 41, and a Daeseonsa at the age of 54. In the 2nd year of Wonjong, he was assigned to the Seonwol-dang temple in Kaekyung by an imperial order, but later returned to the Oeo temple in the south.

Soon afterwards, Ilyeon managed the Inhong temple for 11 years and promoted the religious influence to a great extent. When he was 72, he was appointed the Chief Priest of the Wunmun temple by an imperial order in the 3rd year of King Choongyeol. From the 7th year of the same King, he personally taught the royal families in the Eastern Capital and at the Kwangmyung temple for two years. When he was 78, the monk was sanctioned as the Most Reverend Priest(or Kooksa) by the king. But, as he did not prefer the life in the capital, Ilyeon returned to the Inkak temple in Mt. Ku on the pretext of being with his aged mother ; here he undertook an extensive movement for the revival of Buddhism by conducting twice the evangelical missions in the nine mountain schools of Seon-jong, which were said to have been a great success.

Ilyeon died when he was 84 after leaving his last message to the King and after executing as on any normal day, the catechism with his followers. Upon receipt of the message, the King awarded the priest a posthumous title of Bokak.

According to an inscription in the first edition of the General Library of the Epitaphs in Chosun(Chosun Kumsok Chongram), Ilyeon's personalities and his aptitudes for learning were described to this effect : 'The priest is a man of few humorous remarks, without any affected characteristics, and is always sincere in his encounters with things. For unreasonableness, he is devotional, and, in high position, he is modest··· In his sparehours, he absorbs himself in reading the Buddhist literatures or in researches of the other schools. On the other hand, he also conducted extensive studies of the Confucian books, and became thoroughly versed in a hundred affairs···'

He also left more than a hundred volumes of books including the Samkuk Yoosa that was compiled with the previous historical material of Kokuryo, Baekje and Silla, and some supplementary references up to the middle of Koryo. This is one of the few valuable historical records extant today in Korea.

The Eastward Transmission of the Imje-jong

The Silsang mountain school of the Seon-jong religion, first introduced into Silla during the age of King Heungduk by Priest Hongchuk from the Tang Dynasty in China, was later relayed into Koryo and developed along with the eight other schools. From the middle of Koryo, the Seon-jong schools were integrated into Chokye-jong by Priest Jinul, taking the name of the religion from that of the mountain where the priest lived, and the books the priest had written as its religious doctrines. Aside from the Chokye-jong, Royal Priests Bowoo and Haekun imported the Imje-jong, one of the five branches of the Seon-jong in China, from the Yuan Dynasty during the years of King Kongmin of Koryo after their studies there. This was inherited through the Lee Dynasty as a main branch of the Seon religion.

The Seon-jong was originally initiated in India by Sakya's disciple Kassapa, who perceived the significance when his master silently plucked a flower at a mountain retreat, it was introduced into China by Dharma. In China, the religion was handed down by Haega, Hongin, and, then, by Haeneung and Shinsu. The one Haeneung transmitted in Southern China was called the Nam-jong(or the southern religion) ; it was further disseminated by his two disciples, Namok and Chungwon ; the former relayed his school to Majo and the latter to Sukdu respectively. It was the descendants of the Majo branch that had been introduced in Silla from the time of Majo's successor, Chijang and developed through Koryo by forming the Chokye-jong without further factional disagreements.

However, in China, it was the Majo's Seon religion that prospered exclusively, seceding into the five additional sects of Kyuang, Jodong, Imje, Wunmun, and Bupan. Among these sects, the Imje-jong was especially successful.

The Imje-jong conveyed to Koryo at the end of the Dynasty by Preists Bowoo and Haekun was the one inherited from the religion's 18th successors, Chunghong and Cheorim of China.

Bowoo

The conveyor of the Imje-jong to Koryo, the Most Reverend Priest Bowoo was a man born in the 27th year of King Choongyeol in Hongju from a family of Hong. Originally, he was called Boher with a pen name of Taego. By virtue of Priest Kwangji at the Hoiam temple, he left the world at the age of 13 and, after years of learning through the Seon temples, passed the monk selection examination of the Hwaom-jong at the age of 26. Pursuing his researches through asceticism, Bowoo was accounted to have attained his awakening at the age of 38 from a letter 'Mu' meaning 'Nil' at the Jeondan-won in Songdo in January of the 7th year of King Choongsook. When he was at the Joongheung temple in Mt. Samkak of Hanyang(now Seoul) in the 2nd year of King Choonghae at the request of his followers, a great crowd of disciples came to hear his teachings.

When he was 46, Bowoo went to Yenking(now Bejing) in China and exchanged religious views with the 18th founder, Chunghong, of the Imje-jong. At the request of Emperor Shun of the Yuan Dynasty, he gave religious sermons at the Youngnyung temple, and was awarded the gold-foiled clerical robe and other gifts from the Empress and the Crowned Prince.

After his return from China, he managed the Joongheung temple for a while, then, went to Mt. Soseol, where he labored in the day and practiced Seon(zen) at night for 4 years, refusing the imperial summons of King Kongmin. In April of the 5th year of the king, however, he became a Royal Priest(Wangsa) and stayed at the Kwangmyung temple in the capital, enjoying the reverence of the people. Later, he moved to the Bongam temple on Mt. Huiyang, then to the Borim temple on Mt. Kaji.

At this time, the heretic monk Shindon was at the helm of power under the favor of King Kongmin, eliminating all the loyal officials including Lee, Kong Su, Lee, In Bok, Lee, Su San and Won, Song Su with forefeiture of all their properties, and curtaliling the other priests approach to the king by various means of calumny and plots. Bowoo was also slandered as a vicious monk by Shindon, and was confined to Mt. Sokri by King

Kongmin for a year. But, once his innocense was proven after the death
of the dexterous monk Shindon, the ripentant king appointed Bowoo to
the position of Kooksa and advised the priest to stay at the Yungwon
temple. Declining the royal advice, Bowoo went to the Yangsan temple
in the 7th year of King Shinwoo, dying the following year at Mt. Soseol
at the age of 82.

Hyekun

The Royal Priest Haekun, another importer of Imje-jong, along with
Bowoo, was born in the 7th year of King Choongsook in the Nyunghae
Prefecture. On the occasion of his friend's death, Hyekun decided to become a monk, and, after 4 years of religious pursuits at the Hoiam temple
on Mt. Chonbo, attained the self-realization in the 5th year of King
Choonghae. One year after Bowoo, Hyekun went to Yenking (Bejing) and
studied at the Bupwon temple under priest Jigong, an Indian monk in
Chian who previously raised a great sensation in the fields of the Seon
religion in Koryo with his sermons on inanimation on Mt. Chonbo and
Mt. Kumkang. In March of the 4th year of King Choongmok, Haekun
left Yenking and arrived at the Jongjaseon temple in pingjang Fu in August
of the same year to see the Seon Priest Cheorim, who questioned the visitor
from his sancton.

"Where did you come from, Priest ?"

"From Yenking," replied Haekun.

"Whom did you meet there, then ?"

"High Priest Jigong."

"What does he do everyday ?"

"He uses a thousand swords everyday," Haekun answered. Then,
Cheorim again asked :

"Not to mention a thousand, did you bring what you can use with
even one sword ?"

Resolutely on his feet, Haekun struck his questioner with his sword.
Falling down on the floor, Cheorim called out for help, and Haekun, again

helping him up, said,

"My sword can kill a man and, at the same time, can well save a man."

The chinese priest, smilling, accepted Haekun as his disciple and taught him for over half a year.

After touring various places in China for meetings with the famous Chinese Imje-jong priests and preaching at the Kwangje temple for two years at the request of the Yuan Dynasty's Emperor Shunjong, Haekun returned to Koryo in the spring of the 7th of King Kongmin. At home, he lectured extensively moving auound to one temple after another by an imperial edict to Shinwan temple, Jungyang-am, Chungpyung temple, Youngkam-am, Kwangmyung temple in Kaekyung, and to the Hoiam temple for many years. In the 20th year of King Kongmin, he was appointed Royal Priest and stayed at the Songkwang temple later. He was assigned to manage the Bowon temple by the succeeding King Shinwu, but died enroute to his new assignment at the Shinluk temple in Kangwon province at the age of 57. He was awarded the posthumous title of Seonkak.

The Inactivity of the Kyo-jong

At the end of Koryo, the corruptions of the Kyo-jong was worse than those of the Seon-jong. The irregularities of the monks, the excessiveness of religious services, the monopoly of the farm-lands and the extortion of the fortunes were great and the religion itself became extremely realistic. All the desires of human beings, such as, the desire of having a son, re-covering from sickness, extinguishing riddance of guilt, desiring having peace in a family, depended on the Graces of Buddha. Accordingly, the vitality of the Kyo-jong Buddhist religion as an orthodox branch gradually faded, and the emergence of great Buddhist Priests for mankind could hardly be expected. However, there were a few Kyo-jong priests such as Kyowoong from the Chontae-jong during the age of King Injong ; Jongrin from the Hwaom-jong, Dukso and Jichiung from the Chontae-jong during the age of King Myungjong ;and Haeyoung from the Hwa-om-jong during the King Choongyeol, who revived the religion to some extent, but their fame and achievement were uncomparable with those of the preceeding Seon-jong priests.

Moreover, Confucian learning was on the rise at the closure of the Koryo Dynasty and took the place of declining Buddhism. Althouth there were many reactionary Confucian scholars including Lee, Je Hyeon, some of them converted to the Seon-jong Buddhist denomination, while the Kyo-jong was entirely expelled. The last successor of the Kyo-jong, at any rate, was Priest Jan from the Jaeun-jong branch who came out in the years of King Choongsook, and Priest Heyonkyun from the Chontae-jong during the King Kongmin period.

Chapter 15
The Risings of the Anti-Buddhist Movement

The Emergence of the Confucian Learning

The Confucian development that sprung up at the end of Koryo and played a vital role in abolishing the Buddhist religion in the first part of the Lee Dynasty really began from the period of King Kwangjong of the Koryo Dynasty when the public servece examination system was enforced following the patterns of the Tang Dynasty of China. At the time of Kings Sungjong, Munjong, Yejong and Injong of Koryo, the Confucian learning developed with the establishment of the Kukjakam(a Confucian school, which later became Sungkyunkwan) and other teaching institutes and the appointment of talented students to various official positions and the royal encouragement of the Confucian lectures by the prominent scholars. But, for about a century after King Uijong, the religious influences had been almost completely subdued by the military in power who ruled the people.

Subsequently, the Confucian teachings were resuscitated by King Choongyeol who himself learned and even sent his son to learn the Chineses classics from Choi Ong and seven other instructors he appointed at the Kukhak(National School) its motivation to King Choongyeol and, at the same time, to the contributions made by An, Hyang, who introduced the Sung Dynasty classics in Koryo by bringing back the complete works of Chu-tzu from his tour in Bejing. By establishing the Kukhak Sumhakchon(Sponsorship), An, Hyang not only endeavoured to educate the

Confucian scholars, but also encouraged the learning by procuring the image of Confucian and his disciples and obtaining the books relating to the Confucian classics and history, religion musical instruments from the Yuan Dynasty in China. As a pioneer of Chu-tzu, An also advanced the teachings of the Chinese Confucian philosopher at the local higher learning institutions that later inspired a series of Anti Buddhist movements.

As a result, the number of the Confucian students increased by thousands. Baek, Yi Jung, who also brought the Ch'eng-tzu and Chu-tzu expositions from the Yuan Dynasty, succeeded An, Hyang as a legitimate successor. From Baek, fhe religious lineage ran down through Lee, Jae Hyeon, Lee Saek and then to Kwon, Keun. In the 16th year of King Kongmin, Lee, saek was the superindentent of the Sungkyunkwan institution, where such famous instructors as Kim, Yong ku, Jung, Mong Ju, Park, Yi Joong and Lee, Soong In gave their outstanding lectures which gave a great impetus to the Confucian learning.

The Coming of the Buddhist Expulsion

The movement to expel Buddhism at the closure of the Koryo Dynasty was an inevitable outcome, first, because of the rise of the ideologically different Confucian influences, and secondly, because of the Corruptions and degeneration of Buddhism itself, and, lastly, because of the Confucian's revengeful ambitions and their accumulated grudges from the 400 years of long repression by the Buddhists especially because of the atrocities committed by the monks who monopolized the government affairs at the end of the Dynasty.

The Anti-Buddhism movement became a subject of heated discussion which was lectured at the Confucian insitutions, and storms of letters poured into the imperial palace complaining about the Buddhist encumbrances. In fact, the opposition trends for the once powerful religion became irreversible from the time of King Kongmin.

According to the Dongkuk Tongkam(A Condensed History of Korea), the   cermony-justic Minister of the time Jo, In Ok appealed to King Shinchang as follows ;

The Buddhist religion is aimed at purity, non-avarice and departure from the world, but not at the rule of the state. However, the monks of many temples today, contrary to the teachings of their masters, take the servants and the farm-lands as their own personal belongings rather than those of the temples. Beside, they are corrupting public morals by meeting with the widows and are scheming to bribe the powerful authorities. How in the world, then, can they be expected to profess an unworldly religion; therefore, the virtuous and unselfish monks should be selected to be assigned to the temples, and the profits from the farms and the servants should be managed by the government to prevent further misappropria- tions by the chief priest of a temple. Moreover, the monks staying in a village should be accused of having committed adultery, and the house- wives should not be permitted to visit the temple for any reason. The offenders should be bitterly accused of infidelity ; the priestess should be considered unchaste ; the one who shaved the head of a house-wife should be heavily punished ; all public and private servants should be prohibited from becoming a monk ; and the monk who stays a long time a private house should be called into the army services ;and the house-keeper al- lowing the monk should also be questioned for hi s crime.'

When the feeble King Kongyang ascended to the throne, he attempted to construct the Yeonbok temple and to appoint the monk Chanyoung as a Roy al Priest. At this time, the Confucian scholars from the Sung- kyunkwan institution, in their Anti-Buddhist movements led by the su- perindentent Jung, Mong Ju and an instructor Jung, Do Jeon, severely criticized Buddhism saying that Buddhism was devilish religion and that all the expenses for construction should be saved. As the movement heigh- tened, the King in his 3rd year in office issued a decree banning houes- wives from visiting the temple. Stimulated by the event, the Sungkyun- kwan students riding on the currents, wrote to the King for the rejection of the Buddhist religion. There were those who even insited that whoever have his head tonsured to become a monk should be executed by laws. Some claimed that if one has his faith in Confucianism, he would become a pure gentleman, but the deceitful Buddhism religion would only make a man become a dwarf. But worst of all, some reactionaries even tended to treat the monks as if they were animals. All the Buddhist ceremonies, in the end, were gradually replaced by those of the Confucians.

The Anti-Buddhist movement was accompanied by diversified opinions. But the most dominating ones could be generally summed up in two arguments. The first one was to save the religion, and put it back on its true natures by eliminating and readjusting all the corruptions since its essentials were viewed as not being without sanctity. The other opinion was to prohibit it outright on the grounds that the corruptions arose from Buddhism because its essences were basically wrong. The former views were upheld by Lee, Saek, Kwon, Keun, Lee, Je Hyeon, Choi, Young, Lee, Gok, etc., and the latter by Jung, Mong Ju, Jung, do Jeon and others from the Sungkyunkwan Confucian institute. As the matter progressed, however, the latter opinions gained the control, and the monks became social outcasts with the closure of many Buddhist temples in the first part of the Lee Dynasty.

Jung, Do Jeon

One of the most theoretical critics of Buddhism at the end of Koryo, was Jung, do Jeon, one of the Confucian subjects, who, like Shu Sun-tung of the period of Emperor Kaotsu of the Former Han Dynasty, helped the warrior Lee, Sung Kye in overthrowing the imperial regime of the Koryo Dynasty; he took an important part in instituting on blue prints for state-craft as well as a renewal of works of mercy that had been the principle of administration in the first part of Chosun(the Lee Dynasty).

Jung, whose pen name was Sambong, was a son of the Penal Department of Minister Lee, Woon Kyung. Intelligent from his childhood with a great inclination for learning, Jung studied under Lee, Saek and was acquainted with Jung, Mong Ju, Lee, Jon Oh and Kwon, Keun. Passing the public service examinations for the post of Jinsa in the 12th year of King Kon-gmin, he became famous for his abandant knowledge, not only in Con-fucianism and literatures, but also in musical grammar, medicine and military stratagem. He was later awarded the scholarly title of Taehak Baksa (meaning an erudite of Sungkyunk wan) by King Kongmin. During the years of King Shinwoo because of his pro-Ming Dynasty advocacies, expressed together with Jung, Mong Ju and Lee, Soong In, Jung, Do Jeon was banished of the Hoejin Prefecture, where he occupied himself in teaching the Confucian letters to the village students ; at the same time, he defamed the Buddhist religion by writing a series of Anti-Buddhist books. Later, after his return to the Sungkyunkwan, he became a henchman of the powerful retainer Lee, Sung Kye, betraying his former masters Jung, Mong Ju and Lee, Saek, and helping dethron two Kings, Shinwoo and Shinchang ; he then ascended to the prime ministership by making King Kongyang abdicate his crown in favor of Lee, Sung Kye, who later es-tablished the Lee Dynasty. In the end, Jung was murdered along with his protege, Crown Prince Bangsuk, by Bangwon, another son of Lee, Sung Kye's former Empress.

As compared to the moderate Anti-Buddhist group of Lee, Je Hyeon, Lee, Saek and Lee, Gok, Jung, Do Jeon was thoroughly progressive, attempting to set up the educational system on the exclusive basis of Confucianism.

The most lusterous sections of the works of Jung, in which he gave very logical arguments for the exclusion of Buddhism, were the parts relating to 'Mind, Spirit and Reason,' and the 'Sketch of the Buddhists' contained in his 9th Volume 'The Collection of Sambong'. The 'Sketch of Buddhists', which may be considered an introduction to his Anti-Buddhist stand, consisted of three chapters, mostly dealing with the merits and demerits of both Buddhism and Confucianism or expatiating on the causes of the latter religion. In the latter part which consisted of 19 chapters, however, he gave a detailed discussion from the standpoint of views of the teachings of Chu-tzu, making pointed attacks on all ranges of Buddhist doctrines, deploring that Buddhism was a demon's religion because it destroys the morals of mankind and the structures of society, while breeding monk-parasites and various other falsities.

Part IV

Buddhism(2)

Buddhism(2)

Chapter 1
Lee Taejo and Buddhism

Lee, Sung Kye, the Founder of the Dynasty

The founder of the Lee Dynasty(popularly called Taejo), Lee, Sung
Kye was a man from Youngheunng, Hamkyung province, with a pen
name of Songheon. Due to his imposing air and dauntless youthful vigor,
he entered the government service during the reign of King Kongmin
of Koryo and distinguished himself with various military achievements
while helping defeat the Japanese invaders, the red-turbaned rebels(the
Honggeonjuk) and the army of the Yuan Dynasty. In the years of King
Kongyang, his rising fame and his party-men who held the important
government positions, solidified firmly his standing in the political sphere.
Finally, he usurped the throne by murdering the loyal subject, Jung, Mong
Ju, and by expelling the King, labelled as 'iniquitous', to Wonju, Kangwon
province.

As he grew up in a Buddhist family, Lee Taejo attempted to protect
the religion. It was his belief that the foundation of the Dynasty was
accomplished by virtue of the power of Buddha who would perpetuated
the national destiny if he had devotion to the religion. Thus, in July of
his 2nd year in court, Taejo rebuilt the old tower of the Haein temple,
reprinting the collections of Buddhist Literature and preserving them in
the tower : ··· with the Buddhist expedients, we could keep our ancestors
blessed and our people advantageous. On installing the collections in the
grandly rebuilt tower, I pray for the divine protection of Buddha and for

his abundant blessings for the welfare and prosperity of the people and the country". This was the King prayer-address(cf. The first edition of the Chosun Bulkyo Tongsa, or the General History of Buddhism in Chosun). Beside he was a believer in the theory of cause and effect. For fear of deadly retributions resulting from his ruthless execution of the royal families and their subordinates on his usurpation of power, Taejo prayed for the bliss of the deceased by inscribing the three parts of the Buphwajong, sutras, In order to pacify his guilty conscience and to perpetuate his national destiny Taejo also developed an enthasiastic devotion for the Imje-jong sometimes immersing himself in deep religious exaltation, he appointed the Chontae-jong monk Jacho to the position of Kooksa, praying for blessing upon the death of the Empress Shinduk, a devout Buddhist, by establishing a big Heunchon temple. He ordered the Seon Priest, Jisang, to institute the Suryuk temple within the Jinkwan temple on Mt. Samkak, and removed the letter-blocks of the Buddhist Collections from the Seonwon temple Kanghwa Island to the Jichon temple. Although the Confucians movement for the exclusion of Buddhism was still rising, the manner in which Lee Taejo of Chosun revered Buddhism and treated the monks at this time was not popular in the least, different from the periods of Koryo.

King Taejo and Muhak

Muhak Jacho was a monk revered and respected by Taejo. They were said to have had a long close association from the time when Lee, Sung Kye, a vigorous warrior in his forties, served under King Kongmin.

The relationship between Taejo and Muhak began when Lee, Sung Kye was digging a burial ground for his deceased father, Hangjo, in the 9th year of King Kongmin. Then, two monks, one old and the other younger, passed by, the older one saying to the younger : "The ground he is taking should not bear a man who is no more than a famous general, but the one yonder is a King. On learning the prophecy relayed by the younger monk, Lee was said to have followed the two Buddhists after changing the buria ground. The two monks at the time were the very famous Priest, Haegun, and his disciple, Jacho.

Subsequently, Lee went after Jacho in the cave on Mt. Gumbong, located in Anbyeon, and asked for the interpretations of his dreams. The first dream, it was said, in which Lee, Sung Kye brought out three rafters from a brokendown house, Jacho explained was a sign of his becoming a king in the future ; the second one, in which Lee saw the flowers and the mirrors falling down, was interpreted as his bearing fruit and rising fame. Delighted, Lee, Sung Kye was said to have established a great temple called Sungkwang temple at the site nearby Jacho's cave, although this still remains quite ambiguous.

On assuming the throne, Taejo appointed Jacho to the position of Royal Priest on the occasion of the king's birthday on October 11th, and ordered him to give his sermons in the imperial palace, inviting some 200 other monks to a court festival.

When Taejo went on a trip in the south in search of a new site for the capital, Jacho accompanied the King along with the other royal subjects. After five months of constructional processess on Mt. Kyeryong, which the subjects suggested as the proper location for the capital, Taejo terminated the project and changed the place to Hanyang(now Seoul) on advice from the royal monk that Mt. Inwang could be accepted as the guardian against evil influences, and Mt. Baekak and Mt. Namsan were the White Tiger and Blue Dragon guarding the capital.

Lee Taejo had eight sons, six of them from his former Empress Han and two from his latest Empress Kang. Rivalry erupted among the sons for the imperial succession. In the end, the fifth son, Bangwon, killed his two half brothers, Bangbeon and the Crowned Prince Bangsuk, together with Jung, Do Jeon and Nam, Un, the distinguished contributors of the national foundation. Dissatisfied over such a riotous act, Taejo abdicated his seat in favor of his 2nd son, Bangkwa, whose royal titel was Jungjong, and retreated to Hamheung in Hamkyung province, calling himself the Superior King. The fifth son, Bangwon, however, pressed his brother

Jungjong again for concession of the reign, and obtained it two years after wards. Thus, the third King Taejong, after his enthronment, consecutively sent the messengers to persuade his father in Hamheung to return to the capital, but were consistently and strongly refused. This was finally realized with the help of the monk Jacho.

The monk who had played such a vital role in the background of Taejo was a disciple of the Imje-jong's priest Hyegun. Born in the 14th year of King Choongsook in Samki-kun with a pen name of Muhak, he bacame a monk at the age of 18, and studied under the Buddhist scholars on Mt. Yongmun, Yangpyong-kun, Kyonggi province. Continuing his pursuits at the Budo-am shrine in the 2nd year of King Kongmin, Jacho went to Bejing of the Yuan Dynasty, and studied under Priest Hyekun who was then staying at the Ryongam temple on Mt. Hsi after his meeting with the Chinese Priest Chihkung. He returned to his home country from China in the 5th year of King Kongmin, earlier than Hyekun, and stayed at the Wonhyo-am hermitage on Mt. Chonsung. Although he refused the one previously offered to him in the 4th year of King Kongmin. Later, moving around to the Hoiam temple, Jinbul-am on Mt. Kumkang, be passed away in the 5 th year of Taejong at the age 79.

King Taejo's Exclusion of Buddhism

Though traditionally a devout Buddhist along with his Empress, dedicated to protecting the religion, Taejo was compelled to support Confucianism outwardly, even if tepidly, for the reactionary tides against the excessive corruptions of Buddhism at the end of Koryo were then simply irretrievable. In addition, as he accomplished the revolution of overthrowing the Koryo Dynasty and establishing his new regime entirely in cooperation with the powerful Confucian subjects, Taejo's only alternative was to approve the rejection of Buddhism.

Therefore, on suggestions from the Confucians, King Taejo endeavoured greatly to promote the Sungkyunkwan Confucian institution, increasing the number of authorized students at the local schools in each kuns, building new institutions, and setting up the norms for various ceremonial systems after those of the Confucians.

First of all, however, in order to accomplish both the spiritual and religious reform of Buddhism, some pre-requisites were needed, something more realistic, or something of a loftier philosophical background, that could surpass Buddhism both in logics and theories. The one who held the responsibilities for this spiritual direction was Taejo's brain-trust, Jung, Do Jeon, with his writings based on the teachings of the famous Chinese Confucian scholar named Chu-tzu, as has previously been mentioned.

During the time of Taejo, all the Buddhists, including some of the high priest like Jacho, Deuktong, Joku, etc., only kept silence against the boiling Anti-Buddhist movement without taking any counter-measures like the Chinese Buddhist Chang Sang Yiung of the Sung Dynasty.

Chapter 2
The Persecution of Buddhism

King Taejong's Suppressive Measures for Buddhism

Despite the fact that there was such a strong Anti-Buddhist subject as Jung, Do Jeon, Buddhism did not go through much suffering during the years of King Taejo and Jungjong because of the kings' lukewarm attitudes or dual policies toward the two rivalling religions. It was when the Confucian Taejong assumed the reign that the real Buddhist persecution began.

A man of stout-heart and determined character, Taejong was also fond of learning ; he had the best knowledge of Chinese classics among the other sons of Taejo. He passed the public service examination in the years of King Shinwoo, was promoted to the position of Chief Secretary to Miljiksa(the official in charge of the royal treasury, the guard of the palace and the military installations), and always befriended the Confucians because he had a wideranging information about the Confucian philosophies. As a result, when Taejong took up the power, he carried out decisively his political measures of suppressing Buddhism and promoting Confucianism in coordination with his Confucian associates.

The following illustrates the determined execution of Taejong's Anti Buddhist policies :

1. The Abolition of the Buddhist Services in the Imperial Palace.
   Taejong's Anti-Buddhist measures began by abolishing all the Buddhistic services small or large in the palace. But Taejong's father

Taejo, provided a small feast at the hall of the palace, inviting some 100 monks, when Joku was appointed to the Royal Priest in the 3rd year of the King, even though he realized the illegality of the services and eliminated most of the large ones, such as mass meetings or festivals.   However, Taejong even went so far as to drive all the sutra-reciting monks outside prayer-house. The statue had been enshrined in the palace since the age of Koryo.

2. The Confiscation of the Temple-owned Farm-lands.

In the 2nd year of Taejong, all the farm lands owned by the temples were confiscated and nationalized in order to put financial pressures on the Buddhists. The temples confiscated and the temple-owned slaves delivered to government offices. This was done on the suggestion submitted by the Seonwunkwan(the government office administering astronomy, topography, almanac and weather).

3. The Restriction of the Number of the Temples.

Four years after the confiscation of the lands, that is, in the 6th year of Taejong, the number of temples throughout the country was reduced as follows at the request of the board of state affairs, in Uijongbu.

This was one of the greatest incidents of Taejong's Buddhist supression.

4. The Curtailment of the Religious Sects.

On or about the 7th year of Taejong, the number of the religious sects was also out down from 11 to 7 as they were considered another

The Name of the Religion	Total Number of the Temples
Chokye-jong & Chongji-jong	70
Soja-jong & Bupsang-jong of the Chontae	43
Hwaom-jong & Domun-jong	43
Jaeun-jong(Bupsang-jong)	36
Joongdo-jong & Shinin-jong	30
Namsan-jong(Yul-jong)	10
Shiheung-jong	10
Grand total	242

cause of corruption. The eleven sects consisted of Chokye, Chongji, Chontae Soja, Chontae Bupsa, Hwaom, Domun, Jaeun, Joongdo, Shinin, Namsan and Shiheung ; after the reduction, there were Chontae (a compound of Chontae Soja and Chontae Bupsa), Chongnam (a compound of Chongji-jong and Namsan-jong), Chokye, Hwaom, Jaeun, Joongin(a compound of Joong-do and Shinin) and Shiheung.

5. The Dismissal of the Laborers Employed by the Temples.

In connection with the confiscation of the land, all the laborers, such as farmers and servants, employed by the temples were dismissed and put under public-ownership in the 5th year of Taejong by an appeal from the board of the state with the exception of the following allocations.

Areas	Servants	Permanent Members
Kyungsang & Kaesung ; per each one temple of Seon-jong & Kyo-jong	100	100
Kyungsang & Kaesung per each of others	50	50
Capital city of each province ; per one temple of Seon-jong or Kyo-jong	50	50
Head Temple of each eup	10	10
The Other Temples outside eups	30	30

As a result of this reduction, 6,600 servants were turned over to the hands of the government and an exorbitant amount of assests forfeited.

Beside, Taejong abolished the system of Wangsa and Kooksa, intensified the supervision of the monks, and ordered his successor to prohibit the establishment of any more temples. Therefore, the 19 year rule of Taejong with such Buddhist persecution brought a complete setback to the religion that had been prospering from the Silla period.

Taejong's Buddhist Services

Such a strong Anti-Buddhist though he was, Taejong yielded his usual attitude and conducted some of the Buddhistic services in order to pray for the late Taejo who had passed away in his 8th year of rule, according to an authentic record. In the 10th year of Taejong, the Kaekyung Buddhist temple was set up by the Taejo's mausoleum in Yangju, and the sutra-reciting ceremony was conducted at the Heungduk temple.

The Heungduk temple was originally built as one of the Kyo-jongs by contributing the Taejo's personal residence hall, Dukan-jon ; there was a total of 600 volumes of the Prajna Sutras stored in it. In addition, Taejong ordered the provincial governors of Poonghae, Kyonggi, and Choongchong to supply the paper manufactured in their areas to the Haein temple in Kyongsang province for the printing of Buddhist Literature ; in the 12th year, the Kaekyung temple was consecrated to Buddha. All of these religious activities were conducted by Taejong as a means to pray for the bliss of his deceased father.

The Religious Policy of King Sejong

Known as a benevolent ruler of the Lee Dynasty with his merciful nature and determined character, Sejong succeeded to the pro-Confucian policies of his predecessor, Taejong, and adopted them as firm principles of the state. In the 2nd year of his rule, Sejong established the Jiphyeon-jon (the Royal Research Institute), and appointed 13 of the most prominent scholars of the country to specialize in the classics ; State Affairs, Histories and Confucian learning at the Institute. In the 3rd year, the King appointed his prince Hyang as crown prince in a Confucian ceremony held by having his son bow to the image of Confucius at the Sungkyunkwan Shrine. Also, a number of Confucian students were appointed to government position ; and many talented youth were selected to study Confucian scriptures, astronomy, topography medicine and industrial arts on a government subsidy. Therefore, the morale of the students at the Confucian school became heightened and the Confucianism prospered extensively.

Sejong's persecution against Buddhism, meanwhile, was just as agreesive as his predecessor. Beginning with the closure of the Naebul-dang, a Buddhist shrine in the imperial palace, the year he was enthroned, the

King went on to terminate the "prayer-go-Buddha" activity called 'Yeon-jong Hwanwon' that was held annually in the local provinces in his 3rd year, and prohibited the Kyunghaeng prayer-procession that had been traditionally observed for 400 years since the period of the 4th year Koryo. In the 6th year, on the suggestions of his ministers, Sejong reorganized the sectarian structure of Buddhism in such a way that the seven sects previously reduced by Taejong were divided into the Kyo-jong and the Seon-jong, and only four branch religions of Hwaom, Jaeun, Joongsin and Shiheung were made allowed to belong to the former, while the other three branches of Chokye, Chontae and Chongnam belonged to the latter. The Heungchon temple and the Heungduk temples were respectively designated as the head temple of the Seon and Kyo. Sejong also reduced the number of temples in the country to 36 authorized from the previous number of 242.

The reduction was taken in view of the fact that the most of the temples were vacated by the majority of the monks frequenting the villages and towns for religious purposes or personal ones. According to an official report, then, there were only 7 monks residing at the Youngtong temple while there should have been 200, only 4 at the Youngam temple as apposed to 100, and only 20 at the Heungduk temple as apposed to 125. Along with the reduction, the system of the Seungroksa(the supervising office for the monks) was abolished, and much of the manpower and the real estate was put under the government control.

Afterwards, although it is not very clear about the year, Sejong was said to have executed such a strong anti-Buddhist measure as banning the monks' entrance to the capital, prohibiting the young men from becoming monks and manufacturing arms from the iron-bells and statues requisitioned from the closed Buddhist temples. Against such suppression, the Buddhists neither opposed nor argued.

Though he was such a stout Anti-Buddhist, Sejong converted to Buddhism in his later years. Then, he conducted the rain-festivals by inviting the monks, rebuilt the Heungchon temple, removed the reprints of the

Collections of Buddhist Literatures from the Haein temple to the Heung-chon temple, reinstated the luxurious Naebul-dang, and favored such Seon-jong monks as Haengho and Ilwoon. He even adopted a protective policy for the religion by issuing orders to the local provincial governors to forbid the destruction of the existing temples. All the royal subjects and the ministers stormed the King with letters, suggestions and advice; even the Confucian students at the Jiphyon-jon demonstrated their grievances by boycotting their studies en masse, but the King did not listen. It was because of this sudden turn-about that Sejong's successor, Sejo, the second son of Sejong, moulded his faith in Buddhism.

The Haṃherdang's Kihwa

When the tides of the Buddhist persecution rose high in the first part of the Lee Dynasty, there was no Buddhist like Kihwa, who countered the trend with his arguments and theories for the sake of the dying religion.

Kihwa was a disciple of Muhak with a pseudonym of Deuktong ; his living room was called the Hamherdang. Secularly named Yu, he was born in the 2nd year of King Shinwoo in Choongju. From his early age, Kihwa learned the Chinese classics at the Sungkyunkwan Confucian school, but, after experiencing the transiency of life, became a monk at the Uisang-am on Mt. Kwanak at the age of 21. In the 6th year of Taejo, he met and studied under the monk Muhak at the Hoeam temple. From the 6th year of Taejong, Kihwa went through the Daeseung temple on Mt. Kong-duk, the Kwanum-kul on Mt. Chonma and the Bulhi temple, and became widely known for his religious pursuits. In the 14th year of Taejong, the famous monk went to the Inbong temple on Mt. Jamo, where he spent three years in religious contemplations in a small room of the temple that was given the name of Hamherdang. For his growing reputation, Kihwa was summoned by King Sejong for his subjects and served at the Daeja-am in Kaesung. After 4 years at the Daeja-am, he toured the mountains of Kilsang, Kongduk and Woonak, and passed away at the Bongam temple on Mt. Huiyang in March, the 15th year of Sejong. He was then 58.

Against the Confucians heated expulsion of Buddhism, Kihwa, in order to justify the persecuted religion, produced the work of manifestation, in which he asserted that the Buddhist doctrines coincide with the metaphysical theories of the Chu-tzu teachings, and that the essence of the religion was having the man return to his nature that would bear the Buddhisattva. In the practice of religious morals, he claimed, the fifth commandments of Buddhism and the five principles of Confucianism also were on record. Since the ideal society of Confucianism could be realized on the basis of Buddhist theory of causes and effects, by which the inner world of man could be purified, Kihwa advocated that neither religions should be abolished, but should co-exist in harmony.

Chapter 3
King Sejo and the Revival of Buddhism

Sejo's Admiration in Buddhism

By nature, King Sejo was clear-sighted and determined, wrote many literary works and was expert in military strategy and other inventional works during his father Sejong's rules.

With ambitions to usurp the throne, Sejo killed a loyal subject, Kim, Jong Seo and a royal-descendant sovereign in An Pyong. After holding supreme military power for three years, Sejo dethroned King Danjong ; later, he massacred him and his loyal subject, Sung, Sam Mun, along with their colleagues.

Constantly uneasy about these vicious crimes, Sejo experienced the grief of his son's sudden death in September of his second year in reign. He then initiated various Buddhist services, not only to pray for his deceased son, but also to alleviate his guilty conscience for his past misconducts. His religious works included writing, reprinting, recompiling and inscribing all sorts of Buddhist sutras, along with the renovation of the Dokap Temple in Youngam, where he enshrined another Buddha statue.

The year his son died, Sejo continued the liquidation of the royal lineage prolonging his reign by murdering princes Keumsung and dethroning King Danjong even though he still conducted religious works. As a means of praying for the peace of their souls, he sent 23 volumes of Buddhist books to Japan, and printed some 50 copies of all the Buddhist sutras at the Haein temple for distribution and for storage at the great temples in each province. In addition, he contributed a good sum of crops and cast-iron bells to the temples, sponsored sutra-reciting meetings, established a prayer-house in Koyang-kun for his dead son, and executed great Buddhist rites, touring around the famous temples in the country.

Sejo's inclination toward Buddhism, certainly affected by Sejong's conversion in his late years, was definitely derived from his true wishes to expatiate his sins and to pray for his son.

Sejo's Policy for the Monks

The Buddhist works of King Sejo were not limited to those mentioned in the preceding page, but extended to protect and promote the religion by ceasing former high-handed policies of the government. Sejo enacted and specified in the national code the selection examination for the monks, encouraged the religious devotion by renovating and newly establishing a number of the temples including the Daewonkak temple with its thirteenstoried stone pagoda and attempted to penetrate the religion it into the people by translating the Buddhist scriptures into easy local vernacular called Hankul.

Moreover, to correct the scornful attitude toward the monk, Sejo issued a decree to forbid the arrest of Buddhist monks. According to the historical records, the King had ordered that the arrest of the criminal suspects among the monks should be carried out only by royal permission, and curtailed authoritarian intrusion into the temples without license. This was contrary to the suggestions made by the state council that housewives should be prohibited from visiting the temples for they were the sources of various public demoralization. Also, the King slackened the supervision over the monks, helped the monks in their efforts for religious pursuits by terminating their public obligations, and paved the way for all the servants to become monks.

Above all, the most outstanding achievement Sejo accomplished was the translation of various Buddhist sutras into the Hankul invented by his father, Sejong. Although many of them had been reprinted during the past tencenturies since Buddhism was first introduced, the religious literature was not popularly read by the people because of their difficulty. However, since Sejo's initiation of publishing the Buddhist books and scriptures in local language under the cooperation of such monks as Sumi, Shinmi, Hongjun, and other scholar like Yoon, Sa Ro, Hwang, Su Shin, Kim, Su On, and Han, Kye Hi, the Trinity of Buddhism was revived and revitalized ; rescued from the brink of complete destruction in the first part of the Lee Dynasty. At the same time, Sejo was revered by the Buddhist as a great guardian King of Buddhism regardless of his merciless sins in the past.

The Regulation Handling the Monks and Temples

The draft of the state regulation handling the selection examination of the monks and the management of the temples was completed a few months before Sejo's death, in September of the first year of King Yejong. There were similar states laws promulgated during the years of King Taejo, Taejong and Sejong, but some of their provisions contradicted each other, and were not fit for practical application. Therefore, Sejo ordered Choi, Hang, Kim, Kook Kwang and No, Sa Shin to draft one that could be used as a permanent fundamental law of the state by selecting the proper clauses from the previous examples. The criminal and house laws were thus completed in the 5th year of Sejo, but the ceremonial laws, or Yejon, pertaining to the government official, military, industry and to Buddhism were concluded two months before the death of the King.

The Yejon that came under the state code of laws called Kyungkook Daejon stipulated that the monk candidates should report to the head temple of the Kyo-jong and Seon-jong for the sutra-reciting examinations conducted every three years, and that a total of 30 authorized successful candidates should have to pay some 30 bolts of cotton cloth as a poll-tax to the government office called Yejo in order to obtain government credentials. The one who passed the examinations was given the rank of Daeseon, from which he could be promoted to the next higher ranks of

Jungduk, Seonsa, Daeseonsa and Dodaeseonsa in the Kyo-Jong on the appointment of a chief priest of a temple conducted every 3 years, the law provided that the Yejo should execute the selection from among many candidates recommended by each sect's head temple, and that the retiring chief priest was accountable for all the losses or damages that occurred at the temple. The establishment of new temples was not recognized, but the renovations of the existing ones were approved by the office of Yejo.

Kim, Si Seup

When Sejo was executing the Buddhist promotional policies, there were many scholars and monks rendering their meritorious services for the restoration of the religion under the special favors of the King. But, aside from them, there was only one, Kim, Si Seup, who abhored the King and always stood in opposition to the royal families, but who made a great contribution to the Buddhist religion.

Kim was born in Hansung in the 17th year of Sejong ; he had numberous pen names such Seoljam, Dongbong, Chungbinja, Byoksan, Chungeun and Maewoldang. Writing poems at the age of 3, Kim was recognized as a genius at the higher learning institution at the age of 5. By proving his talents even before King Sejong, he was said to have received 50 bolts of silk as a reward. While studying at the Joongheung temple on Mt. Samkak in the 3 rd year of Danjong, Kim burnt all his books in resentment when he heard that Sejo had usurped the throne by murdering a number of loyal subjects and members of the royal family. From then on, he travelled from one temple after another. By virtue of his erudition and good conduct, Kim soon became famous, and had many followers among the monks. When the Buddhist seminaries were conducted by Sejo after the completion of the Wonkak temple, the participating monks were said to have been questioned about the absence of Kim. The King, accordingly, sent out the order to summon him. but, as Kim pretended to be insane, he was left alone. At the age of 47, Kim started to eat meat, let his hair grew and got married. Following the death of his wife soon afterwards,

Kim went into the mountain against the advice of his associates ; he died at the Muryang temple in the Hongsan Prefecture at the age of 59.

Among the literary works written by Kim, the 'Kumo Shinhwa', depicting the local scenes of the Lee Dynasty, was valued highly as one of the best in Korean literature.

As he was originally of Confucian schooling, Kim's Buddhist standpoint of views, unlike those of the other monks, were the ones from the position taken by a Confucian, as was his interpretation of the Buddhist essences. However, he maintained that the ideals of both Buddhism and Confucianism were not inconsistent, that the blind attitude of the rulers to apply the effects of Buddhism in political fields was basically wrong, and that the true significance of Buddha was in transcending various worldly agonies, including life and death. Not only the rulers, but also the man on the street, he emphasized, should fulfill his role as a constituent of the country ; all should devote themselves to the religion, but not to become so fanatical as to contribute their entire property to the Buddhist shrines. Once the religion was professed in this way, it would not be harmful to either Confucianism or to the state, Kim remarked. Therefore, the indiscreet expulsion of the Buddhists by the Confucians was ill conceived ; it was necessary prevent Buddhism from total extinction. Comparing the monks' participating in the politics to the acts of a beast, Kim also stated that Buddhism and the state should be separated into entirely different spheres, the scope of the monks' activities restricted, and the Confucians and the Buddhists should interact in harmony. Though Kim was not critical about Confucianism, he was very critical of Taoism.

Chapter 4
The Resufferings of Buddhism

King Sungjong's Suppression

By the conversion of Sejo, Buddhism prospered for sometime. But when Sungjong succeeded to the throne after Yejong, it again lost its vitality, for the King adopted the Confucian promotion policy as the principle of the state, and thoroughly persecuted the Buddhist religion.

The first thing Sungjong carried out upon assumption of power was changing the system of the mourning rites from those of the Buddhists to the Confucians. Then, the King banned the establishment of the Buddhist shrines in the capital area, and abolished the system of the monk selection examinations. Those monks who passed the examinations previously and had government-issued credentials were closely scrutinized for their qualifications ; should any of them fail, they were sent back to the common world.

Although he had once conducted some renovations on the temples at the wishes of the Empress Dowager, Sungjong was consistently Anti-Buddhist, tearing down 20 priestess' temples in the capital city, and treating a Confucian subject like Kim, Su On as a criminal for his inclination toward Buddhism. In his later years, Sungjong sent another Confucian named Kwon, Ke Dong into exile in the country-side for his attitude favoring the Buddhist rites as a means to cope with the epidemics then prevalent in the Hwanghae province. Another incident occurred when the Queen Insoe sent the image of Buddha to the Jungup-won temple ; a Confucian student named Lee, byuk took it and burnt it. The Queen Mother insisted on a heavy punishment for the man, but King Sungjong refused her saying that he should be awarded a prize instead.

Far-sighted and determined in his rule, Sungjong also left a number of literary works, including the General History of Korea(Dongkook Tongkam), the Geography of Korea(Dongkook Yoji Seungram), the Literary Selections(Dongmunseon), the Brief History of the Three Kingdoms (Samkooksa Jeoljo), etc.. As the King pursued the consistent policy of approving whatever was profitable in the promotion of Confucianism, and of treating as a traitor of Confucius whatever had a Buddhist tinge, there were some biased-Confucians who advised that all the monks should be executed. But Sungjong was related to have refused them by saying, The Buddhist monks are also human beings. How could we kill innocent people ?'

The Madness of Yeonsankun

King Yeonsankun was the most atrocious but valorous ruler in the history of the Lee Dynasty ; although he had very little concern about religion, he was not satisfied with Buddhism. However, as his grand-mother Empress Dowager Insoe and his mother had such a devotion to the religion Yeonsankun was obliged to perform some of the religious services, i.e., conducting the refine mass at the Jinkwan themple, and Bongsun temples, reprinting the Buddhist scriptures at the Wonkak temple, establishing the Bongeun temple in Kwangju to pray for the ancestors, and copying some 8,000 volumes of the scriptural collections at the Haein temple at the wishes of his grandmother Empress.

Finally, when his mother and grandmother passed away in the 10th year of his rule, the lecherously atrocious King began to show his true colors. He broke the Buddha's statues enshrined in the Jangui temple on Mt. Samkak, closed down the Heungduk temple and Heunchon temple, then the head temples of Kyo-jong and Seon-jong, using them as public offices or stables, and turned the Wonkak temple into a house of Keesaeng

(woman entertainers). According to the Yeonryosil Kisul(a history compiled by Lee, Keung Ik with the historical events from the age of Lee
Taejo to Hyeonjong), Yeonsankun was said to have classified the woman
entertainers selected from each province into four groups : Heungchung,
Woonpyung, Danpyung and Sokhong ; he assigned them to each temple.
The one assigned to the Wonkak temple which was renamed Yonbang-
won, was the Sokhong group entertainers. Beside, the King abolished
and terminated the Buddhist systems concerning the monk selection examinations and thier promotional rank, confiscated the land belonging to
the temples, and even employed the monks as the servants of his or of
the government. As a result of such a harsh suppression, most of the
temples in Seoul were closed, and many of the monks were forced to do
dishonorable work.

The atrocities of the King did not end just with Buddhism. He used
for his own sensual pleasures and amusements, the temples of either Buddhism or Confucianism, public or private house, or Confucian subjects
or monks as he pleased. The oppression the Confucians received was also
unprecedented ; their school Sungkyunkwan, was confiscated as the King's
pleasure house, and some of its students were abused and forced to be
lifters of the King's personal sedan chair along with other civil officials.

The Continued Persecution by Joongjong

The Buddhism that had been tortured by continued oppressions of King
Sungjong and Yeonsankun was pressed to the verge of asphyxiation by
even more severe persecution at the hands of the succeeding King Joongjong.

The year he assumed the reign, Hoongjong changed the Heungchon temple toa public office, and completely abolished the system of
the monk selection examinations. In his 7th year in office, the King broke
down the Wonkak temple, and released the building material to those
who had their houses torn down by Yeonsankun ; he commandered the
bronze statues from Kyungju for the production of arms, and, in the 11th

year, banned the mourning rites on the anniversary of the death-day. Joongjong also demolished a number of the temples and Buddha's statues in Seoul and in the Jungeup Prefectrue , including Youngeung temple, Naejang temple, Sushim temple, etc., and charged that the temples were the dens of monk-robbers.

In his later years, Joongjong, on the false pretext of reviving the old credential system for the monks, and, at the suggestion of Kim, An No, requisitioned the Buddhists to be engaged in such public works projects as bank-revetment in the upper part of the Han River and the tunnel project in Uihang, Choongchong province. Consequently, the majority of the learned and famous Buddhist priests concealed their whereabouts.

The Depreciation of the Monks Qualities

As a result of such consecutive Buddhist persecution by the successive rulers, the entrance of capable and talented men to the priesthood was completely blocked, and the monks' social standing as well as their qualities was extremely lowered.

During the golden age of Buddhism in Koryo, there were throngs of excellent people coming into the religion from the royal lineage, the nobles and from the commoners as well for the special protection and treatment rendered by the imperial courts toward the priests and religion. Beside since the monks were selected through examinations and their high positions of Seonsa or Daesa were obtainable only by the breadth of their respectable knowledge, those in the higher standard of culture strove to succeed in their lives through the means of religion.

However, after the tyrannical rules on Buddhism by the three kings of Sungjong, Yeonsankun and Joongjong, the majority of the monks in the mountain temples were social drop-outs such as the famished, the tax or service evaders and the criminals seeking refuge. The more the number of such straggler-monks increased, the more the quality standard of the monks in general became depreciated. Drinking, smoking, gambling and other licentious deeds were the usual practices of those monks in the temple. Outside the temple, they, as the group of hoodlums today, ran around from the village to village, plundering, injuring and locking up the people who could not possibly report the damages inflicted by them to the government authorities for fear of their vengeance. One of the characteristics of the hooligan Buddhist bands was that whoever became affiliated with the group could hardly sever relations with them because of their harsh punishment. It was for these reasons that Joongjong colsed down the temples and recruited the monks for various social works with a view to eliminate the rescals and to quicken the national construction.

The saying is that each period of time bears a hero ; some devout Buddhists, though they were small in number, absorbed themselves faithfully in the religious pursuits in the moutain dens or temples. They were Priest Jieom, Hyujung, Yujung and Seonsu.

Chapter 5

Empress Munjung's Promotion of Buddhism and Priest Bowoo

The Promotion of Buddhism of Mother Empress Munjung

As King Injong, the successor of Joongjong, died one year after he was enthroned, the throne ascended by Myungjong, the son of Mother Empress Munjung. Because the crowned King Myungjong, was only 12 years of age at the time, most the state affairs were regented by the Mother Empress, the possessor of just as much rigid and practical will as any man. Since she was such a devout Buddhist ; secretly performing the religious mass at the temples even in the years of Joongjong. The Mother Empress in regency adopted protective and promotional policies for Buddhism, bascially uprooting the previously suppressive ones.

The Regina established the Insu temple at the place where it had been the Jeongup-won in the capital, restored the land and the servants for the Wonkak temple in Hongju, and ordered the erection of red gates at the prayer houses called Naewon-dang in various local districts banning unauthorized persons from the gates. Then, the monk selection examinations were revived along with the system of awarding credentials. The Bongeun temple and Bongsun temples were respectively designated the head temples of the Seon- jong and Kyo-jong, while the Dodaeseonsa (the highest rank in Seon) Bowoo was appointed the bench of the Seon religion, and the Dodaesa(the highest one in Kyo) Sujin was selected as the chief priest of the Kyo religion. During this time, the Confucians, of course, entertained doubts, and public opinion became confused. But the reason Munjung revived these systems was primarily to check the increasing number of the vagabond monks by giving them a leader in a position to command them, instead of having them abandoned and uncontrolled. In any case, Priest(Daesa) Hyujung, who could be paralleled with the famous Priest Jinul in the history of Buddhism in Korea, was the one who excelled in the monk examinations resumed at the suggestion of Priest Bowoo at this time.

A monk originally from the Boeun Temple, Bowoo was highly respected by other Buddhists for his outstanding refinement and religious knowledge. For this, he was entrusted by Mother Empress Munjung with the promotion of the Buddhist religion. He earned the trust of Munjung, and infused new vigor for the persecuted religion by suggesting restorations of various former Buddhist systems. When Bowoo was appointed bishop of the Seon religion under the favors of the royal households, his outer appearance gave the impression of a Wangsa or Kooksa of the age of Koryo. Therefore, the Confucians, mostly from the Sungkyunkwan institution, were severely repulsed, criticizing Bowoo as a vicious monk and even petitioning the Empress that he should be executed. As their petitions were incessantly turned down, the Confucian students went on a strike, not coming to school for some time. Despite the Confucian's harsh reaction, Munjung was firm in her conviction and carried out the policies in favor of Buddhism, conducting rituals and dispatching courtiers to the Naewon-dang Buddhist shrines in various palaces. This, in the end, incurred elements of abuse in espenses and some ill-effects, because the local governors or magistrates tended to satisfy Munjung with their presentation of various gifts for the religious services.

Bowoo

Acting as the promoter of Buddhism as a fulcrum in the religious sphere for about 15 years under the shelter of Mother Empress Munjung during the age of King Myungjong, Priest Bowoo not only excelled over the others in his Buddhist learnings, but also was well conversant in the

Confucian classics in both prose and poetry. It was not clear exactly when he had entered into Buddhism, but when the word spread that Bowoo, whose pen names were Her Eungdang or Nan Am, had attained the spiritual awakening on Mt. Kumkang, a crowd of people from all corners of the country came to hear his teachings, and a number of scholars without ranks attempted to associate with him for his far-reaching eloquences. According to one of the story-books called Erwoo Yadam, Bowoo acquired the reputation while he was on Mt. Chungpyung in Chunchon, but this was supposed to have been after he had left Mt. Kumkang.

When there was a report that Munjung was seeking a talented monk to arouse Buddhism, the ambitious Bowoo quickly came down from Mt. Kumkang and awaited the opportunity at the Bongeun temple in Kwangju-kun. It was while he was at this temple that Bowoo gained access to the Mother Empress, earned the royal favor to become bishop of the Seon religion, and accomplished much in the promotion of Buddhism in general. According to the Taechon Jip, a historical commentary, Bowoo planned a magnificient Buddhist rite at the Hoiam temple on April 8 the 20th year of Myungjong, with an exhorbitant amount of national treasure as a means to demonstrate against the reactionary Confucians and to celebrate the Buddhist development. The triumphant monks came up from various parts of the country for the occasion. But, unfortunately, Mother Empress Munjung died a day before the celebration, and all the congregated monks dispersed. A strange story was that when the thousands of pecks of rice prepared for the feast were cooked and made into cakes, they were colored red as if they had been dyed with blood, and the people took it mysteriouly. After the death of the Empress, the situation reverted, and Bowoo was accepted by no temples around the capital Hanyang. On his escape to the Kangwon province, the once influential monk was seized by the authorities and sent into exile on Cheju Island by King Myungjong despite the Confucians insistence that he should be hanged. The story book also related that the magistrate put Bowoo to hard labor, forcing him to clean up the inns. He was finally murdeted in 1565 by several strong men at magistrate Byun Hyup's instigation.

Thus, the 15 years of struggles by Priest Bowoo for the glory of Bud-dhism ended. Although it might be true that he had somewhat diviated from the virtue of modesty by taking advantage of the royal favours, he certainly was a great monk, who resuscitated the religion temporarily in the middle of the Lee Dynasty by reinstating order in the religious field and enhancing the qualities of the monks, previously recognized only as a group of scoundrels. It was from this period, too, that such famous priests as Hyujung, Yujung and Seonsu lived along with those who made great contributions to the country later as bulwarks against the Japanese by arousing voluntary support.

Ilseon and Youngkwan

While Bowoo maintained his fame by taking part in affairs of both the state and religion, there were others who gained their fame only by their religious pursuits and contemplations in the mountains or woods, com-pletely segregated from politics. They were Priest Ilseon and Youngkwan.

With the pseudonyms of Hyuwon and Seonhwaja, Ilseon was born in Ulsan in 1488, the 19th year of Sungjong, and lost his parents in his child-hood.   Realizing that life was mutable, Ilseon went into the Dansuk temple at the age of 13, and practiced asceticism at the Munsu-am temple on Mt. Myohyang at the age of 24. Later, he studied under the famous Priest Jieom on Mt. Chiri, and attained the spiritual awakening after his further searches for the truth on Mt. Kumkang. Then, after making prea-ching tours through such famous mountains as Chonma, Odae, Baekwun and Lungka, he returned to Mt. Myohyang in the 39th year of Joongjong, and engaged himself in lecturing on the Buddhist doctrines or helping others in religious practices at the Naewon temple and Bohyon temple. By this time, his reputation was so wide-spread that Ilseon had a throng of followers. He passed away in the first year of King Sunjo at the age of 81.

With the pseudonym of Eunam or Yeonsun Doin, Priest Youngkwan from Jinju could be regarded as a great star of the Seon religion in the south Chosun(now the Kyungsang and Cholla provinces) just as Priest Ilseon was the crown of the Kyo religion in the Kwanseo(now the Pyong-an and Hwanghae provinces in the north). Although he was born in the 16th year of Sungjong(1485), that is, three years earlier than Ilseon, Youngkwan entered a Buddhist monastery when he was 13, the same age as of Ilseon, and learned the religious doctrines and practiced asceticism from his 17th year. Later, he personally built a small temple in Kuchon-dong and spent 9 years there in pursuit of the truth. In the 4th year of Joongjong, he went to Mt. Yongmun to study under the old priest, Jowu, and, at the same time, to do extensive reading about the teachings of Laotzu- Chengtzu. After further research under the Seon Priest Jowu in Mt. Kumkang in the 14th year of the same King, Youngkwan spent another 9 years in religious contemplation completely secluded from the world at the Naewon-am shrine on Mt. Mihyeok. Then, at the age of 46, that is, in the 25th year of Joongjong, he moved into Mt. Chiri and studied under the old Priest Jieom, for three years after paying homage to his parents in his hometown. Following the death of Jieom, Youngkwan led the followers and spent almost 40 years in preaching through out the mountains and villages until his death in 1571 the 4th year of Sunjo at the Yeonkok temple in Kosung. He was then 87.

Chapter 6
The Toyotomi War and the Loyalty
of The Buddhist Monks

The Toyotomi War and the Monks

During the age of Sunjo, Confucian learning became highly prosperous, while the Buddhist monks were extremely repressed. However, because of their loyalty to the royal household and their voluntary services for the country at the time of the crucial Japanese invasion during this period, the Buddhists regained better social standing.

As a first step to advance into the Asia mainland, Toyotomi Hideyoshi of Japan launched an all-out attack on Korea with a 150 thousand men army separately commanded by Kato Kiyomasa, Konish Yukinaga, Kuroda Nagamasa and Shimatsu Yoshihiro, etc. in the 25th year of Sunjo, 1592 A.D.. The enemy forces that landed on Pusan in April of the same year advanced in three ways, trampling down the regions of Kyongsang, Cholla, Choongchong provinces and closed into the capital as though they were going through a no man's land. King Sunjo, fled to Uiju, a town situated on the northern border, with the royal family and his senior subjects, dispatching his princes to each province in order to stimulate patriotism among the populace. Finally, when the capital fell into the hands of the Japanese army without much difficulty, the social orders crumbled into chaos and the public was filled with panic.

At this critical juncture, the Buddhist priests like Hyujung and Yujung resolutely rose to their feet and led the army of the monks to resist the enemy forces, achieving brilliant victories.

Hyujung, who played the role of a central figure in the resistance, was staying on Mt. Myohyang in Pyongan province. The 73-year-old monk was then summoned by the King to Uiju, was appointed the head bishop of all the Buddhist sects in the country, and was requested to swear fealty. Hyujung, in turn, sent out messages to all the provincial temples to raise a voluntary army of the monks. His disciple, Yujung, rose in the Kwan-dong (now Kangwon province) areas with more than 700 men ; another disciple, Cheoyoung, in the Cholla region answered the call with more than 1,000 volunteers, and Hyujung, despite his age, himself directly commanded 5,000 of his followers in battles at Pyongyang and Kaesung, achieving many successful victories. When the Japanese forces retreated from Seoul, Sunjo returned from Uiju ; Hyujung ushered the King to the Kaesung with his 700 warrior monks. At this time, the commander of the reinforcement from the Ming Dynasty, Lee, Ju Sung, and other generals submitted many written commendations for the old monk for his outstanding war service. After the King was settled again in the imperial palace, Hyujung received royal permission to retreat into Mt. Myohyang for his old age, turning the commanding authority of the monk army over to his closest disciple, Yujung. Famous for his courage, the new commander fought many battles against the Japanese army in various places in the Kyosang region and scored many brilliant results. At the request of Yu jung, the commander of the regular government troops, the monk leader, Yujung, went alone across to the enemy camp in Ulsan and persuaded the Japanese commander Kato to withdraw his troops. At this time, when Kato asked the monk if there was any treasure in Chosun, Yujung completely astonished him by answering, 'Now in our country, we take your head as the most precious treasure.' After the war, Yujung went to Japan as a peace negotiator and came back with some 3,500 war prisoners.

Meanwhile, Youngkyo of Kongju, Choongchongnam province, another disciple of Hyujung, also led an independent fight against the Japanese army. He had his learning from Hyujung, but was staying at the Chung-yon-am temple in his hometown when the war broke out. On learning that the king had taken a refuge in Uiju, Youngkyu himself raised up monk volunteers, armed them with sickles and axes, and attacked the enemy along with the other warrior in Chungju. However, in a heated battle in Kumsan, he was killed with his entire army of 700 men.

The Compensation for the Loyalities

The motivation that made the Buddhist monks rise, all across the country, by their own will and made them volunteer in action without any opposition was derived both from their devotion for the country and, from their intention to regain government assurances for their better social standing.

Since the monk examination systems were not existent at the time, all the higher ranks of the religion such as Seonsa, Daeseonsa or Daeduk and Daesa were meaningless, although the conception still remained among the Buddhists that they were the first steps for their promotion and were, as such, aspired for. The revival of the system, though it was not welcomed by the royal subjects, was requested by the monks as a compensation for their services. The war was still going on, and the army of the monks was composed of better fighters than any government troops. Considering the request as a matter of enhancement for the monk army, the imperial court stimulated their esprit de corps by issuing an edict that those who submitted the head of an enemy should be given the privileges of a successful candidate of the selection examinations, and the others the qualification to be plain monks with government-issued credential.

Accordingly, Yujung was appointed as a Dangsangkwan (or the superior officer of the monks); each one of the head monks from the Seon and Kyo religions engaged in the training of the Buddhist recruits in the rear area were given the titles of Chongsup; the other head monks commanding the troops in the battlefields had the titles of Dochongsup and Buchongsup respectively. Following the war, the great priests, who had rendered meritorious services for the country, were compensated with the ranks of Seonsa, Daeseonsa, Daeduk or Daesa.

Priest Yujung

As a disciple of Hyujung, Yujung might have been inferior in his religious discernments compared to his master, but he certainly performed more distinguished service for the country. In addition, it was through these two famous monks that the restoration of Buddhism in the Lee Dynasty periods seemed to have been rendered successful.

Born in 1544 the 39th year of King Joongjong in Milyang, Yujung had various pseudonym like Samyungdang, Songwun and Jongbongdang. Becoming weary of the Mencius learning he was pursuing at the age of 13, Yujung went to the Jikji temple on Mt. Hwanak, had his head tonsured to be a monk, and studied the deep perceptions about Buddhism under many aged priests. Passing the Seon priestral examinations in the 16th year of Myungjong at the age of 18, he continued reading extensively the Buddhist doctrines, conducted religious asceticism, and broadened his acquaintanceship with literary men. In the 8th year of Sunjo, Yujung, contrary to the popular expectation for him to be the chief priest of a temple, went into Mt. Myohyang, and won the heart of his master Hyujung after two years of ascetic practices under him. After leaving his master in the 11th year of Sunjo, he spent three years at the Boduk temple on Mt. Kumkang, and, then, travelled and preached through the famous mountains in the south. He was once imprisoned, but, later released, on a false accusation from a vicious monk named Mooup in 1589 the 22nd year of Sunjo.

When the Japanese forces assaulted the Youngdong region in 1592 the 25th year of Sunjo, Yujung not only performed a good office for the protection of the residents in the nine provincial kuns by parleying directly with the enemy commanders, but, on receipt of the message from Hyujung, also voluntarily raised a total of 700 patriotic soldiers, and, together with the Buddhist volunteers from the other areas achieved many outstanding victories in battles in Pyongyang, Kaesung, Uinyong, etc.. In addition, he even served to supply 4,000 suks(570 tons) of rice and clothes for more than 10,000 troops fighting in the battles, and greatly contributed in the construction of the mountain fortress on Mts. Palgong, Kumo and Yongki.

In the 36th year of Sunjo, Yujung was sent to Japan for the conclusion of peaceful negotiations. When he returned, victoriously bringing back a total of 3,500 prisoners-of-war, the King bestowed upon the monk the most highest honor of the state, and presented him with the imperial horse and sackclothes as mementoes. After his return from Japan, Yujung went to Mt. Myohyang to pay homages to his deceased master, Hyujung. From the shock he received as a result of the death of Sunjo, the famous warrior monk fell ill and died at the age of 67 at the Haein temple in Hapchon-kun.

Chapter 7
Priest Hyujung and Priest Sunsoo

The Seosan Daesa Hyujung

Priest Hyujung, who served the state with all his loyalty during the Toyotomi War and raised a number of famous Buddhists to mark a brilliant part in the history of Buddhism in Chosun, was secularly known as Choi with a pseudonym of Chungheodang. He was also popularly called the Seosan Daesa (a great priest of the western mountain) for he had such a long soujourn on Mt. Myohyang in the west.

Born in 1590, the 15th year of Joongjong in Anju, Pyongan province, Hyujung lost his mother when he was 9, and his father in the following year ; he was brought to the capital for studies by the Magistrate of his hometown called Lee, Sa Zeung, who had discovered talents in the young orphan. Hyujung, however, was not much attached to study, preferring to travel through the various Buddhist temples and shrines in the south to become a monk in Mt. Duryu, where he conducted research in volumes of the Buddhist scriptures under the old Priest, Sungin. Afterwards, Hyujung continued religious his pursuits for three years under the famous Priest Youngkwan. After spending some more years in the Buddhist sanctums on Mt. Dosol and Mt. Duryu, he was said to have attained self-realization on hearing the mid-day crows on a visit to his monk friend one day in Youksung village of Yongsung (now Namwon-kun). Still in his thirties, Hyujung passed the monk selection examinations with the most outstanding records, especially at a time when King Myungjong, on advice from

Priest Bowoo, was reinstating the Buddhist systems : he was quickly promoted to the highest position of bishop for both the Kyo and Seon religions. Later realizing that it was not the proper way for a monk to engage in the executive administration, he submitted all his official titles and journeyed through the temples on Mts. Myohyang and Kumkang, preaching the Buddhist doctrines and guiding the ascetics. At this time, his fame was nationwide, and his audiences were always jam-packed with followers. In the 22nd year of Sunjo, when there was a revolt master-minded by Jung, Yeon Rip. Hyujung was temporarily imprisoned along with his head disciple, Yujung, on false charges schemed by a vicious monk named Mooup who abominated the former's rising fame.

For his brilliant exploits during the Toyotomi War in spite of his old age, Hyujung was offered by the King Sunjo the most respected entitle of the nation's highest Daeseonsa and the Supreme Bishop of the Seon and Kyo religions, etc., and was honored with the highest government position called Jung-i-pum ; then the monk was allowed to retreat into the mountain. On Mt. Myohyang, after the war services, Hyujung's religious reputation became even more wide-spread so that the number of his disciples reached more than a thousand, among whom more than 70 succeeded. At the age of 85, the famous monk passed away at the Won-sook-am temple in 1604 the 37th year of Sunjo, leaving a number of literary works including the Seonkyo-kyol(the Secrets of the Seon and Kyo), the Seonkyo-seok(the Interpretation of the Seon and Kyo), the Chungherdang works(the Eight Volume Collections of Chungherdang), etc..

The Religious Lines of Hyujung

The legitimate line of Priest Hyujung, acquired a strong influence over the entire monks of the country. This line was the one descended from Prists Bowoo(in the last stage of Koryo), Honsu, Kakwun, Jungshim, Chieom and Youngkwan. Hyujung was so influential, not only because his many followers regarded him as a supreme pontiff for his exceptionally outstanding knowledge, religious preceptions, generosity, loyalty to the country, but also because of his two famous masters, Ilseon and Young-kwan. Ilseon predominated over the religious spheres in the Kangwon, Pyongan and Hwanghae regions, Youngkwan the Kyongsang, Cholla regions respectively. However, there was another religious line inherited by Youngkwan's disciple, Buhyu, and Buhyu's follower, Byokam, in the later years, but they were totally incomparable with the success achieved by Hyujung.

Although there were some other small branches initiated by Chungmae, Joongkwan and Herhan who claimed to be the legal descendants of Hyu-jung, the religious legacy was inherited by four major branches···one by Hyujung's legitimate descendant, Yujung, and the others by Yujung's three highest disciples, Pyunhyang Unki, Jungkwan Ilseon, and Soyo Taeneung.

The Branch of Yujung

The relationship between Yujung and his master Hyujung could be compared with the that of Sakya and his great disciple Kayeh. However, Yujung's line was succeeded by Songwol Eungsang, an uncommon genius with the gifted of purity, sagacity and thoroughness in both the Buddhist and Confucian doctrines. Eungsang pursued asceticism on Mt. Odae, ac-hieving fame through religious preachings for more than 30 years on Mt. Kumkang ; he gained many followers.

Eungsang had, among many others, Herback Myungjo as his legal descendant. Myungjo, in turn, had such a high disciple as Chonpa Ssangun and Kumbong Chono, and some six to seven religious inheritors.

The Branch of Pyunyang

Considered one of the two greatest authorities of Hyujung's religious line along with Yujung, Pyunyang Unki became a monk at the age of 11, studying under Priest Hyeonbo. As he grew up, Unki went to Mt. Myohyang and acquired the power of mind under Hyujung. Afterwards, he became famous for his preachings throughout Mt. Kumkang, Mt.

Kooryong and Mt. Myohyang until he passed away in 1644 the 22nd year of Injo, at a choister on Mt. Myohyang when he was 64.

Among Unki's hundreds of followers, Poongdam Uishim, Chungum Sukmin, Hoekyung Hongbyun, Hamyong Kyejin, Hwanjuk Uichon, Juksang Hyesang and Mokhoung Chonsin were the leading disciples, each forming their own branches. But the branch of Poongdam Uishim, which was again divided into tens of other sub-branches, was the most successful.

The Branch of Jungkwan

When he entered into Buddhism in his early years, Jungkwan Ilseon was no exception to others in his strivings for learning and religious pursuits ; there was few Buddhist sutras that he had not mastered. He received the enlightenment from Hyujung's sermons on Mt. Myohyang, and, up to his later years, taught hundreds of his followers on Mt. Sokri and Mt. Dukyu.

The legitimate descendants of Jungkwan Ilseon were Insung Joongun, Hoyeon Taeho, Mooyeom Kyehun,Wunkok Choonghi and Saan Choongin, who respectively led their own independent branches later.

The Branch of Soyo

One of the high disciples of Hyujung, Soyo Taeneung entered into Buddhism when he was 13. After practicing asceticism came a disciple of Hyujung at the age of 20. On instruction from his master Hyujung after three years of faithful pursuits under him, Soyo set out to preach through Mts. Kumkang, Odae and Koowol for 20 years. He gained many followers and a great reputation due to his eloquence. When the imperial palace was removed to the Mt. Namhan fortress during the Ch'ing Dynasty invasion in the 14th years of Injo, that is, 1636 A.D., the monk on an imperial order, rebuilt the western part of the mountain castle. Soyo passed away at the age of 92 in 1649 the 27th year of Injo.

There were many outstanding followers of Soyo Taeneung, but, among them, Chimkwaeng Hyeonbyun, Jinbaek Kyaewoo, Baekryon, Takok,

Songwol Hyeonjung, Haewoon Kyungyeol, Kyewol Hakul, Bokwang
Cheowoo, Kaeyoung Keukrim, Songpa Chonhae, Ssangwoon Kwanghae,
Poher Damsu, Soowol Sasun, Jinhae Loiwoon, Jaewol Sooil and Soowol
Keukyeon were the 15 most prominent disciples. They also led their respective independant sects, and, although Chimkwaeng Hyeonbyun was
legal descendant, the branch of Haewoon Kyungyeol was the one that
was most prosperous.

Seonsoo

Despite the dominating influences of the Hyujung's religious lines
during the age of King Sunjo of the Lee Dynasty, Priest Seonsoo preserved
his independence in leading a separate Buddhist sect.

With the pen name of Boohyu, Seonsoo was a man Kodaebang, in the
Cholla province. As he was born in 1543 the 38th year of Joongjong,
Seonsoo was about 23 years younger than Hyujung, but because they
studied under Priest Youngkwan, the direct descendant of the Imje-jong's
Bowoo. They were contemporaries. In his earlier age, Seonsoo became
a monk under Priest Shinmyung on Mt. Chiri. Later, he learned the ab-
strustness of Youngkwan and broadended his discernment for 7 years from
the religious books borrowed from No, Su jin, the vice premier of the
government. During the Toyotomi war, he stayed on Mt. Dukyu and,
following the war, on Mt. Kaya and in Koochondong, pursuing and promoting the Seon religion extensively. When King Kwanghaekun assumed
the throne, he was put into jail on a false accusation from a vicious monk,
but, because of his lofty elegance and untainted speeches, he was released
soon to expound the religious fine-points at the imperial palace. For this,
he received a pair of surplices and a set of Buddhist rosaries from the
king as gifts. Seonsoo continued preaching on Mt. Chiri, where he had
more than 700 followers. When he died at the Ssangkae temple on Mt.
Chokey at the age of 73 in 1615 the 7th year of Kwanghae, the king revered
him with the posthumous entitle of Hongkak Deungkye.

Seonsoo also had a number of highly virtuous disciples. Among them,

Byeokam Kaksung, Loijung Eungmook, Hohan Hiun, Daeka Hiok, Song-kye Sunghyeon, Hwansook Inmun and Poher Damsu, who later led their own schools, were the most prominent. The religious school led by Byeokam Kaksung, the direct descendant of Seonsoo, was most prosperous by virtue of his upright religious austerities coupled with his thorough explications of even the Confucian classics. Appointed to the position of supreme bishop of the country by King Injo, Kaksung renovated the fortress on Mt. Namhan, and proved his loyalty to the country by orga-nizing the Hangma Army composed of monks during the Ch'ing Dynasty invasion. For such outstanding patriotism and his religious reputation, there were more than 10,000 mourners, it was said, when Seonsoo Kaksung died at the Hwaom temple on Mt. Chiri. Among the disciples of Kaksung, there were more than 30, including Chuimi Sucho and Baekok Cheoneung, who later attained their success ; a total of 8 schools branched out from them after Kaksung's death, but the one Chuimi Sucho initiated was most prosperous.

Chapter 8
The Military Services of the Monks

The Reconstruction Project of the Capital

With the end of the Toyotomi War that lasted for 7 years, the country was in inexplicably miserable state, whereby the imperial palace was burnt down, all the public offices either burnt down or devastated, and literally everyone, regardless of being nobles or commoners, became street beggars at the expense of the despoilments by the Japanese army and the material requistitions by the Ming Dynasty reinforcements. In addition, nation-wide famine existed as a result of long spells of drought, shortage of man-power, along with widely prevalent diseases which all added to the horrible post-war scene. The exhaustion and devastation of the people were un-imaginable.

Then, King Kwanghaekun ascended to the throne and attempted to reconstruct the capital from the ruins, left undone by his predecessor King Sunjo.

At that time, there was a witchcraft monk named Sungji, who was in close contact with those of the noble class and even with the imperial court. With his magic in topography, he advised the construction of In-kyung Palace at the foot of Mt. Inwang, and, finally, earned the personal favors from the king himself. He was given the official rank of Chumchoo by the king, and he became prestigeous and powerful. On the suggestion and advice from this monk, King Kwanghae, in his 8th year in office, removed thousands of private houses, issued an imperial edict throughout the country to levy taxes and to demand material and manpower of the monks to construct the Kyungduk and Jasoo Palaces. As a compensation, the Buddhist laborer was given credentials, and those in the supervisory level were given the title of Chongsup or Buchongsup. Then there were overwhelming complaints from the people because of these excessive burdens. But the king repressed them in a high-handed manner, trading official appointments for valuables such as gold, silver, iron chloride, wood or stones.

Though he had been such a tyrant, Kwanghaekun also was a symphathizer for Buddhism. Thus, he had a deep respect for a vicious monk like Sungji, and established a number of Buddhist shrines called Naewondang within the imperial palace and local places praying for blessings for the royal family. Kwanghaekun's concubine, named Yu, a commoner was so strictly bound to Buddhism that she made a number of the gold, wooden and stoned statues of Buddha, and distributed them among the temples in the palace.

The Renovation of Mt. Namhan Fortress

As the grievances among the people rose high against the tyranny of Kwanghaekun, persons like Lee, Kui, Kim Yu, Kim, Ja Jum and Lee, Kwal, who belonged to the Seoin Party(the first political group formed during the years of Sunjo), initiated the military movement to oust the tyrannical ruler and to restore the royal successor, Injo, into the seat of power. When about fifty people who made distinguished services in restoring Injo to the throne were rewarded with recognitions, Lee, Kwal was dissatisfied and he led the rebellion in the northern border region in the 2nd year of Injo, and, finally, attacked the capital with the reamnants of the Japanese forces. The King, then, fled to Kongju, Choongchong province. Although Lee, Kwal's revolts were soon quelled the incident stirred up the public opinion to the extent that a defense perimeter was built around the capital. At last, Mt. Namhan fortress was constructed on the suggestions from Lee, Won Ik and Lee, Kui.

With an unfavorable view towards Buddhism, King Injo sent out the order to forbid monks to enter capital castle. But it was necessary to enlist the hands of the Buddhists in order to execute the construction projects. Thus, the King undertook the construction on the mountain fortress in September of his 2nd year of rule by appointing Priest Kaksung to the post of Dochunsup(the supreme bishop) to supervise the subordinate workers who came from all parts of the country, and the construction was completed in July of the 4th year. And, in addition to the two existing temples of Mangwol temple and Okjung temple, a total of seven monasteries such as Kaewon temple, Hanheung temple, Kookchung temple, Jangkyung temple, Chonju temple, Youngwon temple and Dongrim temple were also built as the camps of the monk's army.

The government, then, was ruled by the political party called Seoin which had been entangled with its intra-party factionalism, and the matters of the national security and defense of the capital were abandoned into the hands of some 500 Buddhist troops stationed at the 9 temples. Moreover, the fact that the services of the monks were performed on the conditions that their status would be assured by the state with the credentials and the promotion of their religious ranks represent the weakness of the ruling government. Whatever was the reason and sacrifices, the Buddhist monks had only one intention, to secure their social standing and to convince the people of their valuable raison d'etre.

According to the Annals of Namhan(Volume 4, the Namhanji), the system of the monk's army was instituted in such a way that after the completion of the mountain fortress there was one Seungkun Chongsup (commander), one Seungjoongkun(staff officer), one Kyoryeonkwan (traning officer), three Chokwan(guard officer), one Kibikwan(officer responsible for the colours), 138 troops permanetly assigned to the 10 temples, and 356 additional volunteer monks. Those monks from the provinces of Kyonggi, Kangwon, Samnam and Hwanghae were required to perform their duties at the capital fortress for the two-month period on a rotation basis, but this was abolished from the 32nd year of Youngjo.

After the completion of Mt. Namhan fortress, the defense castle was built at Mt. Juksang, and the monks were recruited to guard it in the 23rd year of Injo at the request of the Governor of the Cholla province.

The Ch'ing Dynasty Invasion and the Monk Volunteers

After the construction and renovation of the defense walls in most of the strategically important positions of the country with the mobilization of the Buddhist manpower, there were two invasions from the Ch'ing Dynasty in the north again requiring the services of the monks.

Prior to the conquest of the Ming Dynasty, Emperor Taechong of the Ch'ing Dynasty launched an attack to subjugate Chosun in January, 1627 the 5th year of King Injo, with Prince Ahmin commanding the 30,000 men army across the Yalu River, This was the beginning of what is now popularly known as Jungmyo Horan(the 1627 Invasion of the Ch'ing). At this time, the defense of the northern border of the country was so neglected that the torrents of the invading troops towards the south were irreversible. Remembering the merits of the monk fighters during the Japan's Toyotomi Invasion, King Injo urged the loyal services from the bonzes, appointing Priest Myungjo of Mt. Myohyang as the commander of the Buddhist army. Myungjo complied, sent out his messages throughout the country, gathered some 4,000 volunteers and resisted the invading enemies in Anju, Pyongan province, but he was completely subdued. The defeat of Myungjo in Anju, caused by the incompetence of the government troops, costed many lives and made the others responsible for the rear defense lines ; the Governor of the Pyongan province Yoon, Sun and the Garrison commander of the Hwanghae province Jung, Ho Seo, deserted their positions.

Although this invasion from the Ch'ing Dynasty ended with a peaceful conclusion with brotherly relations between the two states, Emperor Taechong of the Ch'ing launched another assault on Chosun 9 years later in 1636, the 14th year of Injo, with more powerful forces of 100,000 men. They again pressed into the capital unresisted. King Injo sent his royal family and other royal relatives to take refuge in Kanghwa Island, but he himself and his crowned prince were already blocked enroute by the enemies. Thus, the King and his prince along with other state officials fled to the Mt. Namhan fortress, where some 10,000 monks were on the defense. The King issued the injunctions to all the provinces to raise the royal army against the invaders. In the northern province, Priest Myungjo again rose with the volunteers, and supported the government and other troops with a supply of provisions. In the south, Kaksung of the Mt. Chiri temple beat the drums and sent out his messages through all the Buddhist temples in the Kyongsang and Cholla regions, calling for voluntary spirits. With several thousand of the participants, Kaksung organized the Hangma Army, and advanced northward only to learn to his great lamentation that Injo had alrady surrendered.

After the war, the two Buddhist monks, Myungjo and Kaksung, were cited respectively with the highest honors of the country as a compensation for their loyal services.

The Renovation and Protection of the Mt. Bukhan Fortress

For some time since King Hyojong, the country was in a peaceful state, and there was not much exploitation of the services from the Buddhsit monks. But from April the 37th year of Sookjong, the renovation works of the Mt. Bukhan fortress began with the utilization of their services called in from the entire country, and were completed six months later along with the establishment of the eleven temples, Joongheung temple, Buwang temple, Bokwang temple, Bokook temple, Yongum temple, Wonkak temple, Kooknyong temple, Sangwoon temple, Seoum temple, Taego temple and Jinkook temple these were used as the military camps for the monks. A total of 350 troops, responsible for the defense of the capital castle, was permanently stationed at the camps, and there was one head monk and one commander respectively assigned to each camp, and one commander-in-chief to the entire camps. The permanently assigned troops, whose daily routines consisted of the sutra-reciting practices and the military trainings, were replaced by the local monks on a two-month rotation basis.

Consequently, the burdens and sacrifices of the monks from the local provinces were immense, for the entire expenses to and from their temples and the camps were to be covered by their own means or assisted by the temples where they belonged. Thus, King Youngjo abolished the rotation system, and had the local temples pay only the costs for the maintenance of the permanent troops.

Chapter 9
The Maltreatment for the Monks

Hyeonjong's Ban on Entrance to Priesthood

For about half a century through the ages of Sunjo, Kwanghaekun and Injo, there were so many national crises and the loyal services of the monks were in such demand that the Buddhists could sustain their standings free from intense government suppression. But, when peace continued in the state for about twenty years following the stabilization of the relations with the neighboring countries, the usefulness of the monks was steadily declining, and, at last, the oppressive hands thrust out Buddhism itself.

On his enthronment, King Hyeonjong appointed such famous Confucians as Song, Shi Yeol and Song, Jun Kil to important government positions so that the Confucian learning was extensively stimulated while Buddhism severely persecuted. In December, 1660, the King sent out a religious decree, forbidding the people from entering into the priesthood, and those violating the order were forcibly sent to the world by the aut horities.

Two months after the decree, Hyeonjong, on the written suggestion from a Confucian scholar named Yu Ke, destroyed two temples for Buddhist nuns, Jasu and Insu, in the capital and sent the younger nuns back to the world, and removed the older ones to the temples outside the capital, and buried in the ground various sacred materials enshrined in the two temples. Later, even the Buddhists' entrance to the capital was banned. On evacuation of the temples in the capital, Jung, Tae Hwa, holder

of the highest government position called Younguijung, stopped the King
from carrying out these works saying that those shrines were the places
where many of the aged and shelterless royal harems of the former kings
sought their homes, and that none of the preceding rulers attempted on
such an ill-considered action. Instead of listening to him, the King accepted
flatteries from the Confucian official named Song, Jun Kil who was intent
on winning royal favors, and established two Confucian schools at the
sites of the two temples.

Against such a tyranny on Buddhism by Hyeonjong, Baekok Cheoneung,
the leading disciple of Priest Kaksung, severely criticized the government's
policy in his protest letter submitted to the King. Explaining the relationship between the historical rise and fall of a country and those of the
religion, and quoting the passages from both the Confucian classics and
Buddhist scriptures, the monk clearly stated his conviction in the letter.
He further proved that no kings in succession since Lee Taejo were so
repressive toward Buddhism, and said that the breaking down of the two
temples, the residing places for the former empresses that did not even
belong to the imperial palace, was very regrettable for the King.

The Sufferings of the Buddha's Statues

In May, 1662 the 3rd year of Hyeonjong, there was an incident in which
Cholla Kamsa(the governor of the Cholla province) Lee, Tae Yeon had
been dismissed from his powerful position, for reporting, in an official
letter to the imperial court, that the Buddha's statues of many temples
in the province were perspiring.

Lee, Tae Yeon's reports were explained to the King by a court official
named Min, Jung Jung as nothing more than the water-drops congealed
from the mists and vapors on statues carved out of wood, varnished and
gold-powdered. The official flattered the King that the reports would
only bewitch the people. Thus, the King ordered the dismissal of Lee,
Tae Yeon and the destruction of all the statues that were said to be
sweating.

The Forgery Incident of Cheokyung

During the reign of King Sookjong, the suppressive policy for Budd-hism was alleviated to some degree compared to the previous rules, but the public confidence in the monks was generally degraded following a forgery incident committed by a vicious monk named Cheokyung in the 2nd year of Sookjong.

Cheokyung, a handsome looking son of a subordinate official of Pyung-won-kun, Kangwon province, entered Buddhism in an earlier age, and was taught by the Priest Jieung. In the 12th year of Hyeonjong, he left the priest and roamed around Kyonggi province, calling himself a divine monk, deceiving the others saying that he had given up eating grains but he ate rice cakes and meats at night in a cave. Besides, he always carried a small jeweled Buddha's figure, and fascinated the people by saying that it will surely give a spiritual response if one makes a prayer to it. There were many, especially housewives, bewitched by the story, who followed blindly after the monk, giving scandal. Even the women from the imperial court secretly visited to him.

Then, a house-maid named Myohyang from a noble family came to Cheokyung and told him that his handsome countenance resembled the crowned prince Sohyeon, a posthumous grand child of King Injo ; the humor was that he drowned or was still alive. Out of his malicious in-tentions, the monk learned more details about the child of the prince from an inmate of the house of Bokchangkun, of royal lineage, who came to him for prayers. Then, writing down the name and the birth date of the dead child of the prince, Cheokyung in tears submitted it to the Prime Minister Huh, Juk, who then reported it to the King. But soon afterwards, everything Cheokyung had said about Prince Sohyeon's son's birth date, the hand-writing and so on, was proved to be false as a result of the investigation of his boarding room owner and his previous master Priest Jieung. Finally, the monk was condemned to capital punishment by the court along with the house-maid Myohyang and several other court-ladies of Bokchangkun.

The Buddhist Monks that became Commoners

Although King Youngjo was the most sagacious king of all the rulers of the Lee Dynasty, terminating the factionalism in the government and initiating the Renaissance in Chosun, Youngjo adopted throughly suppressive policies toward Buddhism. In the 25th year in office, King Youngjo prohibited monks' entering the capital castle on writing suggestions from the office of Inspection called Saheon-bu. He erased the famous Buddhist sutras of Leungumkyung from the list of the instructional material for the royal family in the 29th year, condeming then as herectical literature. He ordered his secret agent Lee, Kyung Ok to behead the priestess who was then winning the popular respect and fame in Hwanghae province by claiming herself a living Buddha, in the 36th year. He then forbade the enshrinment of ancestral tablets within the temples in the 39th year, and abolished all the temples for the royal families in the provinces in the 44th year. Again in the 46th year, King Youngjo banned the construction of the hermitages around the royal tombs, for there were a number of vagabond monks running around in groups through such temples, causing much social confusion. The King had the prohibition orders so strictly enforced that the authorities unable to prevent to the hermitage construction were heavily punished.

Subsquent to such oppression bt King Youngjo, the Buddhist religion was gradually regarded by the people as a complete heresy, and the social standing of the monks was plunged into one of the eight lowest classes along with the servant, actor, keesaeng(entertainer), bier bearer, shoemaker, butcher, witch and wizard.

The Extortion

The Confucians of the Lee Dynasty generally regarded the Buddhist monks as merely a group of rascals or parasites and attempted to stamp out their religions as a whole, claiming it ideologically unacceptable. However, a closer study of the lives of the monks at the time would lead one to the conclusion that the Buddhist bands were not all vagabonds.

Among them, there were some highly virtuous, sagacious and ascetic monks included. In fact, what the Buddhist monks contributed to the state during the wars and afterward was much more than the conventional and impractical Confucian achievements.

Aside from the sacrifices they made during the wars, the monks were requisitioned as manual laborers for the construction and renovation of numerous mountain fortresses and for other public works such as building up embankments and excavating tunnels ; they were also called for military services at the mountain camps. There was much burdensome exploitation of the monks, not merely by the imperial court but by the local governments. They were put to miscellaneous labor works and, even worse, were forced to pay tribute to the government with bean-mash, sauce, fruits and crops as, well as large taxes. If they disobeyed any of these difficult demands, they were whipped mercilessly.

The exaction of the government became extremely severe during the years of Youngjo, along with his oppressive policies regarding Buddhism. Therefore, most of the temples experienced extreme difficulties even to provide for their own management. In order to curtail the government pressures, the Buddhists from the temples secretly worked through the royal relatives, princess and concubines to get the Naewon-dang(a shrine for the royal family) established. This served only to increase the burden of the monks later ;all of the shrines that had been opened were again closed in the 6th year of Jungjo.

The Background for the Preservation of Buddhism

Altough the imperial courts and the Confucians strove to eradicate completely the Buddhist religion for hundreds of years, the religion survived because of the virtue of the women, especially the women from the royal and noble families. They had been converting steadily to Buddhism even while the successive kings and governments executed harsh religious persecution.

The empresses, conversion to Buddhism from the time of Empress

Shinmi of King Taejo was invariably handed down in succession through
from the queen's mother to the queen, from the queen to the wives of
the royal subjects, and from the subject wives to the court-ladies or even
to such stout Anti-Buddhist kings as Taejong, Myungjong, Hyeonjong
and Youngjo.

Regardless of what extreme measures were planned and executed by
the court to exclude Buddhism, loyal members made secret contacts with
the temples, and set up the shrines to pray to Buddha for the fulfillment
and satisfaction of their wishes and weaknesses. For such reasons, not
even the atrocious ruler, Yeonsankun, could eliminate the two temples
in the palace, though he destroyed the three great temples of Heungchon,
Heungduk and Wonkak in the capital. Even after the palace temples were
removed and the monks' entrace to the capital was banned by Hyeonjong
and Youngjo, the Buddhists made frequent contacts with the houses of
the nobles and with the ladies of the court through their secret routes.

Chapter 10
Buddhism in the Later Part of Chosun

The Coalition of the songwoon and the Pyungyang Branches

The four Buddhist religious denominations formed by the disciples of Priest Hyujung, Songwoon Yujung, Pyunyang Unki, Jungkwan Ilseon and Soyo Taeneung, separately developed into the Seon-jong and Kyo-jong religions afte the death of Hyujung, according to the first edition, the General History of Buddhism in Chosun(Chosun Bulkyo Tongsa), authored by Lee, Neung Hwa. Originally, What priest Hyujung transmitted was not one of the two sectarian religions , but a compound of the two. In any case, the Kyo-jong religion was developed by Hyujung's legitimate disciple, Yujung, and his followers, Eungsang, Ssangun and Sukjae, while the Seon-jong was preserved by Unki and his followers, Uisim, Suljae and Jian. Such a secession was made without any declared manifestation of the Hyujung's religious preference to the disciples, but from the general acknowledgement that Yujung had access to the Kyo-jong and had been praising the secret principles of the Kyo's Hwaom and Buphwa sects, the others simply thought he belonged to the Seon-jong. With the appearance of Priest Yeoncho, the two religious branches of Songwoon Yujung and Pyungyang Unki were reconciled and restored to unity.

Yeoncho, unifier of the two sects, was a man from Jain prefecture, Kyongsang province ;his pen name was Sulsong. After entering the priesthood at the age of 13 at the Sulmun temple, he made an extensive study of Buddhist literature, practicing great religious asceticism. Then, after studying under Yujung's descendants, Sukjae, of the so-called Kyo sect, and under Unki's disciple, Jian of the Seon, Yeoncho discovered that the two different religions were maintaining the same religious philosophies of Hyujung. He insisted on and achieved the combination of the two. Yeoncho's discernment was so refined that whenever he took the platform, many were converted by his sermons. He died in 1750 the 26th year of Youngjo at the age of 75 ; his body was cremated and sarira was preserved at the Tongdo temple and Woonmun Temples.

King Jungjo's Devotion to Buddhism

The Buddhism of the Lee Dynasty that had been so constantly persecuted by the successive kings was saved from total suffocation by occasional Buddhist rulers like the 6th King Sejo, the Empress Munjung, and later the 22nd King Jungjo.

Jungjo's conversion to Buddhism was motivated by the tragic death of his father, crown prince Jangheon. Although King Youngjo, the father of prince Jangheon, had been such a wise ruler, he was in his later years entangled in indiscreet relations with his young concubine, Youngbin, and other court-ladies. The King disinherited his son, Jangheon, made him a commoner, and starved him to death in a locker. The son of Jangheon, Jungjo, succeeded to the throne later. He constantly lamented his father's death, and removed his grave to Suwon where he established the Yongju temple to pray for his decessed father.

The Yongju temple, built in 1789 the 13th year of Jungjo, a year after Jangheon's tomb was removed, was the biggest one in Kyonggi province. For the construction of this temple , the royal subjects, the local magistrates and the bishop-appointed Sailcollected thousands of yang(then the currency unity), of contribution money from the people. Sail, originally from the Boji temple in Mt. Kaji, was not so famous as a priest, but often frequented the imperial court and accompanied the King to various Buddhist rites under the special favor of the ruler.

The year Yongju temple was built, Jungjo also set up in supplication for a son, an 'Appreciation Monument : He used the inscription he had personally selected at the Sukwang temple, a temple formerly founded by Priest Muhak. On learning there would be a spiritual response if one prayed to the 500 disciples of Buddha enshirned in the Sukwang temple Jungjo and his Empress, who had on child until then, prayed ; they bore the first son three years later. The grateful King admired the Graces of Buddha and granted farm-land to the temple beside setting up the monu-ment.

Jungjo also admired such famous priests as Jigong, Nanong and Muhak, promoting posthumously their religious ranks in his 16th year ; he enshrined the images of Hyujung, Yujung and Cheonyoung at the Daeheung temple and Suchong temple in Mt. Myohyang in his 18th year and contributed the expenses for mourning services annually in their honor. In the 20th year, the King produced the reprints of the Buddhist sutras called Eunjoongkyung in iron, stone and wooden blocks, and preserved them at the Yongju temple.

Despite Jungjo's protective polecies which originated from his sympathy toward his dead father, the Buddhist religion weather-beaten by so many years of oppression, could not regain the power to stand on its feet.

The Mixture of the Buddhist Belief

At times, when Buddhism was dominating the religious life of the people during the age of Koryo, many Confucians like Lee, Yu Bo, Lee, Saek and Lee, Je Hyeon insisted on the harmony of the two religions. On the contrary, when Buddhism was excluded and oppressed by the Confucians and the imperial courts during the periods of the Lee Dynasty, the situation changed. During times, there were so many taking conciliatory stands among the Buddhists that the religious purity of Buddhism was gradually lost, and a mixture of varied beliefs was infused into both Confucianism and Buddhism.

This was especially true when Hyujung, the supreme Buddhist bishop in the middle of the Lee Dynasty, advanced harmonization of the three religions of Confucianism, Taoism and Buddhism ; a great change came about in Buddhist preaching ; most of Hyujung's descendants followed his dictums, claiming that the three religions, though they may differ in their external forms, were similar to each other in so far as their objectives were concerned. There was a similar movement in China to combine the religion when Buddhism was under severe persecution during the epoch of the Division between the North and the South. In addition to the triple combination, the Buddhists of the Lee Dynasty acceded to miscellaneous superstitions such as the theory of divination based on topography, the dual principle of the five primary elements and the orthodox Buddhist belief was nowhere to be found.

The famous priest of the Hwaom-jong during the years of Sookjong, Priest Woljo, Doan, not only conceded the teachings of Laotzu-Chengtzu and Confucianism, but also believed in the departed spirits as well as the Ten Kings of Hades. Hoiam Junghye in the era of Youngjo, became famous for his Buddhist virtues and writings ; he was also a renowned authority on the Book of changes. Sangwol Saebong, a famous monk of the same age, bowed his head to the Polar Star every mid-night. There was even a Buddhist like Inak Uiso of the period of Injo who maintained that Sakya was not a historical figure but a mere fantasy, although he sometimes advocated both Buddhist and Confucian theories. Even such a renowned scholar-monk as Choi, Nu and Yu, Il of the years of Jungjo not only attempted to combine the Seon-jong with Confucianism, but also symphathized with all sorts of Superstitions beliefs.

Buddhism, then, at the end of the Lee Dynasty was infused with various outside elements ; its true religious features and beliefs were last.

Priest Huansun

At the end of the Dynasty, however, there appearred some refinod monks. Among them, Baekpa Huansun, though not entirely pure in thought, became famous through the country as an hoir of the religion at the Kuam temple in soonchang. Born in the Mujang Prefecture in the

Cholla province, Huansun became a monk at the Seuneum temple when he was 12, and elabored for scriptural research and a renewal of religious practices at the Yongmunam on Mt. Cho. Later, he studied under the master of the Kyo-jong, Sulpa Sangon at the Youngwon-am on Mt. Chiri. After the death of Sangon, Huansun began preaching sermons at the Kuam temple on Mt. Youngkye and at the Woonmun-am on Mt. Baekyang ; He met with such success that he later became a recognized figure in the resuscitation of Buddhism. He passed away in 1852 the 3rd year of Chul-jong, at the age of 86.

The religious lineage of Huansun was the one inherited from the Pyun-yang branch of Hyujung by Hwansung Jian, Hoam Chaejung, Sulpa San-gun, Toeam and Sulbongil. Huansun also left several literary works in-cluding 'Junghae Kylsamun', in which he gave various conflicting opinions in order to slacken the Confucians' Buddhist expulsion movement rather than to revive the pure orthodox line of Buddhism.

Chapter 11
The Reincarnation of the Buddhist Graces

The Reincarnation

Since Korea concluded a relationship treaty with the countries of Japan, China and America, etc. were facilitated so that aspirations for liberal democracy were heightened and the unreasonable persecution of the Buddhist monks and temples were seen to be impracticable. At this time, Japan was a powerful Buddhist state ; a number of the bonzes came into Chosun to preach to the residents. Surprised over the maltreatments the local monks were receiving, one of the Japanese monks named Sano Jenlei of the Nichirenshyu branch suggested to King Kojong an improvement of religious policy. Thus, in April, 1895 the 32nd year of the King, the prohibition of the monks' entrance to the capital that had been enforced for about three centuries since King Injo was lifted. In 1899, the Wonheung temple was built outside the capital's east gate (now Seoul) as a head temple for all the Buddhist temples in the country, A responsible bishop was appointed and a head temple was designated in each of the 13 provinces to control the other local temples.

Subsequently, following the public opinions that preferred government protection and guidance for the temples and monks instead of its autonomy, the temple management office was set up in the imperial palace in April, 1902, and, in July the same year, a 36—article ordinance was promulgated to put all the Buddhist temples of the country under government control. The law gave stipulations for the purpose of a temple, the mission and priest's rank of the monks, and the organization and management of the provincial head temple. Along with the enforcement of this law, the rank of the monks was divided into the following three classes :

    The First Class : The internal Buddhist rank for the preachers and lec-
        turers practicing asceticism for self—awakening.

    The Second Class : The external Buddhist rank for those who were older
        than 20 years, earned religious fame or protected a temple.

    The Third Class : The Common monk under 20 years o f age.

The three classes of monks were distinguished by their costumes in the following colours:

    The First Class :Pure red with brocades.

    The Second Class :Pure red without brocades.

    The Third Class :Pure purple without brocades

At the same time, the credential or Dochup system for the monks was revived, and various extortions and requisitions of the monks by the local government authorities were forbidden. In the end, the Buddhist temples and monks were finally guaranteed legal protection and control by the government after about 330 years of sufferings. They had been persecuted since the monk selection system and all the sectarian Buddhist religions were abolished in 1565 the 20th year of Myungjong.

The Japanese Annexation and the Law on the Temple

Although liberation was brought to the local Buddhist sphere at the closure of the Lee Dynasty by virtue of the Japanese bonzes, the Japanese government, with its schemes for territorial aggrandizement at the expense of Chosun established their inspector—general in the Dynasty's capital in 1906 forcing King Kojong to abdicate his throne in the light of his envoy's suicide incident in Taegu ; they concluded a new treaty to dissolve the army of Chosun, and put the Korean people under their police rule by overthrowing the 519 years old Lee Dynasty, concluding with an amalgation treaty in 1910. Even though the local Buddhists regained their delights of beating the bell in the center of the capital and establishing

·their central religious headquarters, the Kaksung tample, the loss of their country was bitter.

Following the annexation treaty, the Japanese government adopted an even a more protective policy for Buddhism, although it had often attempted to restrain Christianity and other religions. Thus, in June, 1911, a year after the treaty, the law on the temple was promulgated by the Japanese governor—general in Chosun to control the disposition of the properties belonging to the temple and to secure freedom for the Buddhist mission. The other detailed regulations in connection with the application of the law were also proclaimed, by which a total of 30 head temples were designated throughtout the country, and the regulations relating to the monks and the religious ceremonies had to be enacted by each respective main temple and approved by the governor—general.

The 30 head temples were:

Yongju temple, Suwon—kun, Kyonggi province,

Jeondeung temple, Kanghwa—kun, Kyonggi province,

Baekyang temple, Jangsung—kun, Chollanam province,

Bongsun temple, Yangju—kun, Kyonggi province,

Songkwang temple, Soonchon—kun, Chollanam province,

Bongeung temple, Kwangju—kun, Kyonggi province,

Seonam temple, Soonchon—kun, Chollanam province,

Bupju temple, Boeun—kun, Choongchongbuk province,

Donghwa temple, Dalsung—kun, Kyongsangbuk province,

Makok temple, Kongju—kun, Choongchongnam province,

Eunhae temple, Youngchon—kun, Kyongsangbuk province,

Uibong temple, Jonju—kun, Chollabuk province,

Kowoon temple, Uisung—kun, Kyongsangbuk province,

Bosuk temple, Kumsan—kun, Chollabuk province,

Kumlyong temple, Munkyung—kun, Kyongsang buk province,

Daeheung temple, Haenam—kun, Chollanam province,

Kirim temple, Kyongju—kun, Kyongsangbuk province,

Haein temple, Hyeopchon—kun, Kyongsangnam province,

Bohyeon temple, Nyeongbyon—kun, Pyongahnbuk province,

Tongdo temple, Yangsan—kun, Kyongsangnam province,

Kunbong temple, Kansung—kun, Kangwon province,

Bumeo temple, Dongrae—kun, Kyongsangnam province,

Yujum temple, Kansung—kun, Kangwon province,

Paeyup temple, Shinchon—kun, Hwanghae province,

Woljung temple, Pyongchang—kun, Kangwon province,

Sungbul temple, Hwangju—kun, Hwanghae province,

Sukwang temple, Anbyun—kun, Kangwon province,

Youngmyung temple, Pyongyang, Pyongahnnam province,

Kuiju temple, Hamheyung—kun, Hamkyongnam province,

Bupheung temple, Pyongwon—kun, Pyongahnnam province,

These more than doubled the 13 head temples de signated in 1899. It was not known how the Japanese government increased the number to 30 temples, which became 31, with the promotion of the Hwaom temple in Koorye in 1918. They were empowered to control some 1,300 other smaller temples scattered throughout the country, beside establishing various laws and regulations for their own jurisdiction.

In addition, the head temple, under the approval of the governor—general, also provided the standards pertaining to the ranks of the monks and the courses of the Buddhist education. Under this system, a commoner could become a monk after completing 4 years of regular courses, and continuing the two year course in the Buddhist acolyte department to learn the basics of Buddhism, followed by three, four, and again three years of higher. educational courses to complete the 16 years of learning to become a monk. And only those who completed at least 13 years of education were qualified to apply for the annual examinations conducted by the head temple for the religious rank of Daeseon and from this one could be promoted to either Joongduk, Daeduk, or Seonsa, Daeseonsa and Daekyosa.

By the application of the laws relating to the temple, many advantages certainly were brought to the over-all improvement of Buddhism in Korea.

But, while maintaining a pro-Buddhist policy on the one hand, the Japanese government on the other hand exploited the religion as a tool for their colonial administration. They established a tablet with an inscription saying, 'Denno Heika Seizyu Banzai'(meaning Long Live the Emperor Denno of Japan) in front of the image of Buddha and urged daily prayers before the tablet, and forced Buddhist services for every festival day of Japan, thus depriving the local monks of their inner freedom. The other disadvantages after the enforcement of the law were that the traditional practices, whereby the senior members of a temple made public discussion and decided the important affairs relating to their sanctum, were replaced by one-man arbitration of the chief priest of a temple, creating a lot of discord among the chief and other monks. Besides, the chief priest was chosen by a popular election in which there were all kinds of evil practices. The monks belonging to the temple which was big enough to be a head temple were treated as one of the lower class and they complained about this status. Taking advantage of these situations, various Buddhist sects of Japan manuevered behind the scene to acquire such temples into their domains. As a result, some of the low-level temples in Korea even assumed their dual relations with a certain Buddhist sect in Japan and another one in the Korea.

The Approval of the Matrimony System for the Monks

Along with the enforcement of the laws governing the local temple, the Japanese Buddhist system Sanctioning the matrimonial life for the monks was also put into effect at this time, sowing the seeds for various religious entanglements in the Buddhist world in Korea which continue today.

Originally, the true character of a monk was in leading a pure life of sobriety, observing the Buddhist commandments in purity, and in refraigning from all the worldly passions and desires. Therefore, once a man becomes a monk, it was unthinkable to eat meat or to lead a sensual life. No famous priests or those called Daeduks could lead such a life, and when worldly monks did not observe Buddhist commandments, they were expelled from the temple. When the religious austerity of the monk was somewhat relaxed in the middle of Koryo, there were some common Buddhist priests who secretly lived a family life. In the last part of the Lee Dynasty, the local monks experienced a great change because of the Japanese Buddhists' philosophy of living. The number of the married monks thus increased in the country.

In 1910, Han, Yong Woon, a new figure of the Buddhist world and one of the 33 draftees of the famous Declaration of Independence from Japan, suggested to legalize matrimony for the monks. This, of course, arouse quite a shock to the world. Han, who was famous for his works 'Thy Silence', theorized that it was not only profitable for the development of the religious power, but also it was not against the will of Buddha to allow the monks to live family lives, and to work their livelihood and property. Neither the Korean government nor the Japanese authorities took any action towards implementing this suggestion at the time. But in October, 1926, the governor-general, overcame by the rising tide of new ideas, finally ordered the head temple to legalize family life for the monks. This was an epochmaking event in the Buddhist History of Korea. About ten years after the reenactment of the law, the majority of the chief priests of the head temples, except perhaps one or two, lived with their wives and families. However, there were some of the conservative bhiku-seung (unmarried) group, who opposed the streams of new thought and acted against the Japanese government authorities, observing the Buddhist doctrines through asceticism or building their own monasteries. At the end of the Japanese occupation, various commotions erupted between the married and unmarried groups of the monks such as filing lawsuits against one another, colliding into tragic events even at the temples, initiating hunger strikes, and committing suicides, President Ree, Seung Man issued a statement in May and in November, 1954, ordering the purification of the Buddhist religion.

Chapter 12
Buddhism under the Japanese Rule

The Central Office for Religious Affairs

Because of the need for a certain central organization to administer various religious affairs of the 30 head temples, the association office was established at the Kakhwang temple in Seoul in February, 1915, as a stan-ding executive body with one chairman, and an annual regular meeting was conducted to discuss the measures for the promotion of Buddhism with the representative from each head temple participating. Along with this, the association regulations pertaining to the missionary district, the method and expenses of mission by each respective head temple, and the management of the central and local Buddhist schools were set up.

Consequently, the central Buddhist school was established in Seoul as a high school, and the local institutes were founded in the provinces by the following temples as middle schools:

Kumlyong temple Local Institute   Eunhae temple Local Institute
Koeun temple Local Institute   Tongdo temple Local Institute
Bumeo temple Local Institute   Haein temple Local Institute
Baekyang temple Local Institute   Daeheung temple Local Institute
Songkwang temple Local Institute   Seonam temple Local Institute

The Buddhist education was enhanced to a great degree by the zeal to begin the normal school by he head temples in addition to the above institutions. Prior to the foundation of the association, there was another Association for Buddhist Promotion organized by the 30 chief priests including Lee, Hoe Kwang, Suh, Jin Ha, Kim, Ku Ha, together with 50 other Buddhists including Lee, Neung Hwa, Kim, Young Jin, Kim, Hong Jo, Park, Du Young, Shin, Il Kyun, etc. at the Kakhwang temple in September, 1914. This Association became an organ for the Buddhist missions for the next five years with the publication of a monthly periodical.

In December, 1922, the association was reorganized as the Central Office for the Religious Affairs of Buddhism in Chosun, incorporated, with a total of 621,000 won (equivalent to some1,850 million won today) collected from the temples, from the head to the lower ones, throughout the country. The reorganization was conducted to give the central organ more authority for decisive administration of the Buddhist missionary and educational policies. The Central Office then consisted of a 7-member board of directors and the standing committee of councilors. Concurrently, various Buddhist movements for the younger generations were undertaken, the Bosung Institute(now Bosung High School) was taken over, and a professional Buddhist college was established by the Office to develop the leaders of the religious platform.

Afterwards, 157 Buddhist representatives from the entire country congregated in Seoul in January, 1928. Then, the new religious constitution was promulgated, and the resolution was adopted to renounce Sakyamuni as the chief principle of the religion, to regard Priest Bowoo as the founder of Buddhism in Chosun both by the Seon-jong and Kyo-jong, and to establish a legislative assembly called Jonghoe to handle various important matters including finances, formality, and the formulation of regulations.

The Confusion and Degradation of the Platforms

With the Japanese annexation and, especially, following the operation of the laws regarding the temple, the local Buddhist sphere regained systematic orders to achieve many outstanding results in the religious mission, but, at the same time, invited just as much confusion and degradation because of alien intervention.

Confusion was further caused by disruption, local factionalism, friction between the head temples and the subordinate ones, and the power struggles at the religious executive center. Such confusions not only hampered the missionary works to a great extent, but also created slander, ensnaring, open bribery, and even bloody melees among the monks of various temples. All who refrained from the struggle, would not only be deprived of their privileges as monks, but would be expelled from the temple.

The fundamental reasons for all these struggles was in the system of appointing the chief priest as well as in permitting a matrimonial life for the monks. For the chief priest, once he was appointed by the governor-general, possessed the exclusive power in his temple to dispose of the properties and the other subordinate monks at his own discretion. Therefore, the rivalry between the ones who held such powerful positions and those who sought to take it developed by whatever ways and means they had at their command.

The main purpose of the appointment system, however, was to stabilize the temples by placing highly virtuous and popular monks in the ruling position. But regardless of how virtuous and famous one might be, once he assumed the power, he became attached to it more than to a just rule and would attempt to prolong his tenure at all costs, thereby, degrading his potential piety. Once he was rejected and lost his power, he had to leave the temple, no matter how long he had served and ruled. However, capable the priest might be, it was often the case that he could be entrapped by some vicious schemes of his fellow monks and be deposed.

Evil practices were made even worse by matrimony for the monks had to support their families. In most cases, the expenses were covered by and came from the temple. For an unmarried single monk, every Buddhist shrine in the country was a place for his meditation and relief from the world. But for the married ones, family problem took a heavier proportion of their time from their religious practices ; they were also obliged to put their hands on properties belonging to the temple and to loosen their religious austerities.

As a result of the 36 years of Japanese rule, the Buddhist followers in the country doubled in number, but the Buddhist platforms and organizations were constantly invalued in disputes and complications and the temples became the places for the wanderers' merriment and holidays.

The Construction of the Central Head Temple

Although the central administrative power of Buddhism was solidified by the establishment of the new religious constitution, the current thoughts of the time under the fascist influence of Japan, Germany and Italy made it inevitable for a construction of powerful regimentation as the core of controlling the 31 local head temples. Thus, in March, 1937, the Construction for the Central Head Temple began at the site of the former Central Office by the resolution passed from the general meeting of the chief priests. Lee, Jung Wook was selected as a representative priest responsible for the constructional project, Lim, Suk Jin and Cha, Sang Myung as members of the standing committee, eleven other Buddhists as non-committee members, and two others as the drafters of the temple charters.

Designed by the experienced Japanese architecture in the old Korean constructions Hayasaki Jihachi, carpentered by Choi, Won Suk, painted by Lim, Bae Kun and the mural patintings done by Kim, Il Sup and two others, the gigantic wooden building, the pillar of which ranged, in fact, to some 21 feet, was completed in October 1938 on the ground of 229 pyungs(763㎡), The total number of manpower mobilized for the construction projects reached more than 72,600, and a sum of 194,200 won was expended, of which 100,000 won was collected from the local head temples and the remaining was covered by special donations from the Buddhist followers and by other income sources. The Buddha's statue enshrined in this grand temple was the one removed from the Doap temple in Youngam-kun.

The Japanese Implementation as a Tool

The Buddhism, though it received a special protection from the Japanese

government since the Japanese annexation, later became a complete tool
for the implementation of the colonial policies by Japan. The setting up
of the monument in honor of the Japanese emperor at the Buddhist shrine
and having the monks conduct the prayers, as mentioned in the preceding
pages, were one example. Also over a thousand patriotic youth were being
severely punished at the prison as a result of their 6,10 Independence
Movement in 1926, and another patriot, La, Suk Ju, killed himself on the
street after he had thrown bombs into the Japanese Industrial Bank and
another of its companies. While these last two events were talking place
the Buddhists, Central Office issued the message to its nation-wide branches to hold three-day special prayer meetings for the sake of the Japanese
emperor. When the Japanese government enforced the volunteer system
to execute their ambitions of invading the Asia mainland, the Woljung
temple of Mt. Odae, where Lee, Jong Wook was the chief priest, selected
15 monks as volunteers. In January, 1942, the Central Head Temple ordered
its subordinate temples throughout the country to submit all iron-material
including the Buddhist bells with the exception of those designated as
national treasures. Afterwards, numerous Buddhist rites praying for the
surrender of the enemies were forced to be held at the temples under
various pretexts and with various means. The Japanese authorities said
that the monks 'should learn the true spirits of the people of the Emperor
like Sakya attained the awakening under the tree of Boddhisattva after
six years of hardships.'

Some of the Buddhist leaders in possession of the national spirits attempted to protect the religious platforms by not complying with such
orders and by pursuing purely their religious practices, but they were
unable to rise against the pressures of the imperial government of Japan
then engaged in war. In the end, along with the proclamation of the new
laws of the Chokye-jong in June, 1943, the Buddhist religion became firmly
framed as an instrument for Japanese imperialism. At this time, the Japanese persecution against the other religions accellerated to such an extent
that many of the Christian and Chondokyo church leaders were imprisoned,

and the Holyness Churches and the Seventh Day Advenlist Churches were closed. Buddhism became the catspaw of the Japanese government, with an increasing number of Buddhist converts that soared up from the total of 170,000 in 1935 to 250,000 in 1943.

The following illustrations show the yearly increase of the Buddhists since the first promulgation of the law regarding the temples.

The Table on the Yearly Statistic of the Buddhist Followers

The Year	Total Number
1920	149,714
1923	170,545
1926	170,354
1929	169,151
1932	168,525
1935	167,891
1938	194,876
1941	196,135
1942	244,795
1943	250,075

The Status of the Buddhist at the Respective Head Temple

(as of December, 1941)

Name of Temple	Location	No of Subtemples	Monks	Followers
Taego-temple	Susong-dong, Seoul	1	13	
Bongeun-temple	Kwangju-kun, Kyonggi	74	487	15,917
Yongju-temple	Suwon-kun, Kyonggi	36	111	1,400
Bongsun-temple	Yangju-kun, Kyonggi	27	119	1,760
Jeondeung-temple	Kanghwa-kun, Kyonggi	34	161	430
Bupju-temple	Boeun-kun, Choongbuk	35	149	4,396
Makok-temple	Kongju-kun, Choongnam	105	851	9,303
Uibong-temple	Wanju-kun, Chonbuk	55	103	9,106
Bosuk-temple	Kumsan-kun, Chonbuk	33	54	1,951
Daeheung-temple	Haenam-kun, Chonnam	33	186	6,002
Baekyang-temple	Jansung-kun, Chonnam	48	221	3,613
Songkwang-temple	Sunchon-kun, Chonnam	31	283	3,603

Name of Temple	Location	No of Subtemples	Monks	Followers
Seonam-temple	Soonchon-cun Chonndn	22	142	1,294
Hwaom-temple	Kurye-kun, Chonnam	16	115	374
Donghwa-temple	Dalsung-kun, Kyongbuk	46	182	11,863
Eunhae-temple	Youngchon-kun, Kyongbuk	28	161	6,789
Koeun-temple	Uisung-kun Kyongbuk	30	87	5,199
Kumlyong-temple	Munkyung-kun, Kyongbuk	43	250	8,195
Kirim-temple	Kyungju-kun, Kyongbuk	15	61	2,917
Haein-temple	Hyupchon-kun, Kyungnam	81	617	13,563
Tongdo-temple	Yangsan-kun, Kyongndm	84	671	24,840
Bumeo-temple	Dongrae-kun, Kyongndm	43	173	29,169
Paeup-temple	Shinchon-kun, Hwanghae	24	37	690
Sungbul-temple	Hwangju-kun Hwanghde	22	15	558
Youngmyung-temple	Pyungyang-bu, Pyongnam	11	23	3,405
Bupheung-temple	Pyungwon-kun, Pyongnam	30	16	362
Bohyeon-temple	Nyungbyun-kun, Pyongbuk	89	131	4,009
Gunbong-temple	Kosung-kun, Kangwon	25	195	2,462
Yujum-temple	Kosung-kun, Kongwon	59	105	800
Woljung-temple	Pyungchang-kun, Kongwon	39	96	840
Sukwang-temple	Anbyun-kun, Hamnam	33	254	5,607
Kuiju-temple	Hamju-kun, Hamndm	74	178	15,718
GRAND TOTAL		1,326	6,246	196,135

Chapter 13
The Propagation of the Japanese Buddhism

The Transmission of the Japanese Buddhism

Although statistics are not very accurate, the introduction of Japanese Buddhism into Korea was attributed a Japanese priest named Himochi Jonin, the head disciple of the Nichiren-shyu's founder Nichiren Jonin, during the age of Koryo Dynasty about 700 years ago. Later, during the years of the Toyotomi War, a monk named Okumura Joshin from the Otani sect of the Shin-shyu(meaning the orthodox Buddhism) came to Korea with the Japanese army in 1587 the 20th year of King Sunjo, and assumed the religious services for the army by building up the Koduk temple in Pusan. A number of other Japanese bonzes accompanied their troops into the country during this period, but their missonary activities were no more than those of army chaplains.

However, with the conclusion of the Otani sect of the Shin-shyu in Japan dispatched Okumura Yenshin, scion of Okumura Joshin, to Pusan for the first propagation of Japanese Buddhism in Korea by establishing its sectarian head temple there. A branch shrine of this temple was set up in Wonsan, Hamkyung province, by Nagadani Tokusen in 1880, another one in Inchon in 1884 and still another one in Seoul in 1890 by Innami Shan-shou. Then, the missionary temples of this sect gradually increased in many of the principle cities.

About four years after the Otani branch, another Buddhist denomination of Japan called Nichiren-shyu began its propagation in Korea by sending

Wadanable Nichiwoong to Pusan ; he set up the first of its temples, Myokakuji temple Then, followed Asahi Hinawa, who established the Chyomyoji temple in Wonsan, Myokakuji temkple in Inchon, and Hokuk temple in Seoul. But the missionary activities of this religion were limited mainly to serving Japanese residents in Korea.

The Joto-shyu, another Buddhist sect of Japan, initiated its first mission in Korea in 1893 by dispatching Yanoue Unkai to Seoul as its first missionary. A number of other monks of the sect also came in, subsequently, to engage in preaching.

When the Sino-Japanese war was over with the victory of Japan, and

The Status of the Followers of the Japanese Buddhism

Nume of Sect	Number of Missions	Number of Temples	Number of Missionaries	Number of Followers
Hongganji of Honpa Branch	43	14	81	54,012
Hongganji of Otami Branch	42	2	56	29,907
Sangen Branch of Shih-shyu	3		4	1,699
Bukkoji Branch of Shin-shyu	3		4	1,311
Joto-Shyu of Shin-shyu	34	13	47	17,941
Singon-shyu	28	6	34	11,870
New Singon-shyu	17	3	12	5,301
Sodo-shyu	26	18	51	6,633
Rinsai-shyu	6		6	2,570
Koheki-shyu	1		1	300
Nichiren-shyu	21	6	23	3,019
Hoke-shyu			1	830
Hoke-shyu of Honmon	3		4	1,670
GRAND TOTAL	227	62	324	137,063

the Japanese position in Chosun became firmly solidified, the number of the Japanese residents in Korea increased conspicuously. Along with this, various Buddhist sects of Japan made headway into the country, establishing many temples in various places. Among them, the Hongganji temple of the Honpa branch was most successful ; the other influential sects were in order of the Hongganji temple of the Otani branch, Joto-shyu, Singon-shyu, etc,. The status of the Japanese Buddhist sects in Korea since 1920 is as follows :

The Mission for the Koreans

Despite the fact that Japanese Buddhism had been introduced into Korea earlier than Protestantism, it was not successful as far as its missionary activities for the Korean people were concerned. For the majority of the Japanese bonzes engaged themselves in religious works exclusively for the small number of Japanese residents in Korea, neglecting the broader Buddhism. Most of the Japanese Buddhist missionaries were swayed by their colonialistic consciousness and biased narrow-mindedness. Consequently, they left almost nothing of religious value when the Japanese made their retreat from the Korean peninsula at the end of World War II.

Some Japanese Buddhists who established the Chosun Buddhist Association in 1920 in Tokyo, attempted to extend the religion to the Koreans by holding lectures and seminar meetings, but were not successful. The head temple Hongganji of the Jodo-shyu set up a few temples for the local people, but, except for the Daesung Church and the Church for the Koreans in Seoul, they did not have many followers.

The only successful result the Japanese Buddhist achieved was the establishment of the Kaesung Commercial School in 1901 by the Joto-shyu. The social services were also conducted by the Joto-shyu with the establishment of the Hwakwang Kyowon in 1920 and the Hongganiji temple of otami Branch, set up the Hyangsang primary school in 1921. The other Buddhist sects of Japan formed the associated social service organization in Seoul, Inchon, Daejon, Kwangju, Pyungyang and Lanam, but did not attain good records.

As can be seen from the following chart, the number of Korean followers of the Japanese Buddhist sects has decreased per annum since 1919.

The Status of the Korean Followers of the Japanese Buddism

Name of Sect	1919	1920	1922	1925	1928	1932
Otami Br. of Shin-shyu	818	1,542	1,669	7,722	596	596
Nichiren-shyu	93	97	127	167	251	124
Hongganji of Shin-shyu	5,942	2,269	2,508	3,157	1,616	2,616
Joto-shyu	9,628	5,903	11,600	3,157	3,884	769
Others	1,515	1,243	1,953	1,547	1,096	3,496
TOTAL	17,996	11,054	17,857	15,747	7,443	7,601

The Development of Japanese Buddhism

Although the Japanese mission among the Korean people had not been so successful, the Japanese suppression in Korea following the end of the Sino-Japanese War became ever more stringent ; many converted to their religion as a means of self-protection, and an increasing number of the people sought residence in Japan. Thus, Japanese Buddhism expanded in proportion.

In 1920, there were eight denominational and 16 sub-denominational religions in Japanese Buddhism with a total of 130,000 followers, but at the end of 1940 they were increased to nine religions and 29 branches with a total of 136 temples and 340, 000 followers. By the enforcement for the religious law in Japan in 1941, the number of the sectarian branches was consolidated in nine denominations and their 17 branches.

Even after this consolidation, the Hongganiji Branch of the Shin-shyu was most influential ; the next powerful ones were the Otani Branch of the Shin-shyu and the Singon-shyu, while the others had meager religious powers with not more than a thousand follwers.

With the outbreak of the Sino-Japanese War in 1937, the Japanese government enforced the policy of exterminating the Korean people, severely suppressing any religions other than Japanese Shintoism and Buddhism. Some of the Koreans, there fore, began to attend the Buddhist shrines in order to demonstrate their loyalty to Japan. As the power of Japan expanded, the Korean followers of Japanese Buddhism increased to some 30,000 at the end of 1941. The status of Japanese Buddhists by the time the Pacific War broke out was asfollows :

The Status of the Japanese Buddhists

Name of Sect	Number of Temple	Number of Missions	Number of Mission	Number of Followers	Number of Koreans
Shin-shyu	43	247	209	186,386	10,998
Nichiren-shyu	19	58	76	27,870	2,185
Joto-shyu	16	46	159	1,327	1,682
Singon-shyu	27	194	175	47,167	5,394
Sodo-shyu	29	13	115	50,855	6,017
Rinsai-shyu	4	25	17	17,166	1,365
Koheki-shyu	1	1	4	890	80
Chontae-jong	1	20	18	5,845	108
Hwaom-jong		5	3	629	
TOTAL	140	719	776	338,135	27,829

Remarks : The number of the Korean followers was based on a statistic conducted in December, 1941. Since then, the separate statistic for the Koreans have not been made.

Part Ⅴ
Christianity(1)

Chapter 1
The Rise of Christianity

Jesus Christ

Christianity, established by Jesus Christ, was the main stream of European Civilization for almost two thousand years. It is devoted to saving human lives. Jesus Christ was born at a humble inn manger at a place called Bethlehem, Judea, some nineteen hundred and ninety years ago. Jesus was the son of David, the scion of Abraham, through Joseph, his foster father, a carpenter, and a young virgin, Mary. According to the Bible, Jesus was conceived to Mary by the Holy Spirit. Jesus, the Savior, was already promised to be born in the Old Testament, and three wise men came to worship Him from the East when He was born. They were led by a strange star in the Heaven. They brought gifts of gold, frankincense, and myrth for the baby Jesus. When Herod, the King of Judea, heard that a New King was born at Bethlehem, he was frightened and sent executioners to search for the child to kill Him. But Joseph took Mary and baby Jesus, and fled to Egypt and remained the retill the death of Herod.

Judea was in hardship both politically and religiously when the Jesus was born ; she was a territory of the Roman Empire, and Jerusalem was ruled by Pontius Pilate, the governor. The Roman Government had very strict laws for the Jews, while the tax collectors' and Saducean's exploitation was extreme. The Old Testament, the Bible tells us, was already formed and showed no more than external forms of marship of God. The

Pharisees, the backborn members of Jews, were very fanatic believers in Yahweh but they were bound by so many formal rules and rituals that their religious life had no spirit in it. Pontius Pilate had judicial power over Judea but he was influenced by the Saducean priests. The Saduceans, however, were not interested in belief but absorbed with maintaining political authority and accumulating property. Moreover, the Pharisees and Saduceans believed that they were the only people chosen by God, and they disregarded the Papans. The Jews were oppressed by political power and pharasaical religion ; thus most of them were expecting the Messiah who was promised in the Old Testament who would come to save them from their troubles. Jesus, the true messiah, was born and emphasized that the formal religion must be reformed, and the people must be saved from the corrupt society. Jesus denied the existing earthly kingdom, and proclaimed the coming of the Kingdom of God.

When Jesus was thirty years of age, John the Baptist went into the regions around the Jordan River, preaching, "Repent, the Kingdom of God is at hand." He also foretold the Messiah saying, "After he comes me who is mightier than I and will give new hope to the people," In those days Jesus cme to Nazareth of Galilee and was baptized by John, the Baptizer, in the Jordan. And when He came up out of water a voice came from heaven, "You are my beloved Son, with you I am well pleased."

Then Jesus was driven by the Holy Spirit out into the wilderness for forty days. He fasted 40 days in the wilderness and was tempted by Satan. After the sufferings and temptations in the wilderness, Jesus came into the villages and towns of Galilee to preach the Gospel. The people were surprised by his great teachings because his teachings were defferent from the priests. Simon and Andrew, the brother of Simon, became the first disciples, and then James and John his brother followed Him. Jesus taught the real meaning of the Law and Way of salvation and the kingdom of heaven. Great multitudes followed Him since He worked numerous miracles, and healed many weak and sick people. Of course his new idea of God was not so a new. It was the same as Judaism. But He showed a God of Love and of Justice. He showed a God of justice and as God of every race, a universal God. He denied the misconception the Jews held that God was intolerant of law and justice. He stressed that God is universal and eternal, and explained the nature of God is love. He Himself lived a life of love and service and all the people who followed Him were comforted by Him and repented of their sins. The Jews thought that He was the Messiah whom they were waiting for, and wanted to make Him their King. As Jesus was becoming famous, the Pharisees, the leader of Judaism, detested Him. They were jealous because the Gospel Jesus preached was completely different from theirs, and Jesus often sat with the publicans who were not allowed to take part in religious ceremonies. He warned the pharisees not to be hypocrites but to lead honest and sincere lives.

The relationship between Jesus and the Pharisees worsened so that he left central regin of Palestine for the northern part of Galilee, east of the Jordan, and preached to the pagans, and later He returned to Jerusalem for the Passover. At this time, Jesus's popularity was great ; many of the people crowd spread their garments on the road, and others cut branches from palm spread them on the road and shouted "Hosanna ! Hosanna in the highest !"

On the other hand, the chief priests and pharisees were searching for a chance to kill Jesus. Jesus foretold his death to His disciples and promised that they will again be united in the future. Then 3 days before he died, He gathered his disciples and had the Last Supper. He took some bread and wine symbolic of His body, blood, and a new promise, and gave them to his disciples after he had given thanks. After the Last Supper, he prayed in the garden of Gethsemane, full of sorrow. Judas Iscariot, one of Jesus' twelve disciples, was plotting to sell his master for thirty pieces of silver to the chief priests and the elders. The next day, Judas went to Gethsemane with a group of men from the high priests and elders, and Jesus was easily caught there. Jesus was taken to Caiaphas the high priest, and was insulted and abused. He was sentenced to be crucified by the high priests. Thus

Jesus was taken to Pilate, the governor, and was crucified at a place called Golgotha(which means the place of a skull).

Jesus's disciples were sure that Jesus was the awaited Messiah, and would rule an earthly Kingdom as Son of God. Contrary from expectations, He was crucified and the disciples were so discouraged that they all left Him, and fled. Only several women were there beneath the Cross, weeping with sorrow. But Jesus rose form the dead after He was buried which was promised in the Scripture. He revealed himself to Mary Magdalene and Peter after His resurrection, and stayed for forth days on the earth, and traveled through Galilee and Jerusalem. He also revealed Himself to his eleven disciples and gave the Great Commision, Saying······ "Go and make disciples of all nations, baptizing them in the name of the Father and the Son and of the Holy Spirit, theaching them to observe all that I have commanded you ; I am with you always, to the end of the age." And then He ascended into Heaven.

Establishment of the Church

Jesus' disciples were fully discouraged when Jesus was crucified by the Pharisees and Saducees ; but their sorrrow was turned into joy and hope when Jesus rose from the dead ; and all his disciples, including Peter, were full of new belief and hope, and zeal to proclaim the Gospel. Especially, Peter, John, and James wanted the their fellow disciples to band together and form the Church of that they could witness to the Resurrection of Jesus Christ and proclaim of salvation through Jesus Christ. There were multitudes of Jews, from every direction gathered in Jerusalem to celebrate Pentecost 50 days after Jesus was risen. The disciples were all gathered in one place and with one accord devoted themselves to praying. And suddenly they were all filled with the Holy Spirit and began to speak in other tongues, as the Spirit gave them utterance. Some people mocking them said, "They had too much new wine." But Peter, rose with the other disciples and said, "Let all the house of Israel therefore know that God has made him both Lord and Christ, this Jesus whom you crucified. Repent, and be baptized every one of you in the name of Jesus Christ." Many received Peter's word and were baptized, and there were added in a day about three thousand believers. The new followers were together and had all things in common, and they sold their possessions and goods and distributed them to the poor and no one was in need.

There were many new followers every day, and the Jewish authorities were worried and arrested some of the disciples and whipped them. Deacon Stephen, the first martyr, was cast out of the city and stoned to death. And on that day the Jewish authorities began a great persecution against the followers in Jerusalem ; and they all scattered throughout the regions of Judea and Samaria and other places. Now those who were scattered went about preaching the Gospel wherever they went and the Gospel was spread throughout the country. Governor Pilate, unlike Jewish aut-horities, did not want to meddle with the new religion because the new religion did not threaten the Great Roman Empire.

Since then, St. Paul, who in the beginning was a great persecutor against the Christian followers, was converted to Christianity and devoted himself to proclaiming the Gospel, and he established Churches in Samaria, Cyprus, Phoenicia, Antioch and Syria ; and many pagans were converted. Antioch was the commercial center between the East and the West, and it was in Antioch in 47 A.D. where Jesus' followers were first called "Christians".

Christianity which was spread to the foreigners through St. Peter and Paul, was also spread to Greece and Rome. The church work proceeded orderly under the Elder system, and some of Christian Doctrines were already formed when Emperor Nero began his persecution of the Chris-tians.

Formation of Christian Doctrine

At the very beginning, the Christian Church did not want to form Doctrine since the Gospel was spread through the disciples who were directly taught by Jesus Christ. But day after day the Gospel was spread to various places and more Churches were established, and had to confront numerous heresies. Therefore, it was necessary for the Christian Church to have concrete Doctrines. For this purpose, Paul and John had strived to form basic Christian Doctrine, and the Synoptic Gospels, the Gospel of John, the Acts of the Apostles, and other Epistles were written in the end of the first Century. After then the christian Doctrine was written by the Christian scholars and Church leaders. Most of the Doctrine were formed by the men who followed Jesus Christ. They urged forming Orthodox doctrines to prevent heresy.

In 325 A.D., the doctrines of the creed, Divinity of Christ, Christology, and Humanity of Christ were formed at the Council of Nicaea. At the Council, the Athanasian Creed difined, the orthodox interpretation of Trinity, saying that the Son is equal to the Father in all ways. But Arianism rejected this, saying that Christ is not equal to the Father in the Divinity; rather, as Son, He was created by the Father. In 381 A. D., some of doctrines we have today were amended and ratified.

God   Christians believe in God and that a mancan be saved through Jesus Christ. God in Christianity is a monotheistic and absolute God. Deuteronomy says, "The Lord our God is one Lord", as Paul said"······for us there is one God, the Father, from whom are all things······." God is an infinite spiritual being, and rules the universe. God is Absolute. And He is in all things and transcended beyond all things, He works in man as a transcendent being. God is also the creator of all things. In the beginning, He created all things ; He does not depend upon the world or human but creates things from nothing with His spiritual power, and is absolutely almighty in the universe. This God is absolutely holy and righteous. He forgives sins, and is pleased with righteousness. He gave his only Son to the World to atone for man's sins and let Him be crucified so that man could be saved from hell. Since Jesus was recognized as the Christ, the Son of God who died to atone for the sins of mankind, acceptance of this belief guaranteed life after death for all.

The Trinity   Christianity believed God as a Trinity, Father, Son and Holy Spirit. The Father is God ; the Son is Jesus Christ, the Ward made flesh ; the Spirit of God, the Love of the Father and the Son for all men. According to the Systimatic Theology of J.C. Crane, "Only God is trinity, equal substance, almighty, and eternity which means God of Father, God of Son, and God of Spirit."

Sin   Christianity says that human life began with sin, being closely related to the first fall of Adam and Eve.

The Westminster Confession says, "Every sin, both original and actual being a Transgression of the righteous law of God, and contrary thereunto, doth, in its own nature, brings guilt upon the sinner, whereby he is bound over to the wrath of God, and curse of the law, and so made, subject to death, with all miseries spiritual, temporal and eternal." (the Westminster Confession for today by George S. Hendry P. 84) Because of this original sin, the communication between God and men was interrupted, and both the flesh and spirit of mankind were corrupted, and man had to confront death ; at the same time corrupted human nature was transmitted to all of Adam and Eve's descendants.

In addition to original sin, there was more proof of evil as sins were multiplied because of man's free will. But God loves man so much and He is willing to save mankind because He is merciful and righteous. Because man needed help to be saved from sin, God sent Jesus to the world and let Him to be crucified to atone for mankind's sins. Therefore, man can not be saved without Jesus who is the Lord of Atonement. The Church is the place where Jesus fulfills the work of Atonement ; salvation is fulfilled through the Church. The theory of Oiginal Sin and the doctrines of Church were deiven from St. Augustine who was a great philosopher and theologian in the period of the Church Fathers.

Dualism   Besides the theory of Original Sin dualism is another thing to notice. The theory of Original Sin is one of the serious theories in Christianity as has already been mentioned ; original sin caused the corruption of mankind. Because man consists of Spirit and flesh, and the Spirit and flesh must be harmonized. The flesh is frequently an obstacle to the good and noble work of Spirit. Sin is caused by weakness of this flesh, and no man can escape from the impure world unless he overcomes the inordinate unclean desires of the flesh. Therefore, the fundamental view of Christianity is that every life which is based solely on fleshly desires must be rejected. Asceticism in Christianity helps man to lead an ascetic life. It is reasonable to live a pure life for happiness in the future.

Love　　Love is one of the most characteristic doctrines in Christianity, and Christianity is counted as a Religion of love. The work done by Jesus Christ on earth was a work of philanthoropy, and his preachings were verses of love. By emphasizing that mankind must love one another, his whole life was a revelation of God's Love. God so loved the world that He gave Jesus as an offering to atone for mankind's lack of love ; Jesus proved God's mercy, grace, and pity throughout his short life. He also showed that God loves mankind just as a father loves his son. The relationship between God and mankind is the same as father and son. Men must love all men as brothers before God as the Son of man loved God and His people. The old Testament says, "You shall love your neighbor and hate your enemy," but Jesus taught us, "Love your enemies and pray for those who persecute you. You shall love your neighbor as yourself." He not only taught us to love our neighbor ; He Himself practiced it. This Love is the foundation of Christian Social morality. The very reason for Christianity to dominate western civilization for many centuries politically and morally was "Love". It is very sure that Christianity would not be able to create such civilization if it simply emphasized obeying God and loving self ; it would then have become extinct.

Repentance　　In Christianity, salvation means deliverance from sin through Jesus Christ with the grace of God and Holy Spirit, thus coming to peace and reconciliation with God. A man, however, needs to repent his sin before he is redeemed. The repentance means confessing oneself to God and asking forgiveness ; he is thus born again and enters into a new life. Jesus wished a man to repent his sin ; He said, "There will be more joy in heaven over one sinner who repents than over ninety-nine righteous persons who need no repentance." Jesus denied scholars and wisemen in favor of the poor and emphasized the purification of man saying, "Unless you turn and become like children, you will never enter the kingdom of heaven."

Ten Commandments   There are Ten Commandments in Christianity which Moses, a great Old Testament prophet, received from God when he had ascended to Mountain of Sinai :

1. Thou shalt have no other gods before me.
2. Thou shalt not make unto thee any graven image, or any likeness of anything that is in heaven above,······thou shalt not bow thyself to them, nor serve them.
3. Thou shalt not take the Name of the Lord thy God in vain.
4. Remember the Sabbath day, to keep it holy.
5. Honor thy father and thy mother.
6. Thou shalt not kill.
7. Thou shalt not commit adultery.
8. Thou shalt not steal.
9. Thou shalt no bear false witness against thy neighbor.
10.Thou shalt no covet thy neighbor's hour or possessions.

Development of the Church

There was a great change in the world's religious circle after Jesus, without resistance, was crucified saying, "Forgive them"to God, the Father about the people who crucified Him. Jesus' surviving disciples proclaimed the Gospel zealously : Jesus rose from the dead, proving He was God. St. Peter and Paul, so zealously proclaimed the Gospel that many churches were established throughout Asia Minor, Greece and Rome. Christianity, however, not only did not accept paganizm but also did not worship the Emperors of the Roman Empire. These Emperors persecuted the Christians for morethan three centuries, and many Christians were martyred. Especially the persecution during the reign of Nero(A.D. 54~68) and Domitian(81~96) against the Christians was cruel ; and even Marcus Aurelius (161~180) persecuted Christians because he understood that

Christianity was an obstacle to the unification of the Roman Empire. Therefore, the Christians had to dig Catacombs inbeneath the ciy of Rome during those days, and there they met secretly. In fact, the Christians seemed to welcome persecution and martyrdom, because the blood of martyrs became the seed of Church. It was impossible for Roman authority to prohibit Christianity. Under such circumstances, the New Testament was written and the Christian followers multiplied year after year. In the first part of the fourth century, Constantine the Great, whose parents were already converted to Christianity, tolerated Christians, permitting them to proclaim the Gospel. In the year 325 Constantine the Great called together the Council of Nicaea and accepted orthodox doctrines of Christianity, banning the Arian heresy and false doctrines. Thus, the Catholic foundation was established ; during the reign of the Great Theodocious the Roman Empire, and Christianity developed vigorously under the protection of state.

At that time, Jerusalem, Antioch, Alexandria, and Constantinople were the chief centers of Christianity ; these Christian centers were administered by bishops. In the later part of the fourth century a bitter dispute arose between church leaders in Rome and in Constantinople over the supreme leadership of the Pope. Moreover, the dispute became more bitter since the East was influenced by Greek culture and the West was influenced by Latin culture. In 476 A.D., the Roman Empire was overthrown by German barbarians. Rome, the mighty political capital, still maintained itself as the center of Europe since the German barbarians were taking a superstitious viewof Rome. Accordingly, the Roman Church was not damaged and the political capital was changed into the holy religious Center. At the same time, St. Augustine called the bishop in Rome the "Pope", "Papa"or "Father"andthe Pope became the visible head of the Church and a ruler of the Vatican in Rome. The Roman church had a most glorious church history since Rome was called a holy place where St. Peter and Paul were martyred, and the Church grew through hundreds of years of persecution. Moreover later, Rome was invaded by the German

Barbarians. After this the Roman Church spread throughout all the European countries under the guidance of many ingenius Popes.

Chapter 2
Transmission of Christianity in Korea

Transmission of Nestorianism

Some of the Christian doctrines were formulated, and some heresies denounced at the Council of Nicea as already mentioned. In 431, however, Nestorius of Constantinople suggested at the Council of Ephesus that the nature of Christ is not of God, but of man close to God. Because of this heresy, hewas banished to Asia Minor, and there he proclaimed his belief. Nestoriusdied, but not Nestorianism. It spread to the Persians and they were called Nestorians, and Nestorianism once became the state religion of Persia. While Nestorianism was at its full glory, Olopen led 21 Christian missionaries of the Nestorian Sect into Changan China, the capital of T'ang, in theninth year of Emperor T'ai Tsung(635 A.D.). The Nestorian Missionaries were welcomed by Emperor T'ai Tsung and the missionaries were asked to translate the Bible into Chinese. Persian temples and branch temples were builtin the provinces(chou), and Olopen became bishop to Chin. Nestorianism greatly developed during one hundred and fifty years. In the reign of Hsuan Tsung, however, the title of the Nestorianism sect was changed into Chingchiao and the Persian temple into Tachin Temple. In 781, Adam, the Nestorian Father of Tachin Temple, built the China Nestorian Headquarters in Changan.

Nestorianism was developing in the reign of Hsuan Tsung of T'ang, at the same time as the reign of King Sungduk(702-736) of Silla ; the time many Nestorian Monuments were built in the reign of Emperor Du

Tsung was the same time as the reign of King Sungduk of Silla. Therefore, it seems that Nestorianism was transmitted to Silla by the envoies since T'ang and Silla were closely related. Furthermore, it appears that Nestorianism was introduced to the Korean envoys and Korean Buddhist students in T'ang during the Silla era since Nestorianism was already firmly spread in Changan and the other provinces. In recent years, however, it was proved that Nestorianism was transmitted to Silla because some Nestorian stone crosses were excavated in Pulkook Temple yard which was built in the tenth year(751 A.D.) of King Kyungduk of Silla. This means that Christianity was transmitted to Silla after 751 A.D., and it is our aim to study how Christianity was transmitted to Silla, and how it had developed during this time.

Toyotomi War(1592-1598) and the Transmission of Catholicism

The man who transmitted Christianity to Korea first is Father Gregorio de Cespedes, who followed the Japanese soldiers in the Toyotomi War. Before Father Gregorio de Cespedes, there was a Jesuit Priest Villela in Japan, who was banished from Kyoto to Kyushu in 1565. He had a plan to transmit Christianity to Korea but this was not accomplished.

In Chosun, during the reign of King Sunjo, violent strife had arisen among the political cliques, and the ruling classes were disrupted and severely corrupted. At this time, Toyotomi Hideyoshi had unified Japan and arbitarily seized the government power. Toyotomi, having done this, now had the ambition to invade Korea and Ming. In the twenty fifth year of King Sunjo(1592), Toyotomi gathered together an enormous force of 150,000, led by Generals Kuroda, Konishi, and Kato. The chief general was Toyotomi. The Imjin War broke out as the Japanese hordes landed in Korea. As the Japanese hordes landed in Pusan, they took Pusan-jin and Tongnai. Seoul was soon taken by a three - route operation ; Kato east route, Konishi central route, and Kuroda-west route. Again, Kato charged up to Hamkyong province, and Konishi charged up to west and took Pyongyang. But reinforcements from Ming and volunteer troops from all parts of Korea counter attacked the Japanese forces, and they retreated down to the southern coast in Kyongsang province. They were stationed there for a long term truce so that most of the Japanese troops felt tired, and their fighting spirit was demoralized as the days wore on.

However, there were many Catholic Christians among the Japanese soldiers, including general Konishi and Kuroda so that Konishi and Kuroda desired that Catholic missionaries come over to Korea and attend to the spiritual needs of the Christians in the army. At that time, Catholicism had already spread in Japan for forty years, and it was still influential though at one time it was prohibited by Hideyoshi in 1587. To this end Konishi asked the Japanese Church to send missionaries to Korea. Thus, Father Gregorio de Cespedes and the Japanese priest Fukan Eion were assigned to Korea inthe twenty sixth year of King Sunjo(1593). Gregorio de Cespedes stopped at Tsushima on way to Korea and stayed there for several months. He baptized four statesmen and many islanders while he was staying at Tsushima. In December 1593, they made their way to Korea and finally reached Konishi's headquarters at Ungchun, Kyongsang province. There they visited soldiers and comforted them. Later, several other missionaries came to Korea but their names are unknown.

They spread the Gospel to Koreans and helped the poor war orphans, and baptized many Koreans in addition to consoling the Japanese troops. The number of Korean converts to Christianity at that time is unknown.

Father Barthelemy C. Bruguiere, the first acting bishop of Korea, and Henrion, the writer of "Historie des Missions", stated that there were many converts after Gregorio de Cespedes and the Japanese priest visited during the war. But, Claude d. Dallet, the author of "History of the Korean Church", says that the Missionaries were not able to make contact with Koreans because most Koreans had taken refuge in the mountains or to the northern parts of the country. Perhaps, the missionaries could make progress with some of Koreans, but they failed in their missionary work because the Koreans had angry feelings towards the Japanese.

Some people can say that the Catholic missionaries failed in their missionary work but we know that thousands of Koreans were imprisoned at Japanese camps. Therefore, there were probably many converts to Christianity in order to save their lives, attracted by the tolerance of missionaires. At the time of the Japanese withdrawal, some of the Korean war-prisoners were taken to Japan. Some of them were sold to Macao, Manila, and Indo-China, and chief Catholic centers in Japan. Most of the settlers became Catholics since they could not bear to live a solitary life in a foreign land. It is true that twenty-one Koreans were martyred by the Shogunate's persecution against Catholics after the war, and there were two hundred and five Japanese martyrs including nine Koreans killed in the 1867 persecution.

Korean Mission to Bejing and Catholicism

The Catholic missionaries from Japan during the Toyotomi War could not complete their missionary work in Korea because they had to withdraw from Korea due of quarrels among the Japanese generals. But the missionary work with the Korean war prisoners who were taken to Japan was somewhat successful. There were probably many Catholic Christians among the returned war prisoners from Japan at the end of the war, but they were not influentialin spreading Catholicism in Korea. After these returned the Dominican and Jesuit missionaries in Japan planned to spread Catholicism over Korea butthey could not fulfill their plan. The Japanese missionary plan for Korea failed but Catholicism in Ming was very influential for the Korean learned men, both in thought and belief, as shown in the churches they built.

As a result of Martin Luther's Reformation against the corruption in Roman Catholic church in the beginning of sixteenth century, some sixty zealous and young German fathers organized a Jesuite Monastery, and they devoted themselves to go overseas to find places in which to witness the Gospel, Among them, the Italian missionary Matteo Ricci had reached Macao, in the Kwangtung province of China in 1580, and there he taught physics and mathematics as he proclaimed the Gospel for about twenty years. Later he went to Bejing of Ming, and he presented a figure of Christ, a cross, map, clock etc. to Emperor Shen Tsung. These gifts were such a curiosity to Emperor Shen Tsung that he asked Matteo Ricci to visit Shen Tsung in the palace, and finally he allowed Matteo Ricci to establish the church. Besides Matteo Ricci there were other learned missionaries : Spanish missionary Nicollas Longobardi and the German missionary Adam Schall, who had come later than the other priests ;and they built many churches and devoted themselves tomissionary work during the last period of the Ming Dynasty. Their dedicated service was the reason many govern-ment officials and court ladies converted to catholicism. Those missiona-ries devoted much to the development of Catholicism and also they enlightened the academic circle of Ming with their knowledge of Astro-nomy, Geography, and Mathematics. Hence a new and vivid European civilization emerged in Ming.

At this time, Korean missions were sent to Bejing several times a year. The Korean mission in Bejing was easily influenced by the new European civilization which had emerged in Bejing, and the new civilization was gradually transmitted to Korea by the Missions.

Whether Korea wanted to or not, Korea had to send groups of missions to Ming on special holidays such as New Year Day, winter solstice, and other national holidays because Ming was Korea's Suzerain state. The missions were called "Mission of winter solstice, or misson of the Emperor's birthday", and were sent to Ming several times each year. Such a policy of dependency upon the powerful state still existed from Ming to Ch'ing even though Ming Dynasty was destroyed. According to Lee, Neung hwa's "History of Christianity in Korea, and History of Diplomacy", a group of missions was formed with 30—40 government officers including chief of the mission group, an interpreter and a doctor. And besides these members therewere about 200—300 merchants who had followed the mission.

From an external political point of view, such a large Korean mission to Bejing was an expression of paying courtesy to the suzerain state but on the other hand, the mission had been transmitting the new civilization from the continent of China to Korea. The new civilization was so interesting to the members of the mission that they easily transmitted it to Korea. The books of Astronomy, Geography, Mathematics, Psysics, Christian Doctrine, and Nobels which were written by western missionaries stationed in China were so interesting to the members of Korean mission that they brought some of those books to Korea and studied them carefully. The Gospel and various Christian books were continuously brought to Korea through the coming and going of missions noble classes, and even to the Buddhists, who had already started to study Christian thoughts.

Huh, Kyun and Lee, Soo Kwang

The Christianity which was called the Study of Heaven or Western Study was transmitted to Korea through numerous mission members but Huh, Kyun, a Confucian, seems the first man who had transmitted it to Korea. Huh, Kyun, son of Huh, Wha, was a Confucian, scholar whose pen name was Kyo San in the reign of King Sunjo. Huh, Kyun, as minister of justice, was also a great Confucian poet, and was a well—known writer of a fantastic story. The Story of Hong Kil Tong tells us what a fantastic writer he was.

He was appointed the Korean envoy to Ming and had gone to Bejing in 1606, the thirty ninth year of King Sunjo. Just then Jesuit father Matteo Ricci was spreading the Gospel in Bejing. There, Huh, Kyun had seen a newly built Catholic church, and he brought home maps and the Teaching of Twelve Doctrines, and finally he believed that Christianity was better than Confucianism. He gave up studying Confucianism, and accepted the Western Learning and was converted to Catholicism. He was admired as "The Transmitter of the Gospel" by the students of Western Learning. In his later years, he was singled out because he foretold the invasion of the Manchurians and was involved in Taebuk Party's plot of purging

King Kwanghae and his widowed mother. Because of this suspicion he was killed in 1618 the tenth year of Kwanghae's reign. His works that remain are Sungso Bok Byungko, Poetry Sungso, Tomoon Taejak, and the story Hong Kil Tong.

Some year later, Lee, Soo Kwang, a Confucian, first introduced Christianity to the public. He held the post of the Minister of Home Affairs throughout the reigns of King Sunjo, Kwanghae, and Injo. He was also a Korean envoy to Bejing in the Ming Dynasty, and brought Matteo Ricci's True Doctrine of God, the Theory of Friendship home and studied them carefully. Chibong Yusul, his writings are a miraculous story, in which he showed the western situation and history of Catholicism. He retired from the government post when Kwanghae's mother was deposed by Lee, Yi Chum in the fifth year of Kwanghae's reign. After the Revolt of Injo, however, he had held the post of Attorney General and the chief secretary of King Injo. His remains are Chibong Yusul, Chaeshin Japrok, Pyung-chok Japki, and Chanrok Kunsuh.

Prince So Hyun and the Gospel

Since the end of the Ming Dynasty, western culture became visible in China through the introduction of Catholic missionaries, and Korea had a chance to make contact with the culture. This was the time when the Ching Dynasty built its foundation in Manchuria and withstood the Ming Dynasty. To rid himself from trouble. King Taejong of the Ching Dynasty invaded Korea in 1636 with a large force of a hundred thousand soldiers. We call this invasion the Byungja Horan. King Injo of the Lee Dynasty was not able to repulse the enemy and finally surrendered himself to King Taejong. After the event, the Lee Dynasty severed relations with the Ming Dynasty and began to offer the so—called Flunkeyism(dependency upon the powerful) to the Ching Dynasty. King Taejong kidnapped two princes of the Lee Dynasty, So Hyun and Bong Rym and took them to China and he killed three high ranking anti—Ching politicians.

King Sejo of the Ching Dynasty finally occupied the mainland of China.

When the Ching Dynasty moved its Capital city to Bejing, the two Korean princes, who were living their banished lives in Shenyang, were taken to the new Capital City. During their banishment, the two princes met Schall, a priest belonging to the Jesuit Society. They learned mathematics, astronomy, and other subjects from the priest. Prince So Hyun was particularly interested in the doctrine of Catholicism and he allowed his men to be baptized.

When prince So Hyun was about to start for Korea after the long banishment, he asked Father Schall to send some Western missionaries to Korea, but because of the lack of missionaries, his dream could not come true. He finally brought back some books on astronomy, mathematics and Catholicism along with crucifixes and devotional objects. When So Hyun left for Korea, he was granted permission to bring several court ladies and five eunuches, who were all Christians. The prince intended to use them for the development of Catholicism and for the study of western culture. This may have been the first time Catholicism was introduced to Korea. Unfortunately, Prince So Hyun who spent his youthful life in exile, suddenly died of an illness seventy days after his arrival home. And his dream for preaching Catholicism to his people had come to nothing. When the Prince died, a rediculous rumour spread in the court, with the result that all materials and books on Catholicism were burned and the Ching's court ladies and eunuches were all sent back to their native country.

It was conveyed to Europe that Prince So Hyun pleaded with Bishop Schall to open missionary work in Korea, during his stay in Bejing. The Holy Body Society sent Paris a messege asking to increase the number of bishops and priests in Asian countries. The Society published a pamphlet, "The Summary of the Chinese Churches", in which they wrote, "When the Korean King (Prince So Hyun) stayed in Bejing and begged for missionaries to be sent to Korea, the Jesuit Society did not have enough missionaries at the request of believers because of the lack of priests" They expressed their sincere regret to the people.

Enthusiasm to Study the Doctrine

After Prince So Hyun died, the Korean government began to realize that the Ching Empire was not so powerful, so they refused to obey the Ching, Instead, King Hyojong of Lee Dynasty worked out a plan to retailate against the Ching Dynasty ; with his men, Song, Shi Yul and Lee, Wan, he prepared to raid the Ching territory. However, this was the time when a great Emperor Kang Hsi, who ascended the throne after King Shun Chih, occupied almost the whole territory of China through his excellent political ability ; his preference for leaning and his desire for construction caused an outstanding development of Ching culture. Although the Korean government hated the Ching Empire, it had to recognize the great accomplishments of Emperor Kang Hsi. The Chosun government decided to follow Ching's asvice and commands and sent envoys to Bejing several times a year as it did during the Ming Dynasty, even though the government indeed did not want to. During the Chosun governments frequent sending of diplomatic envoys to Bejing, there arose a trend for practical learning and for inventions in China. Although it was mainly because of the influence of Western culture, it was also because of the Emperor's promotion of culture.

At that time, the Principle of Chu Tzu was at its height in Korea ; it was also the time when Korea produced two great scholars of the Chu Tzu Teaching, Lee, Hwang and Lee, Yi. In the meantime, Confucianism was so idealistic and so far from practical living that it corrupted the contemporary scholars and finally resulted in a bloody struggle among factions. The Korean envoys to Bejing, whe learned the animate culture of the Ching Dynasty, introduced the Chinese new culture to Korean scholars. The Korean scholars began to be interested in the new culture, reflecting on their own corrupted manner of learning. The envoys did not hesitate to convey Chinese culture and there arose a trend to learn the practical and real things in Korea for the first time. Christianity began to be accepted for its knowledge and wisdom. When Christianity was first introduced to Korea, the attitudes of its scholars including Huh, Kyun,

Lee, Soo Kwang and Yu, In Mong, was nothing more than an interest in a new learning. However, after the Contemcorary Confucian scholars began to study and discuss the doctrine of Western Science profoundly, it came to be characterized not only as knowledge but also as a religion. During the reign of King Yungjo, the enthusiasm for learning Western Study became more zealous and the religious nature of Western Learning became clearer. The Confucian scholars, however, began to criticize those who studied Western Science or became converts to Catholicism. The Confucian scholars called the converts heretics. However, because Western Learning was considered both a religion and a science, and because the knowledge of new learning was required for being a scholar at that time, Western Learning infiltrated deeply into the scholars. There were great scholars of Western Study including Lee, Ik, An, Jung Bok, Lee, Hun Kyung and the like.

Lee, Ik, well known as a man of erudition and power, was a great scholar. His enthusiasm for Western Study was so zealous that he had read Astronomy, Topography, Mathematics, Physics as well as Catholic books. He was proud of himself being versed in Western Learning. At that time, there was a serious conflict among the political factions in Korea in spite of King Yungjo's impartial policy. Because Lee, Ik did not want to be involved in the friction, he retired from political life. While he was living a retired life in Kwangju, Kyonggi province, the King asked him to come back to the political world. He refused the King's plea and continued teaching his disciples. Among them was Lee, Ka Hwan, one of the greatest scholars of Western Science at that time.

An, Jung Bok, one of Lee Ik's followers, was also a man excited about Western Study and, he contributed a great deal to its development. An, Jung Bok was influenced to study Christianity by Lee, Ik. He studied "the Doctrine of God" and "the Story of Ten Strangers." also reading the Seven Subjugation" and "the Self Evidence of the True Way". After he became interested in reading those Catholic books, he neglected to study Confucianism. He was one of the scholars who were proud of themselves for being Western Study scholars. Among his followers, there were those who did not worship their ancestors following the doctrine of Catholicism. However, in his late years, An, Jung Bok became the teacher of the Crown Prince(King Jungjo) He taught the Prince the principle of Chu Tzu. When he realized that some of his disciples did not worship their ancestors because of Catholicism, he made his anti—Catholic attitude clear by publishing two books. "Survey of Heaven" and "Catechetical Study of Heaven". Not to worship ancestors was against the national policy ; besides, it gave the factious people a pretext to make problems.

Shin, Hon Dam and Lee, Hun Kyung, disciples of Lee, Ik, were engrossed in their studies of Catholicism and made a large contribution to its development. The former wrote the Answers to "Western Studies" and the later wrote "the Catethetical Study of Heaven".

Chapter 3
The Rise of Church

Religious Movement

After the reign of King Sunjo, books on Western Learning began to be imported through the Korean envoy to Bejing ; these books satisfied the contemporary scholars' desire for knowledge for about one century. However, Western Science was not characterized as a religion until the beginning of the reign of King Yungjo, for the scholars were not very much interested in the religious contents of Western Thought. During the 50 years of King Yungjo(1725-1777), the doctrines of Western Learning were profoundly studied and Catholicism came to be understood as a religion. From the beginning of King Jungjo, there arose a trend for learning for practical or real things in the world of thought and, on the tide of such a reforming trend, Western Study as a religion came to appear as the rival philosophy against that of Chu Tzu learning, the guiding doctrine of the Lee Dynasty. In other words, there arose a Pragmatic School in Korea through the influence of the new Chinese culture. On the tide of such a trend, the progressive scholars interested in Western Culture first concentrated on studying its doctrine and then launched a religious movement. The scholars attempted to construct a Christian society : they criticized the Confucian School and Confucian Shrine brought up by Confucianism, destroyed the receptacles used in ancestral worship which were inherited from their ancestors, drove all sorts of evil spirits from their homes, criticized the system of social status, insisted on the abolition of conventions, and declared the freedom and the equality of people.

At the point of turning from studying the doctrine to that of launching the religious movement, Lee, Ik made a significant contribution. Lee, Ik was a great scholar of the Pragmatic School in the years of King Yungjo, and most of those who first constructed the Christian society were his successors. Hong, Yu Han was one of his disciples who was eager to read books on Christianity and to practice the doctrine by burning the receptacles used for ancestral worship. He was the first man who enjoyed a holiday every seven days, on the 7th, 14th, 21st and 28th day of each month. He refrained from eating delicious food on these holidays, though there was no such regulation in the Christian way of living.

When he met anyone who was sick while he was out, regardless of their social status, he made the sick person ride his horse while he himself walked. He was always willing to share his property with the poor. Once he repaid the price of land he sold to another when the land was later eroded by flood. Even though he was not baptized, he tried to lead a faithful religious life according to the teachings of the doctrine. Increasingly people came to practice the religious doctrine of Lee, Ik, and they played a great role in the formation of a church society. Lee, Ik's school played the main role in the practical religious movement because the scholars of his school lived very piously. They were all prominent scholars of their time including Kwon, Il Shin, Kwon, Chul Shin and Chung, Yak Yong who tried to structure Christianity into a practical religion at the end of Yungjo.

Most of these scholars belonged to the Namin Faction. They launched a religious movement in the areas of Kwangju, Yangpyong of Kyonggi province. In 1778 the second year of King Jungjo, the scholars, including Kwon, Chul Shin, Chung, Yak Yong, and Chung, Yak Jun, gathered at a quiet temple where they studied and discussed Christianity, science, mathematics and geography for a few weeks. As a result, they began to be much more interested in the doctrine of Christianity. They reached the conclusion that Jesus was great and that the doctrine of Christianity was reasonable, and they agreed among themselves to follow the commandments by having devotions every morning and evening and not working on the 7h, 14th, 21st, 28th of every month. Lee, Pyuk, a leading scholar of the contemporary Western Culture School, who later attended the meetings, also agreed to follow the commandments. They led a religious life for a few years, but they soon faced a conflict between the doctrines and the traditional customs of society. Since they still had many things to learn about the profound doctrines and how to perform the religious ceremonies, they needed many more books and a meeting with a western priest.

The Establishment of the Church

In the 7th year of King Jungjo(1783) when the scholars of the Western Learning were concerned about the problem of doctrines and rites, they received news that Hwang, In Jum, a government official, accompanied by Lee, Dong Wook, and his son, Lee, Seung Hoon, was going to Bejing that winter. Lee, Seung Hoon was born in Pyungchang in Kangwon province, passed the higher public service examination at the age of 24, and was the chief of Pyungtaeck Prefecture. Lee, Pyuk was well acquainted with Lee, Seung Hoon as a friend and as a relative. Lee, Pyuk was pleased to learn that Lee was traveling to Bejing and gathered his scholars for a discussion. They collected some money for Lee, Seung Hoon's travel to Bejing. Lee, Seung Hoon was asked to visit the church in Bejing and to learn of the deep and profound doctrines of Christianity and of its methods of worship. He was also requested to bring some needed books back with him.

During his two month stay in Bejing, Lee, Seung Hoon visited the Southern Church of Alexandre de Gouvea, from whom he learned a great deal about the doctrine and its practice. He was baptized there and was given the Christian name, Peter. He was spiritually converted after being baptized and took back with him many crucifixes, holy pictures, books, including the Doctrine of God, the Seven Subjugations, the Originality of Universal Nature and the Teaching of Christianity. He handed them over to Lee, Pyuk. After studying the books deeply, Lee, Pyuk came to understand the truth of Christianity more profoundly and his heart burnt with belief in the religion. Through his devoted efforts to propagate the religion, the number of converts gradually increased. Most of them came from the Namin Faction and the middle class.

As the preaching movement became more active and the influences became stronger, an anti-movement was attempted under the leadership of Lee, Ka Hwan, one of the leading Confucian scholars at that time. However, the conventional theory of Confucianism was not able to defeat the truth of Christianity ; rather the conflict revealed the absurdness of Confucianism. Through Lee, Pyuk's advice, Kwon, Il Shin was converted to Christianity. Even though Kwon, Il Shin was the leader among those who studied Western Practical Science, he hesitated to convert because he was world-famous as a scholar of Confucianism and had many disciples. Until he was finally influenced to convert by Lee, Pyuk, he had been connected with both Christianity and Confucianism. Later Kwon, Il Shin was baptized with the Christian name, Anbrogio. His younger brother, Kwon, Chul Shin, became a convert a little later, and the Kwon brothers engaged in preaching not only to their family but also to all those whom they knew. The brothers Chung, Yak Yong, Yak Jong and Yak Jun, contemporary leading scholars of Western Learning, were also converted. Through the conversion of these scholars, Christianity became established as a new religion in Korea.

Lee, Seung Hoon baptized Lee, Pyuk and Kwon, Il Shin. Lee, Pyuk was given the Christian name, John, and Kwon, Il Shin the baptismal name, Francisco Savertio. These three baptized men were the real founders of the Catholic Church in Korea. Through their enthusiasm, the religion grew in prosperity day by day. As the numbers of those who confessed their belief in Christianity increased, including Lee, Dan Won, Hong, Rak Min, Choi, In Kil, Chi, Hwang, Choi, Chang Hyun, Kim, Bum Woo, Yoo,

Hwang Kum and the like, there inevitably arose the need for a place to worship. Thus, the first ceremony in the Catholic Church in Korea was conducted by the Priest Lee, Pyuk.

The First Martyrdom and Unrest of the Church

During the five hundred years of the Lee Dynasty, confucianism was the guiding principle upon which the Dynasty was founded, particularly the principle of Chu Tzu learning, which was the index of education and morality. Any theory of principle against that of Chu Tzu learning was regardedas heresy. Christianity was against Confucianism in its origin doctrine and method of worship. Confucianism was very close-fisted regarding fame, prestige and origin, while Christianity demanded philantrophy and equality. Confucianism demanded ancestral worship and did not prohibit the worship of many kinds of spirits, while Christianity prescribed both. It was considered that the expansion of Christianity would violate the Confucian traditions established for about four centuries and would challenge the leading position of the Confucian scholars. This was the main reason why the Confucian scholars did not allow Christianity.

Lee, Pyuk, Lee, Seung Hoon, Chung, Yak Yong and their followers were prominent in the christian movement which resulted in fluctuation of the world of thought, but the exclusive and conservative scholars were not standing by idly. In 1785 the 9th year of King Jungjo, Minister Kim, Hwa Jin sent his man to arrest a Christian official, Kim, Bum Woo, and to torture him until he betrayed his belief. Though he was horribly tortured, Kim, Bum Woo was faithful to his belief in Christianity. In the end he was bahished to Choongchong province, where he led a faithful life until his death a few weeks later. He was the first martyr in the Christian history in Korea.

The news that Kim, Bum Woo had died as a result of the torture surprised other believers. Lee, Seung Hoon, who had been patient with every trouble, was no longer able to withstand his family's teasing to apostatize his faith. At last he burnt all his books on Christianity and made his apostate attitude clear. Lee, Pyuk, the leading man of the Church, was faced with the same problem as Lee, Seung Hoon. Lee, Pyuk's father threatened to kill himself if his son did not give up his faith in Christianity. Lee, Pyuk could not stand against his father, and he too declared himself an apostate. He had serious compunctions over this act, which contributed to his death the following year.

A little later when the cyclone had quieted and the fluctuation of the believers had settled down, the apostates began to come back to the church. One of them was Lee, Seung Hoon. Kwon, Il Shin, the Brothers Chung, Yak Jun, Lee, Seung Hoon and other believers got together to discuss how to develop the church again. They concluded that they should have a priest who could administer the mass and baptize believers, and they selected Kwon, Il Shin as bishop. Lee, Seung Hoon, Lee, Dan Won, Choi, Chang Hyun, Yoo, Hang Kum and others were selected as priests. The bishop in Bejing heard of this movement from a believer who accompanied the envoy to Bejing by pretending to be a merchant. The Bishop sent notice to the Korean church that it was beyond a believer's authority for a layman, Kwon, Il Shin, to ascend to holy orders and that the Bejing church was considering sending a missionary, sooner or latter, to Chosun. The problem concerning holy orders was solved temporarily by his decision. But they faced the dillemma that believers were prescribed from observing ancestral worship by the Bejing church since ancestral worship was also idolatry. But to the Koreans, not observing their ancestral worship was not only a sin against their ancestors but also would give the authorities a pretext to persecute Christianity. This instruction from Bejing placed the Christians in a difficult position. Some Christians whose faith was not very strong left the church. Among them was Lee, Seung Hoon, who gave up his faith and severed all relationships with the belivers.

Serious Persecution

At that time the conservative power of Confucianism again launched an anti-Christian movement and there occurred a considerable number of apostates. However, the remainder of the devoted Christians did not betray their faith even at the risk of their lives. Moreover, during the foundation period of the Catholic church in Korea, the conservative powers, most of whose scholars belonged to Suin Faction, persecuted the Church and attacked Christians openly. This was maily because King Jungjo was a man of magnanimity and because Chai, Je Kong, the leader of Namin Faction, was trusted by the King and was in the position of vice prime minister. There was a man at that time called Yun, Ji Choong who passed the examination for a Jinsa position in the 7th year of King Jungjo and who came to Seoul the following year. There he met Kim, Bum Woo who lent him two books on Christianity, the Doctrine of God and the Seven Subjugations. He was baptized by Chung, Yak Jun, one of his relatives. In the 15th yea of King Jungjo, when Yun, Ji Choong's mother died, Yun, Ji Choong did not worship his dead mother in the Confucian manner and Kwon, Sang Yeun, a Catholic from Kongju, did not bow to the dead body of his mother's sister. This resulted in a serious wave of criticism from his relatives and friends. Hong, Rak An, who seemed to be waiting for the chance, sent a long letter to Chai, Je Kong requesting him to execute Yun, Ji Choong and at the same time, asked the Chief of Jinsan Country to arrest him. The Chief ordered Yun, Ji Choong's arrest, but before the officials reach his house, the two men left the house and escaped to Kwangju in Kyonggi province. The Chief arrested Yun, Ji Choong's uncle in their place.

When the two men heard that Yun, Ji Choong's uncle had been arrested, they decided to give themselves up to the Chief of the Country. They were tortured, but refused to deny their beliefs. Because they refused to renounce their faith, though tortured miserably, they were sent to the Headquarters of Cholla province, where more heinous torture awaited them, but they still were faithful to their religion. At that time, the powers of the Suin Faction pressed the vice prime minister, Chai, Je Kong, to execute them, and he asked King Jungjo for their execution. The King gave his permission, though he did not want to. Yun, Ji Choong walked to the execution-ground in a dignified manner while Kwon, Sang Yeun walked quietly murmuring the names of Jesus and May to himself because he was extremely weak from the torture he had suffered. At the execution ground they were given a last chance to change their minds, but they remained faithful. Finally they were beheaded murmuring the names of Jesus and Mary.

After Lee, Duk Jo and Lee, Seung Hoon left the church, Kwon, Il Shin was busy administering the church alone and was the center of attention of the Suin Faction. Because of his active propagating of the faith, he was finally arrested and tortured severely. But he would not change his mind and was exiled to Cheju Island, where he finally expressed his intention to apostatize for the sake of his 80 year old mother. After he gave up his faith, the King ordered him banished to Choongchong province from Cheju Island, but Kwon, Il Shin died on his way to the new place of banish ment.

Kwon, Il Shin was one of the believers who was severely tortured. Lee, Dan Won in Naipo, the brothers Chung, Yak Jun and Yak Yong, and other prominent Christians were also persecuted by the authorities and, though some Christians' faith waivered, most of them, who were encouraged by the dignified martyrdom of Yun, Ji Choong, were able to tolerate the pressure. Even under such severe persecution, Won Si Jang was able to convert more than 30 Christian families during the two years until he was captured in January of the 17th year of King Jungjo. Although he was tortured and his flesh torn and his body exposed, he stood firm until he froze to death.

Inspite of the cruel persecution, the number of believers gradually increased. In the 18th year of King Jungjo(1794), the total number amounted to 4,000. This was due to a consistent propagation of the faith by general Christians. Although the number of believers increased despite the severe pressure of the authorities, most of the leading persons of the church, who came from good families, passed away, except Kwon, Chul Shin and Chung, Yak Jong. Since they were not strong enough to carry out the hard church work of the day, the development of church was handed to those who came of middle or lower families. From the beginning, Christianity emerged from among the lower class people, as were the 12 disciples of Jesus.

Father Choo, Moon Mo

After the Catholic Church in Korea had gradually expanded, the Bejing Church sent Father J. Dos Remedios to Korea in the 15th year of King Jungjo in 1791, but he was not able to enter the country. For about two years, no special consideration was given to the evangelization of Korea until the 17th year of Jungjo in 1793, when two Korean Christians, Yun, Yu Il and Chi, Hwang, visited Bejing to asked the church to send a missionary to Korea. The Bishop of the Bejing Church was willing to send the priest Choo, Moon Mo of Soochow in Kiangsu State, who was a man of knowledge and virtue.

Father Choo left Bejing in February of the next year and reached the border 20 days later. There he found he could not enter Korea because of the strictly guarded boundary. He engaged in preaching in Manchuria until December of that year. This was the time for the Korean Dongji Mission to pass through the border from Bejing. He accompanied the envoys into the country dressed as a Korean. The great joy of the Korean believers at meeting Choo in January of the next year was beyond expression.

After he came to Seoul, he stayed in a Christian's house in Ankook-dong. There he studied Korean and celebrated the mass. When he went out of the house he wore the Korean mourning dress. So polite and generous did he appear that every believer received a good impression of him and many people wanted to meet the Priesst.

One day, a believer called Han, Yung Ik Came to meet him, and for some unknown reason the believer came to dislike Choo. Upon leaving the house, he reported the Priest to the authorities describing in detail his appearance and the clothes he wore. The authorities ordered Choo to be captured, his believers saw what was going to happen to their priest before the authorities reached the house. They were successful in allowing the Priest to escape, but Choi, In Kil insisted that he was Choo and remained in his place, and Yun, Yu Il and Chi, Hwang, who led the Priest to Korea, were captured and killed.

Therefore, Choo, Moon Mo took shelter in the house of a pious woman believer, Kang, Wan Sook, in Hwa-dong, Seoul and continued to preach with her help. He visited Naipo in Choongchong province and Chunju in Cholla province a few times to baptize believers. He organized the Myung Society for the study of doctrine, and he taught and encouraged the followers of the faith while he also translated the Bible into Korean and prepared preaching materials while he was there. During the 7 years of living in Kang, Wan Sook's house in secret, many believers in the country were captured and Killed. The reason why he could live in safety for so long a time in the house, though many believers in outer world were suffering, was because Kang, Wan Sook was a very wise woman. But a more important reason was that the social customs of the day prohibited strangers from freely entering the house of a noble woman. Also, since women of noble families were exempted from punishment except for high treason, she had the freedom and courage to act.

During the 7 years that Choo lived into Kang, Wan Sook's house, Catholicism had grown steadily, despite numerous martyrdoms because of the persecution by the authorities. Thus the number of believers increased from 4,000 to 10,000 in the first year of King Soonjo in 1801, when the miserable Sinyu Massacre occurred.

Chapter 4
Succession of Massacres

King Jungjo and His Religious Policy

From the beginning of King Jungjo, Catholicism began to grow mainly among the scholars of the Namin Faction, while the scholars of the Suin Faction attempted to persecute it. However, since the King was a liberalist, he had sympathy for the liberalistic Namin scholars. During his reign there were no severe persecutions of the Catholics. Moreover, the disastrous experience of his father's death led him to avoid bloody persecutions ; his reluctant permission to put Catholics to death was due to the strong reguest of the Suin scholars.

In the tenth year of his reign when a certain Suin scholar called Hong, Rak An brought a charge against Lee, Seung Hoon, the chief of Pyungtaek Prefecture at that time. The punishment was not enforced. When Hong, Rak An indicted Lee, Seung Hoon again five years later, the King intended to solve the problem by dismissing him from his official position but a number of Suin scholars appealed to the King to execute him. Instead, Lee, Seung Hoon was eventually banished to Yesan. The following year, when another problem occurred, the King solved it, by exiling Kwon, Il Shin to Cheju Island and by ordering others to write an apology. When Lee, Ka Hwan, leader of the Western Learning was indicted by a government official, Lee, Dong Jik, in 16th year of Jungjo, the King refused to punish him.

Since King Jungjo favored the Namin Faction School, the leader of

the Namin, Chai, Je Kong, was in a high position in the government ;
Catholics, therefore, did not suffer very much despite the Suin Factions
intention to purge those who were connected with Catholicism ; there
were not very many victims during King Jungjo reign. Remarkably, there
were fewer victims in Seoul than in the countryside.

Sinyu Massacre

As soon as the child King Soonjo ascended the throne upon King
Jungjo's death in 1801, a Catholic persecution movement began, instigated
by the Suin scholars. King Soonjo was 12 years of age when he ascended
the throne and his grandmother, Queen Yungjo, was made the regent.
She was a narrow-minded woman and made many mistakes in making
decisions on national affairs. As soon as the Queen took the power, even
before the funeral of King Jungjo was over, the scholars of the Suin
Faction, who had been waiting for the chance for long time, started to
execute the Catholics ; they had the authority of Queen Kim, grandmother
of King Soonjo, to sweep out the heretics. The content of the Queen's
message was that Catholicism was a heresy against the Suin orthodoxist,
dazzled the people with the groundless theory of Heaven and Hell, and
led them into violating the virtue of filial piety and loyalty which resulted
in disorder.   Therefore, its believers must be swept out of the society.
It was the same argument the scholars of the Suin Clique had used when
appealing to the Queen.

The message pleased the Suin Clique, and an order to execute the Catholics was dispatched by a joint message of three government agencies,
Sagan-won, Sahun-boo and Hongmoon-kwan. Execution of the Catholics
started in Kyonggi province, and the persecution quickly spread to every
corner of the country. Believers were captured and killed. Most of the
Catholic leaders belonged to the Namin Faction School. This disatrous
execution of Catholics is called the Sinyu Massacre.

During the miserable massacre, about 300 believers were killed, tortured
to death or died in prison, and almost all of the Namin School leaders

were killed. Lee, Ka Hwan and Kwon, Chul Shin died in prison and other leaders, including Lee, Seung Hoon, Chung, Yak Jong, Hong, Rak Min and Choi, Pil Kong were beheaded ; the deceased, Chai, Je Kong was divested of all his previous positions. The fate of the Namin School was the same as that of Catholicism and, for a while, there was not a breath of Catholicism in Korea.

It is regrettable that the massacre was the product of the scramble for political power between two factions. How could this nation stand for the cold-blood execution ! The Catholics were treated like a group of savages and were executed on the charge of disturbing public morals.

Martyr of Father Choo, Moon Mo

From the time Father Choo had come to Korea in 1874, he had long lived in the shelter of Kang, Wan Sook's house ; his devotion to the expansion of Catholicism was outstanding. However, when the miserable executions occurred in 1801 and the government agencies began to pursue him, he had no place to hide in Korea. Moreover, he was not able to tolerate seeing the believers suffer from the persecution. He thought he had better go back to Bejing and work for the Korean Catholics, and at last left Seoul for Bejing. When he reached the Yalu River, he felt a strong sense of responsibility and returned to Seoul, delivering himself to the authorities on the 27th March, 1801.

Because he answered without resistance everything the authorities questioned him about, he was not tortured severely. He was beheaded on the execution ground in Noryang-jin. It is outstanding in the Christian history of Korea that Father Choo, in the presence of death, felt so proud of 50 years' of consistent devotion of God, even in such serious adversity, that he was able to die calmly on the scaffold. After his death, his head was hung for exhibition for five days and then buried along with the body. There remained nothing of him.

With Choo's death, all his followers were arrested and beheaded. This incident also brought a tragedy to the court. King Jungjo had an elder

brother of half-blood called Lee, Gon, whose son was Lee, Dam. The
son was put to death on the charge of treason and his father was banished
to Kanghwa Island. The wife of Lee, Gon and her daughter-in-law were
permitted to stay in the court. Through the introduction of a court lady,
the women became converts and were baptized by Father Choo, Moon
Mo. They entered the Myung Society and often, enjoyed listening to
Father's preaching in the court. This gave rise to a rumor that some
women in the court had fallen in love with Choo and had love affairs
with him. Of course, it was a groundless rumor. Father Choo was a man
of faith and mature personality and that sort of affair was beyond consideration as far as he was concerned. Although the Priest swore he had
no relations with them, the two women and Lee, Gon were put to death.

Matter of Hwang, Sa yung's Letter

The storm of the Sinyu Massacre was the cause of a letter being written
by Hwang, Sa Yung ; all the people were shocked. Hwang, Sa Yung,
born in Changwon of Kyongsang province, was so brilliant that he could
pass thehigher public service examination while still very young. He even
won the admiration of the King. He was a prominent young man who
could have been promoted to a high position in government. He gave
up the luxury he could have had and instead became a follower of the
Priest Choo. During the Sinyu Massacre when Choo was captured, Hwang
left for Chechun in Choongchong province, where he lived in a cave for
eight months. A certain believer called Hwang, Shim visited him at the
cave, and they discussed methods of rebuilding the church. They continued
to communicate form there with other remaining believers.

Hwang, Sa Yung and his fellows reached the conclusion that rather
than stand by and see the church destroyed, they send a letter requesting
assistance to Bejing, begging for foreign troops to try to recover the
church's power. The contents of the letter were as follows :

1. Since Korea is weak economically, we appeal to the Western countries
   to send funds for the propagation of Christianity.

2. Since Korea is subordinate to Ch'ing, we hope the Emperor will order the Korean government to accept missionaries.

3. We hope Ch'ing will annex Korea and unify the style of clothing.

4. We appeal to the Western countries to send battle-ships with more than 50,000 soldiers armed with weapons and force the Korean King to permit the free activity of the missionaries.

The letter was written on white fabric and was composed of about 13 thousand letters in one hundred and thirty-one lines. Their intention was to win the freedom of religion in Korea. They asked the messenger to deliver the letter secretly to the Bejing church. At that time, a military officer called Lim, Yul heard something about the letter and arrested the messenger and Hwang, Shim. Three days later, Hwang, Sa Yung was also captured in Chechun.

This affair dismayed the government and the people, and the traitorous act of the Catholics changed the minds of many people who had been in favor of the Catholics and who had resented the cruel executions by the Suin Faction. Few people sent sympathy to Hwang, Sa Yung and his followers ; most were against his activity. Two weeks after Hwang, Sa Yung was captured, he was beheaded on the execution-ground outside Susomoon, and his body was torn into six pieces and displayed. Other conspirators, including Yu, Hang Kum and his brother, Yu, Ji Choong, and Lee, Woo Jip were all put to death.

Ulhae Massacre

During the Sinyu Massacre in 1801, most of the leading and most faithful believers were put to death ; it was believed that the church would suffocate and never be able to rise again. However, the young King Soonjo was a man of generosity and hated to see his people killed and injured. Therefore, no severe persecution occurred for a while, though some Catholics were captured and tortured in some of the provinces. As the government loosened its control over Catholics and society settled down, the hidden believers began to study the doctrine again and reorganized the church system. They began to communicate with the Bejing Church, and the devoted preachers of early day began to evangelize in the province of Kyongsang and Kangwon, which had not been cultivated until then.

While the church was on this steady course of reconstruction, there arose suddenly the so-called Ulhae Massacre, and this presented another hurdle to the development of the church. The massacre occurred in the 15th year of King Soonjo, in 1815. During the year of famine in the 14th year of King Soonjo, there was a Catholic called Chun, Ji Soo, who begged from door to door of the Catholics in Kyongsang province. When the believers did not treat him in the way he expected, Chun, Ji Soo developed a grudge against the Catholics and informed against them to the authorities. The government agencies decided to arrest all believers at Easter time when all Catholics were to gather together. The authorities arrested all the Catholics when they had their Easter devotion in certain villages of Chungsong County in Kyongsang province and sent them to the court of Kyungju. A few days later, all the Catholics who were confined in Jinbo village, and in other villages were sent to Andong. These events drove many Catholics to the point of dispair. Most of the Catholics driven to Kyungju Court gained their freedom by renouncing their faith, but the rest stood firm against the torture. Among them were seven believers, including Kim, Sa Il, who all died in prison. The rest were driven to Taegu, where they were put to death.

Most of the Catholics sent to Andong renounced their faith. Others who were very devoted died in prison. The rest were sent to Taegu, where six of them died by cruel torture.

Many Catholics were captured in Kyongsang province, and more than one hundred of them were driven to Taegu.

Most of the victims of the Ulhae Massacre were from Kyongsang province, but the confessions of some of the arrested led to the capture and execution of Catholics in Choongchong and Kangwon provinces. The total number of Catholics arrested during the Ulhae Massacre was over 300.

Junghae Massacre

Twelve years after the Ulhae Massacre, minor trouble among Catholics themselves caused another terrible massacre. The Catholics of Cholla pro-vince had suffered less from the frequent massacres and the number of believers who avoided severe persecution by the authorities increased. At that time there was an earth-ware factory around Goksung County in Cholla province, and all the potters were Catholics who practiced a faithful religious life there. In February of the 27th year of King Soonjo in 1827, they celebrated a festival for their new products. All the villagers drank wine and were in a fine mood. Han, Bak Kyun, one of the earthenware makers whose father was a martyr was not very pious. He got drunk and tried to find fault with the master of the drinking house. He had a fight with the master and beat his wife. The master had been baptized only a few days before and was not very faithful to his new religion. The master finally ran to the authorities in Goksung, taking with him the Catholic books he had, and informed the authorities about the Catholics. The flame of persecution quickly spread to every corner of the province, and the believers were arrested, regardless of age or sex. Those who gave up their faith were freed, but the rest were sent to Chunju, the capital city of cholla province. Most of those initially arrested were from the southern part of the province. The following month, March, the local government agencies began to hunt the Catholics in the northern countries. About two hundred Catholics were captured in Gosan County and sent to Chunju.

During the Junghae Massacre, over five hundred Catholics were cap-tured and the Catholic villages fell into utter confusion. However, the governor of the local government, instead of executing them, decided to wait until their faith grew less enthusiastic and they gave up their faith. He kept them in prison for a long time. Most of the believers became apostates and were freed. King Soonjo also did not want bloody persecu-tion and would not permit the local government officials to execute the captured. The martyrs during the massacre were no more than 10. The flame of the Junghae Massacre spread to a part of Kyongsang province, but the persecution there was not so severe. The Catholics in Cholla province had been hunted for about three months.

Chapter 5
The Establishment of the Korea Parish

Establishment of Parish

After the storm of the Junghae Massacre in Cholla province was over, Catholicism was able to grow in peace, though there were some persecutions in certain counties. This was largely due to the generous personality of King Soonjo. During much of his reign, the people suffered from many natural disasters as flood and draught. These natural disasters also kept the King from considering extreme persecutions. Particularly, after his son, Prince Ho, died at an early age, the King hated any extreme policy which would persecute the people. The King did not eat any delicious food after the prince's death.

Under the benevolent policy of King Soonjo, Catholics were able to continue to read the Bible and have prayer meetings indoors without anxiety and the number of believers increased again. The enthusiastic believers began to preach actively. At that time, the envoys to Bejing brought news that the Western missionaries in Bejing exercised their authority over the Chinese and, of course, such news encouraged the development of Catholicism in Korea. As the political situation settled down and the number of believers increased, the Vatican ordered, at the request of the Korean Catholics, the Society of Foreign Mission in Paris to start to propagate in Korea. On the 9th of September of 1831, Pope Gregory XVI decided to establish a parish in Korea, independent of the Bejing Parish.

Bishop Barthelemy Brugiere

As the risk of carrying on Catholic activity disappeared and the church began to develop in Korea, the leaders of the church sent Korean believers to Bejing and to the Provinces of Shansi and Fukien in China to beg for missionaries. However, the Bishop of the Bejing Parish as well as other Parish bishops were not able to send any missionaries to Korea, even though they realized the need. This was not only because of a shortage of personal and material needs in Korea, but also because of the risk in Korea of such mission activity. The parishes of Shansi and Fukien also had to take the jurisdictional dispute with the Bejing Parish into consideration.

In the 33rd year of King Soonjo in 1833, the Society of Foreign Mission dispatched a Chinese bishop called Liu Fang Chi, a graduate of a mission school in Italy. But, since he was arrogant and eager to win fame and not a man qualified for preaching, he was not able to make a significant contribution to the church's development. At the plea of Korean Catholics, the Vatican resolved to establish the Korea Parish and assigned Brugiere, then a missionary in Siam, to the post of the first Vicar Apostolic of Korea.

Brugiere was born in Raissec in France in February of 1792. Upon graduation from the Carcason Mission School, he lectured at the school for 13 years until he was 33 years old, when he entered the Society and was appointed to perform mission work in Siam.

When the pope nominated him as the Vicar Apostolic of Korea and authorized him to found the Korean church independent of the control of the Bejing church(which was under the care of the Mission Society, and directly attached to the Vatican) the Portuguese missionaries in Bejing and Macao resented Brugiere and expelled him from the Society. But his consistent efforts surmounted the difficulties and at last the Society agreeded to his having sole responsibility for the Korea Parish ; he was able to leave for his new position.

After the problem was resolved, he came to Hsiwantzu in Mongolia Via Manila, Macao, Fukien, and Nanking in order to head for Korea through Shansi State in 1832, where he had been waiting for the chance to enter Korea for about one year. In October of 1835, he left for Korea, but on his way there he died in Palikou in Mongolia. Thus his dream for korea ended without his having set foot on the land. As soon as Father Pierre P. Maubant, his companion in Hsiwantzu heard of the sad news of Brugiere's death, he hurried to Palikou, where he joined the funeral ceremony of Brugiere. On the occasion of the 100th anniversary of Catholic propagation in Korea, which was held in Seoul, the remains of Brugiere were laid to rest in Myungdong Catholic Church in Seoul.

Enterance of the French Missionary

When Brugiere left Hsiwantzu for Korea, Maubant was to have accompanied him, but at the suggestion of the Korean Catholics that it might be more dangerous for two people to pass through the frontier guards at the same time, Maubant decided to follow him later and stayed there until he heard the news of Brugiere's death. After the funeral, Maubant headed for Korea along with the Korean believers. In spite of many dangerous obstacles, he succeeded in passing the frontier by posing as a Korean. He reached Seoul on the 25th of January of the second year of King Hunjong in 1836.

When Father Maubant reached Seoul, the Chinese Priest Liu Fang Chi, who had come to Korea earlier, had to leave. Liu Fang Chi had not been appointed by the Bejing Church, but had volunteered to preach in Korea. When Maubant was appointed as the Korean Parish Father by the Bejing Parish, Liu ostensively had to welcome him, but in fact he did not. Instead of cooperating with Maubant, he tried to disturb Maubant's mission work because he aspired to be the founder of the Korean Catholic Church. Such behavior disappointed the Korean believers and they lost all respect for him. He finally returned to his home country in December of the second year of King Hunjong.

In January of 1837, another French missionary Father Jacques H. Chastan was able to enter the country after surmounting various obstacles.

He joined Maubant in studying Korean and in carrying out the Church's work.

They were very eager to learn Korean and to preach to the believers. They, dressed in sables, visited village after village listening to the villagers' confessions and saying mass for them until late in the night. They were willing to eat the poor food the villagers offered. Such enthusiastic missionary activity filled the villagers with peace and pleasure wherever the two priests went. The believers were very much encouraged and the Church's power began to spread with irresistable force. In order to foster Korean priests, Maubant sent three Korean boys to Macao for the further study of Catholicism. The Korean church was developing gradually and well organized by foreign missionaries, but it needed a leader. The Society assigned Father L. J. Imber to the post of Vicar Apostolic of Korea. He was engaged in preaching in the Province of Ssuchwan in China at the time of his appointment. In December, 1837, seven months later, he left for Korea ; he reached the gate at the border, and there he met three Korean believers who had filtered into the group of those who were on their way to Seoul. Under the guidance of the three Korean believers, he was able to cross the frontier into Korea, and he reached Seoul at the end of the year. They experienced the same risks as had Maubant and Chastan. Through the superhuman efforts of the three French missionaries, the believers regained their zeal, and many of the apostates returned to the church. The numbers of believers increased day by day, and the total number of Catholics was over 10,000 in 1839 the 5th year of King Hunjong, three years after Maubant first came to Seoul, when the believers were around 6,000.

Chapter 6
Recurrence of the Massacres

Kihae Massacre

Due to the generous policy of King Hunjong's regent and the constant efforts of the French missionaries, Catholic believers were increased to over ten thousand. But in the meantime, there arose a strong hatred against Catholicism. The hatred came, not only from the different schools or factions ; it came also as a result of friction between the progressive and conservative camps. The expansion of Catholicism, which declared the freedom and equality of the people, meant the ruin the established ruling class, accordingly, the conservatives did not hesitate to use any means to halt the expansion. The high ranking government officials, mostly from the Confucian school, determined that Catholicism was a threatening and harmful doctrine to the nation and the whole society. They began to persecute Catholicism again, and the persecution resulted in another massacre.

As soon as the regent of King Hunjong abdicated from his position because of illness, Lee, Ji Yeun, one of two vice prime ministers, and Chung, Ki Wha appealed to the King to exterminate the Catholics. One month later, the Queen, grandmother of the King, attended the Hijung-dang hall conference composed of the cabinet members. The Queen censured the high ranking judges and policemen for being unable to control the Catholic believers and permitted them to execute the Catholics. The Confucians designed the drama. In every corner of the country, Catholics were captured and put into prison. The Catholic Church was again wracked by a cyclone of persecution. During this persecution, the leading Catholics, including Lee, Kwang Yul, Hong, Yung Joo, Cho, Sin Chul, Kim, Je Joon, Choi, Yung Hhan, Chung, Ha Sang, Choi, Han Ji, and Yu, Jin Gil, were tortured to death. Eight Catholics who had been captured during the Junghae Massacre and had been imprisoned for over 19 years, were all beheaded.

This sudden persecution drove the believers into chaos. They left their families and properties seeking shelter. Some entered the depths of the mountains and others started on wandering journeys. Catholic Churches were destroyed. During the persecution, the believers were afraid that the French missionaries would be arrested and they tried to hide the foreign missionaries until the persecution was over. However, the government agencies were trying to trace the French missionaries. A Judas-like believer told the authorities where Father Imber was living, but before he was captured, Imber delivered himself to the government agents. Maubant and Chastan were no longer able to stand by while the believers suffered in order to keep their residence a secret. They, too, gave themselves up. After a painful torture, they were all sentenced to death. They were beheaded in the execution ground of Noryang-jin in September of the 5th year of King Hunjong(1839) under the ridiculing eyes of passers-by. Their bodies were left without care for three days and buried in the banks of the Han river. Imber was 43 years old, while Maubant and Chastan were 37 years of age at the time of their deaths.

The day after the French missionaries were beheaded, Chung, Ha Sang and Yu, Jin Gil were tortured to death. The two Catholics were the leading members of the Catholic church at that time. Chung, Ha Sang was the son of Chung, Yak Jong, who as sacrified during the Sinyu Massacre. Chung, Ha Sang had visited Bejing more than ten times to invite foreign missionaries to Korea. His letter to the King appealing for the protection of Catholicism, which contained over 3,400 words, added luster to the Chung family name. The composition of the letter was so good and Chung,

Ha Sang was a man of such great discernment that the people sent him the highest praises. Just before they delivered themselves to the authorities, Maubant and Chastan wrote to the Society of Foreign Missions in Paris and to their friends. The contents of the letter was very noble and full of the spirit of martyrdom. The letter provided encouragement for the Korean Catholics who were suffering under the severe persecution. The Kihae Massacre was more severe than any in the past, and its influence spread into all the corners of the country. During the massacre, about 130 Catholics were beheaded, but the number of captured is unknown. If fifty percent of the total Catholics were captured, over five thousand believers would have been arrested and imprisoned.

Reconstruction of the Church

Because Catholicism suffered so acutely during the Kihae Massacre, the expansion of Catholicism was at a virtual standstill for a while. Many of the masters of the families were killed or banished, and the suvivors were wandering on the streets looking for shelter and for their families. The situation was miserable.

The Society of Foreign Missions in Paris, which had no information about the Kihae Massacre, sent Bishop Jean Joseph Ferreol to help Imber in 1840. However, since he was not able to get in touch with Korean Catholics, he stayed in the outskirts of Fengtien in Manchuria for about two years. Two years later in 1842, he got in touch with Korean Catholics and he was informed about the situation of the Korean church at that time. He was appointed as the successor of Bishop Imber.

Since the entrance of foreign missionaries was very difficult after the Kihae Massacre, his attempts to enter the country failed many times. He sent the Korean Priest Kim, Dae Gun to Korea to get more information from the Korean Catholics. Kim, Dae Gun went to Shanghai accompanied by other Catholics, where they met Bishop Ferreol and Father Daveluy. The Korean believers led the two missionaries to the entrance of the Kum river in central Korea by sailing-vessel. After six years of constant effort, they were able to land at Kangkyung ; there they changed their clothes into mourning dress for the journey to Seoul. They engaged in preaching in Seoul. The next year, Kim, Dae Gun, the first Korean priest, was ar-rested while attempting to arrange to smuggle in another foreign miss-ionary. He was charged with having communicated with Western savages and was put to death in September of 1846 the 12th year of King Hunjong, on the sands of the Han river. Because they were careful in their manners, Ferreol and Daveluy were not captured. They used to act like mourners, wearing bamboo-hats and mourning dress.

When King Hunjong died without leaving an heir. one of the King's relatives came to the throne. The new King was the grandson of Lee, Gon, who had been put to death during the Sinyu Massacre. He was the King Chuljong, the 25th King of Lee Dynasty. During the 15 years of his reign, Catholicism was not persecuted very much, even though mem-bers of the King's mother's family attempted to disturb the political scene.

In the 6th year of King Chuljong, Korean Father Choi, Ryang Up re-turned to Korea and engaged in translating the Bible into Korean and in carrying out missionary work. Two years later, Father F. D. Ridel came to Seoul, and the two missionaries, Ridel and Choi, encouraged each other in missionary work. After Bishop Ferreol died of illness in 1853, Bishop Simon Berneux came to Seoul from Liaotung Peninsula as Ferreol's suc-cessor ; the following year two more French missionaries came to Korea by boat. In order to educate Korean missionaries, Berneux established a mission school in Jechun. During a peaceful period of over seven years, the lives of the Catholics settled down.

In the meantime, there were great changes in the Ch'ing Dynasty. As a result of the Opium War that abased her dignity, the Hoong Syu Chuan's revolt drew the country into the vortex of chaos. Moreover, the Arrow incident in which a British vessel figured, was a source of shame because the ungraceful behavior of Chinese officials insulted the British national flag and the Chinese officials kidnapped the Chinese guests on the boat. The Ch'ing government also executed French missionaries in the province of Kwangtung. These two incidents brought about an unfavorable result: the united armies of the two countries, England and France, occupied Kwangtung Province and Tientsin City in 1857 and eventually took Bejing and overran the Capital city. The Emperor of Ch'ing fled from the city to Joho Province. These changes within the Ch'ing territory were made known to the Korean government through its envoys. The Korean officials were afraid that the Ch'ing government in Korea might again persecute the missionaries. But the authority did not attempt to persecute Catholicism and the Westhern missionaries were free to preach and the believers were able to lead their religious life peacefully. Many people who had previously believed that Catholicism was a heresy of savages which disregarded the virtues of respect for the king, parents and Confucianism as the best prin- ciple on the earth, decided to be converted. They did not hesitate to hang the crucifix around their necks and visited the Western missionaries at their churches. The time of King Chuljong's rule, there were twelve French missionaries and twenty-three thousand Korean Catholics in Korea.

The Byungin Massacre

Freedom of religion during the reign of King Chuljong caused a rapid increase in the number of Catholics. The intention of the converts was not only to obtain spiritual salvation but also to save their lives if the Western soldiers attacked Chosun. When Catholicism was on the way to rapid expansion, King Chuljong died in 1863 without leaving a direct heir to the throne. A distant relative of the king ascended the throne, the infant King Kojong. The King was so young that the power was handed over to his father, Lee, Hung Sun. The regent had kept a close relationship with a Christian, Nam, Jong Sam, who was appointed to a high position in the government. The regent's wife also selected a Christian nurse for the young King. The regent and his wife understood Christianity well. Thus, the foreign missionaries in Korea were offered many advantages at first, but the regent's favorable attitude toward the Christians suddenly changed. As a result of Russia's request for an amity treaty in the second year of King Kojong's rule in 1865, a terrible massacre occurred.

In the first year of King Kojong, the Russian Admiral Rezanov, re-quested the Korean government to conclude a treaty of amity. Since the regent believed that the Russian's intention was to secure a ice-free port, Wonsan, and because he had heard of the cruelty and power of Russia, he did not want Russians coming to the northern part of Korea and in-tended to get rid of the Russian influence with the help of France through the French missionaries in Korea. The French missionaries tried to make the best of this opportunity in order to get legal recognition for their missionary work. Based on a draft by Nam, Jong Sam, they worked out a diplomatic plan and submitted it to the regent.

It was about the time that winter diplomatic missions came back to Korea from Bejing with information that the Ch'ing government had recovered its influence over the English and French in China and already cleared up the Western influences throughtout the territory of China and that the Russian battleships which had been treatening the Korea govern-ment on the northeastern coast had withdrawn of their own accord. It was not necessary for the government to beg for French assistance.

The wise regent feared that China might get angry if the Korean go-vernment entered into a diplomatic relationship with the French govern-ment. He decided to execute the Catholics on a large scale.

On January 12th of third year of King Kojong in 1866, an order pro-hibiting Western religious activity was issued, and the foreign missionaries and Nam, Jong Sam were ordered to be arrested. That evening, the terrible persecution began with the arrest of four French missionaries, including Berneux, and five Korean Catholics. Among the five believers there was one apostate. The next day, the terrible massacre was committed by Lee Kyung Ha's soldiers. No Catholic was granted a reprieve. The whole of Seoul City was thrown into utter confusion. About two thousand believers were killed in three days. It is said that the streams in the city were colored red with the blood of the victims. The storm of the massacre infilterated into every corner of the country, and the people trembled with terror.

The execution lasted for three years, during which over 8,000 Catholics were killed. This massacre gave the whole world the impression that Koreans were cruel:

Nine French missionaries captured during the massacre were ordered to leave the country, but they refused and were all beheaded. Around thirty thousand believers were scattered or killed and the foundations of the Church were thoroughly destroyed. Even so, Dae Won Koon, the regent, could not rest easy. In order to hunt up the hidden believers, he gave orders from a search party of every five families, through which he intended to get information of the survivors. Because the regent feared that Western troops might attack his government, he gave a strict command to blockade the coast line.

The bloody massacre was consistent with the Catholic history of Korea. During the massacres, the government officials executed the weak Catholics with swords and iron hammers. During the entire modernization process recorded in Korean history, the massacres and factional friction were the most unforgettable disgraces, and today, the fresh flood of the martyrs is still shining in a corner of the Korean history.

Protest of French Government

Three missionaries, including Ridel, got together in Chungpa-dong in Seoul. They discussed future problems and agreed to send Ridel to Bejing, where he was to asked to meet the French Minister and give him full information about the execution of the French missionaries during the Byungin Massacre. He was also to request protection from the French government.

The young missionary left Seoul at midnight for Inchon, where he left for China in a boat offered by a pious Catholic. He reached Tientsin in May of 1866. There he met Rose, the Commander of France's Asian Fleet and informed him of the details of the massacres. He also informed the Commander of the desperate plight of Father Feron and Calais, who were able to survive the massacre. The two French missionaries fled from Korea to China a little later. The French Minister in Bejing, who learned of the massacre from Rose, made a protest against the massacre to the government of China. But, the government answered they were not able to interfere in the Korean situation. Thus the French fleet, which had surrendered to China, decided to attack the little kingdom of Korea. They miscalculated and attempted to occupy Korea with only three battle-ships. When the French fleet reached the entrance of the Han river near Inchon, they faced a strong defence by the Chosun troops and gave up their intention to occupy Seoul.

In September of that year, Commander Rose sailed to Inchon Port again with six hundred soldiers and seven battle ships. The troops occupied Kanghwa Island and demanded that the Korean government make clear the details of the Massacre. Surprised, the regent sent a message to the whole country appealing for the voluntary cooperation of the nation. He enlisted soldiers and appointed Lee, Kyung Ha as the commander-in-chief and Lee, Yong Hee as the vice-commander. He ordered Commander Lee, Kyung Ha to defend Tongjin with 3,000 soldiers, and a unit of 500 soldiers was to defend Inchon on the left side and a group of 1,000 soldiers defended Bupyung on the right side. The defense of Kanghwa Island was planned with 3,000 soldiers. The area of Moonsu Mountain was defended by Han Sung Kun, the Jungjok Mountain side of the island was defended by Yang, Hun Soo, and the Kwangsung area by Lee, Ki Jo. After the allocation of soldiers was made, Han Sung Kun, who was in charge of guarding Moonsu Mountain, met the French troops in front of the gate of the mountain castle and defeated the French troops. Yang Hun Soo was odered to infiltrate into Jungjok castle with five hundred soldiers from the valley. The French fleet had to withdraw from the island. They set fire to the village where they had stayed for one month. During the fight on the Jungjok Mountain, four Catholics were beheaded on the charge of secretly communicating with the enemy.

This battle was called Byungin Yangyo. Regent Dae Won Koon, who had defeated the French troops, developed a fierce sense of pride, and his policy of national isolation and persecution of Catholics became more strict.

Enthusiasm of Missionaries

Even though the Korean land was colored with the blood of Catholics, the French missionaries' affection for Korea did not fade away. They waited for the change to begin again their missionary work in Korea. The cruel regent, Dae Won Koon, had to resign from power in the ninth year of King Kojong in 1872 because he failed in the scramble for power with Queen Min-bi. The Min family, from which the Queen came, seized power from the regent, Lee, Hung Sun. This faction of the Min family did not want to change the nations policy of isolation but the world situation forced them to change the direction of the policy. Korean territory was opened for the first time to the world by Japan. At that time, Japan had already concluded several treaties of commerce and amity with the Western countries, and she had tried to conclude such a treaty with Korea. But they could not conclude the treaty with Korea because of Korea's seclusion policy. In the 13th year of King Kojong in 1876, Japan threatened the Korean government by sending a battleship to Kanghwa Island. The Korean government finally signed the Byungja Treaty that year, under which the Korean government agreed to open three ports, Pusan, Inchon and Wonsan. At the time Japan concluded the treaty with Korea, the missionary Ridel was appointed as the Bishop of the Korean church. In the same year, Ridel sent the Father M.J.G. Blangc and another missionary to Korea, and he himself came to Korea the following year with two other missionaries.

For the first time in ten years, the Korean church could associate with French missionaries. However, the order prohibiting Catholic activity was still in effect, and the missionaries were soon arrested and put into prison, and in the end they were expelled from Korea. Through the governments of Japan and China, France had warned that it would consider it as a serious matter if the Korean government were to execute the captured

French missionaries. The Chinese government, which did not want to see any problem with the Western countries, advised Korea not to put them to death. So instead of being executed, the French missionaries were deported from Korea.

After the five missionaries were expelled, Bishop Mutel came to Korea in November of the 17th year of King Kojong in 1880 in order to take care of the believers without a shepherd. As with other foreign missionaries, he had to adjust to the Korean food, language and customs during his missionary work. He used to wear the mourning dress and a bamboo-hat on his head, covering his face with a large fan. In 1885, he was transferred to Paris Mission School, and five years later he returned to Korea as the Bishop of the Korea church.

Chapter 7
Freedom of Religion and the Development of Church

Entrance of the Missionaries

In the 19th year of King Kojong(1882), the United States of America concluded a Treaty of Commerce and Amity with the Korean government, and, naturally, the Korean government had to ease its Catholics persecution policy and of excluding Western people. Korean Catholics would have religious freedom for the first time since the beginning of its history in Korea. When the treaty was signed with the American government, Protestant missionaries began to come to Korea from America. The Holy See heard of this and hurried to appoint Blangc as the Bishop of the Korean church. The Bishop traveled Korea with seven other priests. It was recorded that the number of Catholics in Korea when Blangc returned was about 2,500. Two years later in 1886, the French government also concluded a Treaty of Commerce and Amity with Korea, and Ridel came to Korea again the next year. The French missionaries were also free to do their missionary work without wearing the mourning dress and bamboo-hat, and the believers could praise God in peace without fear.

Two years before the Treaty was signed, Blangc sent four Korean students, including Han, Ki Keun, to the Pennang Mission School in Malaysia, and a little later ten Korean students were sent to Pennang. However, because the climate and customs of Pennang were not fit for Koreans, Bishop Blangc determined to educate Korean priests in Korea, and he established two mission schools, one in Wonju and the other in

Yuju, where he began to educate Korean students. In the spring of 1887, he combined the two schools into one and named it the Holy Spirit Mission School. The school was moved to Yongsan in Seoul within the year. In the same year, he compiled principal doctrines of the Korean Catholic Church. Until then, the printing facilities with which all Korean Catholic writings were published were set up in Nagasaki in Japan. Blangc brought the facilities to Korea and began to publish all the books on Christianity in Korea. It was about this time that the four French nuns belonging to the Saint Paul Society came to Korea from the Chartres Nunnery and began to do charitable work. The foundation of Catholic Church became more secure.

In the 33rd year of King Kojong in 1896 after one hundred and nine years' persecution, the Korean government finally proclaimed the freedom of Western religion. By this time, Catholicism had grown greatly and there were over thirty thousand believers and thirty four missionaries in Korea.

Myungdong Catholic Church

After the Treaty of Commerce and Amity was signed between Korea and America, the Korean government signed similar treaties with Britain, Germany, Russia and France, and in these treaties religious freedom was formally recognized. Foreign Catholic missionaries were now able to buy land in Seoul, Inchon, Pusan, and Wonsan for building churches. The Bishop of the Korean Church, Blangc, decided to build a central church in Seoul. He bought a lot for church construction under the name of a Korean Catholic, and the building was designed by the Vicar Bishop, Coast, who was famous as a church architect. Unfortunately, Bishop Blangc died at 47 years of age, in February of 1890, the year the vicarage was completed. Bishop Mutel was his successor, and he continued construction on the building. After the ceremony of laying the corner-stone in the spring of 1892, construction on the Gothic church building, as designed, was started. During the construction of the building, the Dong Hak Revolt occured in June of 1894, and the Sino-Japanese War broke out a little later.

Moreover, because of an unstable situation in France, construction on the Church was temporarily halted. After the construction was resumed and when the frame of the walls were completed, another tragedy occurred ···the designer and supervisor of the work died. Bishop Poisnet hastily educated himself in architecture and completed the construction in 1898. The building was formally completed in June of the year.

The length of the main building is 213 feet, and the floor covers an area of 15,800 feet sq.. The belfry is 131 feet tall. It is the largest and first Western style church built in Korea.

Accident in Cheju Island

While the expansion of Catholicism was at its peak, there suddenly occurred massacre of about 700 Catholics on Cheju Island. Catholicism had been prospering gradually on the island, and Bishop Mutel sent two French missionaries to the island at the request of the believers on the island. Through the missionary efforts, there were about two hundred baptized Catholics in 1901, and over one thousand were going to convert. Some of these sought only to gain their own profits through the Western missionaries.

At that time, the government sent Kang, Bong Hun to the Island to collect taxes from the fishermen, and he was authorized to sell the government owned land and meadows to the residents of the island. Some of the Catholics bought some land and destroyed the sanctury and cut down the sacred trees on the land that they had bought. This caused a reaction from the non-Christian villagers. The bigoted villagers appealed to the chief of the island, but the officials were so corrupt that they were not able to resolve the conflict. The Catholics were supported by the foreign missionaries who were at that time under the protection of the government.

About 500 non-Christian villagers revolted and marched from Daejung County to Cheju town. The government official, Kang, Bong Hun, fled to the mainland, and the foreign missionaries and believers guarded the gate of the town castle. Both sides were deadlocked for a while but the non-Christians rallied under the agitation of Oh, Dae Hyun and attacked the castle for about one week. They killed about 200 Catholics who were outside the castle. The people in the castle were not able to withstand the revolt because there was insufficent food in the castle. As soon as the gate was opened, the revolutionaries surged into the castle and killed about 500 people whom they believed to be Catholics.

Two French missionaries were able to escape the terrible massacre due to the protection of the magistrate of the island. They left for Seoul and reported to Bishop Mutel what had happened on the island. The French fleet in Shanghai Bay was ordered to head for Cheju Island. When the fleet reached the island, the revolt had subsided and they evacuated the 40 Catholics remaining on the island to Mokpo port.

The Korean government ordered the eleven chief leaders of the revolt brought to Seoul. Among them, three people, Kang, Dae Hyun, Kang, Woo Back and Lee, Jae Soo were beheaded in September. The government official, Kang, Bong Hyun, was able to prove his innocence. After the situation became calm, French missionaries went over the island again and engaged in their missionary work. They established the Jin Sung School on the island.

Expansion of Catholicism

After religious freedom was proclaimed, though there were scattered persecutions in the country, including the unexpected Cheju Massacre, Catholicism had been expanding gradually. In 1910 when Japan annexed Korea, there was one Bishop, 15 foreign priests and 73,000 Catholic believers in Korea, and 69 Catholic Churches.

After the Korea-Japan Annexation was signed in 1910, the Japanese government realized that the Korean churches were the greenhouses for the growth of the Korean nationalism, but they did not persecute the Catholics because they did not want to create problems with the Western countries. The annexation did not cause any hardship to the Catholic development for a while. Moreover, there were many Koreans who preferred to live in the world of the Church waiting for their happiness to come after death rather than to lead a life as a subject of an occupied country. In 1911, the year after the annexation, the number of Catholic believers was eighty thousand. The Vatican divided the Korean Diocese into two, Seoul Diocese and Taegu Diocese. Mutel was appointed as the Bishop who was authorized to be responsible for the believers in the northern portion from Choongchong province and P.F. Demange was assigned as the Taegu Diocese Bishop who was authorized to supervise the southern portion from the Seoul Diocese.

Ten years after the annexation, the number of believers increased to about ninety thousand. Compared to the Protestant preaching activity, the result was not very encouraging. Although Protestantism was first introduced to Korea one hundred years later than Catholicism, it had secured over 200,000 believers by 1920, ten years after the Korea-Japan Annexation. Because the responsibility of the Seoul Parish for over 50,000 believers over a vast area was too heavy for one parish to carry out, the Seoul Diocese had to be divided into two parishes. Wonsan Diocese was established in the northern portion of the Seoul Parish in 1920, which was to be under the direction of the German Saint Society. The Wonsan

The status of Catholicism in 1920

Bishops	2
Priests	71
(Foreigners / Koreans)	(41 / 30)
Monks	26
(Germans / Koreans)	(21 / 5)
Nuns	88
(Foreigners / Koreans)	(10 / 78)
Churches	240
Believers	89,333
Mission School	50

Diocese was to control the churches in the provinces of Hamkyong province and Kanto. Bishop P.B. Sauer of the German Saint Society was assigned to the position of Wonsan Diocese Bishop. The Wonsan Diocese, whose headquarters were located in Dukwon, established a mission school, monastery and hospital, and its preaching activity was very successful. Due to his successful activity as the eight Bishop of the Korea Diocese, Bishop Mutel was made a Count and Cardinal Chamberlain and in 1920 was appointed as the first Archibishop of Korea.

Beatification of the 79 Blessed

The Beatification of the 79 martyrs was held in Rome in July, 1925. The Blessed is the name of those who are virtuous and pious and second in rank after Saints. During the Kihae Massacre in 1839, the Vicar Apostolic Imber wrote of the terrible suffering of the contemporary Catholics in Korea. At that time, he asked a lay believer, Hyun, Sok Moon, to write a detailed church diary.

When the Kihae Massacre was over, Ferreol became the successor of Imber. Since he recognized the significance of the Kihae Massacre, he wrote a detailed record of the Massacre, referring to the records by Imber and Hyun, Sok Moon and also to the evidence of eye witnesses. When the record of the Kihae Massacre was almost completed, the Byungoh Massacre occurred, during which nine believers, including Kim, Dae Kun, were killed. Ferreol added the nine martyrs to the record of the Kihae Massacre and sent it to the Vatican through the Parish Foreign Mission society in 1847. On the basis of the record, the Vatican continued its investigation, and made the final decision in May of 1925 to give the name of the Blessed to the 79 martyrs who had been faithful to death. The decision was made 79 years after the report was submitted. On July 5th, 1925, Pious XI conferred the title of the Blessed on the 79 martyrs in St. Peter's in the beatification ceremony.

On that day, the floor of the St. Peter's Sanetuary was covered with a fine carpet and the hall was decorated gracefully with electrical equipment and a picture of the 79 Blessed was put on the altar. Their spirit of mar-tyrdom was glorified. There were over ten thousand participants and there were seven Catholics from Korean including Mutel, Han Ki Taek and Chang, Myun.

The Beatification was a very honorable event for Korea, but it was very regrettable that the martyrs of Sinyu Massacre, including Yun, Ji Choong, and Choo, Moon Mo, and the victims of the Byungin Massacre, including Berneux, Nam, Jong Sam, Hong, Bong Joo, and the like, were not beatified. We hope they will be beatified some day. Among the 79 blessed, 31 were men and the rest were women.

Classification of the 79 Blessed

Bishops	1
Priests	3 (including 1 Korean)
Catholic students	2
Chairmen	15 (including 2 women)
Believers	58

Rearrangement of Dioceses

In 1923, the Catholic Foreign Mission Society of America sent Father P.J. Byrne to Korea, and the Society sent nuns next year, who engaged in preaching work in Pyongan and Hwanghae provinces. The influence of Protestantism was much stronger than Catholicism in the provinces, and the Catholic preaching activity was not successful. The Pyongyang Parish was established in the north-western portion of the Seoul Arch-diocese territory in March, 1927, and Father Byrne was assigned to the position of Bishop. The diocese was to be the responsibility of the Mary-knoll Society. Although the preaching activity of the Society was successful in the area, the total number of Catholics throughout the Country decreased slightly. This seemed to mean that Catholicism was going to develop qualitatively, while it had been developing in quantity in the past.

In July, 1928, after considering the special situation of the Catholics in Kando of Manchuria, the Yeunkil diocese was separated from Wonsan diocese. The Yeunkil diocese was to superintend the Kando area, and a Swiss, T. Breher, was appointed as Parish Bishop. He did his best to save the spirit of the believers until he was captured by the Communists in May, 1946. He was arrested along with other Christians and imprisoned. He died in November, 1950, on his way to banishment to his native coun- try. In July, 1928, when the Yeunkil diocese was first established, the Vacariate Florane office was established in the province of Hwanghae as a sample case, and a Korean Priest Kim, Myung Je was appointed as the vicar forane. The vicar forane is a position which superintend the church- men and general believers in a certain area, such as a town or city, on behalf of the Parish Bishop. It was the hope of the Pope at that time that the Korean church could be placed in charge of Korean priests, and the establishment of the Vicariate Forane was the first preparatory step.

In April of 1931, another vicariate forane office was established in the province of Chollabuk province in order to set up a Korean self-governing parish in that zone. It was to be under the direction of the Taegu diocese. The Korean priest Kim, Yang Hong was assigned as the vicar forane. In 1937, it was decided that the province should be an autonomous diocese, and the Korean priest Kim, Yang Hong was appointed as the Bishop.

It was one hundred years since the Vatican established the Korean church in 1931, and the one hundredth anniversary was marked in Sep- tember of the year. At the celebration of the anniversary, the remains of the first Bishop of Korea, Bishop Bruguiere, who died in Palikou on his way to Korea, were moved from Palikou to Myungdong Church. During the anniversary, there was a joint conference of all bishops and vicar forane in Korea, and they were determined to reform the Korean Catholic doctrine and to establish a central publishing center. They also decided to found the Catholic athletic center for more positive Catholic preaching activity.

The anniversary celebration was over and the Catholics had established a sound base in Korea. Bishop Mutel, who had been in charge of taking care of the Korean Catholic churches for 43 years, died in January, 1933.

Due to his death, the future of the Korean Catholicism was uncertain. But his successor Bishop Rario, who had been the vicar bishop successfully carried on.

In September, 1937, the Kwangju archdiocese was established in the west portion of the Taegu archdiocese. The Kwangju diocese had jurisdiction over the province of Chollanam province. As mentioned before, the Chollabuk province was under the authority of the Vicariate Forane office established in 1931. An Irish Bishop, Owen McPolin, from the Saint Columban Foreign Mission Society, was appointed as the Bishop of the Kwangju diocese.

Since the number of Catholics in Kangwon province had increased and the believers in the zone had difficulty in communicating with the Seoul archdiocese, the Choonchun diocese was established in 1940 in the eastern area of the Seoul diocese, and Bishop Thomas Quinlan was as signed to the position of Bishop. This diocese was also to be under the authority of the St. Columban Foreign Mission Society, and the established Wonsan diocese was divided into two parishes, Hamhung and Dukwon. At that time, there were eight diocese, five bishops and three diocese bishops in Korea. Two French bishops administered the Seoul and the Taegu dioceses and two Irish bishops superintended the Kwangju Parish and the Choonchun diocese. The Hamhung diocese and Dukwon diocese were administered by a German Bishop and an American Bishop governed the Pyongyang diocese. The Chunju diocese was under Korean bishop. There were 169 foreign and 139 Korean priests assisting them, and catholic churches in Korea had 110,000 believers.

Persecution by the Japanese Colonial Government

In order to occupy the mainland of China, Japan embarked upon the Bukou Chiao Bridge(near Bejing), without clear reason, and began to invade the land. The Nanking Government sent federal troops north and reacted against the Japanese invaders. The Japanese government dispatched a large force to the mainland with the slogan, "Retaliation Against Atrocious China, and they began to occupy Bejing, Nanking and Wuhan by turn. An all-out war between the two countries developed.

The Japanese government began to persecute the Korean people more severely so as to avoid future trouble in Korea, and the Korean people were put on a wartime footing. From 1937 the Japanese government prohibited Koreans to use the Korean language under the policy of "Assimiliation" which was intended to assimiliate Korea into Japan. They forced Koreans to worship at Japanese Shrines and, under the name of a voluntary system, they drove Korean young men to the front line. In 1940, the Japanese government forced Koreans to change their names into Japanese names, and the next year, began to arrest Korean patriots on a large scale upon the promulgation of the Acts of the Temporary Detention of Political Offenders. The Church had no choice but to follow the policy, but no one carried it out seriously.

After the Japanese started a war with America by attacking Pearl Harbor in December, 1941, the churches, mainly administered by the enemies of the Japanese began to be persecuted again. As soon as the Japanese entered the war against America and England, 35 American missionaries in the Pyongyang Parish and 32 Irish missionaries were imprisoned and the Americans were deported to their native land the next year. Since the French missionaries were also prohibited from doing their missionary work, the French Bishop of the Seoul diocese was forced to resign from his position, and a Korean Bishop, Noh, Ki Nam, succeeded the French Bishop. He was to administer the Pyongyang diocese and the Choonchun diocese in addition. Soon after the Korean Bishop took charge of the three dioceses, the Japanese authorities dismissed the French Bishop of the Taegu Parish and appointed a Japanese priest Hayasaka in his place. In February of 1943, the authorities assigned another Japanese priest Kyoda to be Bishop of the Kwangju diocese instead of the previous Irish bishop.

Catholicism receded, and most of the churchermen took part in worshiping the Japanese' Jinja. Because Catholicism did not offer strong resistance like Protestantism or Chonto-kyo, it did not suffer very much. As the war became more desperate in 1944, the Japanese government brought stronger pressure on all Koreans and arrested some Korean bishops who refused to take part in the Jinja worship. In the meantime, the Catholic Churches in Pyongyang, Taejon, Sinkye, Yeunan, Yangyang, and the like, were placed under requisition. It was indeed fortunate that the Catholic Churches did not suffer martyrdom during the Japanese occupation, though there were several persecutions.

A List of Catholic Hierarchy and Believers
(at the end of Dec., 1944)

Bishops and Priests	242
Fathers	56
Nuns	332
Churches	1,163
Believers	183,666(including non-baptized)

A Chronological Classification of the Numbers of Catholics(Exclusive of the non-baptized)

1866	23,000
1900	42,442
1910	73,517
1919	81,504
1922	91,320
1925	89,789
1928	86,026
1931	96,626
1934	100,752
1937	112,610
1939	113,562
1941	108,079
1943	116,687

Chapter 8
Orthodox Church

The right name of the Orthodox Church is the Holy Orthodox Priests Transmission Eastern Chruch. This Orthodox Church produced many martyrs and many famous fathers in the early years of Christian history. The Nicaea and Constantinople conferences which fixed the basic doctrine of Christianity were held in the East, but after the Western Church, which had its center in Rome, developed politically, the Orthodox Church became inactive. Originally the Eastern and Western Churches were different only in their administration and were in a brotherly relation, but in the Middle Ages, the Orthodox Church rejected iconoclastry while the Western Churches upheld it. They quarreled for about 300 years, and finally they divided into the Greek Orthodox and the Roman Catholic Churches respectively. Since then the Orthodox Church has spread to many Balkan Slavic countries and has established individual state churches, such as the Russian Orthodox Church.

The Russian Orthodox Church introduced the Orthodox Church to Korea. The Russian Orthodox Church was the most powerful church among the Orthodox Churches. The Russian Orthodox Church established a church in Korea for the first time in January of 1900, when the two powers, Russia and Japan, were competing with each other in Korea. At this time, Horisanpo, the Bishop, came to Korea with a choir conductor, Jona. He established a church with Siluski and Boriyaski, the Russian consular officers in Korea. As they began to hold services, they named the church as the Nicolai Church. Since Russia wielded great influence in Korea at that time, about 30 Imperial officials and diplomats were converted and attended the service. Realizing this, King Kojong granted state land in Sudaemoon for the church site in January, 1901 and the Russian consulate invited Father Sketokovsky, who built a church and preached the Gospel. Towards the end of the year a new church was completely built and they 'offered the building to God.' About 100 Koreans came to the church ; almost all were from the upper class.

When Russia was defeated in the Russo-Japanese War, the number of believers were temporarily reduced and Sketokovsky returned to his country. But after the war Father Ivanovsky came to Korea ; he was assiduous in preaching the Gospel and taught the ritual of the church to the candidates for the priesthood. The man who became the first Korean father was Kang, Ie Wan. He established 6 churches in Kyonggi province and was able to gather about 500 believers.

He also founded two educational institutes, educated 400 students and engaged in social work. Being recognized for his fine services in preaching the Gospel in Korea, Ivanovsky was promoted to Bishop and was transferred to his country on his promotion. In 1913 Father Iriney came but returned the following year. After that Father Bradimil engaged in preaching the Gospel with Father Kang for about 3 years. Later Father Piotosi arrived, introduced Kim Luke as the second Korean Father, and worked zealously. Since Lenin's Soviet Union had been established, preaching funds were cut from Russia and his preaching activity came to a standstill, while educational and social relief institutes were closed. Father Piotosi remained as the sole Russian Father and continued to preach the Gospel until 1932, striving that churches might attain independence. He fell ill and "ascended to Heaven" after he went to Japan. Father Alexander then came to this country from the Japanese parish and was later replaced by Father Porikav who worked here even after the Liberation of Korea. When World War II broke out, Japanese authorities suppressed even these tiny churches, put Father Kim into prison, and tortured some of the believers. Father

Kim's elder brother died in prison. The number of known believers right after the Korean Liberation was only 20 to 30.

Part VI

Christianity(2)

Part II
Christianity (2)

Chapter 1
The Introduction of Protestantism

Protestantism

Christianity, which made a great contribution in breaking feudalistic customs and in enlightening the people throughout the latter period of Korean history(a period of full of bloody party strife), was that of the Roman Catholic. Since the time Roman Catholicism was introduced to Korea, it became the greatest force in sowing the seed of the Gospel to the people, liberating them from old customs and developing their culture, but because the lingering poison of persecution was not fully abated, the intensity of propagation decreased a little at the end of Lee's reign. At this time when the force of Catholicism became feeble, Protestantism entered this country from America, then a young country in the Western Hemisphere ; it showed its youthful vigor in preaching the Gospel and within 20 years, it surpassed Catholicism in fluence. Today, not even a 100 years, later, Protestant missionaries propagated in Korea so extensively that the number of its adherents can be counted at more than eight million. Protestantism not only occupies the premier position among the religious in Korea, but it also contributes much to the development of our culture.

Protestantism, which left its great footmarks in developing our culture and changed the world of thought since the end of the Lee Dynasty, is essentially in the category of Christianity ; its basic doctrine is not different from that of Catholicism. Its difference lies only in its ritual and other superficial aspects. The Christianity which was persecuted for about 300

years in the Roman Empire, was finally adopted as the state religion of
Rome by Constantine the Great in the early years of 4th century. Papal
rights were established, but Christianity was corrupted internally and lost
the dignity of its religion in the 16th century. A great amount of money
was required in the administration of the Vatican and antipathy was provoked among the people because of the burdensome taxation which was
imposed on them by the Vatican. The believers became weary of the
excessive interference in the churches from the Vatican, and various church
rituals ; they also were more and more discontented with the exploitation
of the rich monastic class. Therefore Christianity had to be converted
wholly into a living religion by many pious and faithful reformers, but
they could not achieve their wishes and many of them were killed at the
hands of the Vatican. When the corruption of the Vatican became greater
and they began to sell Indulgences, for atonement, the good but unenligh-
tened people strove to be the first to buy Indulgences to atone for the
sins they committed in the world. Martin Luther, a German Priest, declared
the famous Faith Confession in 1517 and asserted that Christianity should
be reformed, by giving an explanatory letter in the following year. This
reformation of Martin Luther brought about the Christian reformation
movement in Germany and spread to many European countries, such as
France, England and Switzerland. It became the great power which was
opposed to Roman Catholicism ; the Puritans moved to the New American
Continent and established a new country, ensuring the prosperity of Protestantism.   Since it was reformed by protesting against Christianity, it
is called the Protestant Church as the word protestant means a resistor.
We speak of the Protestant Church as the new church and the Catholic
Church as the old church. Thus Roman Catholicism and Protestantism
are not different in basic doctrine, but only in their process of origin in
worship and in acceptance of the Pope in Rome. Another difference between them lies in that Protestantism allows a little more liberty in inter-
preting the Bible. In any case the Protestants who were suppressed in
England moved to the New American Continent to acquire liberty of faith

and they established a new country with a pioneer and reformative spirit. They extended all possible efforts in overseas preaching work and as soon as they broke new ground to open a mission in Korea, assiduous missionaries entered this country and brought a flourishing Protestantism, breaking the traditional religious power.

Transmission of Protestantism

People who tell the story of Protestantism's first introduction to Korea, know that Robert S. McClay of the American Methodist Church came to Korea in June, 1884, had an audience with King Kojong and got permission to open a mission, but a man from Holland transmitted Protestantism to Korea for the first time. A Nethelandish cruiser, Aubel Kelk, let three of its sailors, including John J. Weltvree, land at Cheju Island due to a shortage of drinking water in the 5th year of King Injo in 1626. They decided to live in Korea. Weltvree changed his name to Park Yeon and preached the Gospel as a Christian. This might be the first time that Protestantism was introduced to Korea. Then the Sparwar, a Dutch trading vessel, was wrecked on the coast of Cheju Island in the 4th year of King Hyojong ; 36 officers and crew were rescued by Korean authorities and were detained at Yosu, Soonchun, Namwon, etc.. 8 crew members among them at length returned to Amsterdam, Holland, after 14 years of detainment, having escaped through Nagasaki, Japan. Hendrick Hamel, one of the escaped crew, published his "quaint and racy account" of his experiences in Korea called Narrative of Hollandes Wrecked Quelpart. It was believed that since these Hollanders were Protestants, they preached the Gospel while they were detained in Cheju Island, Seoul, Yosu, Soonchun, Namwon, etc.. But there is no evidence that they preached in Korea.

It was not for the purpose of preaching Gospel that Weltvree, Hamel and their parties stayed in Korea, but due to the wreck of the ship. The very first man who came to Korea to propagate Protestantism, was Carl A.F. Gutzlaff, a Netherlander of Deutsch lineage. He belonged to the Netherlands Missionary Society and was one of the friends of Robert

Morison, the Pioneer Protestant missionary to China.

When, in the 32nd year of King Soonjo(1832), a British warship, the Lord Amast vayaged to Korea, via the northern coast of China, requesting an opening of commercial intercourse, Gutzlaff also came as interpreter, landed at Hongchun, Kodai Islands and preached the Gospel for about 30 days. This work was made at the request of Morison ; he translated the Lord's prayer into Korea with the help of some Korean fishermen. He presented two Bibles in Chinese and religious tracts to King Soonjo and returned. This preaching work in Choongchong province was believed to be the first time that Protestantism was actually introduced to Korea, but the seeds were sown on such rocky ground.

33 years after Gutzlaff visited Korea, the Rev. Robert J. Thomas, a Walesman, came to the coast of Hwanghae province, on board a Chinese fishing vessel, in September of the second year of King Kojong in 1865. He sojourned there until December of the same year and preached the Gospel at Baikryung Island and other islands for about 3 months. His motive for deciding to preach the Gospel in Korea was as follows : He learned the pathetic status of the papal church in Korea under regent Dai Won Koon from two Koreans who escaped from the severe persecution of Catholics in Korea. This was at the house of Alexander Williamson, the agent of the National Bible Society of Scotland. He thereupon started to Korea to begin a mission, feeling "an oracle from God". He came to Korea with Kim, Moon Pyung, one of the two refugees, as his guide, and intended to meet Dai Won Koon to get permission to preach the Gospel in Korea, while he was propagating the Hwanghae province coasts. But during the voyage the boat was wrecked twice and had to return back to China. But his enthusiasm of opening a mission in Korea could not be dampened and he began to learn the Korean language in Sangdong, employing a Korean. Meanwhile he heard that an American Vessel, the General Sherman, was going to sail to Korea in the hope of opening the country to commerce ; he requested the captain to take him along ; again he had an opportunity to visit Korea in 1866, the third year of King

Kojong. The General Sherman, mistaking the Taitong river, as the Han river, was proceeding toward Pyongyang when the ship anchored at the shore, where Williamson distributed the religious tracts to the people. Since our government had adopted the national isolation policy at that time, the Chief of Pyongyang, Pyongan province requested the General Sherman to retreat from the city. They did not obey, but kidnapped the Korean soldiers, lynched and plundered them.

The angry soldiers burned the ship by a fire attack(which Kongmyng had used to annihilate Tsau Tsau's fleets in old Chinese history) and killed all the sailors in the vessel. Thomas, who boarded the General Sherman, had advised the captain not to do violence, but when he was in a desperate situation when the ship caught fire, he threw the Bibles to the beach, left the vessel with a Chinese, Cho, Nung Bong, and implored the soldiers to save his life. But the outraged military and civilians struck them violently and beheaded them at Suksom Island. Thomas prayed to heaven, and kneeling down, gave the murderer a Bible ; the latter postponed beheading Thomas for a while, being conscience-stricken.

Hesitating for a moment, with the Bible that Thomas gave him in his left hand, he eventually beheaded Thomas. The murderer was converted and became a faithful Christian later when American missionaries entered this country and preached the Gospel in Kwansu Districts. His nephew, Lee, Yong Tae, graduated from Union Christian College in Pyongyang and engaged in translating the Bible. During this time of confusion, a 12 year-old boy, Choi, Chi Ryang, returned home with 3 Bibles that Thomas had given him, but in fear he handed them to a soldier, After being converted to Christianity, he visited the soldier's house and found that the paper of the Bible was being used to cover the wall of his house. In January of the 3rd year of King Kojong, the American government dispatched Admiral Schufelt, the Asia Fleet Commander, to investigate the burning accident of the General Sherman. In Wachuselt, Hunter Corbett, one missionary of the American North Presbyterian Mission came on board with him and preached the Gospel, staying at Mokdong-po in

Hwanghae province for a week. In September of the 4th year of King
Kojong, Williamson, who supported Thomas' preaching work, came to
the Korea Gate in South Manchuria to know Thomas' whereabouts in
person and asked the passing Koreans for some trace of Thomas. At the
same time, he distributed religious tracts and the Bible in Chinese to the
people. Shortly before this, the American govermnent dispatched Admirals
Rowen and Shenandoh for the second time to investigate the burning
accident of the General Sherman. O.C. Mater, a missionary of the American
North Presbyterian Mission, who was staying at Dungchou, Sangung,
came along with the ship and preached the Gospel, tracing Thomas'
whereabouts.

John Ross and McIntyre

John Ross and his brother-in-law John McIntyre, were Scotch Presbyterian missionaries. They had been preaching the Gospel to the Chinese
and Koreans since they came to Manchuria in 1873. Ross reached Linchiang
through Hsingching and Tongwha, looking for opportunities to bring
the Gospel into Korea, but the severity of the precaution along the boundary of the Yalu River prevented him from crossing the Korean boundary;
even to the end, he was not permitted to enter the country. He could
only deliver religious tracts and the Bible to the opposite bank of the
boundary. But none of this were discouraged them from preaching the
Gospel to the Koreans. They met Lee, Ung Chan who came to a market
which was opened at Korea Gate in spring of 1874 (the 11th year of King
Kojong, and told him about their preaching plan. The missionaries invited
Lee to Nyuchuang and employed him as their Korean language teacher.
Originally, Lee Ung Chan was a Euijoo youngman and though he engaged
in business, coming and going through the boundary gate, he was much
interested in studying a different culture and he taught Korean to the
missionaries, devoting his heart and soul to the project. On the other
hand he was not idle in studying the New Culture. He went to the market
again and took Baik, Hong Joon, Kim, Jin Ki and Lee, Sung Ha, who

were of the same mind with him and of the same native place in the fall of the same year. They worked hard for the missionaries and in 1876, deciding to "believe in Jesus", were baptized by McIntyre. They became the first Protestants in Korea. These two missionaries were translating the New Testament with the help of these four Koreans. Su, Sang Ryoon, who was born in Euijoo, was much impressed by the kindness of the two missionaries when he went he went to Myuchuang for the purpose of trade. He confessed his faith, was baptized in 1881 and helped the missionaries translate the Bible with the earlier 4 Koreans. Su, Sang Ryoon, who was the fifth to be baptized became the first Korean pastor. In the spring of 1882 Ross went to Fengtien with Baik, Hong Joon, Kim, Chin Ki and Su, Sang Ryoon installed a printing machine, and succeeded in publishing Luke and John in the fall of the same year. Matthew, Mark and the acts were published in 1883 and then the remaining New Testament under the title of "The Complete Work of Jesus' Holy Teachings". This was the first New Testament which was published in Korean ; it is called the New Testament translated by Ross.

As they published the New Testament, Ross gave the Gospels to Su, Sang Ryoon and Lee, Sung Ha and let them preach the Gospel at the villages of East and South Manchuria where Koreans lived and it was reported that many people wanted to believe in Jesus. They visited their fellow countrymen who scattered in the foreign country at the risk of their lives. After they returned, Ross and McIntyre went round to the East Manchurian districts, and since there were many people who wished to be baptized, they were able to baptize 75. The important part of the Bible was published and was spread to the brethren in Manchuria, but it had to be sent into Korea quickly. But since it had only been several years since Thomas was murdered and the Bible was strictly forbidden in Korea, it was very dangerous to enter the country with the Bible. At this time Su, Sang Ryoon who engaged in preaching the Gospel with Ross departed from his colleague in 1883, the 20th year of King Kojong and arrived at the boundary gate, leaving Fengtien, with the Bibles in Korean and Chinese. Korean and Chinese authorities were stationed there and checked on passers-by. Su, Sang Ryoon was captured at this place, but fortunately one of his relatives was among the Korean authorities and he could return to Euijoo, his native country, tiding over the crisis. Translating the Bible, Ross, who had particular talents in language and writing, wrote "A Guide to Korean and English" and "Corea, It's History, Manners and Customs" and introduced Korea to England for the first time.

The Opening of Isolated Korea

The Korean people led a hard life within small area in this peninsula, served the Chinese nations, Song and Won as their head family, and Ming and Ch'ing as their main family and so could not make contact with Western countries even in the latter period of Lee Dynasty. When Korea began to know about the Western countries, Russia took vast Siberia into her hands by the Ai Hoon Treaty(1858) and was threatening Manchuria and the Ili Districts. England concluded the Namking Treaty with the Chinese, possessed Hong Kong and set up extra territoriality robbing Hong Kong of 21 million dollars as the reward for winning the Opium War. France also overran Bejing and Tienjin together with England suffered loss when the Arrow Accident broke out ; based on the ground that their missionaries were killed ; they snatched an indeminity of 8 million dollars by concluding the Bejing Treaty in 1860. Seeing these accidents, the Korean Government had come to the conclusion that it had better not deal with these Western countries for the sake of national safety. Korea, which was founded on Confucianism, thought that it was not good to conclude a treaty of amity with Western countries who believed in Christianity. In this political calculation, Dai Won Kun put forward the consistent national-isolation policy. However, after his abdication of office, a treaty was inevitably concluded with Japanese due to the Woonyang-ho accident when the Chojichin battery attacked the Japanese battleship in the 12th year of King Kojong. In the following year, the representatives of the two countries concluded a treaty of amity and reached anagreement that each country should exchange missions and Korea should open Pusan and two other ports(1876).

Isolated Korea could make contact with modern culture for the first time by opening its door by the Kangwha Treaty. Since the Korean Government noticed Japan's intention to establish her influence in Korea, she also concluded a Korean-American Amity and Commerce Treaty in Tienjin, between American representative Shupelt and Korean representative Eu, Yoon Choong in 1882. This was with the help of Lee, Hung Chang, who took charge of Chinese foreign policy to keep the international power in balance. Lee, Hung Chang intended to insert the item that America should not recognize the independence of Korea and that missionaries should not engage in preaching the Gospel in Korea, but the two provisions were omitted when the actually signed the treaty due to the strong assertion of America. The Korean-American Amity and Commerce Treaty was the first treaty that Korea concluded with Western countries.

Following the treaty with America, the Amity and Commerce Treaty was concluded with England and Germany 2 or 3 years later and Korea then concluded similar treaties with Italy, France, Austria and Belgium. She opened her door completely to other countries, and religious activity became more liberal. As soon as the long-closed door was opened by the Amity and Commerce Treaty with America and Germany in the 19th year of King Kojong, many of the Evangelistic Missions wanted to propagate the Gospel, taking advantage of this good opportunity.

At this time the first missionaries who attempted to enter this country were the Americans. The American Methodist and Presbyterian missionaries who stayed in Tokyo contacted Kim, Ok Kyoon and Lee, Soo Chung and together they engaged in mission work in Korea and taught the Bible and English to Korean students in the city. The persons that had contact with Koreans at that time, were George W. Knox of the American North Presbyterian Church, Robert S. McClay of Methodist Church and Henry Loomis, the general secretary of the American Bible Society. Of them,

Loomis translated and published Mark to preach the Gospel in Korea with the help of Lee, Soo Chung. At the same time Knox sent a memorial to the North Presbyterian Mission Center and appealed to begin a mission work in Korea, and Gilbert Reid of the American Presbyterian Mission who stayed at Chihfu, China, also asked the Board of Mission to open a mission in Korea.

Chapter 2
The Propagation of Protestantism

Methodist Church

In spite of all the efforts of the missionaries who came to China, the American churches and little knowledge about Korea and very few people who could say they understood Korea. They knew only that Korea was the country which slaughtered many Catholics and killed foreign missionaries and thought that it was very difficult to open a mission in Korea. Besides that, there were no regulations about propagation in the Korean-American Treaty and though there was something like that in the Korean-English Treaty, it was restricted only to the districts in which Englishmen resided to preach the Gospel and didn't guarantee the liberty of doing mission work in Korea. Thus the American churches were hesitant to begin mission work in Korea, but the mission work began quite incidentally in this country. In June, 1882 the Korean Government sent a special mission to the United States consisting of Min, Yung Ik, and his attendants, Su, Kwang Bum and Hong, Yung Shik, and while the party was on its way from San Francisco to the East, they met the Reverend John F. Goucher President of Goucher College, Baltimore, who happened to be travelling with them on the same train.

During the overland journey, Goucher formed a personal acquaintance with Min, Yung Ik and learned much about Korea. Goucher was intensely interested in Korea as a possible mission field and wrote to the Board of the Foreign Missions of the Methodist Church, asking to send missionaries to Korea and produced a donation of two thousand dollars toward securing that result. He also wrote to R.S. Maclay, the Superintendent of the Methodist Mission in Japan, suggesting that he "make a trip to Korea and open a mission in the country". Thus Maclay came to Korea, and had an audience with King Kojong through Kim, Ok Kyoon's good offices, staying about three months. After he got permission to begin a hospital and school work in Korea, he returned to Tokyo and reported to the Board that all went well and it was possible to preach the Gospel in Korea. Allen D. Clark wrote in his book "The History of Korean Church" that this fact was published in the Christian Advocate, the leading church paper of the Methodist Church and in the Gospel in All Lands, a paper on Korea mission work. Therefore the American churches were very much interested in mission work in Korea. Because 5,000 dollars was prepared for the preaching fund, the North Methodist Church decided to begin mission work in Korea and dispatched Mr. and Mrs. Henry D. Appenzeller and Dr. William B. Scranton in Feb., 1885. They departed from San Francisco, made the voyage through a rough sea and finally arrived at Yokohama, Japan. Dr. Scranton and her son began to learn Korean from Park, Young Hyo, a Korean envoy to Japan and the Appenzellers proceeded to Korea, arriving at Inchon on Sunday morning, April 5, 1885.

The Rev. Horace G. Underwood, who made a great contribution to the history of Protestantism in Korea later, was also on the same ship with them. At first he intended to serve in India, but was appointed a missionary in Korea and learned Korean from Lee, Soo Chung for two months, entering the country with the Appenzellers. Besides him, Dr. Taylor and Scutter, on a diplomatic mission to Korea, were also travelling on the at ship. Originally Appenzeller wanted to preach the Gospel in Japan, but since one of his colleague missionaries could not come to Korea on account of his personal situation, he was appointed as the missionary on his behalf and was sent unexpectedly to Korea. It was Easter Sunday, the 5th of April, 1885, when Appenzeller stepped in on Korean Christianity, they "glorified God, pitching their voice high"and prayed that God might bless their mission work in the country.

Mr. Underwood, being single, was permitted to proceed to Seoul, but Mr. Appenzeller was requested to return to Japan because he was accompanied by his wife. The Appenzellers were not permitted to go to Seoul because the American deputy envoy, Foulk, warned them that it was unsafe for a foreign woman to enter Seoul ;the Japanese and Chinese soldiers were gathered together in the city, competing with each other and some event might arise since the Progress Party had taken the helm of state-affairs since the Kapshin political Upheaval in October of the previous year. Maclay, who had been to Korea before, advised Scranton to enter Korea and acting on this advice, Scranton left his wife and mother in Japan and proceed to Korea, arriving there in May ;following him, Mr. Appenzeller also entered the country at the end of June and planned to establish a church by buying a site for that purpose. Then the Rev. D. A. Bunker came to Korea and engaged in school and mission work. Dr. Scranton had worked with Dr. Allen in the Royal Hospital for a while and established a Royal Charity Hospital, Shi Byung Won, in 1886, by himself and took charge of the hospital.

In the meantime Cholera spread throughout the country and Scranton cured many patients, and thus he won the hearts of many people. The gate of preaching opened itself and Dr. Appenzeller established the Cheil Church at Jung-dong, Seoul and Paichai School in June, 1886 making great efforts in missionary and education work. On the other hand, Mrs. Mary Scranton established the first girls' school in Korea in October, 1885, but since at that time the parents did not let their daughters go out of doors, they only could get one student in June of 1886, and named the school Ewha Hakdang, having 7 students in January of the following year. The word "Paichai" means to cultivate generous and capable men and "Ewha"the pure-flower-of-pear which symbolized the Royal House-hold at that time and thus they named the schools.

After the Appenzellers and Scrantons entered Korea, the Revs. Oringer and Jones followed them and ten other missionaries entered the country; thus the missionary and hospital works made rapid progress. Mr. Appenzeller who took the lead of these missionaries was drowned when he saved a Korean when their boat capsized at sea near Kunsan on their way to Cholla province district to preach the Gospel.

While the American North Methodist Church was engaged in mission work for about ten years, the South Methodist Church had the opportunity to preach the Gospel in Korea from Shanghai, China, crossing the West Sea. A young man, Yoon, Chi Ho, who exiled himself avoiding the up-heaval of Korea, became a Christian when he heard the sermon at an American Southern Methodist Church in Shanghai. He went to America, and studied at Vanderbilt University and Emory College and returned to Korea. He sent letters to the Board of American South Methodist Mission many times to send missionaries to Korea as he eagerly preached the Gospel. His earnestness moved the hearts of Candra Bishop and the leading members of the church and the Mission Board asked the missio-naries who stayed in North China to dispatch a group to determine whether it was proper to begin a mission work in Korea or not. Thus Bishop E. A. Hendricks, being accompanied by D.F. Reid, proceeded to Korea and landed at Inchon in 1895 after five days' journey by sea from Shanghai. It was the time that the internal situation was very precarious since Queen Myung Sung had been killed by Japanese terrorists. The Cabinet was reorganized and the people were less haunted with fear. But he decided to enter Seoul in spite of the danger and succeeded in reaching Seoul through the Han River, boarding a small wooden boat. They inspected many interior situations and could attend the Annual Methodists Confe-rences by favor of the American North Methodist Church missionaries. They also met Korean preachers who came up to Seoul from the count-ryside so they could hear about the country situations. They also received in audience with King Kojong and got permission to dispatch missionaries to Korea.

Hendricks, Reid and their company were intending to make Korea one of the Chinese parishes and do the mission work. On the 1st of May of the following year Rev. Reid began to preach the Gospel and he prepared to propagate in the districts from Seoul to Wonsan through Kaesung. The Rev. Collyer came to Korea in January of 1887 and the South Methodist held the first service by the sermon of Yoon, Chi Ho at the Reid's.

The Presbyterian Church

After the Korean and American Amity and Commerce Treaty was concluded, the political situation was still precarious and many of the American North Presbyterian Church missionaries said that it was too early to dispatch missionaries to Korea, but since Dr. F.F. Ellinwood emphasized the mission work in Korea and a lay Christian P.D. McWilliams was so much impressed by it, he donated a great sum of 6,000 dollars for the mission work in Korea. And so American North Presbyterian Mission decided to open a mission in Korea and searched for the missionaries who would go there . A young doctor, John H. Heron applied for the position and they dispatched him to Korea. But on his way to Korea, he inquired about the situation of Korea and being told that it was too early for the missionaries to enter Korea, he remained in Japan until June, 1885 learning Korean.

Some time before this, Dr. H.N. Allen, who worked as a medical missionary of the American North Presbyterian Church in Shanghai, arrived in Seoul in September 1884. He was appointed as physician to the American Legation and later to the English and Japanese Legations, looking for an opportunity to preach the Gospel. In less than three months after entering Seoul, the so-called Kapshin Political Upheavel broke out on the 4th of December ; Seoul was in turmoil due to the discord between the Conservative and Progressive Parties. Min, Yong Ik, the chief of the Conservative Party, who was also the nephew of Queen Myung Sung, was stabbed by an assassin and severely wounded. At this time Allen cured him and was appointed to the office of court physician, thus winning the confidence of the court. As the first step of his mission work, he wanted to establish a modern hospital in Korea and was permitted to build a hospital　he was given a building by the court at Donghyun which could afford to admit 100 patients. It was the Royal hospital and later became Severance Hospital.

In April of the following year when Allen came to Korea, the Rev. H.G. Underwood, who left great footmarks in the history of Korean Christianity, came to Korea. Allen was a physician, not a pastor. Therefore the North Presbyterian Church, recognizing the need for pastors in Korea, dispatched Underwood, who had just graduated from the Theological Seminary and who hoped to do mission work in a foreign country. After entering Seoul, he devoted himself to preach the Gospel ; the adherents increased day by day. In July of the following year, the Korean Government invited three English teachers ; H.B. Hulbert was among them and with his help, Underwood could administer Baptism and Holy Communion on the 11th of July for the first time in Korea. Since the prohibition to Western religion was not yet removed, they made provisions against any emergency by setting a guard at the door as they baptized the Christians. At this time seven persons were baptized by Underwood, the first fruits he "devoted to God" in Korea. Underwood began a mission school called Yook Yung Kongwon at Jung-dong and organized the first Presbyterian Church in 1887.

The Australian Presbyterian Church was represented by J. H. Davis and his sister who came to Korea in October 1889 and began to preach the Gospel in Kyongsang provinces, but after one year, he was taken ill with smallpox and died for the people of our country in a corner of Pusan.

The North American Presbyterian Church began to do mission work in 1892. The American Government planned to open the world exhibition in commemoration of the 400 years since Columbus discovered America and the Executive Committee of Foreign Missions of the American North Presbyterian Church decided to dispatch seven missionaries to Korea. The appointed missionaries were the Rev. W. N. Junkin, the Rev. W. D. Reynolds,　the Rev. L. B. Tate and his sister and Miss Linnie Davis. Prepared to devote themselves in a strange country, they left San Francisco in October, 1892, and arrived in Korea in November of the same year. They settled in Seoul for the time being, learned Korean and began to study the customs of Korea. They chose the beautiful fertile Cholla district as their mission field and settled in Kunsan and Chunju ; after they learned Korean and studied the customs of our country, they engaged positively in mission work.

While they were studying the Korean situation, they preached the Gospel only to the people who visited them from near and far places, but after they could speak Korean well and knew the customs of the country, they visited every village, searching for "the lost lambs", and their religious power developed rapidly.

The Canadian Presbyterian Church opened the path of propagation in Korea through Rev. William J. McKenzie. While he was engaged in the mission work in the eastern coast of Canada, he heard that missionaries were needed in Korea and so he applied to come to our country. He gathered mission funds from his friends and came to Korea, via the Pacific Ocean. After he stayed in Seoul for several months, he proceeded to Songchun at the request of the adherents, though it was difficult to dispatch and station missionaries in a small village due to the shortage of the number of missionaries. McKenzie decided to devote himself to Korea and led an uncomfortable life, wearing Korean clothing and eating Korean food. This sudden change of his mode of living made the time of his death come earlier, and he breathed his last in a poor village of a foreign country after he had propagated the Gospel for 14 months. His great faith won many believers who built a great church by themselves. Songchun Church wrote a letter to the Foreign Mission Board of Canadian Presbyterian Church, admiring his great service in Korea and asked them to send another missionary on behalf of him after his death. In spite of the financial difficulty, the Canadian Presbyterian Church decided to dispatch a new mission group and Rev. W. R. Foote and D. M. McRae with his wife and Dr. Robert G. Grieson and his wife came to Korea in September, 1898. This was the first time that the Canadian Presbyterian Church preached the Gospel in Hamkyong province.

The missionaries from the American North and South Presbyterian Churches and Canadian Presbyterian Church arrived continously and engaged in mission work ; the number of adherents increased by days and months, but since there was no upper organization which controlled these missionaries, there was some handicap in its cooperative work and so the American and Australian Presbyterian Churches organized a consultation in 1889. In January of 1893, the missionaries of each Presbyterian denomination organized the Council of Missions Holding the Presbyterian Form of Government which adopted the Presbyterian Politics ; Reynolds was selected as the first chairman of the organization. We call this the Council of Missions.

Anglican Church

When the Amity and Commerce Treaty was concluded between Korea and England in 1884, the Anglican Church also planned to dispatch missionaries to Korea ; Bishop Scan, who stayed in north China, and Paikelstell in Japan, visited Korea in 1887 and asked the Mission Board of the Anglican Church to help propagate the faith in Korea. Thus Archbishop Benson of the Anglican Church ordained Bishop C. J. Corfe who was working in the navy on all Saint's Day(the first of November) in 1889. Then Corfe ordered Dr. Julius Wiles and Dr. E. B. Landis to go to Korea and to begin medical work, seeking an opportunity to do mission work. They opened a clinic in Inchon in the August of 1890 ; in September Corfe also came to Seoul through Inchon and established a church. Later Wiles and E. H. Boldock built new churches in Seoul and Inchon , consolidating the foundation of propagation of the faith.

The Baptist Church

The Baptist Church is the most powerful Protestant Church in America, but the first Baptist Church which began its mission work in Korea was the Canadian Baptist Church. Rev. M. C. Penwick, who was sent from the Y.M.C.A of Toronto University in Canada as a Baptist missionary in Korea, began to preach the Gospel in Wonsan in 1889. Several other missionaries entered the country later and preached the Gospel in Kongju. In 1894 Rev. C. E. Pauling, who was dispatched by the Ellathing Memorial Mission, and F. W. Steadman, established several churches, but they were not so prosperous.

Seventh-Day Adventist Church

This church was first introduced to Korea by Sohn, Heung Cho and Lim, Ki Ban, the employees of the Hawaiian Cultivating Company in 1904. In April of 1904 Sohn, Heung Cho and Kim, Woon Hyun were baptized by the Rev. Kunikawa in Kobe on their way to Hawaii ; as they were returning home, Lim, Ki Ban who was on the same vessel with them was converted by their preaching. This began the strange relation of Korea with the Seventh-day Adventist Church. They returned to their native places and preached the Gospel. They asked the Seventh-day Adventist Mission in Japan to dispatch missionaries and in August 1904, the Rev. Kunitani and F. W. Field came to Korea ; thus the mission work of the church was regularized.

Taking this opportunity, they succeeded in preaching the Gospel in Kyongsangbuk, and Pyongannam provinces, the native places of Sohn, Heung Cho and Lim, Ki Ban respectively. The first places where the churches were established were Sun Dol, Yongkang-kun and Kwangmoru, Kangsu-kun, Pyongannam province. In September 1904, the first general meeting of the Seventh-day Adventist Church was held at Chinnampo ; Lim, Ki Ban was selected as the chief of the meeting. In 1905 the Rev. W. R. Smith with his wife were sent to Korea, being dispatched by the American Seventh-day Adventist Mission, they opened a Mission Center at Soonan and strove to extend their religious power.

The Holiness Church

The Holiness Church was originally not an independent denomination,

but a religious group which was organized to preach the Gospel in the
Orient ultra-denominationally. Rev. Chas E. Cawman and one of his
friends, E. A. Kilbourne, American Methodists, "experienced God's special
grace" and came to Tokyo, Japan, feeling charged with a mission to propagate the pure Biblical Gospel in the Orient. In 1901 they began work,
setting out a signboard of the Orient Mission Gospel Preaching Center.
Cawman and Kilbourne, the founders of the Orient Mission, were not
going to initiate a denomination. They began the mission work just to
preach the Holy Gospel to the Easterners in 1907, but since its power
was increased by many adherents, they felt the need to direct them systematically and decided to make a new denomination, the Oriental Mission
Holiness Church. The Orient Mission had its headquarters in Tokyo and
Cawman and Kilbourne, but its founders, entered Seoul, established a
Gospel Preaching Center at Mookyo-dong and concentrated their forces
on roadside and house-to-house preaching. They estabished a Bible Institute at Ahyun-dong in 1911 and wanted to develop their religious power
by training preachers. The Orient Mission was re-named "The Holiness
Churches" in 1922.

Salvation Army

The Salvation Army, like the Anglican Church, is a church which has
its headquarters in England. Though they are both Protestant Churches
of England origin, the Anglican Church is an aristocratic church and the
Salvation Army is a democratic one.

The Salvation Army was originally founded by an English General,
William Booth : to fight against sin, this church adopted military systems
and wore military uniforms. In order to approach the general public who
had difficulty in coming the church, and to reach the people who disliked
to come to church, they preached the Gospel by the roadside and marched
through the streets. The Salvation Army began to preach the Gospel in
Korea in October, 1908 : Col. Robert Hoggard from the headquarters
of Salvation Army preached the Gospel in uniform, and since the interior

situation was agitated by the Japanese who occupied Korea, the preaching team of Salvation Army was conceived as English soldiers and were sometimes insulted. In the following year, 1909, they established the Salvation Army officer Training College and began to train Korean cadets, establishing the mission foundation of the Salvation Army Korea Office.

Chapter 3
The Sufferings of Protestant Churches

The Pressure of the Authorities.

Korea, who held fast to its national isolated policy for a long time, inevitably had to conclude Amity and Commerce Treaties with many countries. But not only central authorities, but also local authorities disliked the fact that Christianity was spreading. Protestantism was oppressed materially and spiritually throughout the country. The Korean Government prohibited the preaching of the Gospel in April of 1888, the third year after American missionaries had entered the country, and religious meetings were prohibited until September of the same year ; thus the Christians were much oppressed in certain districts. In 1899 an American and Korean joint venture company began a tram car service in Seoul and by accident a tram car killed a child under its wheel ; the angry mob poured kerosene and set fire to the four tram cars.

Lee, Keun Taik, the minister of the army, and Lee, Yong Il, the minister of Financial affairs, suggested to King Kojong that he order the citizens not to ride the tram cars since their pockets might be emptied by so doing. Perceiving this, the Americans reported to King Kojong through the minister of American Legation and King Kojong admonished the two ministers not to interfere with the matter. The two ministers reported again, enumerating the acts of the Western missionaries and the evil effect of Christianity. They wanted to destroy Christianity ; by the secret orders of the inconstant Kojong, they were going to kill the Christians all at ɔnce on the first of December, 1900. The fate of the church was just like a candle flickering in the wind. Underwood, who was staying in Haijoo, heard of this from a senior official of Hwanghae Province and reported through the minister of the American Legation to the Throne about the impropriety of the scheme. Thus Kojong once again withdrew his order and the Christians escaped misfortune by a hair's breadth. These incidents took place in the capital, but the oppression of the local authorities was more severe. The local authorities were ill-informed about international and Seoul affairs ; they disliked Christianity because of their Confucian inheritence. Besides the local governors held the power of life and death over their people.

Even after missionaries were able to propagate Christianity publicly, the incidents of oppression upon churches were inumerable. For example, Min, Byung Suk, the Pyongan Provincial Governor, had been repudiating Christianity ; in the early summer of 1894, he captured a Methodist deacon, Kim, Chang Shik, a Presbyterian preach, Han, Suk Jin, and 10 odd adherents. He tortured them severely, without inquiring into the rights and wrongs of the case and intended to kill Han, Suk Jin and Kim, Chang Shik as the ringleaders spreading the "evil science"; but the missionaries in Seoul were informed and they barely managed to prevent the deaths by the order of King Kojong. When these two men were released, they hung between death and life due to the severe wounds ; the jailors covered their bodies with white straw-mats, mistaking them for dead.

In 1894 the chief of Joonghwa-kun banned the revival meeting of the Taekiam Church by mobilizing the libertines in the country ; because the missionaries protested, he arrested a believer, Kim, Baik Kyung, imprisoned him for a month and tortured him severely and without cause brought him to the very gate of death. In 1896, when the believers were going to establish a church in Hamheung, the Myun Chief led the abjectors, letting them break the doors of the houses of Christians. Since they struck Christians violently, a feeling of fear was aroused among the Christians. These were some trifling examples. The oppression from the central authorities to the lower officials was so severe that the preachers had much trouble in doing their work.

The Discord with Catholicism

In preaching Protestantism in Korea, the Catholic oppressions were not so small. We would prefer not to tell the story for the sake of harmony between Roman Catholics and Protestants, but the persecution by the Catholics on Protestantism can not be ignored in describing the history of the persecution which the Protestantism received. Soon after the Religious Revolution the persecution by the Catholics of the Protestants was very severe. Furthermore the torture and the cruel punishment of the Inquisition, the religious law-court of Roman Catholicism, which was established to find out heresy, unbelief and sins of the other religions, was very severe. Through the religious trials, innumerable Protestants were killed and in the Religious War lasting some 30 years from 1618, some several millions of Protestants were killed. Because of the fact that believers were sure that their thoughts and acts only were true, their actions were sometimes more cruel than that of non-believers. The persecution by the Roman Catholics of Protestantism when the latter was first introduced to Korea was also severe.

A preacher, Han, Chi Soo, established Sanggu-dong Church in Jai ryung kun of Hwanghae province in 1893, but they could not have service due to the interruption by the Catholics. When Jairyung Church held a service in 1891, 40 or 50 Catholics rushed into the church, kidnapped men and women believers and lashed them severely. In 1898 when the Wunnai Church in Jairyung kun built a new church, about 100 Catholics rushed in and obstructed the building work, taking the building tools away. Lastly, when the believers held service at Taisong-ri Church in Kimje kun in 1906, a Catholic Father took 30 or 40 Catholics along with him, set fire to the church during the service, surprised the congragation, and had them dispersed. These incidents broke out in many places when Protestantism was first introduced to Korea due to the discord between

Catholicism and Protestantism, but as the power of Protestantism increased, the incidents of persecution slowly disappeared and it was most fortunate that the two churches could find harmony.

Persecution by the People

For some time since Protestantism was first introduced to Korea, the persecution by the people was also severe. Even though there was not the bloody calamity as in the case of the Catholics, the persecution by the people was also terrible. In some districts the so-called noblemen conspired with influential people in the village and they purged the preachers form their village ; some countrymen struck at the believers by attacking their houses. Some people did not permit the Christians to do farmwork and some Christians were diprived of their pedigree. A certain man drove his daughter-in-law out of his home after he cut her hair ; incidents of casting stones at the houses of the Christians occurred very frequently. The reason that they persecuted Protestants was just the same as their persecution of the Catholics. First, they believed that the Christians desecrated their ancestors by abolishing the service for ancestors. Secondly Christians did not bow to the village shrine or the ancestral tablets, but destroyed and set fire to them. Third, boys and girls were not allow to sit together after they reached the age of seven according to the traditional custom in Korea, but the Christians held services in one place (though a certain was drawn between the seats of men and women at that time). They asserted that the Christian way of life corrupted the public morals; in any case we should understand that these conflicts arose from a difference in the mode of living and thought between the Christian and Confucian traditions.

Chapter 4
The Development of Christianity

The Activity of Missionaries

In the pioneer days when Protestantism was first introduced to Korea, the activity of missionaries was great : the fact that the number of Protestants increased to more than 1,000,000 persons : within 70 years since the Protestants entered Korea, is ascribed to the superhuman activity of the missionaries who came to this country with Protestantism. They had many difficulties in preaching the Gospel in Korea because they could not understand Korean, the transportation was inconvenient, the customs were different from East and West and the culture of our country was in an underdeveloped state from the Christian point of view. But they put their hearts into learning Korean to overcome the language barrier, and visited even secluded places among the mountains riding on horses or bicycles seeking out the living human beings. The wall of language, the difference of the customs and the inconvenience in travel could be over come to some extent by their own efforts, but they could not endure the physiological unpleasantness of the different culture. They could not endure the unpleasant mouth odor of the beliveres since they did not clean their teeth regularly, the offensive smell often from their bodies and clothes, and the multiplicity of flies and bugs. But in so many hardships and troubles, they devoted themselves to preaching the Gospel with a concentrated mind to save the "dead souls."

The missionary who first began to do mission work in the local districts was Appenzeller of the Methodist Church. In April, 1887, he went on a walkng tour to preach the Gospel to laborers of officials in the Custom House. Hunt, at this time, only investigated the situation in the countryside, not achieving much in mission work. After he returned to Seoul, he engaged in preaching chiefly in the city. Underwood of the Presbyterian Church who could understand Korean a little, was determined to perform mission work in the countryside in spite of the danger to his life. In the fall of 1887 he left Seoul and went around the northwest districts, such as Songdo Songchun, Pyongyang, and Euijoo. He became the first missionary who preached the Gospel in the far countryside. He baptized 20 persons at his first preaching tour, including the seven persons who were Baptized at Songchun. The reason that he could baptize 7 persons at Songchun was that Su, Sang Ryoon and his brother Su, Kyung Jo of Euijoo, who were baptized by McIntyre and engaged in tract preaching under Ross, moved from Euijoo to Songchun where they preached the Gospel ; several persons had gathered together and established a small church. Then, in the spring of 1888, Underwood and Appenzeller reached Pyongyang for a preaching tour to many places in West and North Korea. However, they had to answer a summons by the minister of the American Legation due to a warning from the Korean Government, and so dispatched a preacher for the tract-preaching to Seoul, Songchun, Pyongyang, Euijoo, etc..

In October, 1888, Appenzeller and Scranton roamed through Pyongyang and Euijoo, preaching the Gospel. At Euijoo they bought a tile-roofed house and established a church. In March, 1889, Underwood with his wife and Dr. Horton preached for two months in the northwest provinces of Korea. During the trip, they reached Kangke, through Songdo and Pyongyang, getting on a boat at the Yalu River, and returned to Seoul. The total milage of their journey reached to 4,000 miles ; they cured about 600 patients and when they reached Euijoo on the 27th of April, they baptized 33 persons there.

The Rev. J.S. Gale, who came to Korea in 1888, went to Songchun via Haejoo for the first time in March of 1889, remained there for three month sand returned to Seoul. At the end of the year he went round the southeast province and while he was staying in Pusan, he buried Davis who died of smallpox and who had done mission work as one of the first Australian missionaries at the foot of Bokbyung Mountain.

As of May of 1891, the two missionaries, Gale and Moffet, began an extensive and adventurous preaching tour to the Korean people. They took Chung, Kong Moo and Choi, Myung Ok with them, went round the northwest provinces and preached the Gospel to the Koreans in a foreign country at Fengtien as Tonghwa and they again crossed the Yalu river and went round the Cha Sung and Hoon Chang, the mountainous villages near the river. They came to the east coast through Chang Jin of Hamkyong province and finally they returned to Seoul through Hamheung and Wonsan. Their touring period consisted of 90 days and they traversed a distance of 5,600 miles. Though they experienced great travel difficulties, they thanked God for giving them a good mission field. Through the journey, the missionaries could apprehend much of the interior situation and it helped them greatly in their planning for the preaching program in Korea.

While many missionaries underwent hardships, traveling to many places, Dr. Hall of the Methodist Church made great efforts to preach through a medical work in one place. Since he was most benevolent and of great service, he was one of the missionaries most respected by the people. He opened a hospital in Pyongyang in 1893, treated poor patients and spoke on religious subjects to his callers. But he suffered from fever and dysentry himself due to excessive labor and passed away in November of 1895. The above mentioned stories cover only a part of the activities of the missionaries. The Protestant missionaries put their heart and soul into letting people know "the good news of Jesus", visiting secluded mountain places and overcoming all troubles and dangers. According to the report of Gale who left great footmarks as an itinerant preacher in the early days of Korean Protestantism, he preached the Gospel by going around the

Korean peninsula 12 times through different roads from 1889 to 1897. Also the Rev. M.W. Greenfield stayed for 180 days at one time in the countryside. Their enthusiasm in preaching the Gospel was not inferior to that of apostles of the early years of Christian history.

Dr. Underwood

Underwood, who not only made a great contribution in mission work of Protestantism in Korea, but also contributed much in the educational field, was born in London, England, on the 19th of July, 1857, and went to America in 1872. He had graduated from New York University and New Brunswick Theological Seminary in 1884. While he was still in the Brunswick Seminary he received a letter from a missionary who was in Japan, one of the missionaries of the American North Presbyterian Church who had much interest in Korea, but Underwood wanted to work in the wider stage of India. For some reason Korea was not attractive to him and he wanted someone else to be sent to Korea, but since no one applied for the position he felt remorse and at this time he heard a voice saying "Why not go yourself to Korea ? How about Korea ?" He then detemined to go to Korea and knocked at the door of the Board of Mission of the North Presbyterian Church in New York. If he had gone to India as he hoped to do, he probably would have also accomplished great works there India.

The Mission Board of the North Presbyterian Church was studying the problem of sending missionaries with the mission fund of 6,000 dollars donated by the McWilliams, and they appointed Underwood as the missionary of their choice and let him go to Korea. When he left New York, his elder brother, John T. Underwood, accompanied him as far as Chicago. He was the man who spared no help with money and prayer in the background for about a half century for Underwood and his son to do mission work in Korea. We should never forget his hidden support which enabled the Underwoods to leave great achievement in Korea. After Underwood entered Korea, he not only studied Korean, but also was absorbed in doing mission work and whenever he had time, he cured the patients and gave lectures on Chemistry and Physics to medical students.

To make a preaching plan, he had travelled not only all over the peninsula, but also in South Manchuria (with Gale who entered Korea later), studied geography, transportation, and the customs of Korea, and in rainy or cold seasons, he translated religious tracts and the Bible assiduously. The religious tracts, such as the Christian doctrine which was made by himself were greatly helpful to his mission work. He opened an orphanage in 1886 for the first time in Korea and established Saemoonan Church (Cheil Church in Shinmoon), the first Church in Korea, by building a tile-roofed house of 20 kan(80 m) in Sodaemun. He edited a hymn book of 159 chapters in 1893. Since he poured all his power into preaching the Gospel, with out sparing himself, converts appeared in succession in many places. His activity overwhelmed the religious field in Korea and there were no non-Christians who did not know his name. He showed new light to the people who were annoyed by the extortion of the officials. He believed that the underdevelopment of Korea was due to the backwardness of education and he put his heart and soul into managing educational facilities.

He especially established Yonhee College and was inaugurated as the first Dean of the College. In 1917 he received 50,000 dollars from John T. Underwood and bought 1,140,000 square feet at Yonhee College site and consolidated the foundation of the college by building a modern school house. This superhuman activity of Underwood stemmed from his faithfulness and spirit of service, and the Christians and relatives in his country praised his success of mission work and blessed God's richest blessings in his work. However, he got sick from excessive work and went back to America for relaxation in spring of 1916. He died on the 12th of October, 1916, at the age of 57. His life, devoted to the preaching of Gospel for 37 years in a foreign country and his service to God and to the foreigners must be considered most valuable in the Christian cause. His wife and daughter-in-law sacrificed themselves for the Korean people and now his grandson is working for Koreans. It was a great misfortune that the wife of the younger Underwoods died an unnatural and regrettable death from four rascals in her home in December of 1948 while she was having a tea-party with some famous women. In every respect the Underwood family is the benefactor of our people, but we can not help grieving for the people who returned evil for good.

Division of Mission Area

Every denomination of Protestantism began to do mission work by sending its missionaries, but, since they were different in nationality, denominations and doctrines, unnecessary conflict and friction easily took place. As for the Anglican Church and Baptist Church, not only was their religious influence weak, but they worked independently from the beginning. There were no big problems, but the rest of the denominations, could not help thinking that the best way to achieve a result from mission work, was to avoid friction and disorder between them. Therefore every sect decided to divide the territories of each denomination in a give-and-take spirit, and to do mission work freely in large cities. The agreed preaching area was divided as follows :

American North Presbyterian Church···At first the American North Presbyterian Church thought of the whole nation as their mission field but later it shared Kyongsangnam province with the Austrian Presbyterian Church, Hamkyong district with the Canadian Presbyterian Church and Cholla province with the American South Presbyterian Church ; they also decided on Pyongan province and Kyongsangbuk province as their mission field. The number of total missionaries who came to Korea by 1920 reached 87 and it represented one-third of the total missionaries whom they dispatched for the foreign mission. They also acquired 115,000 believers.

American South Presbyterian Church···When the missionaries of the American South Presbyterian Church entered Korea, they concluded an agreement with American North Presbyterian Church missionaries and decided on Cholla province as their mission field. At first they began to preach the Gospel at Kunsan and increased their parish at Chunju and as the missionaries entered Korea continually, they opened parishes in Mokpo, Kwangju and Soonchun. Around 1920 the number of missionaries in Korea reached to 70 and the number of the believers could be counted to 17,000.

American Methodist Church···American Methodist missionaries who came to Seoul in a crowd established their parishes in Wonsan, Inchon, and Pyongyang for a time, but after the South Methodist Church entered the country, they shared Wonsan parish with them, settled their parishes again and decided on the whole Choongchongnam province, a part of Hwanghae province, a part of Pyongan province and Kyonggi province as their parishes. The parishes of all Protestant churches were put together, with only that of the American North Methodist scattered here and there. Around 1920 the number of missionaries who came to Korea reached 50 and the believers 3,6000. The number of the missionaries were few, compared to the number of believers, but they achieved much in educational and medical works as well as the mission work.

South Methodist Church···The South Methodist Church entered Korea ten years later than the American North Methodist and North Presbyterian Churches and it had trouble in selecting a mission area. Realizing the triangular area, from Seoul to Wonsan via Kaesung was an "untouched mission field", they consulted with the American North Methodist Church and decided on the northern part of Kyonggi province, the southern part of Hamkyongnam province and the northern part of Kangwon province as their preaching field, increasing their religious influence with education, medical and social work. Around 1920 about 60 missionaries came to Korea and the number of believers reached 12,000.

Canadian Presbyterian Church···The Canadian Presbyterian Church decided on Hamkyong province as their mission field. They began to preach the Gospel in a village and extended their preaching area northward, later making Kanto and Haisamui in Manchuria their mission field. Around 1920, 46 missionaries entered the country and were able to count 203 churches and 12,000 Christians.

Australian Presbyterian Church···The Australian Presbyterian Church was handed over the Kyongsangam province from the American Presbyterian Church and expanded its power. Around 1920 they dispatched 30 missionaries and the believers increased to 10,000.

The Council of Missions

A committee or a consultatory meeting was to be established for every denomination to perform their mission work, cooperating with each other and for the division of mission area among Protestant Missions. American North Methodist Church wanted to do mission work together with the South Methodists but the South Methodists were not willing to do it. Only the Presbyterian missionaries organized a union body between the American North and South Presbyterian Churches and the Australian Presbyterian Church in 1889. In the following year, and Australian missionary, Davis, died in Pusan and the function of the Council stopped for a while, but when the South Presbyterian Mission entered Korea, it was reorganized in January of 1893. This was called the Council of Missions Holding the Presbyterian Form of Government. The Council continued for 8 years until 1900 and in 1901, 25 missionaries and 9 Korean elders and preachers formed a Union of Presbyterian Missions. This Council of Missions had no right to settle matters, but aimed to discuss, advise, report the church problems and to make friendship with each other.

Then the Australian Mission entered Korea and the Canadian Mission was established joining the Council of Protestant Missions. Until then the South Presbyterians were to do mission work in Cholla Province and a part of Choongchong Province and the North Presbyterians in the before-mentioned districts, but since the Australian and Canadian Missions entered the country, the Council of Missions decided to cede the area south Nak-dong river to the Australian Mission, the North Presbyterian Church was to undertake the area north of Nakdong Riber and the Canadian Mission the Hamkyong Provinces.

The first meeting of the Union Council of Missions adopted the following mission policy in 1893 and the missionaries in Korea invited
Nevius, who had been long engaged in mission work in China. They
discussed it for about two weeks, and then adopted the policy which
Nevius used.

1. To preach the Gospel to the labor class and then to the upper class.
2. To strive especially to let women be converted and to educate the
   Christian girls(This is due to the fact that the housewives had much
   influence in bringing up their children).
3. Christian education could be carried out by managing primary schools
   in local cities and the children should be trained in the mission school
   to be teachers of the schools.
4. A large number of Korean preachers should be produced in the future
   and therefore the missionaries should pay attention to this fact.
5. Even if there were not able preachers, God's Words could convert
   the people and, to circulate as many Bibles as possible so that people
   could read them, through translating and publishing them quickly.
6. Every new church must be a self-supporting church. To reduce the
   number of the preachers whom Missions subsidize and let each church
   economically become independent from a financial point of view.
7. Every religious tract and pamphlet should be written only in Korean
   not in foreign languages.
8. Koreans should be led to Christ by Koreans themselves. Missionaries
   should educate few people and make them able pastors rather than
   their preaching the Gospel in public themselves.
9. Medical missionaries could teach the doctrines of Christianity and
   give an example in the hospital or in the houses of the patients when
   they cured the sick. The effect of the missionary work was notably
   not so great if they only diagnosed and gave medicine to the patients.

Chapter 5
Cultural Development Activities

Y.M.C.A

After Protestantism entered Korea, every church organized Ebutt Young Men's Associations and Students' Meetings, but the former was just like a young men's group in Sunday School and the latter was only a religious group and so there was no special projects for the youth in general. The missionaries Underwood and Appenzeller, requested the International Committee of American Young Men's Association to organize the YMCA in Korea. In 1901 the International Committee dispatched Mr. Gillette and requested him to inaugurate the work in Korea. Due to the enthusiasm of both American and English missionaries, an inaugural meeting of the YMCA was held. As a result of the proposal of 37 nationals and foreigners in October of 1903. Young Men's Christian Association was organized as a general youth movement body. Though they organized the Association, they had no affiliation, and so they joined together at the Chinese Young Men's Christian Association. H.B. Hulbert was elected President of the Association and P.L. Gillette as the general secretary. With the large sum of contributions from an American Businessman, John Wanamaker and the American YMCA and an Imperial donation, they began to build the Hall at Chongro, Seoul, and finished building it after five years in 1908 since they began the work. The building had a floor space of 3,600 square feet. From that time they acted positively in religion, education, gymnastics, society and social welfare fields. The Hall had an auditorim, a gymnastic room, classrooms, a library, a dining room, bathroom, a te-chnical laboratory, boys rooms and so on. They held monthly meetings, entertainment programs, English social meetings, and charitable entertain-ment parties in the Hall. They also taught English and vocation training. Since there were indoor athletic facilities, the youths could play volleyball, basketball and judo. A dining room, library and bathrooms were opened to the public.

In 1924 the Korean Young Men's Association containing City YMCAs which were organized in the United Association with cities throughout the country, and Students' YMCAs under the direction of central YMCA joined into the world YMCA directly. YMCA was the only recreation centre where young men could develop spiritually and physically, and it contributed much in eradicating social evils and in developing a new civilization. Some famous persons such as Lee, Sang Jai, Lee, Seung Man, Yoon, Chi Ho, Kim, Kyoo Shik, Shin, Heung Woo were connected with the Association.

Women's Movement

As Protestantism developed, women's movements also made great pro-gress. Women's Preaching Meetings in Presbyterian Churches, Women's Propagation Meetings in the Methodist Churches, and Women's Meetings in the Holiness Church and Salvation Army were organized ; they con-tributed much towards enlightening and raising women's status in society. The main object of the Women's Movement was preaching. Besides that, they spread the knowledge of Korean language and the Bible and aided the improvement of the status of living. As the women's movement in the churches developed little by little, they found their way into society through their churches.

In 1899 the women organized a women's group called Women Friend-ship Meeting, of 50 members, led by Chung, Hyun Sook. They raised a movement against concubinage, which was one of the biggest social problems at that time, and presented a memorial to King Kojong and demonstrated in the streets, holding placards. Because women were living their lives secluded chiefly in their rooms, they tended to go to extremes, such as marching in the streets and the conservative people who ignored women and hated the church called the women's group " a fox group" and called the members of the group or the progressive women as "fox-like"women. This demonstration against concubinage of the women's group was a great shock to the feudalistic society at that time and it made the women criticize themselves and became aware of themselves. Protestant women took the lead in liberating and enlightening women who knew only how to live in the shadows. It is important to mention the women when the March First Independence Movement broke out, the leaders of Women's Patriotic Bodies, such as Korea Patriotic Women's Association, Sincere and Patriotic Women's Association and Great Korea Women's Association stemmed from Protestantism.

In March of 1922 the Korea YWCA was organized and was able to contain a women's body which had affiliation with that of the world. This YWCA first originated in England in 1855 and had a worldwide network system. In Korea, Yoo, Kak Kyung, Kim, Helen and Kim, PilRye promoted it and joined the world YWCA later. In June of that year they had the first summer meeting and continued summer meetings, Work Prayer Week, bazaars and managed short training courses for homeless women, orphanages, lodging houses and generally helpful works.

In 1923 they organized the Korea YWCA, uniting 4 city YWCAs and 8 students' YWCAs and joined the world YWCA in 1924. But they had to secede from the world YWCA and join the Japanese YWCA during Japan's suppression. Apart from the YWCA, the church women leaders organized the Women's Christian Moderation Meeting in September of 1923, had a nationwide network system and performed the movement of enlightening women more actively than the YWCA. The activity of this meeting was almost the same as that of YWCA and the leading women of the meeting were Yoo, Kak Kyung. Paik, In Duk, Chung, Maria, Sohn, Mery, Hong, Ae shi Duk, Yang, Mae Ryoon, etc..

New Educational Work

When we spoke of "the education of Korea ", we meant the passing
of the higher civil service examination to enter government service and
the method of education were only to let students learn the Chinese Confucian books, beginning from the "Thousand Letters"to Chinese Classics,
by memorization. But since Protestantism was introduced to Korea, missionaries brought new western style methods of education and a great
revolution was taking place in the educational field. The new education
first began by the establishment Paichai School by Appenzeller, and Yook
yung Kongwon by Underwood in 1885. The teachers taught Chinese,
English, and the Bible in Yookyung Kongwon, but later the school was
renamed as the Jesus School and the two schools supplemented arithmetic,
geography, history, natural history, etc., and also prepared specimens and
experimental tools. As it was the time that the Koreans highly regarded
only Confucianism, not only did the conservative upper class not take
an interest in the new education, but they also questioned its value and
did not send their children to the school. They said that it was the education
that provided the moral principles. And so the school authorities had to
bring wretched children into the school and teach them. Moreover the
difficulty of women's education was a great problem.

The Jesus School that Underwood established continued to do its work,
but through dissention of some missionaries, it was closed in 1897 and
for a while, only two mission schools Paichai Hak Dang and Ewha Hak
Dang existed. But later Jungshin Girls' School, Jungeui Girls' School,
Kwangsung Boys' School, Paihwa Girls' School, Soongeui Girls' School,
and Soongshil Boys' School were established and the Jesus School which
was closed before, was opened again in 1902, under the name of Kyungshin
School. According to the report in 1902, the schools that the Methodists
managed amounted to 11 boys' schools and 15 girls' schools.

At the end of Lee reign, the government could not afford to manage
primary school education properly, not to mention the middle school
education,   but every mission of Protestantism established educational

institutes and thus made a great contribution in developing culture in extending the people's right.

After Korea was annexed to Japan, the savage policy of Japan did not expand common education but all Protestant denominations were sure that the only way to save the Korean people lay in fostering their ability and therefore established many secondary educational institutes, with each church operating common educational institutes and evening schools. We must especially respect the troubles and sacrifices of the managers of Yonhee, Soongshil, Ewha and Severance Medical Colleges. In spite of the interference and persecution from Japan authorities, they cultivated many able men and women by infusing the spirit of patriotism into their minds as well as the propagation of the Gospel, and there are many graduates of the Protestant Colleges who played an active role in every field of our society today. It is understood that when we said education around Korean-Japan Annexation, almost all the educational institutes from common school to college were managed by Protestants.

When we see the number of the schools in the time of the March First Independence Movement, the golden age of private schools, it was as follows:

College	4(3 government schools)
Middle Schools	40(16 Japanese public schools, 7 for Koreans and 21 vocational schools)
Primary Schools	601(268 public school for Japanese, 535 for Koreans)
Bible Schools	40
Other Schools	33

Medical Work

Among the Protestant social works, medical work developed remarkably. In the past, Koreans knew herbal medicine as the only medicine which had been curing their diseases. They depended upon Chinese medical treatment or superstitious treatment and disliked preventive immunizations, disinfection and isolation. But since Western medicine was introduced into Korea, a great renovation was made in the medical field and many lives were saved. When a cholera epidemic was raging in 1896, the Korean Government was in a desperate situation. At this time the whole situation was given over to American missionaries to initiate measures against cholera and through their desperate efforts, many of the Koreans were saved from the terrible epidemic.

The man who first began the medical work since Protestantism entered Korea was H.N. Allen, one of the North Presbyterian missionaries. He was serving as the doctor of many Legations in Korea and when the Kapshin Political Upheaval broke out, he proved the superiority of Western medical art by curing Min, Yung Ik, the chief of Imperial body-guard and became a court physician. When the government opened Kwang Hye Won Hospital in February, 1885, he took charge of the hospital and then established a royal hospital in Dong Hyun and was placed in charge of it. Shortly after this Dr. J.W. Heron came to Korea from America and helped Allen in his medical work. Dr. Scranton, who was working with Allen, retired from the Royal Hospital and established an independent hospital, and a women's hospital. Allen's Royal Hospital became the origin of the Severance Hospital and Scranton's the Dongdaimoon Women's Hospital.

As the medical mission work was achieving its goals, the Board of Missions adopted a policy to distribute a physician in the center of mission work, but later they followed a policy to establish hospitals there instead and in 1920 hospitals were erected in 24 important cities, such as Seoul, Pyongyang, Wonsan, Soonchun, Haijoo, Chinju, Kaesung, Soonan, Choonchun, Hamheung, Inchon, Jairyung, Wonju, Taegu, Pusan, Kwangju and so on. After Korea was annexed to Japan, provincial hospitals and city hospitals were established in large cities, but they existed only for the treatment of Japanese and the special class Koreans, whereas the Protestant hospitals served all people and the poor. They especially established leprosariums in Kwangju, Taegu and Soonchun and engaged in treating lepers whom no one cared for, which was much admired and highly praised. Not only did the missionaries manage hospitals, but they also strove to further train physicians and nurses by publishing medical textbooks. Though they built hospitals, they had no physicians and nurses who could work there. Thus in 1903, Miss Margaret J. Edmund of the Methodist Mission began to train nurses and Presbyterian Mission Board organized a committee for medical education. In 1905 they began a medical college and selected 12 students for the course. This became the founding basis of Severance Medical College.

Literary Work

It was by the translation of the Bible that Protestantism began its literary work in Korea. The British and Foreign Bible Society undertook translating the Bible by the consultation of missionaries in 1881 and they decided to revise the Bible translated by Ross and selected Committees of Bible Revision with Underwood as chairman and Appenzeller as secretary. They completed revising and translating the New Testament by 1910 and concluded the Old Testament by 1910.

The Bibles were published by the Bible Societies and were spread all through the country by the hands of traveling preachers. Since the Bible Society undertook publishing of the Bible, they circulated 25,000 copies of the Old Testament, 152,900 copies of New Testament and 5,593,400 separated volumes of the Bible within 20 years. The spread general books as well and circulation of the Bible contributed greatly in enlightening the Korean people to Christian way of thinking.

We also cannot forget the activities of the Korean Tract Society. This was first suggested by a missionary, Heron, and several missionaries who were gathered together at Underwood's residence in October, 1889 and was inaugurated under the purpose of performing every Christian literary work in order to raise and purify the life of individual, society and state through Jesus' teachings and sacrificial deeds. It was titular for some years after being established, but after four years, they were able to obtain a

source of revenue and published Underwood's Salient Principle on Christianity, Moffet's Two Friends and another 12 religious tracts. The religious
books were published one after another, with the help of Lee, Won Mo,
Lee, Chang Jik, Lee, Kyo Seung and Kim, Dong Myung in 1897, and
Kamok Moonko in 1905. 30years after this Society was inaugurated, its
publications amounted to 400 books and 5 periodicals. This Korean Tract
Society was renamed as the Korea Jesus Tract Society in 1919 and for
20 years beginning in 1920, it published at an average 1,600,000 booklets
every year.

In February, 1897, Appenzeller published "Christian Advocate", a week-
ly, interim sized between newspaper and magazine, ten years before "Independence News" was published. Underwood began "The Christian News"
under his own initiative and in 1915 the "Christian News "of the Presbyterian and the "Christian Advocate "of the Methodists were amalgated,
to form the "Christian News "which continued until 1935, being published
by the Korean Christian Literature Society. The first representative of
the "Christian News "was J.S. Gale and then H.A. Rhodes. As for the
magazines, a monthly, "Church", was first published by Appenzeller in
May, 1889. It continued for about 10 years and was the first monthly
magazine in our country. It was 11 years before "Cho Yang", the organ
of the Korean Self-Support Association was published. Then the missionaries issued the "Theological Review"(Shin Hak Wolpo). These two
magazines were issued by foreigners, but "Public Way", "New Life" ,
"Real Life" and "Living Well" were published by Koreans later and played
an important role in the Christian literature movement. In 1937, "New
Man" by Chun, Young Taik was issued and served as the religious and
educational magazine.

Chapter 6
The Rise of the Church

Wonsan and Pyongyang

The missionaries who came to Korea not only preached the Gospel but also endeavored to be more faithful, and the revival meeting of the missionaries at Wonsan in December 1903 proved a great initiative in raising Korean churches. The revival meeting was held in December of 1903 by the Presbyterian, Methodist, and Baptist missionaries at Changjun Church, Wonsan, and the participants "experienced the Holy Spirit, which descended in the garret at Pentecost". Since then missionaries could work more vigorously and with greater power. In summer of 1906 the "fire of the Holy Spirit descended upon the missionaries revival meeting at Wonsan and they who experienced God's grace confessed all their sins while crying" and it became a great moment to develop the whole chruch in Korea. As soon as this information was related to Pyongyang, Chang Dai Hyun Church invited R.A. Hardie, the central figure of the Wonsan meeting, and held a revival meeting. The Presbyterian and Methodist missionaries and Korean adherents experienced the fire of Holy Spirit in the meeting led by Revs. Kil, Sun Ju and Greham Lee and the fire of faith shined brightly. In the meetings of mission schools, this phenomenon took place. The events in Pyongyang were followed by similar events in the northwest countryside in Korea and all the Christians who had "experienced new life" confessed their sins and engaged in preaching the Gospel by themselves. Kil, Sun Ju who concluded Pyongyang Meeting,

opened great revival meetings in many churches in Seoul and the congregation too "were moved by the Holy Spirit"and all the Protestant churches in our country were greatly developed.

The Million Movement

After the revival of churches in Wonsan and Pyongyang, the Million
Movement was launched for a speedy evangelization of the country. This
movement was first begun by the prayers of C.F.Reid, M.B.S tokes and
Gambles, who kept vigil for several nights with prayers. After these missionaries prayed fervently, there were joint prayer meetings with scores
of missionaries and Korean preachers. In September of 1909 the joint
missionary meeting decided to launch the Million Movement and the resolution was adopted at Presbyterian Council and at the Annual Meeting
of South and North Methodists in the spring of 1910. After the decision
was made, all the Christians prayed assiduously for the success of the
movement and revival missionaries from America came to Korea and held
revival meetings. Korean preachers of every denomination held revial
meetings respectively and got many converts, every adherent striving to
propagate the Gospel ; thus there were no houses which were not visited
by the preachers. A total number of 100,000 days was devoted to the
movement by the adherents and 1,000,000 religious tracts and 700,000
separate volumes of the Gospel were spread throughout the country. The
Million Movement could not get the expected number of adherents and
gained only 20,000 new believers, but it brought many benefits to Koreans.
The time in which the movement was launched was the period that
Koreans had much sorrow because their country was in ruins and they
were in great fear for their lives and properties.

Minister Kil, Sun Ju

A truly unforgettable patron of such a revival movement of the church
was Minister Kil, Sun Ju, who was also known by his pseudonym Yungke.
He was born in March 1869 at Anju, Pyongan South province where he

spent most of his childhood in studying the ancient Chinese classics but failed in his commercial career. He visited famous temples in his attempts to master the Buddhist Truths but no longer finding ascetism to his taste, he indulged himself in Taoism without reaching the inner solace he so desperately sought.

Yungke assumed his career in commerce after mastering the Chinese herb medicine. He was converted to the Christian faith by Kim, Jong Sup and discovered that salvation through Christianity satisfied his thirst for faith in religion. He became an outstanding evangelist of the Christian revival movement.

He was elected as the deacon of the Presbyterian Church in 1898 and became an elder in 1901 ; he was ordained assisting minister in 1902 and commenced his revival movement as a prominent figure and potential leader among the Christian churches. He graduated from the Pyongyang Theological Seminary in 1907 and was renowned as one of the seven early Christian ministers ; he was assigned to the congregation at Changdaihyun Church for 15 years, during which time he highlighted the revival move- ment throughout the country. His sermons were not merely authoritative, fluent and graceful in tone but so inspiring that the audience on the floor repented of their sins. He had a miraculous power of alleviating suffering and the spiritual disease of the congregation. His broad and deep know- ledge of the Holy Scriptures and the profound wisdom of biblical research not only elevated him as a scholar of the Bible but also played an essential role in the interpretation of the Book before the foreign missionaries. Of course, his early theological ideals were extremely orthodox, influenced by Underwood and Gail.

For ten years after 1924, Minister Kil chiefly engaged in the revival movement throughout the country and preached number of sermons on more than 20,000 occasions ; he converted 70,000, 30,200 of whom were baptized ; he established 60 Christian churches. In 1935, while leading a revival service at Kochang Church in Kangsu-kun, he received the call of God at the altar ; he died while leading the morning devotion.

Minister Kil is also a famous patriotist who cannot be forgotten in Korean History. In 1897, he established the Pyongyang Chapter of the Independence Association with An, Chang Ho and other 17 patriots ;after the national disgrace of Korean and Japanese Annexation, he founded Soongduk and Soonghyun schools to teach native Korean faith and to promote the independence of Korea ;he also established the Bible Institutes and Night schools to enlighten his follow citizens. During the March 1st movement for independence, he represented the Christian churches as one of the 33 patrons and signed the proclamation of Korean Independence. He was arrested and imprisoned by the Japanese police.

His literary accomplishments remain in the famous Commentaries on Romans, the Comparison of Korean-Jewish traditions, the Secret of Godly Blessings, A Synthesis of Sermons, the Accomplishment of Man, etc..

Minister Kim, Ik Du

Kim, Ik Du, known as a twin-preacher of Minister Kil in the Christian revival movement in Korean history, was born in November, 1874 in Taiwon, Anak-kun, Hwanghae province. Before his Christian conversion, Kim was a notorious delinquent of the village. He became a reformed Christian in 1900 and was baptized in 1901 in a Presbyterian church, becoming the assisting minister in 1903. Upon his graduation from the Pyongyang Theological Seminary in 1910, he was ordained to ministry at Shinchon Church in Hwanghae province for 20 years and then ministered to the congregation of Seungdong Church in Seoul in 1930. While leading the congregation of Shinchon Church, Minister Kim sponsored the Christian revival movement throughout the country, convening the most important meeting in Seungdong Church in Seoul in 1920. The total congregation on this occasion alone amounted to 6 to 7 thousand, and the offering of the Christians in one evening amounted to 1,700 won(presently equivalent to 30,000,000 won) in case, not to mention, 200 gold-rings, 20 gold watches, 200 either gold or silver hair-pins. Although he was less academic, Kim's sermons reached the common strata and his biblical proficiency caught the audience up in an emotional experience.

While he was assigned to the parish of Seungdong Church in Seoul, Minister Kim continued to motivate the revival movement throughout the country, helping to bring about a remarkable conversion of the people into the Christian churches in Korea. A great number of the multitudes of people in his audiences were both mentally and physically diseased because Kim was widely known to heal and to cure. Many witnessed the miracles ; in fact, he brought sanity to the lunatics, and enabled the dumb and deaf to talk, and the crippled to stand and walk away. When he failed in his healing of the diseased, he was reproached by some of the people.

After the liberation in 1945, he associated himself with the Christian League under the Communists through the deception of the disguised Christian minister Kang, Yang Wook. This brought him infamy in his later years. He passed away during the Korean War, a drastic loss to the Korean Christian churches.

Chapter 7
Christian Churches and the March lst
Independence Movement

Turmoil among the Korean Students in Tokyo

After the Japanese annexed Korea under the pretext of protection and Korean welfare, the Japanese government enforced the military police system to blockade both freedom of speech and assembly of the Korean people. Moreover, in an attempt to monopolize Korean economy, the Japanese merchants, farmers, usurers and entrepreneurs swarmed into Korea ; exploitation increased the suffering of the people under renewed oppression which became all the more severe for the Koreans.

While the people trembled under the Japanese muskets and police, the Christian churches paid little concern for the politics and the critical issues of the time, merely concentrating on the expansion of Christian activities and evangelical missions.

When World War I ended with the defeat of Germany and Austria after four years, a new trend began throughout the world. In such a transitional period, President Thomas Woodrow Wilson of America, in January 1918, proclaimed 14 terms as a principle of world peace ; he emphasized the so-called self-determination of each nation in terms of issues regarding colonialism and his approval of the independence of weaker and dependent nations. The principle of self determination of the nation appealed to all the suppressed nations of the world.

The Korean students in Tokyo upheld the proclamation of independence in 1919 among the staff of the Haku Fellowship Society and the leading membership of the alumni circles of the colleges. The key promoters of the movement were Choi, Pal Yong, Kim, Do Yun, Suh, Choon, Lee, Jong Keun, Baik, Kwan Su, Yun, Chang Suk, Kim, Sang Duk, Choi, Keun U and Kim, Chul Su. The declaration of independence was signed by these nine members and Lee, Kwang Su.

In the meantime the leaders from both the Chonto-kyo sect and the Christian churches promoted the independence movement in Korea, encouraged by the current issues. However, the Korean students in Tokyo sent their message to the leader on mainland somewhat earlier, and on February 8th, 1919, the group of students assembled in the YMCA building in Tokyo to proclaim the declaration of Korean independence, cheering 'Long Live Korea.' While the declaration of independence and the resolution was under process, the students and the Japanese police staged bloody struggles and hundreds of the students gathered in the YMCA were arrested ; the rest of them gradually returned to their motherland as they adopted the resolution.

Rise of Independence Movement

The outbreak of the news of the independent rise of the Korean students in Tokyo affected the leaders of the mainland ; the Christian leaders began their movement at once in conjunction with them. Chonto-kyo sect first drew the attention of Lee, Seung Hoon, the principal of Osan School, a well-known Christian leader, and discussed a petition for the support of the Christian churches. Lee, Seung Hoon at once agreed with the chonto- kyo leaders and went to Sunchon on February 12, where he met with Yang, Jun Baik, Lee, Myung Yong, Yu, Yeo Dai, and Kim, Byung Jo, etc., of Presbyterian churches and came to a decision that they would join with the Chonto-kyo sect for the movement. Lee further went to Pyongyang on February 14 and won the approval of Rev. Kil, Sun Ju and Shin, Hong Shik, and then came to Seoul on February 20 to sommon Oh, Ki Sun, Oh, Hwa Yong, Chung, Choon Su, and Shin, Hong Shik at the residence of Park, Hi Do of the Methodist churches in the evening of the day, they met again at Ham, Tai Yong's with Lee, Kap Sung, An, Se Hwan, Oh, Sang Keun and Hyon, Soon. They decided to mobilize all their fellow patriots throughout the country and to proclaim before the Japanese Government the declaration of Korean Independence.

The general concept of the convention was that the Christians alone were to lead the Independence movement ; however, Choi, Rin insisted that the movement should be supported by the entire nation after he was informed of the resolution of the meeting by Lee, Seung Hoon. After the strong emphasis stressed by Choi, Rin, on the evening of the 21st, Lee, Seung Hoon, Park, Hi Do, Oh, Ki Sun, Shin, Hong Shik, Ham, Tai Yung, Ah, Se Hwan , Oh, Hwa Yong, Hyon, Soon and Kim, Se Hwan, etc., gathered at the residence of Lee, Kap Sung within Severance Hospital to discuss the details of the independence movement to be staged through-out the night. They moved to assign Lee, Seung Hoon and Ham, Tai Yong for the liaison mission to consult with the representatives of the Chonto-kyo sect. The joint discussion of the liaison officers with Choi, Rin from the Chonto-kyo sect led to the fact that the mutual cooperation and unity of Christian Churches and the Chonto-kyo sect was a prerequisite in the joint attempt of mobilizing all the people of different walks of life in Korea in the nation-wide movement for independence. On the 22nd, the Christian leaders met at the residence of Ham, Tai Yong and adopted the consolidation of joint affiliation with the Chonto-kyo sect for the Independence Movement ; 16 Christian leaders affixed their signatures to the Declaration of Independence.

March 1st Movement

On March 1st, 1919, the date of the funeral march of the late King Kwangmu, the thirty-three patrons representing all the stations of the Korean people gathered at Myung Wol Kwan, a restaurant, to proclaim the Independence Declaration while thousands of students and citizens staged a rally at Pagoda Park in Seoul. In unison they declared the in-dependence of Korea and shouted, 'Long Live Korea.' They then staged

a street march in Seoul. In the meantime, the slated independence movement was already instigated throughout the country through the underground network so that every Korean in the entire country rose up to
the call of Seoul citizens. The long-cherished freedom of independence
was voiced on a nation-wide scale, with the genuine spirit of Korea.

Although the movement was motivated by Protestant, Chonto-kyo
Secterians, Catholic churches, Buddhists, Confucian schools and Taijong-
kyo Sectarians, the Protestant led the mobilization. The people and the
majority of the leaders of the movement were Christians themselves and
most of the promotive meetings were held at the Christian churches ;
therefore, the most victimized and persecuted were likewise the Christians
when the Japanese retaliated.

41 churches were destroyed by the Japanese military and police in the
three regions of Pyongyang, Soonchon and Suwon. It was therefore natural
for the local police to accuse the Christians as being innovators of the
movement. Even the foreign missionaries, who swore to remain neutral
in the political issues, helped the Koreans from backstage and further called
attention from overseas when they pleaded to justify the movement of
the Korean people under the oppression of the Japanese imperialism.

More than 7,500 people were killed by the Japanese military and police
during the March 1st movement, 15,900 were wounded, and among the
total of 16,900, only 37,000 were acquitted. 9,458 were condemned to ser-
vitude in prison. The denominations were as follows :

Protestant	2,033
Chonto-kyo sect	1,416
Catholics	57
Confucians School	56
Buddhists	66
Shichon-kyo sect	5
Taijong-kyo sect	5
Chon Li sect	3
Misc.	84

Non-religious	5,731
TOTAL	9,456

a breakdown of the Protestant imprisoned by their respective denominations is as follows :

Presbyterians	1,461
Methodists	475
Salvation Army	10
Church Cooperatives	7
Non-denominational	81

By such statistics, though with a difference in number, it is clear that all the Christian churches were victimized.

One can list some of the exclusive Christian leaders victimized during the March 1st Independence Movement;

Lee, Seung Hoon,	the Principal of Osan High School in Chungju
Oh, Hwa Sup,	Reverend of the Southern Methodist Church
Lee, Myung Yong,	Presbyterian Elder
Park, Dong Wan,	Staff of the Christian Press
Chung, Choon Su,	Reverend of the Southern Methodist Church
Shin, Suk Ku,	Reverend of the Southern Methodist Church
An Se Hwan,	General Secretary of Christian Literature Society, Pyongyang.
Kim, Ji Whan,	Evangelist of the Southern Methodist Church
Ham, Tai Yung,	Presbyterian elder
Park, Hi Do,	Secretary, Central YMCA
Choi, Sung Mo,	Reverend of Northern Methodist Mission
Shin, Hong Shik,	Reverend of Northern Methodist Mission
Yang, Jon Baik,	Reverend, Presbyterian
Kim, Byung Jo,	Presbyterian Minister
Kil, Sun Ju,	Presbyterian Minister
Lee, Kap Sung,	Staff of Severance Hospital
Kim, Chang Jun,	Evangelist of Northern Methodist Church
Lee, Pil Ju,	Northern Methodist Minister

Yu, Yeu Dai,   Presbyterian Minister

With reference to the outline of Christian history written by Pyun, Jong Ho, and according to other references, foreign Christian Missionaries who rendered the most outstanding assistance in the March Independence Movement are as follows :

G. S. McCune	E. M. Mowry
J. S. Gale	H. H. Underwood
S. A. Moffett	S. K. Roberts
W. N. Blair	H. A. Rhodes
E. N. Miller	O. R. Avison
G. F. Genso	P. S. Gillette
M. A. Noble	J. Z. Moore
C. D. Morris	H. G. Appenzeller
A. R. Appenzeller	A. G. Anderson
F. E. Williams	B. B. Billings
A. L. Becker	F. W. Schofield

Adjustment of Churches

Christian churches after the March 1st movement were lethally stricken to a state of weakness as the result of the Japanese massacre of approximately 2,000 Christians. 2,000 more were indicted and 40 odd churches destroyed. However, despite the excessive victimization of the Christians, the political independence was unachieved as was originally designed by the Korean people through the movement. The major achievements the Christians earned for the price of their sacrifice were the strengthening of Christian faith in the state of persecution, closer relations of the Christians with the non-believers who had formerly despised the christian faith and, from a political standpoint, the transition of the Japanese military government into a cultural government.

In the year when the historical movement for independence emerged in Korea, the Japanese citizens of the mainland were also yearning for a democratic government ; as the military government in Korea failed and the massive numbers of Koreans were killed and imprisoned, the Japanese citizens from the mainland emerged to criticize and to agree with the international reproaches. Therefore, the Japanese Governor General Terauchi was summoned back to mainland and Saito, despite his long years pursuing military career as the admiral of the Japanese Naval Forces, was well-known as a man of integrity ; though he himself was not a Christian, his feelings for Christians were far more sympathetic because his wife was a believer.

Knowing that an imperial policy impoced upon the Korean people would not ensure a successful government, Governor Saito, as his first policy after communication, announced his wish to adopt a cultural policy through communique with the Korean people ; he removed the existing military government and eradicated the former discrimination between the Japanese and Korean people. He permitted freedom of publication of the press to an extent and encouraged educational policies. The Japanese police attitude towards the Christian churches was also less crucial as the result of the Japanese Appeasement Policy upon the Korean people altogether.

On the occasion of Governor Saito's arrival, the Episcopal Rev. Lombas was on the same train to establish the Northern Methodist Youth Association. Governor Saito invited Rev. Lombas into his compartment to exchange his views on the politics and religion ; and later on he also invited the religious leaders to share their mutual ideas. After the inauguration of Governor Saito, the foreign missionaries submitted a petition criticizing the previous persecution of the churches and claiming the freedom of faith provided by the Japanese Constitution. This petition was submitted by the Federal Council of the Evangelical Mission in Korea and the contents were as follows :

1. Acknowledgement with commendation to Governor Saito for his transfer and restoration of former Japanese policies in Korea.

2. Inevitable conditions under which the Independence Movement would uprise to detest oppression, discrimination and a military government.

3. Removal of the former persecution of Christian churches.
4. As regards the Evangelical Movement ; the mission claimed :
    a) Mitigation policy on Christian leaders and churches
    b) freedom of Christians from discrimination and fear
    c) freedom of petitions
5. As regards educational programs : the mission claimed :
    a) the permission of Christian schools to include Bible lessons and religious services in their curriculum
    b) abolition of restriction in teaching the native language
    c) removal of police officials intervention in the private schools
    d) freedom of each individual student in his conscience of holding faith either in church attendance or the worship of the emperor of Japan
    e) abolition of restriction in teaching Korean History and world history in the curriculum
    f) abolition of discrimination of the private school graduates
6. Freedom of medical works by the mission without the intervention of police and officials of Japanese Government.
7. As regards to religious literature : the mission claimed :
    a) abolition of censorship on all Christian literatures
    b) removal of police intervention upon the articles of all publications of Christian churches
    c) all disturbance to be removed on the distributors of the Holy Script tracts and other church publications
8. All church properties to be registered and protected under legislation.
9. Abolition of restriction solicited against public prostitution and opium production.
10. Renovation and restriction on increasing brewry products.
11. Enactment of new laws solicited to protect the interest of laborers.
12. Prevention of cruelty for all political offenses.
miscellaneous items deleted.
After this petition was submitted directly to Governor Saito, irrational

oppression upon the Christian churches by the Japanese government at large was discontinued and many items specified in the petition were approved and realized by the government. On the other hand, as previously stated, with the March Independence movement, the faith in Christianity was strengthened and closer relations were achieved with the non-Christians. Thus, the churches, in general reference, began to readjust themselves to design the restoration of evangelical and educational movement. They revived the victims of the churches during the Movement and saw the increase of Christian members by the end of 1925 reaching 260,000.

Chapter 8
Union of the Christian Churches

Korea Christians Association

The evangelical movement of the individual denominations saw the collective benefit of uniting all the sectarian activities into one major flow of Christian movement to resolve the inter-church struggles and ensure better godly purposes. All the foreign missionaries in Korea by September 1905 established the Federal Council of Evangelical Mission in Korea which affiliated all the four Presbyterian Missions with the missionaries of both the Northern and Southern Methodist Missions. The Mission thus achieved uniformity in all the Sunday School text books and hymnals. As its organ the Mission published the Christian journal "Korea Mission Field."and, in addition, organized a joint administrative body to operate together the boys schools in Seoul and Pyongyang, and the medical facilities in Seoul. Moreover, the Mission sponsored joint discussions to design the principle policies of evangelical movement in Korea, while sponsoring gospel activities for the Korean students in Japan.

As the conformity of the Missionary Union progressed, along with the foundation of the Korean churches, all the representatives of the denominations and the leaders of the Korean churches in 1911 organized the Joint Committee of Presbyterian and Methodist Churches of Korea to assume the works of the previous Missionary Union. However, the new committe of the Presbyterian and Methodist Churches was confronted with the difficulty of administering all the other remaining Christian denominations prospering in Korea. In February 1919, the Chosun Christian Joint Council was organized to design the international organization among the delegates of all Christian denominations, churches and the Korean Christian leaders. There were 20 delegates from the Presbyterian and Methodist churches and 25 from other denominations.

This Joint Council affiliated itself with the International Mission of Christian Churches, renominated as the National Council Church of Korea in 1924. According to the constitution adopted by this united body, "All the Christian churches are to cooperate with the evangelical movement and coordinate their mission in the promotion of public morality and to promote the Christian culture". The supreme objective was to realize all the churches into one denomination. Therefore, this joint council is internally an organization to unite all the churches in Korea, serving externally a relaying system between the International church authority and the domestic church. After the Council was organized, in 1929 and in 1932, its delegation attended two renowned International Missionary Conferences in Jerusalem and Herrnfult, Germany, and promoted a great consolidation within Korea for cooperation among the churches. They sponsored hundreds of evangelical conventions, while publishing an extensive amount of gospel brochures. The Council also sponsored a number of gospel movements amongst the Korean residents in Japan, and Dr. C.A. Clark in 1932 succeeded in establishing the Korean Christian United Church. However, the National Council of Churches lost its function due to the severe persecution by the Japanese Government in 1938.

Affiliation of Four Presbyterian Churches

When the four Presbyterian Missions entered the country, they all had individually different administrative channels in the evangelical movement; however, as the Korean churches became firmer in their foundation, the questions of their independence and affiliation was often discussed among the representatives.

All the Presbyterian church missions in Korea sent their inquiries to the head mission overseas regarding the amalgamation of all the evangelical missions of Presbyterian churches in Korea ; they received the approval from their headquarters to organize the joint Presbyterian church. In Pyongyang in September, 1907, during the Missionary Council Meeting, it was resolved to establish Chosun Jesus Presbyterian Elders' Council and to vest all the previous authority of respective Presbyterian Missions in this Council. All the missionaries from the Southern and Northern Presbyterian Church of America, and the Australian and Canadian Presbyterian Missions were in unison present at a session and agreed to organize their joint Council. Thus the four Presbyterian missions in Korea were successfully united in their evangelical mission and the Korean Christian leaders could also participate in the Christian heraldic policy.

During the Conference convened to establish the Chosun Jesus Presbyterian Council, 40 Korean elders and 38 foreign missionaries were present. Rev. Moffet was elected as the chairman and Bang, Ki Chang as vice-chairman. The exclusive items discussed and passed at this meeting were:

1. To ordain the seven first-year graduates (Suh, Kyung Jo, Bang, Ki Chang, Han, Suk Jin, Yang, Jun Baik, Song, Lin Su, Kil, Sun Ju, Lee, Ki Poong). They were the first Presbyterian ministers ordained in Korea.

2. To send Lee, Ki Poong as a missionary to Cheju Island.

3. To establish seven chapters as proxy to the Head Council in the districts Kyonggi, Choongchong, Pyongbuk, Pyongnam, Kyongsang, Hamkyong and Cholla provinces in consideration of the geographical difficulty of its administration.

4. Approval of establishment of the Chosun Presbyterian Church to be authorized by the International Presbyterian Headquarters, and thereto registered.

5. To issue letters of Appreciation to the Northern and Southern Presbyterian churches of America and the Canadian Presbyterian Mission.

6. Expenses for the councils and organized Church to be borne by

individual churches under the administration of the Head Council.

7. Inform Rev. Underwood in the United States of the Organization of the Church Mission, etc..

Lee, Ki Poong, as the first missionary of the graduates from the Pyong yang Theological Seminary, was sent to Cheju Island to express the gratitude to the Lord for the organization of the Chosun Presbyterian Mission. In 1909, Rev. Choi, Kwang Hul was sent to Vladivostock while Rev. Han, Suk Jin was sent to Tokyo to engage in the heroic movement for the native residents in Japan, and in 1910 Rev. Kim, Yung Je was sent to Manchuria as a Christian missionary.

In 1911, all the seven Promotive Committees of the Church were promoted to seven Chapters of the Presbyterian Councils, and, in September the following year, the Chosun Jesus Presbyterian Headquarters was organized where 52 Korean ministers, 125 church elders and 44 missionaries met together. In appreciation of the establishment of this Presbyterian Conference, it was unanimously resolved that the Conference would despatch Kim, Yung Hoon, Sa, Byung Soon and Park, No Tai to initiate the gospel movement in Shan Tung, China, as the first foreign mission of Christian Evangelism.

The Union of the Southern and Northern Methodist Missions

Although the four Presbyterian missions amalgamated themselves and launched the joint Christian mission work through the independent organization of the Chosun Jesus Presbyterian Council, the Southern and Northern Methodist Mission in Korea saw no efficient joint-work but had to sponsor separate evangelic movement. However, in 1924 when the two leading missions motioned for the exceceutive meeting of the representatives of both Northern and Southern Methodist mission for the joint Annual Conference at the Pierson's Bible School, the uniting of the two missions was discussed and generally agreed upon. In 1926, the two missions organized the promotive committee represented by five each of the members of the two missions who exerted collective efforts to highlight both Northern American Methodist Conference held in 1928, and the Southern American Methodist Council convened in 1930. With the recognition by the American Methodist authorities, the Joint Methodist Council in Korea was authorized to sponsor the independent joint annual conference. Thus, in November 1930, five delegates plenipotentiary from both the Southern and Northern American Methodist Missions came to Korea to discuss the conference with the Korean Methodist Church leaders and established the Chosun Christian Methodist Mission. In December of the same year, the first joint conference was held to adopt a new charter of the Church, and Rev. Yang, Ju Sam was the first presidentelect. Thus, the two Methodist missions united their heraldic movement in Korea in joint efforts.

United Administration of the Professional Educational Organization

By 1930, there were four colleges under the joint operation of all the Christian Churches in Korea. In October 1906, by the joint efforts of the Northern Methodist Mission and the Northern Presbyterian Mission, Pyongyang Soongshil college and Seoul Severance Medical College were established, and by 1910 Soongshil College turned out two graduates while Severance Medical College graduated seven. These 9 graduates were the first graduates of the college education stipulated in Korea. Two years later, the Australian Mission of the Presbyterian Church and the Southern Presbyterian Mission also joined in the operation of the Soongshil College and somewhat later the Canadian Presbyterian Mission also joined in the administration, but in 1915 the Northern Methodist Mission seceded from the joint project. According to the report of 1932, the existing graduates of Soongshil College amounted to 232 and undergraduates 170. Since 1913, Severance Medical College was operated by 5 Christian Missions and in 1923 Severance became authorized as the college by the government, and by 1934 the doctorate licenses of the graduates were recognized as medical doctors within the territory of all the Japanese colonies.

Ewha Women's College was established by the Northern Methodist Church Mission in 1910, but by 1925 the operation was co-sponsored by Southern Methodist Mission, and in 1930 the Unitarian Canadian Mission also joined in the operation. Thus it is still under the joint administration of these three missions to this date. Ewha Women's College found its present school site in Shinchon in 1932 and the number of students then totaled approximately 240.

Yunhee College was established in Seoul in 1915 ; the college inaugurated its name from the tomb of Prince Yunhee buried within the first campus of the school. Although this college was under the joint operation of the different Christian Missions in Korea, the main resource of the foundation was supported by John T. Underwood. The total graduates of the Yunhee College toward the end of 1932 were 2,500 and the undergraduates amounted to 250.

Thus, all the Christian Churches in Korea exerted their joint efforts in the operation of the four early Christian colleges in a united body for the Christian Movement in Korea.

Remarkable Increase of the Christian Converts

As the Korean people recovered from the wound of the March lst Incident, the Korean Christian Churches also revived at a remarkable pace. The belief and faith of the Chrisitans strengthened, and the people who previously disapproved of Christianity began to come to the church while the Christian leaders who were imprisoned experienced the spiritual blessings of the Lord and this testimony of their holy experiences in the churches gave rise to the Christian movement.

One of the major causes for the Christian development after the March lst Movement was the enforcement of Japanese colonialism. Although Governor Minami claimed the Cultural policy upon Korea, it was not the transfer of the colonialism of the Japanese government. The feudalistic exploitation, capitalistic oppression of the Korean economy expedited the classification of the social class system and impoverished the Korean people of their opportunity to survive.

In 1919, during the March Independence Movement, the total number of yeomen house-holds were 525,000 and the half-tenant farming yeomen houses 1,045,000, but by 1932 the number of the yeomen class decreased to 470,000 and the half-tenant farming yeomen houses to 743,000. And, on the other hand, the tenant farmer households increased from 1,003,000 in 1919 to 1,546,000 by 1932.

In the other words, the yeomen class degenerated into the half-tenant yeomen and the latter to the tenant farmers, thus the extensive farm-lands formerly owned by the Korean farmers gradually were transferred to the ownership of the Japanese landlords. The farmers, deprived of their farm-lands began to sworm into the urban areas but, due to the deterioration of the progress in the second industry, there were no opportunity for employment and no means of living was provided. Confronted with the vast national bankruptcy, the Korean people had but three choices to select; either to immigrate with the entire family to Manchuria, or to join in the social revolution against the Japanese government to open a better system for the benefit of safe living, or to convert themselves into the Christian faith in which they may achieve peace of mind in the secular life. Many took refuge in Manchuria to open up new life, likewise many joined the underground forces to plan social revolts, and also many converted themselves to find solace and peace in the Christian churches. Coincidentally, a hugh number of the Christian leaders were released from prison after the March Independence Movement, and they staged a nationwide evangelism; especially Kim, Ik Du and Kil, Sun Ju who campaigned their revival movement throughout the country as the highlight of all the Christian churches in Korea. The result of the enthusiasm of the contemporary Christian leaders doubled the number of the people coming into the Christian churches. The rate of increase of Christian converts is from 196,000, Protestants in 1919 increased to 260,000 in 1925, and in the gradual process the number totally increased to 330,000 by 1934, and the Protestant churches became the hegemony of all religious orders. Gigantic church buildings went up in the urban areas, and many people crowded into the churches on Sundays with the Holy Scriptures and Hymnals in their hands. Many also sang hymns in the streets and still more prayed a blessing while dining in the restaurants. Many people still lived in the hope of salvation amid poverty, loss of their country and their precarious condition of life.

Chapter 9
Japanese Persecution of Churches

Japanese Policy of Korean Erosion

While the Korean people suffered from economic bankruptcy, the Japanese military conquered Manchuria in September 1931 and established their puppet regime to open a better way for Japanese people to live. Again the Japanese imperialists increased their arms and forces in an attempt to put Asia entirely under its sway. Indeed Japan grew and was empowered in Asia to withstand the power of the western hemisphere.

A crucial issue was the incident of the erasure of the Japanese emblem which occurred in Korean giving way for Japan to enforce their oppression. Upon the inauguration of Governor-General Minami in August 1936, who was ambitious for a chance to enforce the oppression upon Korea, Son, Ki Jung of Korea won the gold medal in the Mararthon at the World Olympic Games held in Berlin. The Editorial staff of the Dong-A Ilbo erased deliberately the Japanese symbol from the breast of the winner before the photo release of the highlighting news. It was long after Japan withdrew herself from the international League of Nations therefore she no longer paid any heed to international opinion. However, for Japan this was the best opportunity she could ever have to impose upon the Korean people their loyalty to the Japanese Imperor and, by closing the Dong-A Ilbo, Minami Governor enforced his policy of Japanizing the Korean people under the pretext of inter-state unity and the promotion of annexation that would design the complete erasure of the national spirit of Korea.

In July 1937, through the well-schedmed Incident of Lu-Kou-Chiao the Japanese government instigated the Sino-Japanese War, as previously stated, and began to occupy the Chinese mainland. Japan, in its attempt to secure military power from the rear, had to prevent the possible recurrence of political revolts from Korea. They therefore imposed the policy of Janpanizing the Korean people, and desperately administered the issue of Korean erasure, for which the Korean people had to suffer massive trials.

The Japanese policy of Korean erasure began by the use of the Japanese Language ; this was used to gradually destroy the Korean native tongue. All the native language taught in the school curriculum was at once abolished. They posted in the schools, governmental offices, and private enterprises "the use of National Language"and powerfully abused the Koreans for speaking their mother tongue. Later this policy was imposed on the Christians and Japanese became the language of worship services in the churches. They also urged the Koreans to swear the oath of becoming citizens of the Japanese Empire. This oath was what they termed as "The Oath of Imperial Citizen."

1. We are the citizens of the Imperial State. With loyalty, shall we serve the lord-country.

2. We Imperial citizens shall mutually assist in unity.

3. We Imperial citizens shall indure hardship and cultivate power to promote the national prestige and the Imperial virtue.

The Korean people were forced to recite these three pledges in schools and governmental offices during the morning formation, and they were recited by the congregation before the worship began in all the churches. The farmers who had no command of the Japanese language and who were unable to recite the Pledge of the Imperial Citizen were deprived by the local officials of the privilege of grain allocation or ferry-rides.

The Japanese government also enforced the change of names for all Korean people. The change of the Korean name applied to adoption of new Japanese names in place of the original surname of the Korean family traditionally inherited throughout history, i.e. Nakamura or Hoojida. As a result of the Japanese way of christening, all the Korean blood brothers were subject to different names and therefore suffered from the breach of the family system. The breach of the family system added to the diss-missal of the native spirit.

The conscription policy was then enforced on all the Korean youths who were needlessly led into the battle ground and were forced into the war through what they termed the 'Student Militia System'. Moreover, Korean men were mobilized to meet the demand of labor forces in Japan by compulsion, and grains were taken by force while the white mourning dress of the national tradition was forbidden by law and thus further di-minished the Korean spirit.

The Issue of Shintoist Worship

Though it had been one of the long pending religious issues, the worship at the shintoist shrine was not as stronly enforced on the Christians by the Japanese authorities as on the public servants living on the stipend from the Japanese government and the faculty and students of the public schools.

However, the problem emerged as a trying case for the Christian faith ever since the Manchurian Conflict(1931-1937). The Potentiality of Japan became powerful enough to entertain an ambition of conquering the Asia mainland, and the Japanese government attempted to deprive the Koreans of their national spirit by forcing attendance at the Shinto shrines set up across the country and even in small towns in countless numbers. A certain form of Shinto rite was conducted at the shrine on every national occasion of Japan, and, soon, the students and faculty of the private schools and the schools that belonged to the Christian mission were all ordered out to participate in the religious event. The churches were uneasy, hesitant, and showed negative a attitude toward this Japanese action. But, in the winter of 1935, the Japanese governor-general came out with a more stringent measure, dismissing Dr. G. S. McCune, Dean of the Soongshil College and Miss V. L. Snook, principal of the Soongshil Girls' School, from their positions, and expelling them from the country on the ground of their denying Shinto worship.

The churches were again caught in a flurry. They had to make a choice; whether to stand fast to their own religious faith or entirely succumb to the forced worship of the Japanese god at the Shinto shrine. Meanwhile, the Japanese government mobilized its police forces and employed various means of threats to make the Christians worship at the shrine.

Finally, the day of humiliation came. The Presbyterian Church that had the most conservative creed and the largest number of followers among the other Protestant denominations convened its 27th general assembly in Pyongyang in September, 1938. Before the convention, the police superintendent of Pyongannam province summoned the foreign missionaries and threatened them to pass the issue on the Shinto worship, saying that if anyone should make an opposing remark at the meeting against it, he would be severely punished on a charge of blasphemy. In addition, the local police went after each assembly representative and warned them that anyone who opposed the issue would be arrested. Some 20 churchmen including Ministers Joo, Ki Chul, Lee, Ki Sun and Chae, Jung Min, who had been vigorous opponents to the Shintoist practice, were already under tentative arrest during this time. The meeting, however, proceeded under the watchful eyes of hundreds of policemen and plainclothesmen. At the outset, one representative named Park raised the motion relating to the religious issue, and the chairman Hon, as if on a premeditated compromise, brought it up as a formal agenda and asked for a resolution by yes or no without going through the procedural discussion. There were only a few favoring the motion, but the chairman proclaimed it adopted. Then, a missionary, W. N. Blair, stood up for an objection, but, because of the police repression, could only leave a statement that he wanted it to be recorded on the minutes of the meeting that he had opposed the action that was in opposition to the constitution of the church and the discipline of God. Another missionary cried out, "I am going to make an appeal to the will of God. This was a tragic event. The Japanese authorities propagandized that the issue had been passed unanimously, charged the Christian ministers and elders not attending the shrines as herectics and tortured them in prison, and relentlessly closed down the schools that were not complying with the worship.

Following the convention, most of the vigorous anti-Shintoists were arrested by the Japanese police, some of the clergymen who were holding on to their faith and conscious had to go into seclusion, or some disappeared into the Manchurian areas. Some others remained at home, attending the Shintoist merely for the purpose of maintaining their livelihood. And to these remnants of the Christian fellows came another trial. The Japanese dictated that the spirit house enshrining their god, Amateras Omikami should be built within the church for everyone to make a bow before it, and that the Old Testament and the Book of Revelation should be removed from the bilical code for they were not the Bibles. This invited a head-on collision between the churches and the Japanese authorities, and, eventually, some 2,000 church leaders were imprisoned, of whom 50 died in prison, and about 200 churches were closed down during WarII.

The Appearance of the Puppet Religious Group

While they were wrangling over the issue concerning the Shintoist worship, the so-called Christians Fraternity Association was organized in Pyongyang, often referred to as the Jerusalem of Korea, and 'the Reformed Religious Body' in Seoul. These were the puppet religious groups betraying their fellow Christians to the governor-general or declaring that it was scriptural to enshrine and worship the Japanese god in the church. Some renowned clergymen also took part in these groups at the persuasion of the police.

In fact, they were a group of people most unchaste and short-sighted, especially at a time when the churches were undergoing a great hardship.

Among these weak faith Christians, there were two categories of people, the ones who tried to rise up in the world by holding on to religious power, and the others who tried to maintain the status quo by rendering camouflaged cooperation for fear of the pressures from the Japanese police. But, in any case, they were the people who voluntarily offered the Japanese army the holy bells taken from more than 3,000 churches for the production of arms to be used in destroying England and America ; who claimed that the Japanese god, Amateras Omikami was superior to Jehovah or Heavenly Father, and who bowed before the Japanese shrines set up in the church every morning. What was more, they even set up traps for, and threw into prison, their own fellow ministers, and sold off their own churches. The entire Christian society was shocked by their endless evil action.

Discovering that the Christian religious platform became so completely powerless and at their disposal, the Japanese imperial government made all the Protestant denominations discard their native names in 1942 and had them subjected to the Japanese Christian Order of Chosun. The whole religious power and the actual helm of the local Christian schools had been completely turned over to the hands of the Japanese-sided people, and the churches which belonged to Seventh-Day Adventist, Holiness and Baptist Church underwent the bitter experience of disembodying their denominations in 1943.

Then, the puppet ministers at the helm of the religious power even built up a sort of Japanese spiritual training institute called Daehwasook of Imperial Cultural Center, and contributed more glories to the Japanese god than the Lord in Heaven by forcing innocent clergymen to offer sacrifices at the Shintoist shrines.

The number of the Christian believers before the Liberation in 1945 had changed as follows since the independence movement of March 1st, 1919 :

The Number of the Christian by Each Denomination

(as of Dec. 1943)

Denomination	Number of Churches	Number of Ministers	Number of Followers
Presbyterian	3,044	2,765	160,717
Methodist	794	350	31,914
Holiness	204	Closed	5,000(Approx.)
Seventh-Day Adventist	185	Closed	3,000(Approx.)
Anglican	127	99	5,923
Salvation Army	89	112	2,204
Church of Pentecost	4		
Christian Church of Chosun	23	10	2,897
Church of Assembled	26	25	207
Church of Christ	6	3	309
Church of Jesus, Chosun	8	5	395
Church of Jesus	8	7	725
Evangelical Church of Chosun	19	7	294
Church of Nazareth	3	3	35
Assembly of God	1	1	40
Christian Church of Dong-A	29	32	145

Remarks : The sudden drop in number since the year-end 1941 was attributable to Japanese persecution to ward the churches.

The Status of Change in Number of Christians by Each Denomination

Year	Presbyterian	Methodist	Holiness	Anglican	Seventh-Day	Salvation
1919	141,044	43,856	850	4,264	1,839	4,725
1922	194,037	64,112	1,833	4,127	953	5,718
1925	182,650	58,434	5,413	4,805	1,542	8,909
1928	186,880	42,513	4,926	5,993	3,998	3,443
1931	197,538	45,142	5,626	6,448	4,202	4,173
1934	248,812	52,674	9,004	5,516	5,018	4,527
1939	286,268	53,002	11,135	8,016	5,984	6,057
1941	256,575	50,286	9,165	7,535	4,510	4,536
1943	160,717	31,914	5,000	5,923	3,000	2,204
		(app.)		(app.)		

Part VII

Other Religions

Chapter 1
The Chonto-kyo(天道教)

The Founder, Choi, Je Woo

The Chonto-kyo religion was originally advocated by Choi, Je Woo from Kanjung-ri, Kyongju-kun, Kyongsang Province in 1860. Choi, Chi Won, a celebrated man of letters in the Sylla Dynasty, and Choi, Null, who had assumed an official position called Sasung at the Sungkyunkwan Institution, were Choi's distant forefathers. His father, Choi, Oak, was said to have been famous for his Confucian learning in his home province, and he gave up his public career to engage in educating the younger generation in Yongdam at the foot of Mt. Kuimbong in the outskirt of Kyongju. It was from such a beginning that Yongdam later became a holy-land for the Chonto-kyo religion.

Born in October 1924, the 24th year of King Soonjo, Choi, Je Woo was considered to have been intelligent and magnanimous from his childhood. Choi's family seemed to be in an adverse condition. Losing his mother when he was 6 and his father when 16, Choi, was unable to attend the private school called Sudang, and spend most of his adolescent year busily eeking out as canty living.

His youth, however, was not all spent in insipidity. Despite business, he read extensively the Buddhist and Confucian books, and conducted a profound research in Western learning. Not satisfied only with these studies, Choi set out for a tour of the world with a view to acquaint himself with the public morale, popular sentiment, luck and cycle of life. He returned to Kyongju in 1844 to lead his family, and continued his meditation to find the truth about life and the universe.

When he was 32, Choi obtained a book explaining about the three religions of Confucianism, Buddhism and Taoism from a strange monk who came from the Yujom temple in Mt. Kumkang. After three days of deliberations on the contents, Choi grasped the concurrent point of the three religions as well as an outlook on the universe ranging from man to heaven. The following year, he pursued his asceticism at the Tongdo temple in Mt. Yangsan for 40 days, continuing his religious austerities, and avoiding the contacts with others so that he was in rapport with heaven, and at the Yongdam-jung under Mt. Kuimi in his hometown of Kyongju when he was 36. Then, one day in April 1,860, when he was 37, Choi, felling a strange development in his spirit with his body and mind shaking, grasped the truth about the law of the relation of man-to-heaven, and, thence, began the mission for the cardinal principles of his religion ; calling for the preservation of peace for the country and people, and world-wide propagation and extensive salvation of the people.

After drawing up a brief formula for his tenets, Choi endeavored to train his followers on one hand, and to compile such works as Yongdan-ka, Kyohun-Ka and Cheosa-ka on the other. When he was 43, he devoted himself exclusively to the work of the religious propagation, entrusting Choi, Shi Hyung with the other matters relating to his religion.

The Advocacy of Donghak

It was in 1860, when Choi, Je Woo first advocated this school, Donghak, under the slogan of his religion, Conto ; which he widely spread to save the people. The word Donghak, meaning an Eastern learning, stands out against the Seohak, the Western learning implying Catholicism. The political corruption and degradation at the end of Chosun period plunged the whole society into the verge of complete hopelessness, and, in addition, Catholicism, considered to be endangering the destiny of the state, was overwhelming the spiritual realm of the country and was extending its influence even to the imperial court. Our old faith is languishing, and, taking advantage of this, the Seokyo(meaning the Western religion) is on the rise, and our national destiny is in Jeopardy. I am graced with the divine revelation from the Supreme God. Thus, should anyone profess in my religion, he will be exempt illness and enjoy the life endowed by Heaven. The Seokyo is a perverse religion that will ruin the people and country, said Choi, Je Woo in his propagation literatures. It was from such a stern rejection of Catholicism, or Seohak, that Choi named his religion Donghak.

Nevertheless, the immediate motive that made Choi rise and call for the salvation of the people had been stimulated by the martydom spirit of the Catholic church, taking into account what he had said about Catholic principles. However, his religious practices and doctrines seemed to have their basis on the harmonized combination of those of Confucianism, Buddhism and Taoism. This could be supported by the following examples. In a question-answer interview with an old Buddhist monk named Song-wol-dang, Choi said :

'I am fond of Buddhism. Though I am not a monk, I am awakened to the teachings of Buddha.'

'I do not belive in Taoism, but I am fond of it.'

Choi, Je Woo, on his 44th birthday, also said to his legitimate heir, Choi, Shi Hyung :

'Our religion essentially is neither Confucianism, nor Buddhism nor Taoism,' but the one that put the three together in oneness. That is, Chonto which is not Confucius, Buddha or Tao but, instead, they are a part belonging to the Chonto meaning the Heavenly Way. The Confucian ethics, the Buddhist introspection and the Taoist mental cultivation are the gifted parts of human nature, the very native property of the Chonto. My religion is, thus, founded on the Great Origin of Infinity······

It is also plain that Choi attempted to adopt only the merits of the three religions. He stressed the five cardinal principles of morality of Confucianism, the mercy and equality of Buddhism, and the non-avarice and purity of Taoism. However he criticized them because : they lack the art of peace and tranquility : Confucianism is too adherent to the moral ob- ligations, to reach the stage of occultness ; Buddhism, once in its nirvana, totally breaks away from the morals and disciplines ; and Taoism idles away in nature.

The heart of Choi's religion, however, was in believing the Chonto, the Great Principle of Infinity, which had its essence in the natural sub- limation from an inactivity of life that would finally concur with the pro- vidence of Chonju(Lord in Heaven), the great master of the universe. That is to say, if one should protect his innermost feeling for the just conduct of his body and spirit, lead his Heaven-given nature and receive the teaching from Heaven, the essense of change would naturally appear to make him in oneness with Heaven, and the spirits of the two would be so united that they would become inseparable. Thus, the protection of the innermost mind, just spirit, initiative nature and heavenly teachings were the principal guidelines for the Donghaks in their religious asceticism. If man, the wisest of all beings, should understand and follow the truth of the Chonto, he would continue his life in peace, and if he lived with the will of the Lord in Heaven in his mind and integrated his actions with those of the Chonto, man will not only become an angel, but the entire world will become an earthly paradise.

But before his religious ideals of completely driving out the Catholics and saving the people were substantiated, Choi's Donghak, with its similar incantation and definition of God with those of the Christians, earned much misunderstanding from the Confucian group. Choi made every effort for his defense, but the more his followers increased, the greater the jea- lousy of the Confucians became. Finally, Choi, knowing his tragic dooms- day was forthcoming, turned over the legitimacy of the religion to his superior disciple, Choi, Shi Hyung. He was later arrested by the authorities in Taegu and was questioned on charges of bewitching the people with paganism. In a query at the court, Choi, Je Woo cried out unflinchingly, 'I have tried to save our declining country and our troubled world by teaching the Chonto to the people. This Chonto principle has revealed the Will of God, and my enlightenment originated from the Nature of God, but not from any artificial manipulation. I am ready to sacrifice my body for the cause of religion and virtue that will be known through the generations to come. So, do as you please !' As he had given no sign of surrendering, Choi was tortured 21 times in a month of his imprisonment, but was still dauntless. At last, Choi died at the age of 41 on the execution-ground in Taegu March 10, 1864. Three days after his death, his disciples, Kim, Kyong Pil, Kim, Kyong Sook, Jung, Yong Seo and Kwak, Du Kwon, took the body out for burial, but found that there was still some warmth in it. They waited for a possible resurrection, but it did not come even though there was some perspiration from the corpse. So, they buried the body in Yongdam at the foot of Mt. Kuimi.

Following the execution of the founder of Donghak, there was a great set-back in the expansion of Donghak, as the followers shunned their public recognition and the number of new patrons decreased conspicuously.

The Sincere Devotion of Choi, Shi Hyung

If it were not for the superhuman efforts made by Choi, Shi Hyung, the heir of Choi, Je Woo, the Donghak religion could not possibly have been saved from the brink of its total dissolution since the death of its founder.

For the establishment of the Donghak religious organ, Choi, Shi Hyung had been a great contributor as in the case of St. Paul in the first Christian church and Sariputra and Maudglyayana of Buddha. Like his predecessor, Choi was born in March 21, 1927, in Dongchon, Kyongju, and was originally called Kyongsang with a pseudonym of Haewol. In the Chontokyo, he is revered as the Divine Priest Haewol after his pseudonym. Choi, Shi Hyung also lost his mother when he was 5 and his father when 12, and had to lead a frugal life, working for his distant relative in a paper mill in his hometown. After marriage at the age of 19 with a girl from

the Sohn family, he moved to Seungkwang-myon of Kyongju and worked
for the local people for six years. At that time, the propagation of Donghak
religion was in full swing, and Choi, then 35, became a convert after hearing
a sermon given by the religious founder, Choi, Je Woo.

From this time, Choi, Shi Hyung strained himself to hear the Voice
from Heaven, visiting Choi, Je Woo, at least, 3 to 4 times every month
for his preachings, and learning religious manners, sitting in contemplation,
or performing purification. Thus, he came to realize the secret principle
of Donghak earlier than the others, and often was graced with Heavenly
inspirations. Choi, then, intended to set off for the evangelical mission,
but did not have enough funds of his own for the work. Finally, using
the 120 suks of rice offered by a rich man named Kim, I Seo, he went
on preaching tours through the counties of Younghae, Youngduk, Sangju,
Heunghae, Yechon and Chungdo, and organized religious networks by
setting up the missionary centers in the important parts of the country.

Choi, Shi Hyung, after the death of his master, was pursued by the
authorities, but continuously engaged himself in preaching through the
towns of Pyonghae, Uijin and Youngyang, and strived to revive the religious influence by secretly dispatching his men throughout the country
to stimulate the faith of the followers and by spreading reprinted copies
of the religious literature. In 1866, the third year of Kojong, there was
a great massacre of the Catholics by the atrocious ruler, Dae Won Kun,
and, as it became ever more difficult for the mission, Choi retreated into
the seclusion in Youngyang, and no one knew his whereabouts except
a few of his close associates. Only a few of the disciples of Choi, Je Woo,
therefore, could attend the posthumous birthday ceremony of their master
on October 28th of the same year. Thus, in order to avoid the authorities'
pursuit, Choi moved his master's remaining family to Kongkwan-am in
Sangju and himself to Sansu-ri of Poongchon the following year. When
Choi, loitered through the ravine after seeing off Choi, Je Woo's widow,
his exhausted spirit heard : 'It was by the Providence of Heaven that you
are vested with the obligation of the Great Principle. Not be distressed

even if you are not admissible to the world. Do try to build up the foundation of the Principle, for there shall be the divine Judgement.' Taking this as a spiritual revelation of the late Choi, Je Woo, Choi, Shi Hyung continued the mission in secret through Youngyang and Yangyang with a more determined will.

At this time, a man named Lee, Pil, claiming himself a Donghak and saying he would exonerate the late founder of his false accusations, sent a notice in March the 6th year of Kojong(1869) to the followers in Munkyung, Younghae, Youngduk and Sangju, and spearheaded a riot with about 500 men, killing a local government chief of Munkyung. They attempted to advance into Sangju to eliminate the corrupt officials. Surprised by the incident, the government authorities repressed the revolt by deploying troops, and executed more than a hundred of the followers. Choi, Shi Hyung, escaped the mishap and wandered from one place to another. In August of the same year, Lee, Pil again led the revolt in Munkyung city, but his men were dispersed by the government troop's counter-attack. Lee was arrested this time and was given capital punishment. This incident is referred to as 1869 uprising in the Chonto-kyo religion.

Subsequently, the authorities intensified their control and investigation of the Donghak adherents. For more than 4 years, Choi, Shi Hyung lived in hiding in the mountains and the residential quarters, but led a comparatively stabilized life by occupying himself by the farming in Songbu, Danyang, after he had moved his residence there in February 1871, the 10th year of Kojong. In the meantime, the authorities slackened the rigid control of the Donghak, thinking the religious organ had completely vanished since there was no sign of its latent activities or Choi's existence. Taking this opportunity, Choi changed his original name Kyungsang to Shi Hyung and revived the religious propagation, setting up a printing plant, and distributing religious literature called Yongdam Yusa and Dongkyung Daejeon to various local districts. Around the 20th year of King Kojong, the Donghak religion regained its strength from a stalemate period and spread through the Kyongsang and Cholla provinces. Among the many followers Choi converted this time, there were brilliant figures as Sohn, Byung Hee, Sohn, Chon Min, Kim, Yeon Kook, Park, In Ho, Hwang, Ha Il, Suh, In Ju and Ahn, Kyo Sun. Choi spent 49 days at the Saja-am temple in Iksan, studying the religion together with Sohn, Byung Hee.

Choi, Shi Hyung lived in Boeun-kun, Choongchong province, in 1885. Detecting the gradual expansion of the religious power, the provincial governor Shim, Sang Hoon, accompanied by the county head Choi, Hi Jin of Dan yang-kun and their subjects, stormed into the religious meeting place and arrested three Donghak followers including Kang, Si Won. Choi, who was now known as 'Choi with Bundle' for his extraordinary skill of escaping narrowly dodged the risk of being caught, fled to Kongju, and made his elusive appearance in various parts of the country for missionary activity.

The Exoneration Movement

Although the Donghak religion had originally been initiated against the extortions from the Yangban and power classes as well as the overall unfair condition of society, the followers became complete prey for the corrupt officials who, under the pretext of stamping out heresy, raided their houses, plundered their properties, pressed them for the bribes, or inflicted severe punishments. The Donghak patrons everywhere were panic-stricken, and there was a growing tendency that they should unite together to rise against the government rather than become helpless victims of the officials. Thus, the movement developed the intention to prevent the official persecution by basically securing the rightful status of the religion through the exoneration of its prime initiator Choi, Je Woo. This was finally carried into action by the consistent demand from Choi, Shi Hyung's two disciples, Suh, Kae Ju and Suh, Byong Hak in 1892, the 29th year of Kojong while Choi was in seclusion in Sangju. Choi, who at first did not approve of the proposed movement for fear of the possible ill-effects, issued manifestos to all parts of the country, and filed a letter of complaint explaining the atrocities of the local government officials with the governor Cho, Byung Sik of Choongchong province. As was anticipated, no effective result came from this initial movement. Then, Choi sent another appeal to governor Lee, Kyung Sik of Cholla province, and at the same time, gathered some thousands of Donghaks at the Chamlye station of the province for a demonstration on November 1. The appeal read in part :

'It is indeed deplorable that our master Choi, Je Woo in Yongdam had unfortunately been accused of heresy and martyred in Taegu while he, at the command of the Supreme God, was trying to transmit to the world the Principle of uniting man and heaven in oneness and to save the people from distress. . . . Our master was not a Western pagan, but tried to discern right from wrong. We swear we shall bear any sacrifices even if death comes to us thousands of times······ Truly, it was on account of the lack of sagacity and sincerity on our part that we were unable to assuage our resentment and to bring our Great Principal to light in the past 30 years, despite the long perseverance of our lasting rancour and sorrow······ Taking our Principle as an off-shoot of the Western creed, the local magistrates and the corrupt officials of various towns at present are inflicting intolerable damages on our people by arrests, brutalities and pillages without any reservation. The damages and casualties are increasing, and there is no shelter for our safety······ Our faith in this religion means no harm whatever, but only that will make man, into what is humanly possible, repentance, loyalty to his sovereign, pious to his parents, respectful to his teacher, and to be sociable with his friends. And, accordingly, there is nothing else so greatly wished in our day-and-night prayers to Heaven than the welfare and peace of the state and people, and the broad propagation of our religion······ Be especially merciful enough to report this appeal to Sangkam(His Majesty) in order to purge our master of his chagrin, and to issue your decree to save our impoverished people from dying in your province.'

No favorable action was taken immediately by the governor after he received this letter. But about 5 days later, he sent out an order not to be bewitched by this perverse religion. Exasperated, the Donghak followers filed a more resolute appeal and continued their demonstrations. The governor became a little uneasy about this, and, instructed the local government of the counties that there should be no plunderings of the property of the people under the pretext of religious control on the Donghak, and that those bewitched by this religion should be persuaded to give it up. The demonstrators returned home, satisfied that they had attained, at least, one of their goals. After this movement, the popularity of Choi, Shi Hyung together with the spirit of the religious followers was greatly heightened. But the authorities' atrocities continued unchanged. It seemed that there was not the slightest favorable consideration from the government for the repeated appeals made by the Donghaks for exoneration of their religious founder. Thus, in February 1893, hundreds of Donghaks, who disguised themselves as the Confucians going up for public examination, went to the capital, and pleaded for a royal action, wailing loudly before the Kwanghwamun Gate. The King Kojong, personally came out to the gate and pacified the demonstrators to retreat, saying, "Your wishes shall be fulfilled only if you would return to your homes and remain faithful to your respective works."

Later, however, there was no instruction of any kind ever sent down to the local government from the imperial court, and the authorities' harrassment continued. Finally, a massive demonstration was planned by the religious leaders like Sohn, Byung Hee, Lee, Kwang Yong and Kwon, Jae Jo, and carried out in an orderly manner on the death-day anniversary of the late Choi, Je Woo in Boeun, Choongchong province, in which Choi, Shi Hyung himself and tens of thousands of the religious followers participated. This was reported in the capital as if "the Donghaks rose in revolt." The imperial court even attempted to mobilize the army to repress it, but, instead, dispersed the demonstrators by having an official read to them an imperial instruction of good conciliatory phrases. Afterwards, the imperial government did not show any favorable signs. The Donghaks were imbued strongly with a sense of resistance to the government, whereby some thousands of them provoked an uprising in Echon-kun, Kyong-gi province, and several of the riot leaders were arrested and executed while trying to attack a local government office.

The Donghak Uprising

In the midst of such a riotous spirit among the Donghaks after the unsuccessful movement to attain the rightful public recognition for their religion with an exoneration of their religious founder, another Donghak named Jon, Bong Joon sparked a popular uprising in Kobu-kun, Cholla province, in January 1894, under the banner of eliminating the atrocious rule and saving the people. The immediate cause of this revolt were the brutal requisitions and extortions imposed by the country head Jo, Byung Kap of Kobu-kun. Jon, who originally had harboured al ill-feeling against the brutal administration and, stood for political reform, distributed through the missionary centers in the provinces a notice calling for a religious assembly at Mahangsi, Kobu-kun on Jan. 1st. Thousands of followers led by Choi, Kyung Sun, Jung, Il Seo and Sohn, Hwa Joong thronged the place. Jon led the explosion of the rightful indignation of the massive crowd at the assembly by exposing various crimes of the country head and stressing the need for a coup for the exoneration of the religious founder. In addition to the Donghaks, the impoverished farming mass, who had been equally discontented, were also agitated and joined the ranks. They, at last turned to rioting, charging into the Kobu-kun county office, wresting the military weapons, breaking down the grain-warehouse, and demolishing the reservior that had been an instrument for the exploitation of the private resources.

The imperial court, at the news of this outbreak, dispatched Lee, Yong Tae, the head official of Jangheung-bu, to investigate the event. Leading his 800 men, Lee made the situation worse by manhandling the rioting people and burning down the houses of the Donghaks. As a result, the

Donghaks became even more indignant and broke out into a nationwide uprising in March, the same year, under the leadership of Jon, Bong Joon. The other leaders of this religious coup who chanted the slogans, 'the peace and welfare for the state and people, and the elimination of the corrupt of ficials', were Jung, Jong Hyeok and Cha, Chi Ku from Jungeup, Kim, Kae Nam and Choi, Young Chan from Taein, Chin, Wo Bum and Kim, Kong Sun from Mankyung, Kim, Duk Myung and Kim, Sa Hwa from Kumkang, Oh, Ha Young and Oh, Shi Young from Kochang, Kim, Bong Nyon and Lee, Chik Kown from Kimjae, Bae, Kyu In and Bae, Kyun Chang from Mooan, Song, Mun Soo and Kang, Kyung Joong from Moojang, Choi, Seung Woo and Choi, Jon Ha from Imsil, Kim, Hong Ki and Kim Mak Ki from Namwon, Yang, Hae Il from Soonchang, Jon, Sam Yung from Jinan, and Yoo, Chi from Mooju. With the long-suppressed farming and servant classes joining in, the Donghak uprising expanded into a war ; all of its people seemed to support it as the rioters everywhere attempted to correct the hundreds of years of accumulated corruption and mal-administration by executing the greedy and brutal local magistrates, retrieving the property taken by the power-hungry classes, and freeing the slaves and the other innocent people held in confinement.

The imperial government, confused by these developments, ordered Hong, Kae Hoon and his army to attack the revolutionary arms from the capital ; the other government troops advanced to Kobu-kun county from Jonju. The Donghak army of Jon, Bong Joon fought with government troops from Jonju and killed more than a thousand of the royal troops at the Hwangto-hyeon battle ; it destroyed the army led by Hong, Kae Hoon from the capital in another battle at Hwangryong-jang, capturing three cannons. Now, confident of victory for the army of justice, the Donghak army of tens of thousands of men reorganized its ranks, overan most of the entire Cholla region without resistance, and caputred the capital city, Jonju, of Cholla province on April 27. At this time, Choi, Shi Hyung, the supreme commander of Donghak, issued a warning against political involvement in the movement, but this was no more than a distant cry to the raging waves. In the end, Choi, on hearing the report of a great massacre of the Donghak believers, could no longer sit aloof. He called together all the religious leaders from the local parishes to instruct them, 'this is the destiny of Heaven. Help Jon, Bong Joon with all your fellows to clear away the resentment against our founder and to fulfill the great wishes of our religion.' He then turned his pontifical flag over to Sohn, Byung Hee.

The imperial government, being anxious about the growing intensity of the Donghak uprising, requested reinforcements from the Ch'ing Dynasty through its consul-general to Seoul. The Ch'ing government on the pretext of rescuing its vassal state, landed their army in Asanpo in June, and notified Japan of their intention in accordance with their Ti' enchin Treaties of 1871 and 1885. The Japanese government, which had constantly been on the lookout for such an opportunity since the 1884 political upheaval in Korea, also landed 7,000 troops loaded on seven warships at the port of Inchon with an excuse of protecting their residents in the country. A division of the Japanese troops moved into the capital with cannons. For fear of a more dangerous war with the powerful neighboring countries, the imperial government issued a decree promising ·no harmful retaliation for the Donghaks should they disband their army and retreat from the Jonju fortress. Considering the imminent danger of the entire country, the Donghak army withdrew voluntarily. But from this incident eventuated the Sino-Japanese War(1894-95) that caused great affliction for Korea. As the Japanese ambition for Chosun became explicit, the leaders of Donghak, including Choi, Shi Hyung, rose up en masse in September the same year, calling for the expulsion of the foreigners and the peaceful welfare of the state and people ; they attacked the logistic bases of the Japanese army in various parts of the country. The Japanese army, collaborating with the government troops, came up to the front and inflicted great casualities on the Donghaks. The Donghak army Commanded by Jon, Bong Joon was also continously defeated in the battles at Kongju, Nonsan, Taein, Jangsung and Noryoung, and became completely demoralized. Finally, the religious rebellion was brought to an end when Jon was arrested in Yongji-ri of Soonchang in December, the same year, and executed in Seoul. According to an estimate by the Chonto-kyo religion, the total death of Donghaks in this last stage of the revolt had been more than 200,000.

The Establishment of the Chonto-kyo

Following the end of the bloody uprising, Choi, Shi Hyung was ready, for martyrdom and chose Sohn, Byung Hee, Kim, Yeon Kook and Sohn, Chon Min among his many other disciples as successors of the religion in January, 1896. In April, two years later, Choi was captured in Yeoju and executed in Seoul. Sohn, Chon Min followed suit, voluntarily accepting martyrdom ; Kim, Yeon Kook remined in the country to control the religious regime, Sohn, Byung Hee went to Japan with Lee, Yong Koo and Sohn, Byung Heum to take refuge and to learn the trends of the international situation. Under the alias of Lee Sang Heon, Sohn, Byung Hee associated with powerful figures in and out of the government in Japan, paved the way for Korean youth to study there, and discussed the affairs of the home country with the other exiles like Park, Young Hyu, Kwon, Dong Jin, Oh, Se Chang and Jo, Ui Yeon.

Afterwards, when there was a wide-spread rumour about an imminent Russo-Japanese war, Lee, Yong Koo and his clans organized their political circle called 'Jinbohoe' at the expense of the Donghak religious organ, and established their nation-wide systems. At this time, the pro-Japanese political party, Iljinhoe, led by Song, Byung Jun, absorbed te Jinbohoe by threats, supported the military action of Japan, claimed that Korea should be under the Japanese protection, and issued a statement favoring the conclusion of the 1905 Protectorate Treaty with Japan. On learning about such a movement at home, Sohn, Byung Hee, still in Japan, severed his connection with his colleague Lee, Yong Koo and persuaded the other Donghaks to secede from the Iljinhoe to devote themselves only in the religion. As an orthodox sect of Donghak, Sohn, then 46, newly initiated the Chonto-kyo religion on December 1, 1905. When he returned to the coutnry the following year, there were more than 40,000 religious patrons welcoming him on the street, and his residence in Seoul was always crow-ded with visitors. Sohn immediately set to work, proclaiming the charter of the religion, establishing the central headquarters of the Chonto-kyo in Seoul and 72 parishes in the locality, and making himself the supreme pontiff. He then went on to formally oust Lee, Yong Koo and 62 other former leaders of Donghak from his religion as they still involved them-selves in the pro-Japanese political activities with the Iljinhoe. This ousted group later founded the Sichon-kyo religion.

In August, 1907, Sohn relinguished his seat to Kim, Yeon Kook and appointed Park, In Ho as assistant pontiff, but, as Kim was cajoled in to a post of Daeyesa in the Sichon-kyo by Lee, Yong Koo, Park, Su suc-ceeded to the supreme position of the Chonto-kyo. Ever since, Sohn played an active role behind-the-scene for the religion without taking a religious post. Accompanied by the key members of Chonto-kyo, he toured around the country preaching, setting creed schools, conducting memorial rites in honor of the martyrs, publishing peridicals, taking charge of and ope-rating the Dongduk Girls' School, Bosung College and Bosung Middle Schools, and giving sermons for hundreds of the religious leaders. As a result of Sohn's strenuous efforts for both the religious expansion and the national movement, the followers of Chonto-kyo increased to a million throughout the country during this time.

The Independence Movement of March 1st, 1919 and the Chonto- kyo

When the religious power of Chonto-kyo was on the rise, the First World War (1914-1918) broke out, and a new world order was impending after the war as Germany was flushed with victories. Sohn, Byung Hee ordered a million followers at the 37 parishes of the country to be prepared for any possible crises. But the war ended, instead, with the defeat of

Germany and her league of states, Austria and Bulgaria, after more than
4 years of persistent fightings. Prior to the end of the war, President
Woodrow Wilson of America proclaimed self-determination for the people
as one of his principles for the peace settlement of the world. Prepared
to cope with such an international development, Sohn, Byung Hee advocated the declaration of independence movement from Japan by having
secret conferences with his leading disciples, Choi, Rin, Oh, Se Chang
and Kwon, Dong Jin. Such a movement was also planned by the Christian
church and the Korean students in Tokyo. In secret rendevous with the
three leading members of Chonto-kyo at his house, Sang Choon Won,
in January, 1919, Sohn, Byung Hee gave the following instruction, 'this
is the very opportunity to launch the great undertaking for our national
independence. Be prompt in the preparation, and Choi, Rin should take
the responsibility to see to it that everything goes right and to arouse
everyone from all walks of life'. Later, in the first part of February, Choi,
Rin discussed the detailed methods for the movement with Song, Jin Woo,
Hyeon, Sang Yung and Choi, Nam Sun secretly at his house on several
occasions. Meanwhile, the Chonto-kyo and the Christian church could
make joint cooperation as there was not much difference in their plans
and methods. Besides, the Chonto-kyo leaders even supplied their Christian
counterparts with an exhorbitant amount of 5,000 won as an expense for
the mobilization of their people. The two Buddhist representatives also
took part in the joint effort for the national independence. The Confucian
organ was uncertain, and it was no longer possible to wait for further
collaboration for fear of a possible abortion of the plan.

The declaration was jointly signed February 27th at the house of Choi,
Rin in Jae-dong, Seoul, by Sohn, Byung Hee and 14 other leaders from
Chonto-kyo, Lee, Seung Hoon and 15 others from the Christian church,
and Han, Yong Woon and another from the Buddhist organ. There was
a brief discussion on who should be the first signatory, but, at the suggestion of Choi, Nam Sun, Sohn led the others in an alphabetic order.

Finally, the day came. From the early morning of March 1st, 1919, two days before the imperial funeral of King Kwangmoo, the manifesto of independence signed by the 33 partriotic leaders was widely diffused in Seoul. At 2 p.m. that day, 29 of the 33 leaders met at the Taehwa-kwan and pronounced their declarations. Tens of thousands of people led by the students rallied at the Pagoda Park and gave loud cheers, 'Long Live the Independence of Korea !' The students then staged demonstrations through the streets in an orderly fashion, chanting 'Mansei !'(Long Live), and even the general public sympathized with the demonstrators. The capital Seoul, became literally a center of crying excitement for national independence.

As had been planned, the movement extended throughout the country with more than 2 million people participating. The total number of Japanese authorities during this time was 46,000, of whom 1,461 Chonto-kyo followers were indicted as guilty. Among the 47 leaders convicted as prime initiators of the independence movement and thus sentenced to three years of hardship in prison were Sohn, Byung Hee, Choi, Rin, Kwon, Dong Jin, Oh, Se Chang, Lee, Jong Il, Lim, Ye Hwan, Kim, Wan Ku, La, In Hyeop, Hong, Ki Jo, Choi, Young Hwan, Lee, Hong Hoon, Hong, Byung Ki, Park, Jeung Seung and Kwon Byung, Duk from the Chonto-kyo religion.

The Religious Complication

As soon as Sohn, Byung Hee, the leader of the national independence movement of March 1, 1919, and initiator of the Chonto-kyo religion, died in May, 1922, after he was released from the prison on bail the previous October due to his ailment, the religious organ plunged into a great confusion. This, however, was not new, for the Chonto-kyo had long been suffering from its intra-religious factionalism that had not come to the fore because of the influence of Sohn, Byung Hee. When the new religious charter was passed at the end of 1921, there was a great conflict between the two rival factions, the one, led by Kim, Bong Kook and Oh Ji Young, opposing the constitution and the system of the religious founder, and the other of the central religious headquarters favoring their legitimacies. Then, the situation did not deteriorate further because of the existence of Sohn. But, within a month after his death, the factional strife became so aggravated that the religious founder Park, In Ho declared his resignation in a key-member meeting held June 2 at the Sang Choon Won. In a special meeting of the religious representatives soon thereafter, the charter was revised to abolish the system of the founder and to select the elders and hold the assembly under the new system of representation.

When the revision was announced, Oh, Ji Young and Kim, Bong Kook were dissatisfied, and attempted to organize the union church by having the local religious powers seceded from the mainstream of their church. This was unsuccessful, but Oh, Ji Young's sect branched out anyway from the religion and established the United church.

In a general session of the elders in April, 1925, the standard formality and decorum for the church were passed, stipulating the observation of the birthday and death-day of the three religious founders as memorial days of the religion excluding the other anniversaries of the latest founder, Park, In Ho, as observed previously. Park himself and 30 other elders including Oh, Young Chang opposed the new proprieties and launched a movement to revive the old system. They held protest meetings and stopped sending up. their offered rice to the central headquarters. This group was called the old faction, and the others at the headquarters the new faction. The strife between these two factions continued heatedly, and some of the authoritative figures like Choi, Hoon Mo, Lee, Jong Rin and Kwon, Dong Jin organized the association for realization of unity to arbitrate the two rival parties, but, instead, they were absorbed into the main line of the old faction as Park, In Ho wished. Later, there was anoher disagreement between Park and Oh, Young Chang who again founded his own Church in Sariwon. All told, the Chonto-kyo religion was divided by the four branches of the Union Church, Sariwon Church, and the Old and New Factions.

Such factional dissension within the Chonto-kyo had amounted to

nothing more than a sheer struggle for religious power and had served
no benefit at all for the religion itself through the ensuing five years. Thus,
in October, 1930, Choi, Rin suggested the coalition between the rival factions, and brought the discords under control by arranging an equal
number of the religious posts for the factions in a joint-meeting held in
December the same year.

In August of the following year, Park, In Ho, the leader of the old
faction regarded as the fourth-founder of the Chonto-kyo, distributed
the literature explaining that he and Sohn, Byung Hee were the legitimate
successors of Choi, Je Woo and Choi, Shi Hyung, and awarded the religious name for devout woman believers. This aroused an immediate reaction from the new faction, and the discords of the two parties became
so heated over the issue at the April 1932 regular meeting that the assembly
hall was turned into shambles and the police had to be called in to keep
order. The two factions continued their fight, exchanging accusative state-
ments, purging the old faction of the other elements, or even partitioning

The Status of the Chonto-kyo Strength (as of August, 1934)

Name of Province	Number of Parishes	Number of Mission Centers	Number of Followers
Kyonggi-province	13	30	2,458
Choongchongbuk-province	9	10	415
Chongchongnam-province	8	14	837
Chollabuk-province	12	11	986
Chollanam-province	20	38	2,544
Kyongsangbuk-province	10	3	221
Kyongsdngnam-province	12	16	912
Hwanghae-province	18	115	10,282
Pyonganbuk-province	23	312	38,491
Pyongannam-province	21	111	15,030
Kangwon-province	17	15	495
Hamkyungbuk-province	11	15	2,092
Hankyongnam-province	19	91	18,643
TOTAL	193	781	93,406

their religious headquarters in one building under the two separate sign-boards 'The Central Church of Chonto-kyo' for the Old Factions and 'The Headquarters of the Chonto-kyo' for the New Faction. Afterwards, there was another brief skirmish between the Old Faction and the Sariwon Church of Oh, Young Chang over Oh's statement that he had been appointed to succeed the legitimacy of the fifth founder by the forth founder Park, In Ho, who, instead, had earlier offered him a religious post in his faction. The feud between these groups was brought under control by Park's explanation of the fact.

The Social Improvement Activity

The Chonto-kyo religion made its efforts for the new cultural movement immediately after the March 1st, 1919, Independence Movement by organizing the youth creed club that was reorganized as the Chonto-kyo Youth Association in 1920 with its nation-wide structure, and by publishing such magazines as 'Shin Yeosung'(The New Woman) or 'Eorini'(The Children). Along with the trends of the time and the expansion of the religion, and for the formation of more powerful organization that could be the core of a national movement to construct a paradise on earth, the Chonto-kyo Youth Party was established in September 1923 with the offices of general affairs, organization, training and propagation under the control of the party leader, and various other academic research departments including the publication of the paper, 'Dangsung'(The Voice of the Party). The total strength of the party was brought up at the end of 1925 to more than 120 local chapters with some 30,000 in membership. In addition, there were other group activities such as the Boys Association, Youth Association, Students Association, the Farmers Society of Chosun and the Laborers Society of Chosun. Among these diversified social improvement activities, the movement of the Boys Assn. attained most remarkable effects under the leadership of Bang, Jung Hwan. The Farmers Society, organized with more than 200 chapters throughout the country, launched its project in September, 1925, under the joint auspieces of Lee, Don Hwa and Kim,

Ki Jeon of the New Faction, and Lee, Sung Hwan, Kim, Jun Yeon and Yu, Kwang Yeol from the non-religious group. With the secession of this non-religious group from the Society since the convention in April, 1930 , the Chonto-kyo's social organ made a great contribution for the social economical interest of the rural people. It also executed the work projects relating to production, consumption, trust and utilization of the farmers by establishing the farmers' cooperative union. The laborers' society of Chosun was the last one formed in May, 1931, by the resolution adopted at the convention of the Chonto-kyo's Youth Party to promote the welfare and cultural training of the workers, and it had its local branches in most of the important cities of the country.

The Oshim-dang Incident and the Prayer Incident

The leading members of the Chonto-kyo's New Faction including Kim, Ki Jeon, Jo, Ki Kan and Park, Sa Jik organized the Oshim-dang Party, an underground national movement front, in 1929 in Seoul. Their plans were detected by the police department of the Pyongannam Province in 1934 while they were trying to expand the organization through their churches across the country, and some 170 party leaders were arrested and tortured for more than 60 days. Fortunately, since they had done nothing that was against the Japanese government, the case was dropped from prosecution and all the detainees were released on an excuse that the activity of the party had been nothing more than a religious movement.

As the Japanese oppression toward the Korean people became ever more stringent after the eruption of the Sino-Japanese war, a special prayer-meeting was planned by the Chonto-kyo religion for 21 days beginning January 11, 1938. The meeting was to confess the pledges of 'destroying the Japanese for revenge and for the earliest achievement of independence' in terms of reciting the religious incantations.

The meeting began at 5. P.M. that day at all the places as planned. But the contents of the prayer were revealed by the Shinchon parish in Hwanghae province, and some 200 religious followers were confined and tortured at the Haeju police station for 72 days. The leaders of this abortive meeting were mostly from the Old Faction of Chonto-kyo including Park, In Ho, who received severe interrogation while on his sick-bed, and Suh, Pil Kyu and Kim, Jae Kyu, who died of torture in the prison. The others who completed the prison term were Choi, Jun Mo, Han, Sun Hoe, Jung, Hwan Pil, Hong, Hun Ui and Kim, jung Eun.

The Coalition of the Churches and the Japanese Persecution

The factional strife having served no advantage but self-destruction to the religion itself since the disruption over the issue of the religious founder in April, 1932, the leaders of the New Faction, Choi, Rin and Lee, Don Hwa, proposed an unconditional coalition with the Old Faction in January, 1940. The Old Faction leaders like Lee, Jong Rin, Kwon, Dong Jin, Oh, Se Chang, Choi, Jun Mo and Han, Sun Hoe welcomed the move and agreed to hold the joint-convention on the religious anniversary of April 5.

A day before the convention, Park, In Ho died of a long sickness, saying, 'Now that our churches will be united, I shall bear no more smouldering grudges'. The two parties decided to hold the joint funeral services for Park and held the convention as planned in peace and harmony for the first time in eight years. At the convention, the mutual agreement was passed, and, according to the majority of the public opinion, Lee, Jong Rin, Choi, An Kook, Jo, Ki Kan, Park, Suk Hong, Jon, Ui Chan, Sohn, Jae Ki, Choi, Jun Mo, Jung, Kwang Jo and Lee, Don Hwa of both factions were selected for various executive positions of the religion, and Choi, Rin, Kwon, Dong Jin and Oh, Se Chang for the eldership. In addition, all the local churches together with the other religious organization of the two factions were consolidated under the single banner of the Central Religious Chamber of Chonto-kyo. When the general assembly was held at the Central Church two years later in April, 1942, at which the executive members were reshuffled, the two parties maintained peace and harmony.

Then, the Pacific War broke out, and the Japanese army swept over

most of the Southeast Asian countries. As a means to enforce their colo-
nialization policy, the Japanese government closed down the vernacular
papers, prohibited the use of the Korean language, and added pressures
in all categories. The Chonto-kyo religion, the hot-bed of nationalism,
was no exception. Although Choi, Rin, an authoritative figure of the religion, led the van of pro-Japanese activity in such a capacity as the
commander of the War-Ready Patriotic Corps for Japan, the Japanese
persecution toward the Chonto-kyo was by no means lessened. Thus, the
central cathedral of the religion was requisitioned in May, 1943, as an army
uniform manufacturing plant, and the Sohn, Byung Hee memorial hall
as the district office of Chongro-ku, and a number of other local churches
closed.

Upon Liberation from the Japanese occupation August 15, 1945, then
executive members of the religion, Lee, Jong Rin and Jo, Ki Kan, together
with the two elders, Kwon, Dong Jin and Oh, Se Chang, conducted
memorial services before the grave of the late Sohn, Byung Hee, and,
later, persuaded Choi, Rin to retire.

The List of Change in the Religious Strength of Chonto-kyo

Year	Number of Parishes	Number of Followers
1895	21	9,054
1900	36	30,282
1905	78	88,678
1910	129	112,767
1915	154	121,995
1920	165	130,884
1925	173	84,503
1930	191	104,550
1934	193	93,406
1938	196	75,676
1942	-	50,000 (Approx.)

Remarks : This information is based on the statistics compiled by the Japanese government-general
in Seoul, but the Chonto-kyo authority estimates more than five times the total of these
numbers.

Chapter 2
Japanese Shintoism

Shintoism

This was one of the established folklore beliefs of Japan, worshipping nature, ancestors and the emperor of the state, and was also referred to as the 'Great Principle of Kaminagara' by the Japanese people. The ancient records were used as the scriptures by this religion, which believed that a god existed in the things that are pure, superior and mysterious. There were some 800,000 or 8 million such gods worshipped by Shintoism according to the records, but, among them, Amateras Omikami, the center of the universe, was believed to be their superintendent.

And among the many natural, personified and ancestrial gods, the emperor of the state was regarded and worshipped as the real and living divine lineage of the Amateras-Omikami. Shintoiom, thus, had assumed a central role in developing the imperial rule of Japan.

Generally speaking, Shintoism can be divided into two categories, the one that had developed through the government-established shrines, and the other through the sects. For example, a certain deified object or place of the Japanese was tended with sacrifices, the public was made to attend the services, the relic of the sacrificial god revered, the national conviction stimulated, and the government-appointed priest would officiate at the religious ceremonies. Besides the many shrines set up by the government, there are countless numbers of other such private sanctums, both small and large in scale, built up in various parts of Japan. The sectarian Shintoism, however, was the product of the last period, and there were some 13 different denominations. Although the origins and gods of these branches may differ, they had similar practical ethics and religious behavior in that they revere the imperial household of Japan and express loyalty and patriotism.

Shintoism had been merely a national belief of Japan, but not a supranational one. Its mission in Korea, thus, was something that could hardly be expected with any remarkable effects. However, it made its way into Korea immediately the Japanese occupation of the country, but no sectarian Shintoism other than the Tenri-kyo had ever been successful.

The Introduction of the Sectarian Shintoism

The Tenri-kyo was the first Shintoist sect that had launched its propagation in Korea. At the closure of Chosun Dynasty when the three foreign powers of Japan, Russia and China contested their might in the Seoul political arena the Japanese businessmen came consecutively into Korea for what opportunity they could seize. It was during this time, that is, in September, the 30th year of Kojong(1893), that the first missionary of the Tenri-kyo named Kuromi arrived in Pusan and initiated his work, and, in the following year, his son came over to help him. Their works were not successful then. But, as the Japanese position was heightened with their victory over the Sino-Japanese War in 1893, another Tenri-kyo missionary named Aoki was dispatched to Pusan, who succeeded in drawing some 100 Korean converts during his one and half years of mission.

On learning of the Tenri-kyo's successful mission in Korea, the other Shinto sects such Shinri-kyo, Konggo-kyo and Daisya-kyo followed suit in dispatching their pioneers to Pusan from 1897. Following the Korea-Japan amalgamation treaty in 1910, there was a total of 10 Shinto denominations engaged in the missionary activity in Korea including Fuso-kyo, Jikke-kyo, Shindo Sinsyu-kyo, Kurozumi-kyo and Midake-kyo.

The Tenri-kyo, among others, concerted much of its efforts in winning the Korean believers by formally setting up its missionary center in Pusan in June, 1904, and another one in Seoul in 1908. As the number of the Japanese residents increased in most of the principle cities after the end of the Russo-Japanese war, its center for the Korea mission was established in Seoul in April, 1909 with Matsumura Yoshitaro appointed to the first director. After the amalgamation treaty, Sato Matsuhito was appointed to the position, and the directorate office underwent a new construction, during which time there was some 13 Tenri-kyo churches with about 1,300 Korean followers.

The Development of the Tenri-kyo

Even if the other Shinto sects conducted missions solely for the sake of the Japanese residents in Korea without paying much interest to winning the Koreans, the Tenri-kyo, as a result of its extensive work through Kyonggi province, Seoul and Kyongsangnam province, earned some 13,000 local converted in 1912, and some 15,000 in 1918. When the anti-Ja-

The List of the Tenri-kyo Strength by Each Province in 1921

Province	Number of Temples	Number of Koreans	Number of Japanese
Kyonggi-province	15	3,690	8,636
Choongchongbuk-province	1	80	190
Choongchungnam-province	2	99	630
Chollabuk-province	3	146	749
Choolanam-province	1	517	640
Kyongsangbuk-province	3	130	517
Kyongsangnam-province	15	1,796	4,826
Hwanghae-province	2	107	46
Pyonganbuk-province	-	-	300
Pyongannam-province	4	52	1,247
Hamkyunmgbuk-province	2	16	561
Hamkyongnam-province	2	155	595
TOTAL	50	6,788	18,937

panese spirit was high among the people immediately after the independence movement of March 1st, 1919, the Tenri-kyo met a great setback.
It exerted more of its efforts for the local mission beginning October,
1919, by setting up educational and training schools both the Japanese
and Korean missionaries with a Korean language department to boost
the language proficiency of the Japanese, and by establishing the churches
in various places, but it could only maintain the strength of the Korean
believers as enumerated in the following table, which was quite lower
than the level prior to the independence movement.

The Principle of the Tenri-kyo

The Tenri-kyo that had been most successful in Korea was the most
powerful Shintoist sect among the others. Founded by a woman named
Nakayama Miki, it was originally called the Shinto Tenri-kyo in 1885,
an order belonging to the Shintoist headquarters of the Japanese government ; renamed the Church of Tenri-kyo in 1888, and gradually developed to form an independent branch in October, 1908. By 1935, the total
number of the followers reached some 5 million. In Tenri-kyo, the Denriounomikoto, the so-called master god of the universe, was believed
to be the principal god consisting of ten other gods including the parents
of the Amateras Omikami.

The Tenri-kyo's doctrines were in realizing the plateau of nectar, considered as a happy and peaceful paradise of god, by eliminating attachments,
following the almighty Denriounomikoto and fulfilling the truth with
sincerily, mercy, generosity and self-reflection. To put it a little more
concretely, man constantly becomes egoistically attached to the eight vices
of avarice, miserliness, hatred, evil desire, resentment, anxiety, arrogance
and vanity that cause various diseases and calamities, not realizing the
fact that his body is something that had been borrowed from the Denriounomikoto. It was, therefore, believed that man could be saved from
disease and calamity only by ridding himself of the attachments and having
his mind awakened to the principle of the lone. As a practical compendium,

the religion thus stressed that man ought to keep his mind and nature pure, rise up early, and be honest and diligent. In addition, he ought to return the graces of the Denriounomikoto, to the empire and his parents.

In view of the fact that the Denriounomikoto, the principle god of the Tenri-kyo religion, was not a unique god, but a body of the ten others, most of which were of Japanese origin except one, the Sakkodevendra, which might have had been included under the influence of Buddhism, the Tenri-kyo can be treated as no more than a pan-national and racial religion of Japan. Even if the Buddhist principle of cause and effect was widely discussed by the religion, its attitude in worshipping the Amateras Omikami, and the empire and emperor of Japan had not been changed.

The Mission by Each Shintoist Sect

The ten Shintoist sects out of thirteen launched their missions in Korea since Japan carried out her colonial policy, but with the exception of Tenri-kyo, Konggo-kyo, Oyasiro-kyo and Sinri-kyo, they were all comparatively inactive. Some of these branches remained only titular in the country without any activity until the Liberation in 1945.

The Tenri-kyo, as discussed in the preceding page, had been most conspicuously active in its mission for the local people, while the others remained completely indifferent. Beside the mission centers set up in many places, the Tenri-kyo trained some 40 to 50 Korean missionaries annually at the creed training institute in Seoul and attempted to maintain fellowship between the Koreans and Japanese by organizing a fraternity association called Naesun Dongkyunghoe in Taegu. Along with the expansion of Japan's potentiality following the Manchurian Conflict, the Tenri-kyo's religious strength also increased, and the total number of the Korean followers reached some 16,000 by 1935 and close to 20,000 just before the Liberation.

The following table shows the strength of each Shintoist sect in Korea as of the end of 1943.

The Religious Strength of Each Shintoist Denominations
(as of December, 1943)

Name of Sect	Number of Mission Temples	Number of workers	Number of Follower
Tenri-kyo	196	476	31,414
Shinri-kyo	44	60	7,996
Konggo-Kyo	40	62	17,186
Shinto Syusei-ha	1	62	210
Oyasiro-kyo	13	28	15,635
Fuso-kyo	15	29	1,097
Shinto	4	5	1,012
Kurozumi-kyo	6		
Jikko-kyo	7	5	2,035
Midake-kyo	7	9	1,054
TOTAL	313	684	78,580

Remarks : A total of 15,822 Koreans as of the end of 1941 included A total
of 1,009 Koreans as of   the end of 1941   included A total of 44
Koreans as of the end of 1941 included

The Kinto Shrine

This was the first Shintoist shrine established in Korea. When King
Sejong sanctioned the beginning of international commerce and trade by
inaugurating the three ports of Pusan, Jaepo and Yeompo, there were
about 1,600 Japanese residents living in those towns. As the number of
the residents increased later, the imperial court subjected them to their
control many times. The uneasy Japanese emmigrants provoked a riot
together with some 300 troops sent from the Daema-do (Tsushima) Island
in 1510, the 5th year of King Joongjong. Since then, the Japanese people
withdrew, as their residential area was entirely abolished, and there were
only a few island people frequenting to the port of Jaepo, as it was the
only place where a reception center was allowed for the Japanese from
Tsushima.

With the resumption of the normal relations between Korea and Japan after the Toyotomi invasion, the commercial vessel and merchant from the island state were permitted into Pusan, and there were again a growing number of Japanese residents in the country. As a means to pray for their safe voyage and prosperity, a Shintoist clan from the island built up the Kinto Shrine in March of 1678, the 4th year of Sookjong, on the 13,200 m² ground in Mt. Yongdu of Pusan mobilizing about 1.2 million man-power, and enshrined their sacrificial god called Oumono Nusino Kami. The Miyajima Shrine and the Kato Shrine were also constructed outside the boundary as Kinto's auxiliaries.

The Kinto Shrine, or called the Kinto Bira Shrine built during this time, is assumed to have been the first of its kind ever established in the Korean peninsula. It had been maintained and operated by the people from Tsushima Island with its designations changed a few times to the Residen-tial Shrine in 1894 by the resolution of the Japanese residents and to memorial tablets of this shrine later, and there was a total of eleven gods enshrined including Amateras Omikami and Toyotomi Hideyoshi just before the Liberation.

The Shintoist Shrines before the 1910 Japanese Annexation

The establishment of the first Japanese Shinto shrine in Pusan, Korea, was spoken about three centuries ago as mentioned in the preceding pages. But when the power of Chosun became incompetent during the ages of King Kojong, the foreign temples increased in most of the principle cities of Korea as the Japanese residents swelled radically.

In the 19th year of Kojong(1882), when there was a great turbulence in the domestic scene, whereby the progressives and the conservatives fought each other, the armed rebellion broke out, and the rioters attacked the Japanese legation and the imperial court. The Japanese residents in Wonsan built up their Wonsan Shrine enshrining the Amateras Omikami, and solidified their spiritual foundation as if they were unaware of the wide spread commotion.

Afterwards, they established the Inchon Shrine in Inchon in the 27th year of Kojong(1890), the Kyongsung Shrine in Seoul in 1898 enshring the four gods including Amateras Omikami and the Kunitamasino Kami, the Jinampo Shrine in Jinampo in 1900, the Kunsan Shrine in Kunsan in 1902, the Yongampo Shrine in Yongchon in 1904, the Daejon Shrine in Daejon in 1907, the Sungjin and Masan Shrines in Sungjin and Masan in 1909, and the Songdo Shrine in Mokpo in 1910. In other words, the Shintoist shrines were set up in the eleven principle cities throughout the country before the Korea-Japan annexation treaty was concluded in 1910 in addition to the Shinto altars built up in Taegu and Samrangjin for worship.

The Administration of the Shrine and the Shinto Palace of Chosun

Many more Shintoist shrines and altars were established in Korea even after the 1910 Japanese annexation. The government-general in Seoul, therefore, enacted the regulation in August, 1915, to enable its control over the establishment, removal and consolidation of the shrines in the country.

Among the many shrines so far built in Korea, the Shinto Palace of Chosun in Seoul occupied the highest position. The construction of this central shrine in Korea enshrining Amateras Omikami and Emperor Meiji was launched in July, 1919, and completed in October, 1925, with a total expenditure amounting to 1,570,000 Yen(equivalent to about $10,000,000). The regular religious festival, followed by the so-called Praising Shrine athletic meeting in which the selected representatives from each province competed for victory, was conducted at the shrine on October 17 annually after its inauguration.

As a Royal Court-subsidized shrine, the Shinto Palace of Chosun was in the highest class among many others. However, the Japanese government, under a special addict from its Emperor, undertook construction of another similar class temple in Booyeo, Choongnam province, which had been the old capital site of the Baekje Dynasty. Japan had a close connection with it during the age of the Three States, by mobilizing the service corps from all the provinces. But the project was suspended after three years of construction due to the Japanese surrender in the Pacific War in 1945. Besides these two grand Shintoist monasteries, six other smaller ones such as the Mt, Yongdu Shrine, Kyongsung Shrine, Taegu Shrine, Pyongyang Shrine, Kwangju Shrine and Kangwon Shrine belonged to an important category receiving subsidy from the Japanese treasury every year.

From the time when the first Kindo Shrine was established in 1678, the 4th year of Sookjong in Pusan to the Korean Liberation of August 15, 1945, there were a total of 59 shrines accredited by the government regulations in the country and over 870 smaller non-accredited ones set up for private worship.

Having become powerful after its invasion of Manchuria, the Japanese government forced the Korean people to worship at the shrines in order to weaken their national spirit through religious concentration. The Japanese authorities also maintained that all the Koreans should attend the shrine to manifest their sincerity as the people of Japan. At first, the local people, except the public servants, hesitated or took somewhat negative attitude toward the Japanese order, but, in the end, they could not escape from it.

It was against the doctrine of the lacal Christians to attend the shrine and bow before the Japanese idol. But ever since the issue was brought up and unjustly passed by a few pro-Japanese members at the 27th general assembly of the Presbyterian Church in Pyongyang in 1938, the Japanese authorities succeeded in having the Christians worship the Shinto gods by sending the many vigorous opponents to Shintoism to prison or closing down a number of the churches or schools.

The number of the Shintoist shrines established in the country as of the end of December of 1944 was as follows :

The Status of the Shintoist Shrines

Rank of Shrine	Number of Shrines	Number of Exorcists
Royal Court-sponsored	2	12
National-sponsored	6	28
Others accredited	59	66
Others non-accredited	875	-

Romark : Because the Booyeo Shinto Palace was not completed, the official from Chosun
Shinto Palace assumed the work there

Chapter 3
Quasi-Religions

The Gregarious Growth of Quasi-Religions

Originally no form of imitation religion existed in Korea. A religion, if any reference were made, would generally mean either Buddhism, Confucianism or Taoism. But in about a century after Choi, Je Woo founded Donghak, the forerunner of Chonto-kyo religion in 1860, various forms of analogous religions sprung up gregariously like mushrooms after rain.

As it was always the case with the beginnings of other religion, the gregarious growth of many similar religious orders at the end of the Lee Dynasty were stimulated by certain particular social phenomena, that is, the corruption and decadence of the existing religion and politics along with absolute despair of the living condition of the people.

The people, then, could obtain no spiritual comfort from Buddhism as it was not only corrupt but also treated as a heresy, nor from Confucianism as it was an exclusive religion for the Yangban (upper) class to sustain their privilege and nobility even if it had dominated both the political and cultural sphere of the time, nor from Catholicism as it was considered traitorous to the country. In addition, the social condition at the time was such that the mass of the people were plunged into an extreme distress and hopelessness at the expense of constant oppression and extortion from the privileged Yangbans. The exhausted mass, in the end, was growing to be rebellious toward the privileged class, pessimistic toward the world and, above all, was beginning to yearn for an ideal society as the rumour spread from a superstitutious book called Jungkam-rok that the Lee Dynasty would soon be perished and the Jung Dynasty would be born in its place under Mt. Kyeryong.

The people were cherishing their only hope in the forthcoming new world in the midst of despair and hopelessness, and if anyone should emerge with a certain philosophy that might satisfy the discontentment of the people or offer spiritual comfort and promise the revival of the old traditions, he could certainly win sympathy from the populace. This was the very opportunity which most of founders of the pseudo-religions seized to their advantage in establishing the pseudo-religions at the end of Chosun Dynasty. Thus, the majority of these orders had many things in common in their doctrinal contents. For instance, the contents were generally combined with the three elements of Buddhism, Confucianism and Taoism with equal attempt to revive the old folklore belief of Korea and, at the same time, to give new hope for the masses.

The folklore belief meant the old Shinkyo faith, in which the witches and wizards were believed to be capable of conjuring the misfortunes from various Shamanistic spirits, or inviting the blessings from the heavenly gods by acting as mediums, or becoming deified themselves by virtue of the spiritual power of god. But coming into the end of Chosun Dynasty, it was popularly believed that any man, who attained a spiritual enlightenment through earnest asceticism, would be graced with the spiritual power of a god to be deified. Once deified, he would become omnipotent, foreseeing the things, that are a thousand miles or thousand years away or enjoying an eternal life. That is to say, he could become a man like the almighty, Hong Kil Dong.

Choi, je Woo also attempted to revive this sort of popular faith with the combination of the three religious merits···the Confucian ethic, the Buddhist introspection and the Taoist Self-Culture···in advocating the Chonto-kyo religion with a view to give more appeal to the masses. Such doctrines had been commonly adopted by the other religious orders formed later.

In addition to such a mixed combination of the doctrines, another cha-racteristic of the analogous orders was that they also attempted to divide the mundane human affairs into the past and future world by proper coordination of various superstitious theories including the principles of topography and astronomy. According to this compound doctrine, the troubled past ends up as of yesterday, and the new, happy ideal world unfolds realistically from today, but not in such a distant future that anyone could experience this during his life-time.

The Influence of the Analogous Orders

Some of these pseudo-religious orders gregariously formed at the end of Chosun Dynasty against the social corruption and government extortion made a great contribution in enlightening the masses both socially and politically through various popular movements. This was particularly so with the Donghak religious organ. Under the Japanese rule, most of them made no cooperation with the government-general, but led their people in an extraordinary direction of their own, while some contributed to the advancement of the people through the farmers, youth and women's social activities.

With the exception of a few like Donghak, however, these religions generally provided no advantages and caused more harm for society. Some of the orders like Sichon-kyo led the traitorous movement against the country, while some bound the people into too conservative disciplines or bewitched them with various unscientific superstitions. Some vicious ones even sold their religious posts as a means to gain followers or indulged in numerous savage deeds ranging from swindling to murder.

The reason that the most of the orders had not been helpful to society could be attributed to their dependence on their realistic doctrines. The attitude of the followers was also responsible, in that they strived more for what was considered the immediate interest in their living than in the religious doctrines or practices. To them, such things as certain religious privileges, mundane positions, or blindfold longevity meant more than anything else.

Many people, therefore, have had their property squandered or even had their lives sacrificed in pursuit of such a perverse religion as Baekbaek-kyo or Bochon-kyo. With elapse of time, people began to realize that these quasi-religions which had fascinated them could no longer provide any benefit for their living or had no useful purpose for the future. Then, the religious organs also began to shake and crumble as the followers gradually turned their backs against them.

The Status of Quasi-Religions

In about 80 years after Choi, Je Woo first initiated the Donghak religion, there was some 80 different quasi-religious organs newly established in the country and about 60 at the time of Korean Liberation in 1945. They could be mainly classfied into the Donghak, Hoomchi, Shinto and Confucian religions, but, except for the Donghak, generally they were not seen as successful, nor being useful to the society.

According to a classification made by the Japanese authorities in 1934, the year religious orders reached the peak of prosperity, there were some 18 branches belonging to the Donghak, 10 to Buddhist, 7 to Confucianism, 16 to the Shinkyo and 5 to other miscellaneous religions with a total of 1,157 churches and 173,000 followers.

The Strength of the Quasi-Religions

(as of August, 1934. cf. The publication, 'Chosun' dtd Apr. 635)

Religion	Number of Branches	Number of Followers	Number of Churches	Number of Parishes
Donghak	18	117,585	970	436
Hoomchi-kyo	11	20,216	118	200
Buddhism	10	23,054	26	25
Confucianism	7	6,702	12	16
Shinkyo	16	4,707	29	32
Others	5	594	2	2
Total	67	172,858	1,157	811

The Sichon-kyo

This was the first branch to secede from the Donghak religion by its prime initiator Lee, Yong Koo, a beloved disciple of Choi, Je Woo, in 1906 as a result of his disagreement with Sohn, Byung Hee, the influential leader of Donghak.

Although he had been imprisoned after the Donghak Uprising and had endeavored to expand the religion after he was released from prison, Lee, Yong Koo constantly led a pro-Japanese political group along with Song, Byung Jun and Kim, In Kook, supporting the Japanese annexation of the country, and the Japanese military action in the Russo-Japanese war or other traitorous activity. After Lee and his 50 other adherents were expelled from the Donghak by Sohn, Byung Hee, they founded their independent branch, Sichon-kyo, which did not gain much strength due to its constant pro-Japanese stand even though the 1919 Independence Movement. Its influence was thus drastically reduced especially after 1919, from sbout 10,000 followers at the peak of its development to some 500 at the end of 1940.

The Sangjae-kyo

This was a branch of the Sichon-kyo initiated by Kim, In Kook, a head disciple of the Donghak's second founder Choi, Shi Hyung. Kim once held the supreme position in Donghak, but abandoned it to collaborate with the Sichon-kyo's founder Lee, Yong Koo. Dissatisfied over Song, Byung Jun's exclusive control of the Sichon-kyo organ after Lee's death in Japan, Kim established his independent sect in June, 1925, at Mt. Kyeryong of Choongnam province, under the name of Sangjae-kyo, claiming he had been given the revelation Sangjae, the Supreme God. The total number of followers for this branch, by which various religious scriptures of the Donghak were used and the pro-Japanese prayers recitated, was estimated at 5,000 at the end of 1940.

The chungrim-kyo

Originated from an order established by Nam Jung, a disciple of Choi, Je Woo, in 1913 with the doctrines based on the combined superstitutions including those of the Jungkam-rok. The religious designation was taken after Namjung's pseudonym, Chungrim. This branch had some prosperity after its foundation, but the Japanese persecution, especially since Namjung became a suspect of spreading the groundless rumour about the coming establishment of the Jung Dynasty in Mt. Kyeryong, compelled it to almost complete destruction.

Later, however, the persons like Han, Byung Soo, Kim, Sang Woo and Lee, Ok Haeng managed to revive this religion by holding the first successful gathering in Jangchoongdan, Seoul, in which 20,000 people participated, and conducted the mission under the pretense of correcting the wrong idea of Koreans in order to avoid Japanese persecution.

For once, the Chungrim-kyo had been quite prosperous with its head-quarters in Seoul, 42 chapters in locality, and its followers reaching 10,000. But since the leading members of the religion including the founder were arrested for some illicit affairs, the organ crumbled completely, and there was only about 400 to 500 followers in 1940.

The Sooun-kyo

Established in 1914, as one of the analogous religious orders by a man named Lee, Sang Yong, this religion should rather be classified as a branch of the Donghak despite its affluent Buddhist contents. Lee, Sang Yong became a monk at an early age and completed his Buddhist asceticism at the Yujom temple in Mt. Kumkang, but initiated this separate branch that revered its principle follower as a descendant of Buddha, while he was preaching through Chungyang, Choongnam province. The main tenets of this religion were based on the combination of those of Confucianism, Buddhism and Taoism, and its head temple was set up in Seoul in 1923 but removed to Kuntan-dong in Taejon as the followers increased rapidly to be about 3,000 in 1940.

The Baekbaek-kyo

A man named Cha, Byung Kan originated this quasi-religious group in 1918 in Kapyung, kyonggi province, seceding from the Baekdo-kyo religion. Its tenets were in realizing a bright world through purification of public morals and popular sentiment, and by the grace of a spiritual influence from Heave, and, as its norm of discipline, the 15 commandments were stressed against all evil conducts.

Jon, Hae Yong became the founder, and the religious leaders, despite their tenets to save the corrupt world, defrauded properties of the foolish followers, violated the chastity of the woman, took the law into their hands and committed all sorts of vicious crimes. Fearing possible exposure of their crimes, they murdered a number of persons in secret. But when their crime was finally detected by the police in 1937, the founder Jon, Hae Yong took his own life, and most of the leaders were captured and given to capital punishment. Then, it was discovered, to the complete astonishment of the world, that over 150 people were murdered and the total sum swindled by this religious organ exceeded one million won (equivalent to some 6 million dollars now). The skull of Jon, Hae Yong is preserved at the National Scientific Criminal Investigation Laboratory.

The Daehwa-kyo

Sohn, Eun Suk, who once was a Donghak, originally found it as Jewoo-kyo but renamed it to Yonghwa-kyo later. This was again changed to the Daehwa-kyo by the second founder Yoon, Kyung Joong in 1923, based on the doctrines of the Donghak religion with much Buddhist influence. Setting up the head churches in Kaedong, Seoul and in Mt. Kyeryong, Yoon once made a great effort to expand the religion even through Manchuria with procurement of a large area of land there to establish a magnificient religious city. But following yoon's death, the order became only titular. Despite its exaggeratied clain of 50,000 members, the actual srength of the religion reached about 2,000 in 1930 when its prosperity was in decline, but there were almost none remaining before the

Liberation

The quasi-religious orders described above were the ones which belonged to the Donghak. The others which belonged to this category were the Daedong-kyo, Chonok-kyo, Inchon-kyo, Chongmyung-kyo, Pyunghwa-kyo, Chonbup-kyo, Daede-kyo, Samsung Mookook-do, Mookyung-do and Donghak-kyo.

The Tongchon-kyo

This was established in 1920 in Seoul by a patriotic leader, Yang, Ki Taek, who stimulated patriotism greatly through his writings.

After the Japanese annexation was put into effect, Yang went into Manchuria to engage himself in the independence movement, but returned to assume an editorial position with the daily Dong-A Ilbo inaugurated in 1920. He soon resigned from the newspaper because of his disagreement with the Chang, Duk Soo faction and, then initiated the religious movement. Binding up the then powerful Chonto-kyo religion and others such as Sichon-kyo, Chungrim-kyo, Hoomchi-kyo, Jyese-kyo, and Kyungchon-kyo, yang attempted to make his religion the strongest one in the country with the intention of doing away with all the foreign religious creeds. The other purposes of the religion were to revive the old Shinkyo and to transform the whole world into a state of heavenly spirit by revealing the principal of Heaven and correcting the morals of the people. For some time since its successful inauguration, the Dongchon-kyo advanced vigorously, but became inactive as soon as Yang, Ki Taek left and took refuge into China.

The Kija-kyo

This was another quasi-religious group founded in 1910 in Pyongyang to revere Kija, the founder of the Kija Chosun Dynasty. It once had several local chapters throughout the country, but was generally only nominal. Han, Tae Ri, the leader of the Haeju Chapter, assumed leadership of the religion, which had no activity in the 1940's.

The Kwansung-kyo

This was established in 1920 in Seoul jointly by Kim, Yong Shik and Park, Ki Hong to worship Kuan Yu, a famous general during the epoch of the Three States of China. The idea of worshipping the deified Chinese warrior was first introduced into Korea during the Toyotomi invasion by the Ming Dynasty reinforcements, but it seemed to have been forgotten at the closure of the Lee Dynasty. Since the foundation of the religion, however, the followers increased to some 2,000 in 1941, and there were seven temples in the country. At the religious service, they would recite the Sacred books of Myungsungkyung, Kaksejikkyung or Samsungkung.

The Hoomchi-kyo

With the combination of the contents of the old Shinkyo and Donghak religious, Kang, Il Soon established the order. Born in September, 1871, in Jungeup, Chollabuk province, Kang believed in Donghak because of his abhorance for Catholicism from his earlier age. When the country was plunged into uneasiness and disorder following the Donghak uprising, in which he did not participate, Kang devoured the books relating to Confucianism, Buddhism, Taoism and the principle of duality and topography with a determination to save the troubled world.

When he was 31 years of age, Kang, Il Soon came to the grip of truth as he was striving in religious practice at the Daewon temple in Mt. Moak, Chonju, and established the Hoomchi-kyo with the formulation of its doctrines. According to his tenets, man can become a real god and, thus a fairy-land, where there is no bodily sickness or spiritual discomfort, will be possible in the reality only when he reaches the stage where his body and spirit would coincide by having his mind at peace and tranquility. And for this process, man should act humanely with justice, not being exclusive or jealous of each other, and be cooperative for the common prosperity.

This religion was also called as Hoomchi-kyo or Taeeul-kyo, for the good, Hoomchi of Taeeul, was often chanted in the religious incantation.

But, afterwards, it became known a Hoomchiri-kyo or Hoomchiki-do (meaning 'stealing' religion) as its believers indulged in pillage of the property of the followers.

Due to Kang, Il Soon's effective mission with his magic formulas of healing the sick, the number of the followers was said to have increased conspicuously. In 1907, therefore, Kang selected five leading disciples including Cha, Kyung Suk. But when Kang, who considered himself as an eternal deity, died at age 39 at the house of his disciple, Kim, Kyung Kon, his followers were shokcked and his religion split into a number of branches.

The Bochon-Kyo

This was founded by Cha, Kyung Suk, a head disciple of the Hoomchi-kyo's founder Kang, Il Soon. When his master died, whom he regarded as an immortal and from whom he inherited the religious reign of the Hoomchi-kyo, Cha entertained a great suspicion about his faith. After months of writing and trying to realize the true principle about the universe and the life and death of mankind, Cha attained an enlightenment which ended his torments. Thus, he set up a new religious order under the name of Sundo-kyo to launch a secret propagation, and redesignated it as Boh-wa-kyo in 1925 and as Bochon-kyo the following year. The religious believers developed to the extent that they could make an exaggeration of the total followers as exceeding 500,000 to one million, but, in fact, there were more than 30,000.

Along with the religious expansion, cha built up a giant temple in Jungeup-kun, Chollabuk province, attracting simple people by saying that a fairy-land will be realized there. While many of the followers were starving to death as their assets were either dwindling or plundered, Cha, Kyung Suk drove a carriage with a great banner in the front, on a carpeted road as a means to demonstrate his authority. Seeing this, the people revered him as a son of Heaven, and the followers were loyal to him hoping attain certain religious privileges. Upon Cha's death in April, 1936, the religious organ was completely disbanded by the authorities. By 1945, there was a total of 15,000 followers.

The fundamental tenets of the Bochon-kyo were belief in humanity and justice and in reverence for Heaven with the similar magic formulas of the Hoomchi-kyo.

The Mookook Daedo-kyo

Founded in 1919 in Taein-myon, Jungeup-kun, by Jo, Chul Je, who as a devout follower of the Hoomchi-kyo ;s Kang, Il Soon. After Kang died, Jo, Chul Je married Kang's sister. Jo once worked as a leading member of another religious organ set up by one of Kang's head disciples, Kim, Hyung Yeol, but initiated his independent sect, the Chonin-kyo, with his followers and reestablished it as Mookook Daedo-kyo in 1925.

The special feature of this religion was in trying to secure the stability of life through industry, economy and religious life. In this sense, the leaders of the religion launched a reclamation project in Anmin-do and Wosan-do islands in Choongchongnam province, and initiated a labor organization called Jinup-dan to provide employment for and to improve the living condition of the followers.

This was also disbanded along with the Bochon-kyo in summer of 1936 by the government authorities, at which time there were about 2,000 followers.

The Jeungsan-kyo

One of the Hoomchi-kyo followers named Chae, Kyung Dae separated from the branch and established this religion in 1924 along with Kim, Un Soon, stressing the supremacy of the religious founder. By persecution of the authorities, this was again dissolved in the summer of 1936 with about 700 to 800 followers at the time.

The following were off shoots of the Buddhistic religion.

The Kumkang-do

The so-called 18th generation of the famous Buddhist priest Mokeun, Lee, Sang Kook established this order in 1926 in Yeonki-kun, combining the contents of Buddhism, Confucianism and Taoism. Lee was originally a believer of Kuan Yu, but was dissatisfied, and attained enlightenment from the research of the three religions. Thus, the religious view toward the universe and human life were those of the three religions, except that the founder Lee, Sang Kook was regarded as the unique saviour to whom an absolute subordination must be made. As an analogous order in the locality, the Kumgang-do, by which practical deeds were more stressed than research and asceticism, had been comparatively superior with about 5,000 converts in 1940.

The Daekak-kyo

This was founded in 1922 by Baek, Sang Kyu, an authoritative Buddhist who had been chief priest of the temple for many years and participated in the 1919 independence movement. When he formally established the order under the banner of revolutionary Buddhism, maintaing that the essence of the principle was in Kak (consciousness), there was much opposition from the other Buddhists, but, at the same time, there were some sympathizers. This religion once had a few local chapters and about 1,000 followers in 1940

The Bulbup Yeonku-hoe(The Research Association of Buddhism)

Originally initiated as an association in 1916 by Park, Joong Bin, this Buddhist branch was redesignated as above by the resolution of the 30 association members in 1924. Taking the universal substance into the four components of heaven and earth, parents, brethren and law, the religious group maintained that man lives to repay the favours of the four components, and that this is the very true nature of man's social existence. The members of this association wore uniforms, observed the ten commandments and rejected idolatry. Their headquarters were located in Iksan-kun, Chollabuk province, and the total strength was estimated at 1,000 in 1940.

The Kwanghwa-kyo

This originated from a Buddhist branch, Obangbul, established by Kim, Chi Yeon at Jinan-kun, Chollabuk province, in 1888 (25th year of King Kojong). When Kim, Chi Yeon was executed later as he opposed the intention of the government, his disciple s, Kim, Sun Ki and Kim, Huan Bae, continued the religious trend, carrying out the missionary works secretly. Since Kwon, Chae Kyo became the founder in 1930, he redesignated the religion as Kwanghwa-kyo, consolidating the followers from other branches such as Jungdo-kyo and Chungrim-kyo. The headquarter of the religion was set up in Nonsan and its members reached about 3,000 in 1940. The doctrine of the religion was that man's mind itself was a Buddha and that man ought to remedy eccentricity and injustice for the cause of humanity and righteousness. Through the chanting of the invocation prayers they eliminated sickness and misfortune.

The other quasi-religious groups that belonged to the Buddhistic religion, in addition to the above-mentioned ones, were the Jungdo-kyo, Wontong-do, Bulkyo Keuknak-hoe and Wonkak Heyonwon-kyo, the last of which had been extremely pro-Japanese, enbracing about 3,000 followers before the Liberation in 1945.

The Chronology of a History of Religions in Korea

The Year of Grace	The Dankun era	Age	The important matter of the domestic	The contrast of a foreign
	1		Dankun Wanggum found the ancient Chosun in theocracy period	
B.C 604	1730			The birth of Laotzu
B.C 565	1769			The birth of Sakya
B.C 552	1782			The birth of Confucius
A.D 4	2330			The birth of Jesus Christ
64	2397			Nero massacred Christians
118	2451			The prohibition of Christianity
142	2475			Chang Taoling organized Wutaomi religion
303	2636			Diocletianus persecuted Christianity
311	2644			Constantinus persuaded the propagation of Christianity

The Year of Grace	The Dankun era	Age	The important matter of the domestic	The contrast of a foreign
325	2658			The opening of Christian council in Nicaea
372	2705	King Sosoorim, 2nd	Ch'in's King, Fuchien dispatched to Kokuryo a monk named Shuntao and introduced Buddhism	
374	2707	King Sosoorim, 4th	Ado came to Kokuryo	
375	2708	King Sosoorim, 5th	Sungmoon temple and Ibulan temple set up in Kokuryo	The Prohibition of Laotzu-Chuangtzu Learning in Former Ch'in Dynasty
381	2714			The 2nd Christianity Council in Constantinople
384	2717	King Chimryu, 1st	Monk Maranandha came to Baekje from Chin Dynasty	
385	2718	King Chimryu, 2nd	Baekje set up Buddhist temples in Hansan and received ten monks.	
391	2724	King Kwangkaeto, 1st	The King of Kokuryo ordered worship of Buddhism religion to seek fortune	
392	2725	King Kwangkaeto, 2nd	The establishment of nine temples in Pyongyang	

The Year of Grace	The Dankun era	Age	The important matter of the domestic	The contrast of a foreign
395	2728	King Kwangkaeto, 5th	The coming of monk Damshi of Chin Dynasty to Kokuryo	
400	2733			Hieronymus translated the Bible into Latin
		The time of King Nulji	Mookhoja came to Silla from Kokuryo and teaching the Buddhist Trinity of Buddha, Dharma and Sutra	
		The time of King Choji	Monk Ado came in Silla with his three followers	
485	2818			The Prohibition of Chamwuiwoojun in Wei
498	2831	King Moonja, 7th	The establishment of the Kumkang temple in Kokuryo	
518	2851			Wei Dynasty send Songwoon Hyesaena to India to collect the Buddhist Scriptures
526	2859	King Sung, 4th	Kyumik of Baekje went into India	
528	2861	King Bupheung, 15th	The monk of Silla, Yi, Cha Don died a martyr and the Buddhism was prevailed	The Buddhist Temples were nearly 32,000 and Buddhist priests were about two millions

The Year of Grace	The Dankun era	Age	The important matter of the domestic	The contrast of a foreign
529	2862	King Bupheung, 16th	The prohibition of Killing lives in Silla	
544	2877	King Jinheung, 5th	The establishment of Heungryun-temple in Silla with growth of temples	
549	2882	King Jinheung, 10th	The Liang Dynasty conveied the Buddha's Sariva. The Monk of Silla, Kakduk returned from Liang Dynasty	
	2884	King Jinheung, 12th	The monk of Kokuryo Hyeryang was naturalized in Silla and became the chief priest established the Pal-kwan Festival in Silla	
552	2885	King Sung, 30th	The King of Baekje sent the Buddhist Status and Scriptures to Japan	
553	2886	King Jinheung, 14th	Hwangryong temple became as the new palace in Silla	The 5th Councilin in Constantinople
554	2887	King Sung, 32nd	Baekje sent 16 priests including Damhae and Doism to Japan	
565	2898	King Jinheung, 26th	The envoy Lyussu of Ch'en Dynasty came wth monk, Myungkwan to Silla and brought about the 2700 volumes of Buddhist Scriptures	

The Year of Grace	The Dankun era	Age	The important matter of the domestic	The contrast of a foreign
566	2899	King Jinheung, 27th	The completion of Hwangryong temple in Silla	
574	2907	King Jinheung, 35th	The Six-Feet Tall Bronze statue was made in Silla	Taoism and Buddhism were abolished and the lewd shrine were destroyed in the Northern Chou Dynasty
576	2909	King Jinheung, 37th	Wonhwa became the Hwarang of Silla	The Emperor John III
577	2910	King Uiduk, 24th	Baekje dispatched the Buddhist literatures, scholars, priests, architects and stone masons to Japan	
579	2912			The North Chou allowed the Buddhism and Taoism
587	2920	King Uiduk, 34th	Baekje dispatched the Buddhist relics, monk, architect, painter to Japan Japanese Buddhists like Zenshin came to Baekje for learning the Buddhist Precepts	Goth converted to Christianity
589	2922	King Jinpyung, 11th	The priest of Silla, Wonkwang went to Ch'en Dynasty to search for the truth of Buddhism	

The Year of Grace	The Dankun era	Age	The important matter of the domestic	The contrast of a foreign
599	2932	King Bup, 1st	Baekje forbad the Killings and released all the captive animals	
600	2933	King Bup, 2nd	The establishment of Wangheung temple in Baekje	Gregory I was gradually established the ecclesiastical authority
601	2934	King Moo, 2nd	The priest of Baekje, Kwon Reuk went to Japan and presented astrology, topography, and calendar	
607	2940			The establishment of Horyu-Ji in Japan
616	2949	King Jinpyung, 38th	The birth of Wonhyo	
620	2953	King Jinpyung, 42nd	The birth of Uisang	King Kao Tzu of Tang Dynasty established the Temple of Laotzu
624	2957	King Youngryu, 7th	A Taoist came from Tang Dynasty to Kokuryo and lectured Laotzu	
625	2958	King Youngryu, 8th	The King of Kokuryo sent persons to Tang Dynasty to learn Buddhism and Laotzu	
630	2963			Mahomet occupied the Holy Land, Mecca

The Year of Grace	The Dankun era	Age	The important matter of the domestic	The contrast of a foreign
635	2968	Queen Sunduk 4th	The priest of Silla, Myungrang came back and established Youngmyo temple	Ahlabon of Persia introduced the Nestorian Tablet to China
636	2969	Queen Sunduk, 5th	The priest of Silla, Jajang entered into Tang Dynasty to seek after the Buddhism	
643	2976	King Bojang, 2nd	The transmission of Taoism from Tang to Kokuryo	
		The time of Queen Sunduk	The priest of Silla, Buprang first introduced the Seon Religion to Silla	
645	2978	Queen Sunduk, 14th	The construction of Nine Storeyed Pagoda at Hwangryong temple	The coming of Tang priest Hyunjang from India
649	2982	Queen Jinduk, 3rd	As the suggestion of priest Jajang, Silla became use the attire of Tang Dynasty	
650	2983	King Bojang, 9th	The moving of Kokuryo priest, Boduk to Baekje	
659	2992	King Mooyeol, 6th	Silla established of Jangui temple in Hansanju	
660	2993	King Uija, 20th	The falldown of Baekje	

The Year of Grace	The Dankun era	Age	The important matter of the domestic	The contrast of a foreign
668	3001	King Bojang, 27th	The falldown of Kokuryo	
671	3004	King Moonmoo, 11th	The coming of priest Uisang from Tang Dynasty	The Tang priest went to India to collect the Buddhism Scriptures
676	3009	King Moonmoo, 16th	The foundation of Boosuk temple	
679	3012	King Moonmoo, 19th	For the expelling of the Tang army, the Sachonwang temples were established	
682	3015	King Shinmoon, 2nd	To protect from Japanese army, Kameun temple was established in the East Sea	
692	3025	King Hyoso, 1st	Doching came from Tang and presented the astronomical chart Seungchon came from Tang and set up the Hwaom-Jong sect	
693	3026	King Hyoso, 2nd	The King Contributed 25,000 acres to Baekryul temple	
694	3027			Manichaeanism was transmitted to Tang Dynasty
726	3059			The Emperor of Eastern Rome prohibit the worship of Idol

The Year of Grace	The Dankun era	Age	The important matter of the domestic	The contrast of a foreign
727	3060	King Seongduk, 26th		Silla priest, Hyecho came back to Tang from India
731	3065			The Roman Emperor excommunicated the destroyers of the sacred image
742	3075	King Hyosung, 6th	The coffin of King cremated and shed the ashes to the East Sea	The Tang priest, Wukung went into India
751	3084	King Kyungduk, 10th	The establishment of Bulkook temple and Sukbool temple	The Tadai-Ji in Japan was completed
752	3085			The Emperor Stephan II was oil painted Pippine
754	3087	King Kyungduk, 13th	The founding of the bell of Hwangryong temple and its weight was about 470,000 Gun	Bonifatius was murdered by a Pagan
755	3088	King Kyungdug, 14th	The founding of Bronze Statue of the Medicine Buddha in Bunhwang temple	Pippine invaded the Kingdom and presented to the Emperor
768	3101			Daejong of the Tang Dynasty appointed 1000 Buddhist priests
771	3104	King Hyekong, 7th	The Grand-Bell was made for the King Seongduk at Bongduk temple	

The Year of Grace	The Dankun era	Age	The important matter of the domestic	The contrast of a foreign
787	3120			The worship of the icon was permitted in the 2nd council of Nicaea (The 7th Council)
799	3132	King Wonsung, 15th	Priest, Bumsoo entered into Tang Dynasty	The Emperor Leo Ⅲ was expelled from Rome and returned by the Emperor Charles
802	3135	King Aejang, 3rd	The establishment of Haein temple	
804	3137	King Aejang, 5th	Hyesho sought after the Buddhist Truth of Buddhism to Tang	Two priests Mosumi and Kookai of Japan went to Tang
806	3139	King Aejang, 7th	The prohibition that newly built and the making of attire and table ware with valuables	Kookai of Japan established the Shinggon-Shyu Mosumi of Japan transmitted the Tendai-Shyu
810	3143	King Hunduk, 2nd	Prince, Kim, Heon Jang contributed the Golden Statue of Buddha and Scriptures to Tang	
821	3154	King Hunduk, 13th	Priest, Doui came back and transmitted the Seon-religion of China	
828	3161	King Heungduk, 3rd	Priest, Hong Chuk found Mt. Silsang	

The Year of Grace	The Dankun era	Age	The important matter of the domestic	The contrast of a foreign
831	3164	King Heungduk, 6th	Prince, Kim, Nung Yoo and the nine priests envoyed to Tang	
839	3172	King Shinmoo, 1st	Priest, Hyechol introduced the Seon religion of the Seodang	
840	3173	King Moonsung, 2nd	Priest, Chejeung came from Tang and found Mt. Kaji	
845	3178	King Moonsung, 7th	Priest, Muyeom came back and transmitted the Seon religion of Mt. Makok	The Emperor Wu of Tang destroied about the 40,000 Buddhist temples and made the 260,000 Buddhist priest return to secular life
847	3180	King Moonsung, 9th	Priest, Bumil came back and introduced the Seon religion of Yumkwan (Mt. Dokul)	
851	3184	King Moonsung, 13th	Wonhong who envoyed to the Tang came back with the Buddhist Scriptures and the Buddha's Tooth	
867	3200			The last separation of the Roman Church, The excommunication between the Roman Emperor and the chief of Constantinople

The Year of Grace	The Dankun era	Age	The important matter of the domestic	The contrast of a foreign
873	3206	King Kyungmoon, 13th	Improved the tower of Hwangryong temple and built the Nine Storeyd Pagoda	
877	3210			Bandit Hwang Shou massacred 120,000 of Religious Adherents
879	3212	King Hunkang, 5th	The establishment of Manghae temple	
882	3215	King Hunkang, 8th	Jisun of Mt. Uiyang entered nirvana	
891	3224	King Jinsung, 5th	Priest, Sunjiong of Sedal temple surrendered to bandit, Yangkil in Nothern Silla	
898	3231	King Hyokong, 2nd	Priest, Dosun entered nirvana	
911	3244	King Hyokong, 15th	Priest, Ieom came back Tang Dynasty and transmitted Todong-chung sect	
918	3251	King Kyungmyung, 2nd	Wangkun moved to Songak and established the ten Buddhist monasteries	
924	3257	King Kyungmyung, 8th	Wangkun established Wejaesukwon, Shinjung-won, Heungkook temples	

The Year of Grace	The Dankun era	Age	The important matter of the domestic	The contrast of a foreign
935	3268	King Kyungsoon, 9th	The Silla King Kyungsoon reverted to Koryo	
938	3271	King Taejo, 2nd	Indian Priest, Hongbum came from Chin Dynasty	
943	3276	King Taejo, 6th	King Taejo presented the ten articles of instruction	
946	3279	King Jungjong, 1st	King Jungjong distributed 70,000 suks of grains to promote the Buddhist Learning	
951	3283	King Kwangjong, 2nd	The establishment of Bongyeun temple for King Taejo / The burning of Nine Storeyed Pagoda of Jungheung temple in Namkyung	
953	3286	King Kwangjong, 4th	The burning of the Nine Storeyed Pagoda of Hwangryong temple	
958	3291	King Kwangjong, 9th	Established the System of Civil Service Examination	
967	3300	King Kwangjong, 18th	The establishment of Kwibup temple for an earnest prayer	The first king of Sung Dynasty promoted Buddhism to King

The Year of Grace	The Dankun era	Age	The important matter of the domestic	The contrast of a foreign
968	3301	King Kwangjong, 19th	The King had regrets to Killed the innocent lives, so that prohibit the killings and extensively hole the Buddhist mass The establishment of the system of Wangsa (Royal Priest) and Kooksa (State Priest) The establishment of Honghwa, Yooum and Samkwi temple	
970	3303	King Kwangjong, 21st	Jijong came from Sung and transmitted Bupan-jong	
987	3320	King Kyungjong, 6th	The abolition of Palkwan and Lantern Festivals	
988	3321	King Kyungjong, 7th	The forced prohibition of killings in January, May and September	Vladimir Converted to Christianity
1004	3337	King Mokjong, 7th	The publication of Teaching Books for Buddhism	
1010	3343	King Hyunjong, 1st	The teaching of reprinting of the letter-blocks of the great collections The re-establishment of Palkwan and Lantern Festivals	

The Year of Grace	The Dankun era	Age	The important matter of the domestic	The contrast of a foreign
1018	3351	King Hyunjong, 9th	The repairing of the tower of Kaekook temple and accommodated 3,200 priests The seeking of Daejangkyung in the time of Sung	
1047	3380	King Munjong, 1st	The forced prohibition of Lunkyung ceremony in Provinces	
1052	3385	King Moonjong 6th	Performed Buddhist mass at the Hoekyung-Jun Pavillion	
1054	3387			The perfect separation between the Rome Church and Greek Church
1055	3388	King Moonjong, 9th	The birth of Uichun	
1063	3396	King Moonjong, 17th	The Khital Tartarsent the collection of Buddhist Scriptures	
1067	3400	King Moonjong, 21st	Heungwang temple was eatablished after 12 years of work	
1068	3401	King Moonjong, 22nd	The death of Choi, Chooung	
1078	3411	King Moonjong, 32nd	The completion of the Gold Pagoda at Heungwang temple	

The Year of Grace	The Dankun era	Age	The important matter of the domestic	The contrast of a foreign
1086	3419	King Soonjong, 3rd	Uichon came from sung and advocates Chontae sect	
1096	3429		The office of the Sutras was established	The Rising of the first Crusadesand the Procession toward the Holy Land
1101	3434	King Sookjong, 6th	Manbulhoi service was prohibited, and Inwang Kyung-Dojang service was held for 50,000 priests	
1109	3442	King Yejong, 4th	Performed a religious service at Dongmyung in Mokmyuk of Pyogyang	King Huijong of Sung promoted the Taoism and suppressed the Buddhism
1110	3443	King Yejong, 5th	King Huijong of Sung Sent the two Taoists to construct the Bokwon-Kuang Shrine	
1112	3445	King Yejong, 7th	Exiled the Chief priest Chingum to Keoje Island	
1131	3464	King Injong, 9th	The learning of Laotzu-Chuangtzu was prohibited The establishment of Palsung-dang at Imwon-kung at Sukyung	

The Year of Grace	The Dankun era	Age	The important matter of the domestic	The contrast of a foreign
1135	3468	King Ingong, 13th	Priest, Myochung in the Sukyung rose in revolt	
1141	3474	King Injong, 19th	Priest, Chingyeon entered nirvana	
1143	3476			The anti Pope revolution happened in Rome
1147	3480	King Uijong, 1st	King prayed to beget a Prince at Youngtong temple and was lectured the Scriptures for 50 days	The Rising of the 2nd Crusades
1158	3491	King Uijong, 12th	King liked the Buddhist services so priests were crowded at palace	
1174	3507	King Myungjong, 4th	Encountered between the 2000 priests and the army Lee, Ui Bang was murdered by a priest	
1189	3522			The Rising of the 3rd Crusades
1200	3533	King Shinjong 3rd	Jinul established the Junghye temple at Mt. Jokye	Chootzu was dead
1210	3543	King Heejong, 6th	Jinul entered nirvana	
1211	3544	King Heejong, 7th	King made a priest to murder Choi, Choong Heon but failed	

The Year of Grace	The Dankun era	Age	The important matter of the domestic	The contrast of a foreign
1216	3549	King Kojong, 3rd	The Khitai Tartarbo invaded and burnt Bohyun temple	
1217	3550	King Kojong, 4th	Choi, Choong Heon Slaughtered 800 priests	
1224	3557			Shinran of Japan eatablished the Aodo-Shinshyu
1230	3563			The 2nd Frerderick reconciled with the Pope
1232	3565	King Kojong, 19th	The Mongolian army burnt the Buddhist Scriptures board of Buin temple	
1238	3571	King Kojong, 25th	The Mongolian army burnt the Pagoda of Hwangryong temple	
1251	3584	King Kojong, 38th	The reprinting of all Buddhist Scriptures finished after the 16th years of work	
1253	3586	King Kojong, 40th	Choi, Hang established Kooyodang	Nichiren of Japan established Nichiren Shyu
1270	3603			The Rising of the 7th Crusades

The Year of Grace	The Dankun era	Age	The important matter of the domestic	The contrast of a foreign
1271	3604	King Wonjong, 21st	The coming of the 4 priests from Tibet	
1284	3617	King Choongyeol 10th	Priest Ilyeon wrote the Samkookyusa	
1290	3623	King Choogyeol, 16th	The 35 priests were sent to Yuen Dynasty	
1311	3644	King Choongsun, 3rd	Sent the Collection of Buddhist Scriptures to Yuen Dynasty	The Capital city Pandia in India was occupied by Islamite
1327	3660	King Choongsook, 14th	The coming of Indian priest Jikong	
1348	3681	King Choongmok, 4th	Bowoo came back from Yuen and transmitted Imjejong sect	
1365	3698	King Kongmin, 14th	King made Pyunjo as the King's tutor	
1370	3703	King Kongmin, 19th	The coming of Ming's Taoist Seo, Saho	
1378	3711			The serious separation of the Roman Church
1382	3715	King Woo, 8th	Bowoo entered nirvana	Wicklife translated the New and Old Testament to English

The Year of Grace	The Dankun era	Age	The important matter of the domestic	The contrast of a foreign
1389	3722	King Chang, 1st	Jo, In Ok appealed the king for the anti-Buddhism	
1390	3723	King Kongyang, 2nd	Jung, Mong Ju suggested the anti-Buddhism	
1391	3724	King Kongyang, 3rd	Women and girls were prohibited coming and going of of Buddhist temples	
1392	3725	King Kongyang, 4th	The falldown of Koryo Dynasty Established Sungkyunkwan in Seoul	The Emperor(of Japan) Kameyama transmitted the Sacrificial vesssl to the Emperor Komatsu
1396	3729	King Taejo, 5th	Established Sokyokjun in Seoul	
1399	3732	King Jungjong, 1st	Established Obu Hakdang School in Seoul	
1401	3734	King Taejong 1st	Reinforced for Confucianism and the persecutide Buddhism	
1405	3738	King Taejong, 5th	Wangsa Moohak entered Nirvana	
1406	3739	King Taejong, 6th	Reduced temples and limited the male and female servants	

The Year of Grace	The Dankun era	Age	The important matter of the domestic	The contrast of a foreign
1407	3740	King Taejong, 7th	The Buddhism sect reduced to the seven sects. The Shrine of Confucius was newly constructed	
1413	3746	King Taejong, 13th	The burning of Cosmic Dual Books	
1419	3752	King Sejong, 1st	Eatablished Kija's monument	
1422	3755	King Sejong, 4th	The abolition of Kyunghaeng (Demonstration Service)	
1423	3756	King Sejong, 5th	Buddhism only left the two sects Seonjong and Kyo-jong, Forced prohibition of the new construction of Buddhist Temples	
1425	3758	King Sejong, 7th	The men who concealed the wicked books were punished. The shrine of Dankun established in Pyongyang	
1444	3777	King Sejong, 26th	The increase of the believers for the theory of Configuration	
1459	3792	King Sejo, 5th	King Sejo went to Western for worship Dankun, Kija	
1464	3797	King Sejo, 10th	Established Wonkak temple	

The Year of Grace	The Dankun era	Age	The important matter of the domestic	The contrast of a foreign
1466	3799	King Sejo, 12th	Sokyukjun was transformed Sokyukseo	
1469	3802			The birth of Nanak, founder of Sikh
1471	3804	King Sungjong, 2nd	The praying for Buddhism was prohibited and the Shamans were expelled to the outside of Seoul	
1488	3821	King Sungjong, 19th	The repairing of Wonkak temple and the constructed a house for Daejangkyung scriptures	
1490	3823	King Sungjong, 21st	Monks who had not government issued credentials was arrested	
1501	3834	King Yeonsankun, 7th	The birth of Lee, Hwang	
1504	3837	King Yeonsankun, 10th	Sungkyunkwan was used as the king's pleasure house	
1514	3847	King Joongjong, 9th	The new construction of Buddhist Temples was strongly prohibited	
1517	3850			Luther asserted the Religious Reformation
1518	3851	King Joongjong, 13th	Demolished Sokyukseo	Zwingli asserted the Religious Reformation

The Year of Grace	The Dankun era	Age	The important matter of the domestic	The contrast of a foreign
1522	3855	King Joongjong, 17th	Re-established Sokyukseo	Ths first edition of New Testament was published, that was translated by Luther
1535	3868	King Joongjong, 30th	Worshiped the Royal Tomb of King Taejo and Worshiped at Sungkyunkwan	
1536	3869	King Joongjong, 31st	The birth of Lee, Yi	
1537	3870	King Joongjong, 32nd	Demolished Shaman's houses and Buddhist Temples	
1543	3876	King Joongjong, 38th	Established Baekwundong School in Poongki	
1551	3884	King Myungjong, 6th	Appointed Bowoo as the Bishop of Seon sect	
1563	3896			Calvin proclaimed the creed of Heidelberg
1565	3898	King Myungjong, 20th	Clubed Bowoo to death in Cheju Island	
1572	3905			About 30,000 Protestants were massacred in France
1587	3920			The prohibited Roman Catholicism in Japan

The Year of Grace	The Dankun era	Age	The important matter of the domestic	The contrast of a foreign
1598	3931			The equal authority was approved to Protestant and Roman Catholics by the Imperial Ordinance of Nante
1599	3932	King Seonjo, 32nd	Established Kwanyu's Shrine	
1601	3934			Matteo Ricci established Christian Church in Peking
1604	3937	King Seonjo, 37th	Hyujung entered Nirvana	
1608	3941			Organized German Protestant Alliance
1610	3943	King Kwanghaekun, 2nd	Yujung entered Nirvana The five wise were worshiped at the shrine of Confucius	
1615	3948	King Kwanghaekun, 7th	Seonsoo entered Nirvana	
1616	3949	King Kwanghaekun, 8th	Based on Priest Sungji's Configuration, Inkyung Palace was constructed	
1618	3951			The rising of the 30 years Religion War

The Year of Grace	The Dankun era	Age	The important matter of the domestic	The contrast of a foreign
1628	3961			The second prohibition of Roman Catholic in Japan
1629	3962			The ordiance of Religious Restoration was proclaimed in German
	3963			Swedish King invaded German for the rescue of Protestants
1645	3978	King Injo, 23rd	Prince Sohyun came back with the books of Western Religion, Roman Catholic Status and terrestrial globe given by Adam Schall	
1660	3993	King Hyunjong, 1st	Forbidding the people to become to priesthood with haircutting	The Presbyterian Church was recognized in the Scotland Council
1661	3994	King Hyunjong, 2nd	Destroyed two temples, Jasoo and Insoo in the Capital and established the Confucian School	
1678	4011	King Sookjong, 4th	Japanese Shrine was established in Busan	
1682	4015	King Sookjong, 8th	Lee, Yi and Sunghon were worshiped at the shrine of Confucius	

The Year of Grace	The Dankun era	Age	The important matter of the domestic	The contrast of a foreign
1687	4020	King Sookjong, 13th	Drove away Shamans from Seoul	The shrine of Confucius was completed at the ridge of Shoheisaka in Japan
1690	4023			
1701	4034	King Sookjong, 27th	Specified the great Hwaom temple of Mt. Chiri as the great Buddhist Temple	
1712	4045			The conflict broke out between Catholics and Protestants in Swiss
1720	4053	King Sookjong, 46th	Withdrew the expulsion command of shamans in Seoul	
1738	4071			Methodist Church wad founded by Wesley
1741	4074	King Youngjo, 17th	The personal running Confucius School was banned	
1749	4082	King Youngjo, 25th	King Taejo of Ming, Shinjong and Uijong were worshiped in Daebodan Shrine	
1764	4097	King Youngjo, 40th	The death of Lee, IK	
1765	4098	King Yougio, 41st	Repaired the board of Samsung	

The Year of Grace	The Dankun era	Age	The important matter of the domestic	The contrast of a foreign
1783	4116	King Jungjo, 7th	at Mt. Koowol and worshiped King Dongmyung at the shrine	
1784	4117	King Jungjo, 8th	The entrance of Buddhists to capital was strongly banned Lee, Seung Hoon was baptized in Peking and came back with the Western Religion books, Cross and Status	Moslems in Kansoo, China rised the revolt
1786	4119	King Jungjo, 10th	The buying of Western religion Scriptures from Peking was banned Western Learning was flourished	
1790	4123	King Junjo, 14th	Yongjoo temple was established in Suwon	
1791	4124	King Jungjo, 15th	The Western Learning was called as heresy Yun, Ji Chung was executed for Western	
1795	4128	King Junjo, 19th	Father Choo, Moon Mo entered the country	
1796	4129			The believers of Bailien-Chyao rised the Revolt in China

The Year of Grace	The Dankun era	Age	The important matter of the domestic	The contrast of a foreign
1801	4134	King Soonjo, 1st	The miserable Sinyu Massacre 300 believers were executed Father Choo, Moon Mo was gibbeted The Matter of Hwang, Sa Yung's Letter was occured	
1805	4138			Westerner's mission work was prohibited in China
1813	4146			The flourishing of Tenri-CHyao in china
1815	4148	King Soonjo, 15th	Ulhae Massacre	The leader of oxford Movement in England converted to Catholicism
1829	4162			The approval Bill of Catholicism was adopted in England
1831	4164	King Soonjo, 31st	The Vatican established the Chosun Parish	Tenri-kyo was founded in Japan
1833	4166			Baptist Church was founded in German
1834	4167	King Soonjo, 34th	Expelled Shamans to outside of Capital	

The Year of Grace	The Dankun era	Age	The important matter of the domestic	The contrast of a foreign
1836	4169	King Hunjong, 2nd	The French missionary Maubant entered the country	
1837	4170	King Hunjong, 3rd	The French missionary Chastan entered the country	
1839	4172	King Hunjong, 5th	Kihae massacre occured, and 130 Catholic believers were executed Three French Fathers were gibbeted The exclusion of Western Learning was commanded	
1844	4177			The establishment of Y.M.C.A
1846	4179	King Hunjong, 12th	The first Korean Father Kim, Dae Kun was arrested and sentenced to death	
1849	4182			Miller, the founder of the Seventh-Day Adventist Church was dead
1850	4183			Hung, Syu Chuan rose the Revolt of Taiping Chun Established the Church of Christ in America

The Year of Grace	The Dankun era	Age	The important matter of the domestic	The contrast of a foreign
1860	4193	King Chuljong, 2nd	Choi, Je Woo advocated Donghak in Kyongju	
1864	4197	King Kojong, 1st	Choi, Je Woo, the founder of Donghak was executed in Taegu	
1866	4199.	King Kojong, 3rd	Daewonkun's massacre of Catholics	Moslem invaded Suiting
1870	4203			Burned Christian Churches and murdered French Consul in Tienchin
1871	4204	King Kojong, 8th	The Confucian Schools recognized by the court were left 47 places abolished all of its rest	The abolition of Catholic bureau in German
1876	4209	King Kojong, 13th	Lee, Yeung Chan and Kim, Jin Ki were baptized by Protestant missionary in Niw Chuang	
1878	4211			Booth found the Salvation Army
1882	4215	King Kojong, 19th	Luke and Mark were translated and published	The death of Darwin
1884	4217	King Kojong, 21st	Dr. McRae entered for the missionary work	The foundation of Watch Tower
1885	4218	King Kojong, 22nd	The two American missionaries,	

The Year of Grace	The Dankun era	Age	The important matter of the domestic	The contrast of a foreign
1886	4219	King Kojong, 23rd	Apenzeller and Underwood came to Chosun Kwanghyewon Hospital and Yukyoung School were founded (The predecessors of Kyungshin School) Baejae School was founded Ehwa girls school was founded	Organized Christian evangelical confederation in German
1889	4222	King Kojong, 26th	Yukyoung Kongwon changed the name to Jesus School Australian missionary, Davis and his sister came to Korea. The Baptist Church started the missionary works	
1890	4223	King Kojong, 27th	Chosun Parish's Bishop, Mutel came to Korea. Bishop of Anglican Church, Corfe came to Korea	
1893	4226	King Kojong, 30th	Tenri-kyo of Japan transmitted to Korea	
1894	4227	King Kojong, 31st	Donghak uprised	
1895	4228	King Kojong, 32nd	Lifted of the ban for monk's entrance to Capital.	

The Year of Grace	The Dankun era	Age	The important matter of the domestic	The contrast of a foreign
1896	4229	King Kojong, 33rd	The first Korean Christian Church was established in Songchun	
1898	4231	Kwangmoo, 2nd	Choi, Shi Hyung, the second bishop of Donghak was executed	The serious collision between Christians and Moslems was occured in Crete Island
1901	4234	Kwangmoo, 5th	Myongdong Catholic Church was built	
1901	4234	Kwangmoo, 5th	700 Catholics was slaughtered in Cheju Island	The organization of Orient mission meeting in America (the Holiness Church)
1902	4235	Kwangmoo, 6th	The temple Administration Law was proclaimed The Russian Orthodox Church was built in Seoul	
1903	4236	Kwangmoo, 7th	Hwangsung(Seoul) Y.M.C.A. was founded	
1904	4237	Kwangmoo, 8th	The Seventh-Day Adventist Church was transmitted	The break of friendship between France and the Vatican
1905	4238	Kwangmoo, 9th	Sohn, Byung Hee changed the name of Donghak to Chonto-kyo	France abolished the religious schools and was possessed

The Year of Grace	The Dankun era	Age	The important matter of the domestic	The contrast of a foreign
1907	4240	Yunghee, 1st	The six missionaries organized the Federal Council of Protestant Evangerical Mission	by the nation
1908	4241	Yunghee, 2nd	The Presbyterian Church organized the parish The Holiness Church started the Evangelism Canadian started mission work in Hamheung The salvation Army started the evangelism work in Korea The Methodist Church held the annual meeting The Sichon-kyo was founded	The pantheistic philosopher Eucken recieved the Novel Prize
1909	4242	Yunghee, 3rd	La, Chol and Jung, Yeol Mo founded Dankun-kyo The Christian Church extended the movement of salvation for one hundred million soul	
1910	4243	Yunghee, 4th	Japan invaded Korea Dankun-kyo	Tolstoi died remote country

The Year of Grace	The Dankun era	Age	The important matter of the domestic	The contrast of a foreign
1911	4244		changed the name to Daejong-kyo Apart remained as the name of Dankun-kyo	
			Japanese Governor General proclaimed the temple administration law	The monists criticized the Christian Church in Germany
			30 Head temples were appointed Divided the Catholic parish into two parishes of Seoul and Taegu	
1913	4246		Chungrim-kyo was founded	
1914	4277		Sooeunkyo was founded	The inauguration of Pope Benedicte XV
1915	4248		The foundation of Yeonhee College	
1918	4251		Korea Christian Association was organized	
			The murder club Baekbaek-kyo was founded	
1919	4252		March, 1. Independent Movement was took place lead by the each religious leaders Mookook Daedo-kyo was founded	Gandhi urgently appealed to harmony between Moslem and Hindu

The Year of Grace	The Dankun era	Age	The important matter of the domestic	The contrast of a foreign
1920	4253		Kwangsung-kyo was founded Catholic's Wonsan Parish was established	
1922	4255		Y.W.C.A. was organized Established Central Office for Buddhist Administration	The inauguration of Pope XI Pius
1923	4256		As the death of Sohn, Byung Hee, Chondo-kyo was divided Ortanized Chonto-kyo Youngman's party	The start of German evangelical Church Federation Gogarten wrote "The Faith and the revelation"
1925	4258		The beatification ceremony for the 79 Chosun martyrs performed Established Japanese Shrine, Chosen Jinggu The Sangjae-kyo was founded	Christian Church Friendship meeting was held in Stockholm
1926	4259		Bochon-kyo was founded	International League of Moslem was held in Cairo
1927	4260		Established Catholic Pyongyang Parish Shinkanhoi and Keunwoohoi were organized	World Christian Rolly was held in Lausanne World Holiness Body Mass Meeting was held in Sidney

The Year of Grace	The Dankun era	Age	The important matter of the domestic	The contrast of a foreign
1928	4261		Established Catholic Yeonkil Parish	
1930	4263		The Union of Southern and Northern Methodist Churches were united Dr. Yang Joo Sam was elected as the first Methodist Bishop The Coalition of the new and old faction of Chonto-kyo	
1931	4264		The performance of the Centennial Anniversary for the establishment of Catholic parish	Spain decalred the execution of Republicanism and the nationalization of the religious establishments
1933	4266		The new establishment of Catholic Kwangju Parish Chonto-kyo again separated in the new and the old faction	
1934	4267		The performance of the 50th Anniversary of the Christian mission The uprising of Oshim-dang Incident of Chonto-kyo	
1937	4270		Baekbaek-kyo murdered about 150 believers	The beginning of China-Japanese War

The Year of Grace	The Dankun era	Age	The important matter of the domestic	The contrast of a foreign
1938	4271		Prayer Incident of Chonto-kyo The issue of Japanese Shrine Worship was illegally adopted in the general assembly of Presbyterian Church Accomplished the headquarter of the Buddhist administration	The repulsion of the officers group about the religion in Germany
1939	4272			The inauguration of Pope XII Pius
1940	4273		Established Catholic's Choonchun Parish Anti-Japanese Christians were largely imprisoned The new and old Chonto-kyo faction was reseparated	The Moslem adopted proposal that make Pakistan the Independance Nation
1941	4274		The mass imprisonment of foreign missionaries The 14 leaders of Backbaek-kyo were sentenced to death	The beginning of World War II
1942	4275		The missionaries of England,	

The Year of Grace	The Dankun era	Age	The important matter of the domestic	The contrast of a foreign
1943	4276		America and France were expelled The inauguration ceremony of Bishop, Noh, Ki Nam, the first Korean Bishop was performed Y.M.C.A. and Y.W.C.A. were under the control of the Federation of Japan All the leaders of Daejong-kyo were arrested in Manchuria Leaders of Christianity were continuously arrested The leaders of Christianity who refused to worship Shintoist were continuously arrested The dissolved Holiness Church Seventh-Day Adventism and the Baptist Church The Holy Bells of and Churches Buddhism Temples were confuscated	
1944	4277		Large number of churches were placed under requisition for military use	

The Year of Grace	The Dankun era	Age	The important matter of the domestic	The contrast of a foreign
1945	4278		Japanese ancestral tablet was enshrined in the church Christian Churches were belonged to Japanese Federation August, 15 Liberation	The Japanese Emperor said that I am not living God

A History of Religions in Korea

Copyright ©1988 by Duk-Hwang Kim ph.D.
Publisher Ju-Sung Lee
Published by arrangement with **Daeji Moonhwa-sa**
Publishing Company
268-11 Shuyu-2dong, Kangbuk-gu, Seoul
Tel : 903-7745, 992-5462
Fax : 903-7028
Registered Date : November, 1, 1950
Registered No : 7-20

First Books Publication : July, 30, 1988
Fourth Books Publication : January, 20, 2000

Printed in Korea   **₩15,000**
ISBN 89-85202-22-7